Configuring and Tuning Databases on the Solaris™ Platform

Allan N. Packer
Sun Microsystems, Inc.

Sun Microsystems Press
A Prentice Hall Title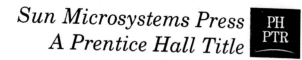

Production Editor: Kathleen M. Caren
Acquisitions Editor: Eileen Clark
Marketing Manager: Debby van Dijk
Manufacturing Manager: Alexis Heydt-Long
Cover Design Director: Jerry Votta

Sun Microsystems Press:
Marketing Manager: Michael Llwyd Alread
Publisher: Rachel Borden

Sun Microsystems Press
A Prentice Hall Title

DEDICATION

This book is dedicated to my father, Ken Packer. Without the inspiration of his passion for writing I might never have started myself. Most importantly, he has demonstrated that in writing and in life, little of value can be achieved without discipline and perseverance.

TABLE OF CONTENTS

LIST OF FIGURES

LIST OF TABLES

FOREWORD

Modern corporations demand a high level of service from their IT environments. Today's successful datacenter architectures consist of multiple tiers that use well-tuned and high-performance servers at every level.

Sun refers to this as the "end-to-end architecture." Typical tiers include powerful database servers connected to many application servers, front-ended by web servers that service a wide variety of desktop, thin-client, and wireless devices. This architecture is effective for both Online Transaction Processing and Data Warehousing applications.

The end-to-end architecture is appropriate for environments ranging from large implementations with thousands of processors and hundreds of servers, all the way down to small single-server implementations. Sun is committed to understanding user requirements regardless of the datacenter's size and to making sure that customers can effectively utilize all of the systems in their datacenters. The business of many of Sun's customers depends on mission-critical commercial applications. Sun understands this dependence and treats it very seriously.

Performance is not typically at the top of the three things that keep datacenter managers awake at night, but running systems efficiently at high performance is an important factor in delivering excellent service levels and doing more with less.

Sun has led the world in making larger servers than anyone thought possible and driving these to new levels of performance. This has been done often contrary to popular wisdom. Many thought that Sun's now popular Sun Starfire system could never scale to use 64 processors. But the capabilities of the hardware and the skill of the engineers at Sun and Sun's software partners soon proved that at first 40 CPUs and then 64 CPUs could be effectively used in a system. Near-linear scalability has been achieved on a wide range of applications. Another common myth was that an SMP system could not handle databases over 1 terabyte. Again, with a great system and intelligent system configuration and tuning, this is now a commonplace database size. Each of these efforts at pushing the bounds of what is possible provided an excellent vehicle for Sun to learn and make improvements before such deployments became commonplace at customers' datacenters. The process of working through the issues in these new situations also allowed the engineering team to simplify tuning techniques and make them easier to understand and implement.

This book contains the collective wisdom of many talented engineers both at Sun and those at Sun's many software partners (Oracle, Sybase, DB2, SAP, Peoplesoft, etc.). The best practices contained in this book provide an excellent framework that will allow readers to start with the best performance ideas for almost every case they will encounter. The author draws on his experience in Performance and Applications Engineering (earlier called Database Engineering) and also draws upon the techniques established by Strategic Applications Engineering (SAE), whose focus was creating world-record performance on high-end systems. Sun will keep pushing the bounds in understanding and demonstrating the performance of commercial applications, while focusing on the singular vision of a consistent product line from the smallest to the largest servers.

Enjoy!

> Brad Carlile
> Director Enterprise Benchmarking
> Strategic Applications Engineering (SAE)
> Sun Microsystems, Inc.

PREFACE

Many books have been written on database tuning—I personally own enough volumes on Oracle tuning to fill a small shelf. Very few, though, approach configuring, tuning, monitoring, and troubleshooting from the perspective of the system as a whole, treating the database as one of a number of key components. I have set out to approach database configuration and tuning from this broader context.

To my knowledge, this book is the first attempt at tackling database tuning for multiple databases. Since many aspects of database architecture and tuning are common across the major products, I have separated out generic topics such as database concepts, hardware architectures, the buffer cache and the optimizer. I hope that the opportunity to see the big picture and to compare and contrast the different implementations outweighs the inconvenience of having to follow cross-references at times.

This book is also the first published guide to database configuring and tuning for Solaris users (although most of the principles and much of the detail should be applicable to other UNIX systems). I trust that it will enhance your experience of running databases on the Solaris Operating Environment.

My aim has been to identify the highlights. An overwhelming array of statistics are reported by Solaris and the various databases; rather than attempting to define every statistic and tunable parameter, I focus on those likely to have the most impact on common database workloads.

Finally, no one person could claim a full mastery of all the topics covered in this book, and I certainly make no such assertion on my own behalf. I have tried to distill the knowledge I have acquired during my 12 years with Sun— 5 years in the field organization as a Systems Engineer specializing in databases, followed by 7 years in Database Engineering (now Performance and

Availability Engineering)—and add to it the research and insights of my colleagues.

I was fortunate to join an engineering group that actively pursued engineering relationships with all four database vendors. This involvement has offered me direct participation in performance projects with the engineering groups at Oracle in Redwood Shores, IBM at the DB2 Development Lab in Toronto, and Sybase at Emeryville. My contact with Informix has been peripheral, and in writing the Informix chapters I have relied heavily on the wisdom and experience of my colleagues.

Intended Audience

This book should appeal to the following groups of readers:

- **Database administrators** looking for practical tuning advice and for a broader understanding of the system as a whole.
- **System administrators and other technical staff** wanting to expand their understanding of the architecture and management of databases.
- **Developers** hoping to better understand the context in which their applications are used. The suggestions on benchmarking applications during the entire development cycle should be of particular interest.
- **Specialists in one database** wanting to learn more about other databases. I know many people who have expressed a desire to better understand the other major databases, but found the task too daunting. I hope this book will simplify that process by providing enough material to answer the important questions without being overwhelming.
- **System users** who simply want to understand the jargon associated with databases and the servers on which they run.

I have tried to go into enough depth to satisfy those looking for detailed configuration and tuning suggestions, while still making the content accessible to people who are not database or Solaris gurus.

Organization of This Book

This book is organized in five parts. Parts One, Two, and Five are best viewed as reference material. Parts Three and Four lend themselves to hands-on tuning.

Part One: Databases on Sun Servers — Provides background information on Sun's relationship with database vendors and Sun's Database Engineering organization, and discusses the optimizations made to the Solaris Operating Environment to improve database performance and availability. The section concludes with a review of the major hardware architectures (including those not supported by Sun) and their implications for database deployment.

Part Two: Database Architecture — Addresses database concepts, database workloads, and explores in detail the database optimizer and the role and sizing of the database buffer cache. Separate chapters discuss the architecture of Oracle, Sybase, Informix XPS, and DB2 for Solaris; for these chapters I provide a consistent format to make it easier for those wanting to contrast an unfamiliar database with one that is more familiar.

Part Three: Sizing and Configuring Sun DBMS Servers — Focuses on system sizing and configuring the CPUs, memory, and networks of a database server. The section concludes with a detailed discussion of data layout technologies, strategies, and recommendations.

Part Four: Performance Monitoring and Tuning — Deals with the issues and tools associated with performance monitoring and tuning, and offers a drill-down method for identifying and resolving system bottlenecks. Detailed configuration and tuning advice is provided for each of Oracle, Sybase, Informix XPS, and DB2 for Solaris, and the section concludes with a discussion on how to monitor applications and what metrics to collect.

Part Five: Other Topics — The final section of the book covers benchmarks and the role of Java technology in databases. The first chapter examines the pros and cons of industry-standard benchmarks and investigates the process and potential pitfalls involved in developing your own benchmark. The final chapter explores direct support for Java technology in databases and the Java 2 Enterprise Edition (J2EE) technology that is central to the burgeoning middleware market.

An appendix lists sources for supplementary information.

Book Website

The scripts and utilities referred to in the book are available on the book website, and I will also use this site to post updates to the material in the book. The website can be found at:

http://www.solarisdatabases.com

Conventions Used in the Book

For consistency, the book uses the notational conventions described in the following list:

- `Courier font` designates code, computer output, directory names, environment variables, file names.

- **Courier bold** designates user input in response to a system prompt.
- A C-shell prompt is shown as hostname%.
- A superuser prompt is shown as hostname#.
- Italics designate the first instance of a new term, emphasis, or a code variable to be replaced by the user.

I sometimes opt for commonly used variants of formal technical terms. For example, I opted for *indexes* rather than the more formal *indices*, *tables* rather than *relations*, *rows* rather than *tuples*, and *columns* rather than *attributes*. Although the noun *data* is a plural with a singular form of *datum*, I follow common usage and treat it as a singular (for example, "key column data is stored in a B-tree structure").

A Note from the Author

I welcome your feedback, suggestions, and general comments. If you like the book, please let me know! If you find flaws, errors, or omissions, I would also be glad to hear of them. In reading *Configuring and Tuning Databases for the Solaris Platform*, I hope you receive even a small proportion of the benefit I have gained from writing it.

Allan Packer

Allan.Packer@Sun.COM

ACKNOWLEDGMENTS

I would like to thank a number of people who have contributed directly or indirectly to this book. The technical content reflects the efforts and research of a large number of people, and especially my colleagues in Performance and Availability Engineering (PAE).

First, my grateful thanks to Brad Carlile for writing the foreword. He has achieved a great deal on Sun's behalf in this segment of the market, and I am honored by his participation.

With respect to the technical content, let me begin by acknowledging material contributed by various colleagues at Sun. Much of the content in the Sybase chapters had its origins in a substantial whitepaper by Anand Atre and Lisa Elser. The Database Optimizer chapter borrowed material from a whitepaper and presentation by Bob Lane and a presentation by Berni Schiefer from IBM (used with permission). A whitepaper by Thin-Fong Tsuei was the source of the research study results and graphs reported in the Chapter 7 section on "Sizing the Buffer Cache". The Informix XPS chapters owe a significant debt to a substantial whitepaper by Denis Sheahan. Some of the description of Enterprise Java Beans in Chapter 28 was lifted from Damian Guy's Honors thesis introduction (used with permission).

I also drew on material from various whitepapers and field notes contributed to by various PAE engineers: Sriram Gummuluru, Nicolai Kosche, Bob Lane, Tony Li, Tariq Magdon-Ismail, Jim Mauro, Richard McDougall, Paul Riethmuller, Denis Sheahan, Jim Skeen, Shanti Subramanyam, Ravindra Talashikar, and Yufei Zhu. My apologies to anyone I have left out!

I have also referred to technical material put together by Brad Carlile and his group, Strategic Applications Engineering, and in particular Glenn Fawcett, Bob Larson, Daryl Madura, and Dave Miller.

I'm especially grateful to those who reviewed substantial chunks of the book. Bob Lane brought to bear his considerable experience and technical insight as well as his skills with the English language. Our lively debates over both grammar and content were fun as well as useful! Jim Mauro and Sriram Gummuluru each worked through several chapters and made many valuable suggestions. Tony Shoumack offered a useful critique of multiple chapters of the book.

Thanks, too, to a number of other people who provided feedback. From Sun, Tom Daly, Bob Larson, Daryl Madura, Richard McDougall, Paul Riethmuller, Ravindra Talashikar, and Thin-Fong Tsuei reviewed focused sections of the book. Connie Dialeris Green and Sumanta Chatterjee from Oracle, Scott Logan from IBM, and Prasanta Ghosh from Sybase reviewed the Oracle, DB2, and Sybase chapters respectively, and John Hornibrook and Berni Schiefer from IBM reviewed the optimizer chapter. I'm grateful to each of them for their helpful suggestions.

An early snapshot of some of the material from the book found its way into a class I developed for SunU. Alan Mayer from Integra Solutions, who ably took over the class, provided insightful reviews of several chapters.

Although the feedback, suggestions, and corrections offered by the reviewers have improved the content of this book, the responsibility is mine for any flaws, errors, and omissions that remain.

A big vote of thanks goes to my wonderful copy editor, Mary Lou Nohr, who provided copious help with layout, patiently hunted down my inconsistencies in style and my grammatical indiscretions, and greatly improved the readability of the book. Thanks, too, to Eileen Clark, Kathleen Caren, and Greg Doench at Prentice Hall for bringing it all together, and to Rachel Borden and Michael Alread for capably handling the issues at Sun Microsystems Press.

On a more general note, my thanks to Brian Wong, Adrian Cockcroft, and Jim Skeen, each of whom played a role in my move into engineering in Menlo Park in 1994 and who have continued to offer encouragement. Special thanks are also due to Bob Lane, Richard McDougall, Tom Daly, Paul Riethmuller, Phil Harman, Brodie James, and Jim Mauro for their inspiration and friendship over the years.

I would particularly like to thank the senior managers of Performance and Availability Engineering (PAE): John Bongiovanni, PAE Director, for his strong and able leadership and for building an outstanding team environment; Ganesh Ramamurthy, my current manager, for sharing his considerable knowledge and astuteness; and Keng-Tai Ko, my former manager. I am indebted to them for their support, past and present.

Many thanks to Sun Microsystems Australia, and to everyone in the Adelaide office in particular, for so readily hosting me and making me welcome upon my relocation to Australia from Palo Alto.

Last but not least, I would like to thank Merilyn, my wonderful wife and best friend, for her unfailing love and support and for always believing in me, and my precious children, James, Melanie, Stephen, and Deborah, thanks to whom my life is never dull! All of them have graciously put up with considerable distraction on my part as a result of this book.

Part One

Databases on Sun Servers

- Sun's Relationship with Database Vendors
- The Role of Database Engineering at Sun
- Solaris Optimizations for Databases
- Hardware Architecture and Databases

1

SUN'S RELATIONSHIP WITH DATABASE VENDORS

Since the inception of Sun Microsystems in 1982, the company's remarkable success has been based on partnerships. This strategy has made it natural for Sun to pursue effective alliances with independent software vendors (ISVs).

The close partnerships Sun has enjoyed, with the major database vendors in particular, don't just happen—they are maintained through hard work and substantial common business interests. Market forces determine the strength and, ultimately, the ongoing existence of the mutual support between hardware and software platforms.

From Sun's perspective, a large proportion of its revenue comes from the sale of database servers. And since Sun is the major UNIX platform, the long-established open systems database vendors (Oracle, Sybase, and Informix) have over the years developed significant customer bases on Sun servers. For DB2 as a more recent arrival on the open systems scene, as well as for the other ISVs, Sun offers a substantial and growing installed base upon which to build database revenue.

Further, Sun's base encompasses everything from small, single-CPU servers to large mainframe-class servers like the Enterprise 10000 (Starfire) and its successors. And, best of all from the database vendors' point of view, software developed on any of Sun's systems runs across all its systems.

The ultimate winners are Sun's customers; strategic focus by Sun backed up by market support ensures that their chosen platform continues to enjoy preferred treatment from the database vendors.

The Nature of the Relationship

Sun maintains ongoing relationships with the major UNIX database vendors: Oracle, Sybase, and IBM (IBM encompasses Informix as well as DB2
since IBM's purchase of the database business of Informix in 2001). Sun
workstations were the original development platform for Sybase and Informix and for Oracle's range of UNIX products. These early involvements provided opportunities for Sun to develop relationships with these companies.

Eventually those partnerships broadened as users installed Sun servers to
run their database applications. While DB2 is not developed on Sun, the Sun
platform is widely used within IBM for porting and performance work. The
development group's nightly DB2 source code build is run on the Solaris
Operating Environment as well as AIX.

Today the partnerships encompass a number of different areas.

Engineering

The engineering relationship Sun has with its database partners is expressed
in the following ways:

- Dedicated engineers within Sun's Database Engineering organization
  work on database engine performance with each of the four major
  RDBMS products.

- Each of the database companies has engineers focused on the Sun platform. The scope of these groups is broader than just engineering—they
  are also tasked with marketing and supporting their respective products on Sun.

- Sun has jointly published a large number of competitive benchmark
  results with each of the database vendors. These benchmarks are
  defined by the Transaction Processing Performance Council (TPC) and
  cover online transaction processing (TPC-C) and decision support (TPC-
  H and TPC-R). The more recently released web-based benchmark (TPC-
  W) is likely to be an important focus in the future. The TPC benchmarks are described in more detail in Chapter 27.

- By agreement, Sun also has access to the source code for all four of the
  major databases. Having source code in the Database Engineering lab
  allows experimentation and testing that would not otherwise be possible.

- Sun engineering staff often present at Oracle, Sybase, DB2, and Informix international and regional user group conferences. These partners
  in turn have traditionally presented training to Sun's specialist Systems Engineers (Ambassadors).

Marketing

Sun works with the marketing organizations of the database companies. The relationship includes the following elements:

- Joint marketing programs are developed to promote the products.

- Senior executives from each company meet regularly to plan strategy and marketing direction.

- Each company briefs the other on product plans to ensure that support will be readily available for new products as soon as possible after their launch and that pricing policies will not cause difficulties in the respective field organizations.

Joint Sales Activities

An effective relationship must be expressed in the field organizations as well as in central groups like engineering and marketing. Joint activities take many forms, including the following examples:

- The sales organizations of Sun and its major ISV partners often participate in joint sales and promotional activities at the local branch or regional level.

- Some local offices have arranged mutual training for Systems Engineers. Staff from database vendors receive training in the Solaris Operating Environment and Java technology, and staff from Sun receive database product training.

The Major Database Suppliers

One of the difficulties in describing Sun's relationship with the major database suppliers is that most of the relationships are of such long standing that the detail is overwhelming. In this section I have chosen DB2 for Solaris for a more detailed discussion for two reasons: first, the relationship is relatively recent and therefore easier to track, and second, I was directly involved in the joint engineering effort for three years from its inception and so have detailed knowledge both of the relationship and of the progress achieved during that time.

The relationship between Sun and IBM regarding DB2 for Solaris should illustrate the kind of work carried out by Database Engineering in cooperation with its database partners.

Sun and DB2 for Solaris

Although IBM ported DB2 Version 1 to the Solaris Operating Environment, IBM and Sun first initiated a joint engineering performance project in July 1995, soon after the release of DB2 Version 2. A permanent team was established within the Database Engineering group at Sun with a charter to focus on DB2 for Solaris performance and scalability and to work closely with the DB2 group within IBM tasked with DB2 for Solaris porting and performance.

The objectives of the joint engineering project were

- To ensure that DB2 was well tuned for the SPARC environment.
- To ensure that DB2 took advantage of the features in the Solaris Operating Environment designed to benefit database performance.
- To publish joint TPC benchmarks as milestones to demonstrate the performance benefits of running DB2 on SPARC/Solaris systems.

Both companies invested heavily in Sun hardware for DB2 performance and testing work. The nightly DB2 build is run on Solaris as well as AIX to allow early identification of platform-specific problems resulting from ongoing product development.

DB2 for Solaris has also been used within Sun engineering for testing and research. For example, at the May 1997 SIGMOD Conference, Thin-Fong Tsuei, a senior Sun engineer, presented a research paper titled "Database Buffer Size Investigation for OLTP Workloads." The research was based on DB2 for Solaris on a Sun platform.

Sun and IBM senior executives meet regularly to ensure that maximum leverage is obtained from the partnership. At the engineering level, regular review meetings ensure that each team is aware of new products and schedules. These reviews allow both companies to plan for the testing and support of upcoming operating system and DBMS releases and to take advantage of testing and benchmark opportunities with new hardware platforms.

Finally, IBM and Sun have also initiated a number of joint marketing programs designed to highlight the benefits available to customers from the Sun/IBM partnership.

History of DB2 on Sun Systems

The September 1997 release of DB2 Universal Database for Solaris V5.0 Enterprise Edition (DB2 UDB EE) for the first time gave Sun customers access to a DB2 product that addressed both OLTP and DSS database applications on Solaris. DB2 UDB Enterprise-Extended Edition (EEE), released at the end of March 1998, further extended the DSS capabilities of DB2 into large data warehouse environments.

The previous version of DB2 on Sun, DB2 Common Server for Solaris V2.1.2, established Sun as a high-performance and cost-effective platform for DB2 OLTP customers. The Sun/DB2 combination offered users the scalability and robustness of SPARC/Solaris along with DB2's features, reliability, and proven track record in mainframe connectivity.

The DSS functionality introduced in DB2 UDB had its origins in DB2 Parallel Edition (PE), which ran only on AIX. DB2 Universal Database Enterprise Edition represented a merge of the code lines of DB2 Common Server and DB2 PE.

DB2 Performance and Scalability on Sun

The first phase of the joint engineering performance project resulted in a *threefold* improvement in performance and led in December 1995 to the first DB2 TPC-C result on a non-IBM platform, the highest DB2 TPC-C result at the time. Since that time a number of other TPC results have been published.

DB2 has demonstrated impressive scalability on Solaris. Figure 1.1 shows the DB2 V2.1 TPC-C results published on an 8-CPU SPARCserver 1000E (December 1995) and subsequently on a 16-CPU SPARCcenter 2000E (April 1996).

Figure 1.1 *Early TPC-C scalability with DB2 for Solaris V2.1*

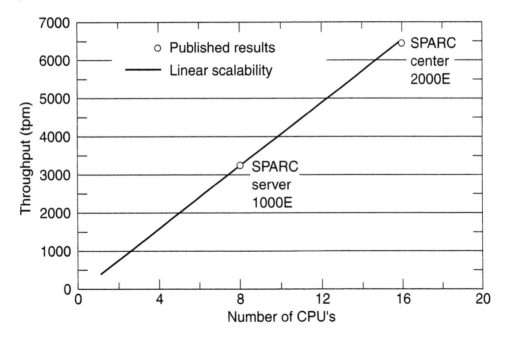

The circles show the published results, and the line shows linear scalability. OLTP workloads do not normally scale linearly; in this case the scalability was achieved thanks to the bufferpool doubling in size from 2 Gbytes to 4 Gbytes, the system bus doubling in capacity, and the database engine being further enhanced for performance.

In November 1997, Sun and IBM published an industry first: a TPC-C and a multistream TPC-D workload both run and audited on the same Sun Enterprise 6000 server at the same time. This result effectively demonstrated the ability of Solaris and DB2 UDB to concurrently manage radically different workloads, even without separating the workloads into different hardware domains. Compared to equivalent standalone runs, the combined workloads showed a degradation of just 1% for each of TPC-C and TPC-D.

The performance improvements resulting from the joint engineering project have been used to good effect in releasing competitive TPC results. Moreover, the changes have progressively been integrated into the releases of DB2 that ship to customers. Providing benefits to end users is the ultimate goal of the engineering partnership between IBM and Sun.

Platform-Specific Modifications to DB2   IBM maintains a common source tree for all open systems versions of DB2 Universal Database. A common source code base means that any new features added to the product are made available automatically across all supported platforms. However, the OS-specific layer of DB2 accommodates differences in the way database operations are implemented on different operating systems. This approach has a number of benefits. It allows IBM these options:

- To take advantage of features available on Solaris that might not be available on other operating systems.

- To choose the optimal method of implementation where a choice is offered, even though the same method may not be the optimal choice on another operating system.

Since the changes are made at a low level, they are transparent to the end user. The benefit is that optimal performance is achieved on Solaris while the functionality of DB2 is not affected at all.

I/O Modifications to DB2 for Solaris   Database performance is intimately connected to the efficiency of disk input and output (I/O). Accordingly, a number of enhancements have been made to DB2 for Solaris to ensure that disk I/O is carried out as efficiently as possible. The enhancements include the following:

- One of the most significant changes to DB2 made for Solaris users was support for raw log files. When raw devices are used, a small number of large log files are preferable to many small files; the maximum log file size was accordingly increased from 64 Mbytes to 256 Mbytes in DB2 V2.1.1.

- A more efficient form of asynchronous I/O, called Kernel Asynchronous I/O (KAIO), is automatically enabled in Solaris when asynchronous I/O is carried out against raw devices. However, DB2 V2 used only synchronous I/O (not to be confused with asynchronous behavior, as in the pagecleaners and prefetchers). The pagecleaners were modified to use asynchronous I/O. This change results in substantial performance gains when tablespaces are placed on raw devices.

- Solaris supports pread(2) and pwrite(2), more efficient forms of the read(2) and write(2) system calls. Their benefit lies in saving one system call per read and write. DB2 was modified to take advantage of pread and pwrite.

- In DB2 UDB V5.0 and later releases as of Solaris 2.6, tablespace containers larger than 2 Gbytes in size were supported. As databases continue to grow in size and disk capacities increase, larger containers can simplify system administration.

Other changes that improved performance included:

- Modification of the number of I/O writes carried out by the pagecleaners each time they were invoked.

- Modification of the delays used by the pagecleaners between issuing asynchronous I/O requests and "reaping" the completed requests.

Other Modifications to DB2 for Solaris The examples below illustrate some of the highlights.

- Intimate shared memory (ISM) allows kernel address translation structures to be shared between processes connecting to commonly accessed shared memory areas. ISM locks memory to eliminate paging and significantly reduces system overhead during context switching. This trivial code change yielded instant performance improvements in DB2 for Solaris. ISM is discussed in more detail under "Intimate Shared Memory" on page 24.

- As demonstrated in Figure 1.1, the TPC-C throughput on the 16-CPU SPARCcenter 2000E more than doubled that on the 8-CPU SPARC-server 1000E. This scalability was partly achieved by a doubling of the number of database buffer pages. Doubling BUFFPAGE was possible only after the DB2 shared memory limit was raised from 2 Gbytes to 4 Gbytes.

- Latch costs vary from platform to platform. Experiments on Sun systems suggested optimal values different from those used on AIX. DB2 for Solaris behavior was modified accordingly.

Many other features in Solaris that benefit database performance, such as large-page support (operating system pages up to 4 Mbytes in size rather than the default 8 Kbytes) for intimate shared memory on Solaris 2.6 and later releases, are available to DB2 without the need for any modification.

This brief history should give an insight into the engineering relationship between Sun and IBM and the benefits that ultimately flow to end users as a result of the relationship. The details also illustrate the way the Performance and Availability Engineering group at Sun works with its partners.

Sun and Oracle

Oracle is able to claim the largest database market share in the UNIX market and thus is an important partner for Sun. The engineering relationship between Sun and Oracle is of such long standing that it would be difficult to enumerate the many product changes that have resulted from the partnership. Nonetheless, the end result has been direct benefits in performance, availability, and functionality to customers of Oracle on the Sun platform.

Sun is itself a major Oracle user: Sun's financial and manufacturing applications run on Sun hardware, using the Oracle Applications software. And Oracle uses Sun hardware to run a number of Oracle's business applications.

Today Sun is the primary RDBMS development platform within Oracle as well as a first-tier release platform. Oracle's Sun Business Unit has worked closely with Sun's Database Engineering group for many years and with Sun's marketing organization.

Sun and Oracle have jointly published many TPC benchmarks, including leading TPC-C, TPC-D, and TPC-H results, on a range of server systems and clusters. Other benchmarks have included APB-1 (which demonstrates OLAP performance, with Oracle Express), and the Oracle Applications benchmark. A number of these benchmarks have resulted in world-record performance results.

Joint Engineering

The joint engineering relationship between Oracle and Sun has allowed each party to enjoy early access to the products and technologies of the other. Technology exchange sessions involving management and senior engineers are regularly scheduled to keep both companies up-to-date on product developments, both current and future.

Joint engineering work between Sun and Oracle has included the following projects:

- Real Application Clusters (previously Oracle Parallel Server) performance (the SunCluster Parallel Database group).

- Oracle parallel data query performance and related benchmark efforts (an example is the published Oracle9i 3-terabyte TPC-H result based on a 2-node Enterprise 10000 Sun Cluster).

- OLTP scalability investigations and related TPC-C benchmark efforts.

- Performance work with very large databases for data warehousing.

- Sun's Oracle Applications Technology Center (SOATC), which focuses on performance of Oracle applications on Sun systems.

- High availability performance and testing work, using Oracle Parallel Server and the Solaris HA-Oracle agent on Sun Clusters.

- Oracle "Test-to-Scale" certification by Sun, along with a 5.5-terabyte data warehouse demonstration.

- Oracle8i Multi-Threaded Server scaling study and recommendations.

As a result of a strategic vendor contract signed with Oracle, Sun has access to Oracle source code, a factor that has helped significantly in joint engineering projects. Oracle, too, shares a strong partnership with Sun products; Oracle is a Java 2 Enterprise Edition (J2EE) licensee and a strong contributor to ongoing Java development.

Sun is Oracle's development platform for its Oracle Applications and Oracle Application Server (iAS), as well as for the Oracle RDBMS. Design, development, and testing work are carried out on the Sun platform. The engineering staff in the Sun Business Unit at Oracle work closely with Sun engineers from Performance and Availability Engineering and other groups.

Sun Engineering

Sun invests heavily in its engineering relationship with Oracle. A dedicated Database Engineering team within the Performance and Availability Engineering group works on Oracle-related projects, and Oracle-based workloads are used for performance testing of the latest server platforms and Solaris. Other engineering groups within Sun also actively work with Oracle, including Strategic Applications Engineering and Market Development Engineering.

Many Solaris improvements, including the following features, have benefited Oracle performance transparently:

- Kernel Asynchronous I/O, available as of Solaris 2.5.1.

- Large page support for intimate shared memory (ISM), available as of Solaris 2.6.

- Solaris I/O (ssd) driver performance improvements, available as of Solaris 2.6.

- In-kernel sockets, available as of Solaris 2.6.

- Direct I/O (which bypasses the file system page cache when accessing files), available as of Solaris 2.6.

- 64-bit address space, available as of Solaris 7.

- Threads library performance improvements, available as of Solaris 8. These improvements resulted in significant benefits to Oracle Express performance.

- PCI I/O subsystem scalability improvements, available as of the 1/01 release of Solaris 8. These changes particularly help I/O scaling and throughput on Sun Fire servers.

- Solaris VM subsystem scaling, available as of the 1/01 release of Solaris 8. Oracle performance is improved by improved E-cache utilization for Oracle shadow processes.

- High-end SMP scaling improvements due to a reduction in CPU cache false sharing effects, available as of the 4/01 release of Solaris 8.

Solaris enhancements specifically implemented by Oracle include the following features:

- List Asynchronous I/O (which submits a list of I/Os to the kernel for processing asynchronously), available as of Solaris 2.5.1, first implemented in Oracle7.3.

- Preemption control (which notifies the kernel that a process is executing a critical section of code and does not want to be preempted), available as of Solaris 2.6, implemented in Oracle8i.

- Process synchronization optimization, available as of the 4/01 release of Solaris 8, implemented in Oracle9i. The effect is to reduce the number of system calls associated with semaphore operations.

- Support for the Dynamic ISM (DISM) and Reconfiguration Coordination Manager (RCM) interfaces, available as of the 4/01 release of Solaris 8, implemented in Oracle9i. DISM allows Oracle to support extending and shrinking the Oracle System Global Area (SGA) and Process Global Area (PGA) when RCM notifies Oracle of CPU and memory changes.

Solaris optimizations are discussed in more detail in Chapter 3.

The list of currently active engineering projects is a long and significant one covering a wide range of issues including performance, availability, resource management, compiler enhancements, and CPU architecture.

Sun and Sybase

Sybase's early meteoric rise to the status of a major database player was largely achieved on Sun systems.

The relationship remains an important one. The banking sector in particular has long been a major user of Sybase and Sun technology. Sybase is used widely within Sun: for example, Sun's sales and support organizations use applications based on Sybase.

Sun has access to Sybase source code. After the release of a 64-bit version of Sybase on Solaris 7, a port actively contributed to by Sun engineers, Sun and Sybase released a world-record TPC-C benchmark result, at the time the largest on an SMP platform. Sun and Sybase have actively participated in performance engineering work on the Starfire platform also.

While Sybase Adaptive Server Enterprise is primarily used for OLTP applications, Sybase Adaptive Server IQ with Multiplex (the original release of which was initially available only on the Sun platform), has also been successfully deployed in data warehouse environments by Sun customers.

Sun and Informix

Sun has always been a major revenue platform for Informix and was the original Informix development platform. Today Sun is a first-tier platform for both Informix Dynamic Server (IDS) and Extended Parallel Server (XPS). IBM's purchase of Informix's database products in 2001 enables Sun to build on the existing relationship with IBM based on DB2 as well on as the engineering work carried out jointly with Informix on its database products.

Sun has had access to Informix source code over many years, contributing to the engineering performance work carried out between the two companies.

Industry-leading TPC-D results have been published on Sun servers, ranging from the low-end Enterprise 450 to the Enterprise 10000 systems, and on 4-way Sun Clusters as well.

The following list illustrates some of the joint Sun and Informix engineering achievements:

- The best TPC-D performance for Informix XPS at 1 terabyte on any platform (based on a 4-node Sun Cluster running XPS 8.2 over the Sun Cluster interconnect). Scalability was enhanced by the use of multiple coservers on each node.

- The best TPC-D performance for Informix at 100 Gbytes on any platform (based on a Sun E450 and XPS 8.2).

- Scalability work resulting in outstanding scalability to 64 CPUs on a Starfire with the TPC-D workload. As part of this exercise, a 300-Gbyte TPC-D result was published with 24 CPUs on an Enterprise 6500 server, followed by a published result on a 64-CPU Starfire (Enterprise 10000).

The 64-bit IDS prototype was developed on Solaris 7 with active participation by Sun. Sun also participated in 64-bit enhancements for XPS 8.3.

IDS 9.2 incorporated OLTP performance enhancements resulting from joint engineering efforts. XPS 8.2 shipped with compiler profile feedback optimizations resulting from compiler testing at Sun.

Other Databases on Sun

Sun has worked with a number of other database vendors in the past. Ingres, now owned by Computer Associates, was one of Sun's strategic DBMS partners for several years.

Software AG and Sun Database Engineering also worked together to ensure that Adabas ran effectively on Solaris.

A number of other relational database products (Progress, for example), also run on SPARC/Solaris along with several object-oriented databases. Database Engineering is not currently involved with these products; instead, the products are supported out of Sun's ISV group. Some of them have large customer bases with Sun hardware.

2

THE ROLE OF DATABASE ENGINEERING AT SUN

The commercial success enjoyed by Sun in the database market is not due just to the strength of Sun's hardware and software offerings. The consistent effort applied within the marketing and sales organizations has borne significant fruit. But the engineering effort, centered around Sun's Database Engineering Group, has yielded consistent and often spectacular improvements in database performance over the years and has brought Sun many world records in competitive benchmarks.

Sun's Database Engineering Group

From small beginnings in 1988, the Database Engineering (DBE) group at Sun Microsystems Computer Division has grown into a substantial organization, now called Performance and Availability Engineering (PAE). The name change reflects a broader scope for the group. As databases increasingly become commodity products, related technologies such as middleware and Internet applications assume more significant roles. Databases have not ceased to be important, though—they are still at the heart of these new applications.

Database and commercial applications engineering teams work full time with the major database vendors, and a Network Applications Engineering team extends the engineering effort to the network stack. Another closely related team works with Solaris software to enhance the operating system with features that improve the robustness, scalability, and performance of database applications. The same team also cooperates with Sun's compiler group to ensure that database workloads are well represented in the ongoing efforts to enhance Sun's compiler technology.

A more recently established group optimizes applications in emerging technology areas. Anticipating rapidly developing markets, such as those catered to by Internet service providers (ISPs) and applications service providers, Sun proactively collaborates with key independent software vendors (ISVs) to identify and resolve application performance and availability issues before they become problems in the user community.

Another team focuses on a comprehensive availability strategy that includes specialized benchmarks with fault injection and recovery monitoring and measurement.

An ongoing project captures and analyzes low-level hardware traces and feeds the results back to the CPU design group at Sun Microsystems Electronics (SME) and the server hardware design group at Sun. Other projects explore the performance and configuration implications of running different types of real-world workloads on databases running on Sun systems.

The charter of Performance and Availability Engineering is the following:

- Provide strategic engineering support for Oracle, Sybase, DB2, Informix, and selected major middleware ISVs.

- Initiate improvements in strategic vendor software and the Solaris Operating Environment to ensure the highest possible performance on the SPARC/Solaris platform for the selected applications. This goal is achieved by measurement, analysis, and tuning.

- Participate in the hardware design process by providing insights into the nature and performance characteristics of a range of database workloads.

- Develop, run, optimize, and support the publishing of database benchmarks, especially TPC benchmarks, to demonstrate the capabilities of Sun servers when running with database workloads. For example, a Java 2 Enterprise Edition (J2EE) benchmark has been developed with a number of Java industry partners.

- Participate in, influence, and lead the TPC standards effort.

- Train and support Sun's worldwide Enterprise Systems Ambassadors (the Enterprise Systems Ambassador Program is described below).

- Improve system availability by increasing the robustness and recoverability of Sun's server products.

- Communicate Sun's achievements in performance optimization and availability enhancements to the Sun field organization and customers.

Related Efforts Within Sun

The Database Engineering group works closely with a number of related organizations within Sun to ensure that databases run well on the Sun platform. One important complementary engineering team is the Strategic Applications Engineering (SAE) group based in Portland, Oregon. SAE originally specialized in benchmarking and performance work on the Starfire (Enterprise 10000) platform and now focuses on publishing and evangelizing benchmarks based on various strategic application workloads across the Sun server range. SAE engineers have many years of experience tuning and configuring commercial workloads on large systems and have significantly contributed to Sun's success in this marketplace. Database Engineering has also worked with the SunCluster group, which works with Real Application Clusters (previously known as Oracle Parallel Server), Informix XPS, and DB2 on Sun clusters.

Other related groups within Sun are the Tactical Benchmarking Group, which runs customer database benchmarks on behalf of the Sun field organization and the competency centers, which specialize in SAP, Peoplesoft, Oracle applications (the Sun Oracle Applications Technology Center, or SOATC), and Baan. Corresponding groups are located in Europe and the Asia-Pacific region.

The Ambassador Program

Sun's Ambassador Program is probably unique in the industry in its scope and effectiveness. Selected systems engineers from Sun's field organization are encouraged to specialize in one of a number of ambassador programs. They in turn become resources available to sales representatives and other systems engineers in their region. This specialization has allowed many ambassadors to become experienced in dealing with issues faced by customers in their area of expertise.

Enterprise Systems ambassadors focus on enterprise systems, which typically involve databases. Ambassador programs are also held for the Solaris operating system, the SPARC hardware architecture, and networking, among others. Ambassadors worldwide are brought together at SunU in California once or twice each year for training.

The Enterprise Systems Ambassador sessions include intensive training from the Performance and Availability Engineering group within Sun as well as input from the database suppliers. Attendees also receive advance information on new hardware and software products from Sun and from third parties with products relevant to enterprise customers.

Performance and Availability Engineering also sponsors job rotations for Enterprise Systems ambassadors. These rotations typically allow ambassadors to participate in a short-term (typically four to eight weeks) project onsite with the PAE group. The information and perspectives flowing in both directions benefit both the engineers and the ambassadors.

Directly interfacing with customers is not part of the charter of PAE. The vast number of Sun customers and prospects interested in enterprise systems necessitates a degree of knowledge and expertise within Sun worldwide. By supporting ambassadors rather than customers directly, PAE is able to leverage its skills more effectively.

3

SOLARIS OPTIMIZATIONS FOR DATABASES

The Solaris Operating Environment (Solaris) includes a number of features and optimizations designed to enhance database performance and availability. These features have been added over a period of years, and new optimizations continue to be applied. Some of these benefits are transparent; that is, they are realized by the database suppliers without any need for code changes. In other cases, database suppliers have modified their products to take advantage of these optimizations.

The performance impact of some of these changes is significant. Researching internal workloads, for example, Performance and Availability Engineering measured a 30% improvement in OLTP performance from Solaris 2.6 to Solaris 8. This speedup came on top of an already substantial performance increase of 16% to 32% (depending on the configuration) from Solaris 2.5.1 to Solaris 2.6.

Most of the features and optimizations outlined in this chapter are described in more detail in the excellent *Solaris Internals* by Jim Mauro and Richard McDougall, published by Sun Microsystems Press. This discussion specifically focuses on the features as they apply to relational databases.

Scheduling Optimizations

Efficient scheduling of processes can make a big difference to database performance, especially for databases like Oracle and DB2 that use a 2n architecture (described in "2n Architectures" on page 58). In this section we discuss the features offered by Solaris to improve scheduling efficiency for database applications.

Preemption Control

Preemption control was introduced to reduce contention on database latches. Database processes use latches—database-specific mutual exclusion locks (mutexes)—to serialize access to critical sections of code or data structures. Each process is granted a time quantum when it is scheduled to run on a CPU. When this quantum expires or when the process is preempted by another process with a higher priority, the process is context-switched out. If the process is preempted while it is holding a database latch, the latch becomes unavailable until the process once again receives CPU time and releases the latch. In the meantime, all other processes that require the latch are stalled.

Solaris 2.6 introduced a new capability called preemption control; Oracle8i was the first database release to implement it. Preemption control allows a database process holding a critical latch to advise Solaris that it does not want to be preempted. If possible, Solaris will grant the process some extra time on the CPU beyond its normal allowance.

Preemption control must be enabled programmatically (with `schedctl_start`(3X) and `schedctl_stop`(3X)).

Dispatch Table Modifications

The introduction of preemption control requires program modifications by database suppliers. An alternative way to reduce the impact of latch contention is to use the appropriate dispatch table for the Solaris TimeShare (TS) Scheduling class (Solaris uses different TS dispatch tables on midrange and high-end platforms). Dispatch table modifications do not represent Solaris optimizations as such; they are better described as effectively exploiting standard Solaris features to benefit database applications.

The dispatch table and its implications for database performance are discussed in "Solaris Scheduling Classes" on page 219.

I/O Optimizations

Solaris includes a range of I/O enhancements that directly benefit databases. Some of the more important optimizations are described in this section.

The pread and pwrite System Calls

Much database activity involves reading from and writing to database tables on disk and to the database log file. The `pread`(2) and `pwrite`(2) system calls were introduced into Solaris to eliminate the need for a separate `lseek`(2) system call to position a file pointer before a `read`(2) or `write`(2) system call. Both `pread` and `pwrite` take the offset within the file as an additional argument. Eliminating system calls frees up CPU cycles for more useful work.

Kernel Asynchronous I/O

When disk I/O is carried out with the read, pread, write, and pwrite system calls, the thread of execution stalls, waiting until the I/O is completed before proceeding. Consequently, these calls are referred to as *blocking* system calls. To allow other work to be done in the meantime, the process yields the CPU while waiting for the I/O to complete. I/O of this type is also referred to as *synchronous I/O*.

An alternative form of I/O used by both multithreaded and process-based databases is *asynchronous I/O*. Asynchronous I/O library calls, aioread(3) and aiowrite(3), return control to the program immediately, without blocking, even though the I/O is not yet completed. The program either expects to be notified of the I/O completion by a signal (SIGIO), or it "reaps" the I/O, often after a delay, by blocking with a special library call, aiowait(3).

Pagecleaners (Database Writers in Oracle terms) typically use asynchronous I/O to fire off multiple writes at one time. This approach is more efficient than waiting individually for each write to complete before initiating the next. Synchronous I/O concurrency can be improved if multiple pagecleaners are used simultaneously, but asynchronous I/O is the more efficient solution.

Asynchronous I/O is implemented with the libaio.so user library. Since the original implementation depends on user threads, an asynchronous I/O call involves multiple switches between kernel and user mode. To improve the efficiency of asynchronous I/O, a special kernel module, /kernel/sys/kaio, handles asynchronous I/O entirely in kernel mode. This feature, known as Kernel Asynchronous I/O (KAIO), was introduced in Solaris 2.4. KAIO requires no software changes by developers—it is invoked transparently on behalf of the calling program.

When asynchronous I/O is carried out, the library attempts to use KAIO to process it. If the database file is implemented on a raw device of some kind (such as a raw disk partition or raw volumes from a volume manager), the I/O will be carried out with KAIO. If the database files reside on file systems, the KAIO attempt will fail (with an ENOTSUP error) and the library will instead create a user thread to complete the I/O.

KAIO delivers performance improvements for database files on raw devices by reducing the length of the code path required to complete an asynchronous I/O. The availability of KAIO is one of many reasons why raw devices are a more efficient choice for database files than are file systems.

Unix File System Enhancements

The broad deployment of database files on the Unix File System (UFS) has resulted in a number of performance challenges. The Solaris file system page cache adds another layer of caching on top of the database buffer cache, often with negative performance implications, especially for large batch jobs where caching offers little or no benefit (these issues are explored in more detail in

"Raw Devices vs. UFS" on page 242). Placing database files on raw devices almost always yields better, and sometimes significantly better, performance than placing them on UFS files.

To eliminate the cache bottleneck, a new feature referred to as Direct I/O was introduced in Solaris 2.6. Direct I/O allows files to be used in the normal way for database files while the Solaris file system page cache is bypassed. An application can enable direct I/O programmatically for individual files with the directio(3C) system call, or an administrator can forceably enable it for an entire file system by mounting with the forcedirectio option.

Note that Direct I/O will not bypass the file system page cache if reads or writes are not aligned with 512-byte sectors or if files have holes. Neither of these situations is likely to occur with databases.

Direct I/O also affects the size of read and write I/Os. Since databases normally open files with the O_SYNC (or O_DSYNC flag), normal UFS behavior for database files is to carry out reads and writes in 8-Kbyte I/Os. That means, for example, that a 2-Kbyte database read results in an 8-Kbyte read I/O and that a 32-Kbyte write is broken up into four 8-Kbyte I/Os. The performance of writes to the log file can be negatively affected by this behavior since transaction commit data is often aggregated by the database to allow a single large write to the log file. Direct I/O frees both read and write I/Os from the 8-Kbyte constraint imposed by the UFS.

Direct I/O as originally implemented did not always result in performance improvements, and consequently a more comprehensive set of optimizations was undertaken to bring the performance of database files on UFS closer to that achievable with raw devices. The improvements resulting from this project became available in the Solaris 8 1/01 release.

One of the most important changes incorporated in this new Direct I/O implementation was the elimination of the single writer lock. Since this lock can have major implications for performance, it deserves some explanation.

For data integrity reasons, the POSIX standard mandates that synchronous writes to files occur in the order submitted. Synchronous writes (write(2) and pwrite(2) calls to files opened with the O_SYNC flag) are used by some databases to flush modified pages from the buffer cache to tables stored in database files on UFS. For raw devices, the database expects to be the sole owner of the device and determines the order in which reads and writes take place. By contrast, Solaris manages writes to file system pages, and the operating system must allow for writes to a file that potentially come from many different sources.

To ensure POSIX compliance, Solaris maintains a single writer lock for each file. While a write is taking place, all reads and writes to the file are blocked until the write completes. If the file access is read-only, this behavior has no impact. For update-intensive workloads generating multiple writes to the same file, the impact can be very significant.

The new implementation of Direct I/O overcomes the limitation imposed by the single reader/writer lock. Tests with write-intensive internal workloads have shown that Direct I/O is able to achieve up to 90% of the performance delivered with raw devices.

The implications of UFS in monitoring database performance is further discussed beginning with "Normal Paging Behavior Prior to Solaris 8" on page 284.

Other I/O Optimizations

A few of the many other Solaris I/O optimizations are outlined below.

UFS Logging

Consistency checking for a large file system can be very time consuming (taking hours in some cases), increasing boot time significantly and delaying recovery after a power outage or system failure. To overcome this problem, Solaris 7 introduced metadata logging support for UFS files.

File system logging is similar in concept to database logging (described in "Logger" on page 54). File system changes are written to a free blocks in the file system, and the log is rolled forward during a system restart. The result is very fast recovery (typically taking seconds).

Enable UFS logging with the `logging` option in `/etc/vfstab`. Refer to the `mount_ufs`(1M) man page for more information.

Large File Support

Even before a full 64-bit version of Solaris became available with Solaris 7, support for large files (greater than 2 Gbytes in size) was delivered in Solaris 2.5.1. This enhancement was made necessary by the rapid increase in the capacity of disk drives, and database suppliers quickly delivered product releases that took advantage of it.

List I/O

In the section titled "Pagecleaners" on page 55, we consider the role of the page cleaners or database writers in flushing modified pages from the database buffer cache to disk. This activity typically involves many asynchronous write I/Os being launched in a short time.

To improve the efficiency of asynchronous I/Os, Solaris made available the List Asynchronous I/O feature. Rather than managing each asynchronous I/O individually, an application can submit a list of I/Os to the kernel with the `lio_listio`(3RT) function call. This approach reduces the number of system calls and allows the I/Os to be processed more efficiently.

List I/O became available in the Solaris 2.5.1 release.

Other Optimizations

A small sample of the many other Solaris optimizations is explored in this section.

Compiler Optimizations

Considerable engineering work has been invested in improving the performance of database code generated by Sun compilers and in ensuring that
database binaries take advantage of the compiler optimizations already available. Examples of the areas focused on are given in the following list:

- **Compiler optimizations.** After research into the assembler code generated during database compilation, developers reduced the instruction
  count and therefore the CPU Instruction Cache miss rate for databases.
  Other optimizations were carried out to reduce CPU Data Cache misses
  on the UltraSPARC III architecture.

- **Profile feedback optimization.** Sun compilers support profile feedback optimization. They use a special compiler feature to capture details
  of block usage within a binary during the running of a workload. The
  code is recompiled with the profile data to achieve better organization of
  blocks within the binary. The result is improvements in the CPU
  Instruction Cache hit rate.

- **Analyzer mapfiles.** Mapfiles reorder functions according to data collected by a sampling analyzer. The objective is to create an executable
  with a smaller working set size, resulting in more efficient use of the
  CPU Instruction Cache.

- **Compiler optimization levels.** Database suppliers have been encouraged to compile with higher optimization levels when preparing database versions for release. Achieving clean compilations with higher
  optimization levels sometimes requires changes to database source code.

Intimate Shared Memory

All major databases use shared memory for database buffer caches, SQL
statement caching, and other uses. Solaris offers a special form of shared
memory called *intimate shared memory* (ISM) with features of particular benefit to databases. ISM was introduced in Solaris 2.2.

ISM offers the following major benefits:

- Processes attaching to the ISM segment share virtual-to-physical
  address data structures related to the shared memory segment, saving
  kernel memory and improving performance.

- Pages are locked, significantly improving performance by reducing the
  kernel code path as well as preventing pages from being swapped out.

- As of Solaris 2.6, ISM memory can take advantage of large pages (up to
  4 Mbytes) supported in the UltraSPARC Memory Management Unit
  (MMU), resulting in a performance benefit that increases with the
  shared memory size. For example, since Solaris pages are typically 8

Kbytes in size, a 3.5-Gbyte database cache would require 458,752 kernel memory pointers. With 4-Mbyte pages, the number of pointers is reduced by a factor of 512, to just 896.

• Since Solaris 2.6, swap space is not required to back the ISM segment, saving disk space. Swap is unnecessary since the memory is locked.

Figure 3.1 illustrates address translation for a regular shared memory segment.

Figure 3.1 *Regular shared memory address translation*

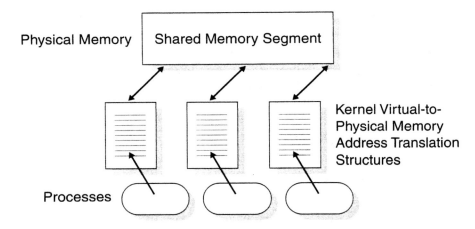

As the figure demonstrates, each process maintains its own address translation structures.

Figure 3.2 illustrates address translation for an ISM segment.

Figure 3.2 *ISM address translation*

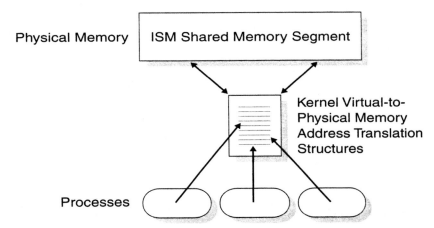

Sharing the same address translation structures among all processes attaching to an ISM segment introduces efficiencies that lead to memory and CPU time savings.

ISM is invoked programmatically by addition of the parameter SHM_SHARE_MMU to the shmat(2) call.

All the major relational databases take advantage of ISM. Note that an attempted ISM attach can fail, though, if insufficient contiguous physical memory is available. Most of the database products will note such a failure in their error log file and quietly attach regular shared memory. The result can be an unexpected drop in performance.

Dynamic Reconfiguration

Dynamic reconfiguration (DR)—the ability to change the hardware resources of a server without shutting it down—is an important capability in any environment where application uptime is a priority. The Solaris Operating Environment and Sun's midrange and high-end servers have supported DR since the mid-1990s (as of Solaris 2.5.1 on the Starfire and as of Solaris 2.6 on the Enterprise product range).

Hardware and operating system support is not enough, though. Unless applications are also aware of and can respond to changes in underlying system resources, DR events may be unable to complete successfully or may cause undesirable consequences.

Consider, for example, a Solaris instance running within a Starfire domain that contains two system boards, each with four CPUs and 4 Gbytes of memory. Imagine that the domain is hosting two database instances, each of which uses 2.5 Gbytes of shared memory. Suppose that the system administrator wants to temporarily remove a system board to allow replacement of a faulty I/O adapter.

DR is a complex undertaking. The hardware needs electrical support for the insertion or removal of components during live operation, and the operating system must be able to support it as well. If a system board with CPUs and memory is to be removed, for example, all processes running on the CPUs must be relocated to CPUs on another board, and all active memory pages must be relocated to memory elsewhere or swapped to disk. I/O boards cannot be detached unless alternate pathing (AP) has been configured to provide another access path to affected disks and networks. Solaris automatically relocates processes and memory pages and also supports alternate pathing.

Databases introduce additional complexity since they use intimate shared memory (described on page 24), which means the shared memory pages are locked in physical memory. Locked pages cannot be swapped to disk—they must be relocated to physical memory on another board.

In the scenario outlined above, 5 of the 8 Gbytes of memory contain locked shared memory pages. Clearly, a board with 4 Gbytes of memory cannot be removed, since the locked memory will not fit on the remaining board. Under normal circumstances Solaris will cancel the requested DR event.

If ISM segments could be resized dynamically, the amount of locked memory could be reduced. Since that is not possible, a more drastic solution is necessary to release locked memory: users must be disconnected from the database and the database must be shut down. Database parameters can then be modified, the database restarted, and users reconnected.

Dynamic Intimate Shared Memory

To allow databases to respond more flexibly to DR events, the 1/01 release of Solaris 8 introduced a modified version of intimate shared memory (ISM) called dynamic ISM (DISM). DISM allows active shared memory segments to be resized dynamically. DISM is invoked programmatically by addition of the SHM_PAGEABLE parameter to the shmat(2) call.

The expectation with ISM is that the size of the initial segment will be suitable throughout the life of the database instance. By contrast, DISM segments are created very large, with only a subset of the shared memory actually used by the database for much of the time. The segment size can then be dynamically grown or shrunk up to the limit of the initial size. DISM segments must be backed by swap space; if a segment is created larger than necessary, the only cost is the wasted swap disk space.

Processes attached to DISM segments share kernel address translation data structures, as do ISM segments. DISM memory is also locked, but the locking is done by the application with mlock(3C), rather than by the operating system as is the case with ISM. Since the application does the locking, it can lock additional memory when the segment needs to grow in size and unlock memory when the segment needs to shrink. Swap space is needed to back the full segment size since memory is not automatically locked, so DISM requires additional disk space for swap compared to ISM.

Returning to the scenario presented earlier, the shared memory segments of one or both databases could be reduced in size to free up locked memory, allowing the system board to be removed without users being disconnected. Reducing the shared memory size could have some impact on performance, but it is far less disruptive than forcing the users off the system.

At the time of this writing, DISM segments do not enjoy large-page MMU support, so some performance impact can be experienced in moving from ISM to DISM. The performance penalty is small for DISM segments up to about 4 Gbytes in size and increases gradually as the segment size grows. This impact can typically be offset by addition of more CPUs if necessary. For absolute best performance, ISM is the better choice; for maximum flexibility in environments with high availability requirements, DISM is the better choice.

The first database supplier to support DISM was Oracle, with the dynamic SGA capability introduced in Oracle9i (described under "Reconfiguring Oracle9i Dynamically" on page 344). Note that Solaris patches are required for DISM, and an Oracle patch is required for the first release of Oracle9i (version 9.0.1).

Reconfiguration Coordination Manager

DISM increases the availability options for databases that implement it. Database shared memory segments can be dynamically reconfigured as required, although the reconfiguration still requires manual intervention.

The Reconfiguration Coordination Manager (RCM) introduced in the 4/01 release of Solaris 8 offers the potential for the entire process to be automated. RCM provides a framework for managing resource-related events such as changes in memory and CPU as a result of DR events like adding or removing system boards. Although RCM is mostly aimed at other Solaris subsystems, a scripting interface was also introduced to allow databases to be notified about RCM events. When a relevant event takes place, the RCM daemon invokes a script, owned by the database instance, to carry out a predefined set of actions on behalf of the database.

This RCM mechanism is supported on Starfire servers as of the 4/01 release of Solaris 8 and on Sun Fire servers as of the 10/01 release of Solaris 8, and Oracle9i is able to take advantage of it thanks to its dynamic SGA feature. Refer to "Reconfiguring Oracle9i Dynamically" on page 344 for more information.

Note that memory interleaving across system boards must be disabled to allow DR to take place. Sun Fire servers still allow 8-way interleaving within a system board, and Starfire servers allow 4-way interleaving within a board.

Thanks to RCM, DR events that would otherwise have required manual intervention from a database administrator can be automatically completed. The combination of RCM, DISM, and complementary database features like Oracle9i's dynamic SGA allow successful completion, without disruption to end users, of DR events that would otherwise have required the database to be shut down.

4

HARDWARE ARCHITECTURE AND DATABASES

Choosing a computer system often involves more than a choice between hardware vendors—it involves a choice between hardware architectures and competing claims about their effectiveness in running database workloads. In this chapter we explore the major hardware architectures and then consider the implications of them for database workloads.

Hardware Architectures

Competing hardware architectures are differentiated by price, performance, availability features, ease of operation (in particular, system administration), and the availability of applications software, including programming languages.

System resources can only be used effectively if the operating system, and possibly also the applications software, understands the design characteristics of the hardware architecture and can schedule resources accordingly. In an ideal world the operating system would hide all such complexity from the end user; the reality is that both system administrators and programmers need some understanding of the architecture. The complexity varies with different hardware architectures, though; the complexity differences will become clear as we consider the major hardware architectures.

Symmetric Multiprocessor (SMP) Systems

Sun was not the first vendor to ship *symmetric multiprocessor (SMP)* systems, but following its initial foray into SMP systems with the SPARCserver 600MP series and the SPARCstation 10, Sun quickly became one of the most vigorous and effective suppliers of SMP systems. The 64-CPU Enterprise 10000 (Starfire) server, in particular, raised the bar significantly with its excellent performance, scalability, and availability features. Sun has also been aided by the maturity, stability, and scalability of its 64-bit-capable Solaris Operating Environment, which has evolved into one of the most robust and popular UNIX operating systems in the market.

As suggested by the use of "multiprocessor" in the name, SMP systems support multiple processors. SMP systems have also been referred to as *uniform memory model (UMM)* or *uniform memory architecture (UMA)* systems, reflecting that all of the main memory on the system is equally accessible by all processors, and with the same performance characteristics. Other major subsystems, such as disk and network, are also equally accessible from all processors.

SMP systems host a single instance of the operating system. Some SMP systems, though, including Sun's Starfire and Sun Fire servers, can be subdivided into domains, which are hardware partitions within a single chassis that comprise CPUs, memory, and I/O controllers. Each domain runs a separate instance of Solaris. For all practical purposes, a domain can be treated as a separate SMP system.

The uniformity of access to resources makes SMP systems some of the simplest to administer and program. Some understanding is still required by the system administrator, though, and major applications, such as databases, do take into account such specifics as how many processors are available.

SMP systems support application parallelism in the following ways:

- Multiple applications can execute simultaneously on different CPUs.

- A single application can take advantage of multiple CPUs to reduce its completion time. You can either break the task into smaller subtasks that can be completed by multiple processes running in parallel, or program a single application to use multiple operating system threads that can run simultaneously on multiple CPUs.

SMP systems can also be combined to form *clusters*—small groups of SMP systems connected by switches or fast networks, with each cluster member running its own operating system instance. Disks are shared among cluster members. Clusters are primarily used to improve system availability; if the cluster heartbeat monitor detects the failure of any cluster member, the role of the failed system is assigned to another cluster member.

The challenges associated with building large, fast SMPs has increased over the years as the number of CPUs and I/O devices increases and places greater demands on the backplane of the system. Since electrons travel at close to the speed of light, it is necessary to reduce the physical bus length as backplane buses become faster. One strategy has been to turn the bus into a "centerplane" and plug in boards from both sides. Crossbar switches have also been used to increase bandwidth by making the bus more parallel, and wider buses have also increased bandwidth (at the cost of latency). NUMA systems, discussed in the next section, offer one possible way of responding to these challenges.

All Sun multiprocessor servers were SMP-based up to and including the Enterprise server product range.

Nonuniform Memory Architecture (NUMA) Systems

As suggested by the name, *nonuniform memory architecture (NUMA)* systems do not provide uniform access times to main memory. The system is typically made up of a number of nodes, each of which includes CPUs, memory, and I/O devices. Within a node, CPU access to memory is uniform, but access takes longer when a CPU needs to access memory within another node.

NUMA systems still provide direct access to all memory and all disk and network devices from all CPUs, although latencies vary, depending on whether the memory or I/O devices are local to the node or on other nodes.

NUMA nodes could be physically separate systems connected by a network or a switch, or boards within the same system connected by a switch but not all sharing the same backplane. Some NUMA implementations include dedicated hardware that keeps memory cache lines coherent across all nodes in the system. The purpose of cache coherence is to ensure that data integrity is maintained when memory is shared across nodes. Maintaining coherency in hardware typically delivers better performance than doing so in software. Such systems are referred to as cache coherent NUMA (ccNUMA) systems.

As for SMP systems, NUMA systems host a single instance of the operating system, spanning multiple nodes. Consequently, application parallelism is supported in the same way as for an SMP system (that is, multiple applications can be run in parallel, or multithreaded applications can concurrently use multiple CPUs). The operating system on a NUMA system needs to be aware of the disparity in memory access times to effectively schedule tasks and allocate resources. Applications that consume large amounts of resource, such as Decision Support System (DSS) applications, also need to take the NUMA architecture into account to achieve optimal performance.

Members of the Sun Fire 3800 to 6800 product range were the first systems shipped by Sun with NUMA characteristics. Note, though, that the latency difference between local and remote memory references is small on these systems.

Massively Parallel Processor (MPP) Systems

Massively parallel processor (MPP) systems are based on independent nodes that contain CPUs, memory, and I/O devices, such as disks and networks. The nodes can be tightly clustered and connected by a switch, as is the case with the IBM SP system, or loosely clustered and connected by standard networks, as is the case with the Linux Beowulf cluster design.

MPP systems differ from NUMA systems, though, in that nodes are unable to directly access the memory and devices on all other nodes. Since devices and memory are not shared, access to remote nodes is achieved indirectly, through the system interconnect. For this reason the MPP architecture is also referred to as a *shared-nothing* architecture.

Another difference from SMP and NUMA systems is that each node hosts an independent instance of the operating system. System administration is consequently more complicated for MPP systems.

Application parallelism is more difficult to achieve with MPP architectures than with SMP or NUMA architectures since applications must be explicitly partitioned into subtasks aware of the underlying architecture. Consequently, parallelism is usually more coarse grained on MPP systems. Databases on MPP systems are typically vertically partitioned to split data rows across different nodes. This is difficult to achieve efficiently for many Online Transaction Processing (OLTP) applications, so MPP architectures are rarely used to deploy OLTP applications.

DSS applications are better suited to shared-nothing architectures provided data can be readily split across multiple nodes. Table scans can be efficiently delegated to the nodes hosting the table to be scanned; the scans can proceed in parallel on all the nodes, reducing the completion time of the scan.

Unfortunately, joins can be significantly less efficient. Suppose Table A has 800 rows to be joined to 2,000 rows from Table B on an MPP system with eight nodes. The table data will probably be evenly split across the eight nodes (approximately), so 100 Table A rows will need to be joined to 250 Table B rows on each node. Unless the joins are colocated, that is, the data in both tables has been split on the join column, data will have to be shipped between nodes to complete the join. Usually data will be shipped from the table with the lesser amount of data to be joined. On average, only one-eighth of the 100 Table A rows on node 1 will be joined with the 250 Table B rows on that node. The other seven-eighths of the Table A rows on node 1 will be needed on the other seven nodes, and an equivalent number of rows will need to be shipped to node 1 from the other nodes to complete the join.

Figure 4.1 illustrates the data movement that will be required when three nodes are involved in a join that is not colocated.

Figure 4.1 *Data shipping between MPP nodes*

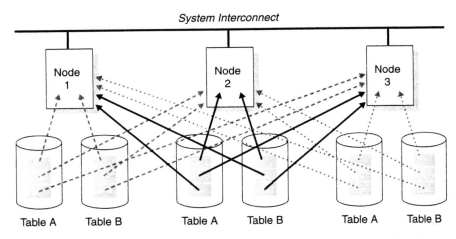

Although the diagram does not make it obvious, data transfer between nodes takes place through the system interconnect.

The amount of data to be shipped increases as the number of rows to be joined increases, and the amount increases further with the number of tables to be joined. Worse still, the amount of data shipped increases with the number of nodes participating in the join. In general, for a system with n nodes, one nth of the join data will remain local, and the rest of the data must be shipped.

MPP vendors initially began selling systems with "thin" nodes containing a single CPU. These systems were touted as "infinitely scalable" for DSS applications: additional nodes could be added as required (although at the cost of repartitioning the data). While this claim had some credibility for table and index scans, the same was not true for join scalability, as we have seen. Not surprisingly, thin nodes became fatter over time as vendors worked to increase processing power without increasing the number of nodes. "Fat" nodes are simply SMP systems, and MPP vendors were soon shipping their largest available SMP as a single MPP node. Processing carried out within an SMP node has the additional advantage of using a fast backplane bus for data transfers, rather than the much slower switch or network used when shipping data to other nodes.

From the perspective of data locality, each node in an MPP system with 64 single-CPU nodes will have 1.5% local references, and a 64-CPU SMP system will have 100% local references.

Sun has never sold MPP systems.

Chip-Level Multiprocessing (CLMP) Systems

A more recent approach to increasing processing power is *chip-level multiprocessing (CLMP or CMP)* systems. CLMP designs place multiple CPUs in a single chip, offering a novel way of overcoming the problem of connecting large numbers of CPUs to a single backplane.

CLMP-based systems are not yet mainstream but could become so in the future.

Databases on SMP and NUMA Systems

Suppose you're on an extended vacation and driving through several countries. As you reach yet another border crossing, an immigration officer approaches and asks for passports. You remain in your vehicle as passport photos are matched with each occupant and an online check carried out just in case you're a well-known criminal stupid enough to use a legitimate passport. The process takes five minutes a person, so, on average, cars are delayed by 15 to 20 minutes, plus any time spent waiting in line.

When a bus arrives, an immigration officer boards the bus to carry out the checks. You don't have to be a rocket scientist to figure out that a three-hour border crossing will not be a pleasant experience for any unlucky bus driver with a full load of 40 impatient passengers. It won't help if the passengers can see from their windows other immigration officers taking a coffee break.

The task will be completed faster if arriving vehicles are directed into multiple queues. If only one officer attends to each queue, though, don't get stuck behind a bus!

If border crossing checks are to proceed smoothly, every eventuality, ranging from individuals on foot to large bus loads, needs to be taken into account. The bus problem can be broken down into smaller pieces if the passengers are asked to disembark for the passport check or if several officers are sent onto each bus. Some way of efficiently redirecting traffic to an idle queue will also be needed.

Similar issues apply when database workloads are run on SMP systems. CPUs may have to deal with large numbers of small transactions (for example, Online Transaction Processing workloads) and very large transactions (for example, decision support workloads). The hardware supplier must provide fast SMP systems and an operating system that offers efficient queueing and resource allocation. The database must present the operating system with a process model that efficiently caters to small transactions and breaks large transactions down into more manageable pieces.

Major database suppliers have optimized their products on Sun's SMP platforms over many years. The Solaris Operating Environment is a mature and robust operating system that delivers efficient scheduling and excellent scalability as the number of CPUs and the load increases.

Apart from uniprocessor systems, SMP systems probably offer the simplest framework for database suppliers to build on. Large numbers of processes are queued and distributed by the OS across available CPUs, so the database primarily needs to ensure that each task is chopped into appropriately sized pieces. Although memory latencies are not uniform on NUMA systems, for all practical purposes databases can treat them like SMP systems, provided the nonuniform behavior does not significantly interfere with performance.

A number of challenges remain. In particular, access and transfer times for disks are considerably slower than for memory, and memory access and transfer times in turn are considerably slower than for CPU caches. Databases must provide efficient caching of database pages to minimize disk access. Program code should be optimized to make efficient use of CPU caches. Database page caching is the responsibility of the database supplier; efficient program code is a shared responsibility between the database and OS.

Sun's compilers offer a number of advanced features to help optimize program code, for example, profile feedback optimization (bringing together the most frequently used blocks of code to improve CPU cache utilization), inlining (replacing function calls by the body of the function), loop unrolling (repeating loop-body instructions inside a single loop iteration to reduce stalls and overall loop overhead), and the use of mapfiles (grouping the most frequently used functions).

Oracle is a good example of a database architecture that has been optimized to efficiently handle both online transaction processing and decision support workloads on SMP systems. Even 32-bit versions of Oracle and Solaris can effectively use much more than 4 Gbytes of memory, too, since the 4-Gbyte address space limit applies to each process, not to the system as a whole.

Although the other major databases also efficiently handle OLTP workloads on SMP systems, some have chosen more complex architectures to deal with DSS systems in an effort to optimize the processing on shared-nothing systems.

Shared-Disk Databases on SMPs

One way of extending a database beyond a single SMP system is to use a shared-disk architecture. Real Application Clusters (previously known as Oracle Parallel Server) is a good example of this model. An SMP cluster is the most common shared-disk hardware platform, although MPP systems that support disk sharing can also be used.

Shared-disk databases run a separate database instance on each SMP in the cluster, but they differ from the shared-nothing model in that all data disks are accessible from all the SMP servers. Further, all of the instances have simultaneous access to the entire data set of the database. In other words, multiple instances share a single database. Since the database is shared among instances, a Distributed Lock Manager (DLM) coordinates access to the data to ensure that cache coherency is maintained and that data integrity is not compromised by the shared access.

Shared-disk databases are primarily used to improve database availability. If a node fails, user applications can be redirected to a live instance running on one of the other nodes of the cluster. Shared-disk environments can also be used to extend the system resources available to a database beyond those available on the single largest SMP system.

For Online Transaction Processing (OLTP) systems, optimal performance on shared-disk databases is achieved by accessing subsets of the data primarily (or even solely) through one node of the cluster. For example, suppose that access to data in an insurance database naturally centers around a six-digit insurance ID. In a two-node cluster, all transactions relating to insurance IDs 0 through 499999 could be directed to the first system, while transactions related to insurance IDs 500000 to 999999 are directed to the second system. Although both systems are capable of accessing all the data, rows associated with a specific insurance ID would only be accessed and cached on one system, eliminating data sharing and hence traffic between the systems to synchronize caches. If one node fails, though, the other is able to take over access to the entire data set. It is important to note that the data itself is not partitioned, only access to the data.

In practice, many OLTP databases do not lend themselves to the neatly partitioned access described in this example. In a sales environment, for example, you might be able to direct transactions to a cluster node on the basis of customer ID. If any customer can purchase any stock item, though, a customer order processed on one system will still need access to the full range of stock IDs.

Shared-disk databases on clusters should not be confused with high availability database configurations on clusters. Many clusters are implemented to support HA database environments: a database instance runs on one cluster node, and if the node fails, another node recovers the instance and takes over the role.

This failover process is greatly simplified by the fact that both nodes share access to the same disks. The environment is not the same as a shared-disk database, though, since only one instance opens and accesses the database at any one time.

Shared-Nothing Databases on SMPs

Which is the better way to transport thirty people from Seattle to Los Angeles: in six cars with five people each or in a bus that accommodates thirty passengers? The answer, of course, is "it depends."

What if you were offered the opportunity to direct a retail operation? Would you prefer a Wal-Mart or a shopping mall full of specialty stores like a clothing boutique, a sporting goods store, a Tandy franchise, a toy store, and a book store?

Such questions often have no right or wrong answer, although sometimes the circumstances favor one alternative over another. Each approach has its benefits and its disadvantages.

The common element between the two scenarios is the choice between managing the problem as a single entity or breaking it into smaller pieces. Database administrators face similar choices with DB2 Universal Database

Enterprise-Extended Edition (EEE) and Informix Extended Parallel Server (XPS), since both products offer the possibility of implementing DSS databases on SMP and NUMA systems with a shared-nothing database architecture.

We examine this architecture here in detail for two reasons: first, people experienced with SMP systems may not be familiar with the shared-nothing approach, and second, people enthusiastic about shared-nothing database architectures may not have considered implementing them on SMP systems.

This concept may seem confusing, since many people automatically associate the term "shared nothing" with a hardware architecture (MPP). I am making a distinction between the shared-nothing hardware architecture (as implemented in MPP systems), and the shared-nothing database architecture (as implemented in DB2 UDB EEE and Informix XPS). Shared-nothing databases were originally designed to run on MPP systems, but they can just as readily be implemented on large single SMP systems.

Should You Split Up?

The decision to partition data or not is no longer tied to a hardware choice between a massively parallel processor (MPP) system consisting of relatively small interconnected systems and alternatives like a cluster of SMP systems, a NUMA system, and an SMP system with a large number of processors in a single server. Even on a single SMP system, DB2 UDB EEE and Informix XPS make it possible to partition data into multiple logical nodes. The key issue is to identify the factors that can help an administrator decide whether or not to partition data for a data warehouse.

Characteristics of Logical Nodes

If you decide to partition your data across *multiple database partitions*, or *coservers* in Informix XPS terminology, you must split each table by using one or more of its columns, such as the primary key, to determine the partition where it should be located. On a cluster of SMPs or an MPP system, these partitions are associated with physical nodes and consequently are spread across multiple servers. On a large SMP system, the partitions simply coexist on the same server as logical nodes.

Logical nodes share the following characteristics:

- The nodes operate in shared-nothing mode. If they were implemented on physical nodes (that is, physically separate servers) they would behave in exactly the same way, with one significant exception: logical nodes communicate by fast interprocess communication (IPC) mechanisms such as shared memory, rather than by an external network or switch as do physical nodes.

- Just as for physical nodes, each logical node has its own independent instance of the database, including shared memory, data disks, and log disks. A subset of the CPUs on the server, such as a processor set, may also be dedicated to the logical node.

- The data is partitioned, or split, or fragmented in Informix XPS terminology, with a subset of rows allocated to each node (in other words, vertical partitioning is used). All access to the rows in a particular node is delegated to that node.

- The database hides the complexity of the node structure from the end user. The logical view of the database makes it appear to be a single entity. A single query will automatically be processed in parallel on all nodes that host data required by the query.

- Where queries require access to data from multiple nodes, the data must be shipped between the nodes to allow database operations like joins to proceed. The final result set must also be shipped to the initiating node.

The Single Data Image Alternative

Both DB2 UDB and Informix XPS allow you to parallelize queries within a single node, so even with these products you can choose to maintain a single data image rather than create multiple logical nodes by partitioning your data.

If you don't split your data into partitions, you can still parallelize individual queries by farming out the work to multiple subagents (DB2) or threads (Informix), which work cooperatively and use the same shared memory segments.

The greatest advantage of this model is its simplicity. Since there's no need to split the data, both initial and ongoing data administration become more straightforward. It's like hiring a bus to L.A. and finding you've avoided the hassle of figuring out who should travel in which car.

Query Scalability

If you intend to deploy a large DSS database on a large SMP system with either DB2 or XPS, you will probably find yourself wondering which is more effective: logical nodes with partitioned data or one node with a single data image? There is no absolute answer to that question; the effectiveness of query parallelism in each case will depend largely on the optimizer.

The major tasks of an optimizer are to minimize the query completion time and to minimize the CPU and disk activity required to complete a query. Assuming the optimizer chooses an efficient plan, scalability will depend on the following factors:

- The degree to which each phase of the query plan can be parallelized.

- The extent to which the work can be divided in practice across the CPUs and disks involved in executing the query plan. Imagine processing all the names in the telephone directory—a subagent or thread ploughing through the "Smiths" will have a lot more to do than a subagent or thread working on the "Entwhistles."

- The likelihood of timely delivery of the required data and index pages to the subagents or threads.

- The location of the performance bottleneck. In this context a bottleneck is the system component that limits performance because it is 100% busy while other system components lie idle or relatively idle as a result.

In an ideal world, your system will not be disk-bound. In other words, performance will not be limited either because your disk I/O is unevenly balanced (some disks idle while others are fully utilized) or because you don't have enough disk throughput capacity to keep your CPUs busy.

If you don't have a disk or memory bottleneck, you should be CPU-bound. That being the case, table scans should parallelize well both for single and multiple logical nodes and should scale well as you add CPUs. Next time you see a DBMS vendor demonstrating scalability as CPUs are added, don't be fooled by how complex the SQL looks at a casual glance. You can bet the vendor is doing some variation of a single table scan, maybe with some CPU-intensive aggregation thrown in.

All bets are off, though, once you do multiple table joins. It is much harder to predict both the scalability of the query as you add CPUs and the degree to which the various phases of the query will parallelize. Our shared-nothing database performance testing at Sun, though, suggests that parallelism within a logical node does not scale well much beyond about 8 to 12 CPUs, whereas scalability for parallelism across nodes extends well beyond that. On the other hand, complex multiple-table joins on multiple logical nodes can involve a costly process of shipping data between partitions, a task that is unnecessary with a single data image. Data shipping is described in "Massively Parallel Processor (MPP) Systems" on page 32.

To Partition or Not to Partition?

Deciding whether or not to partition your DSS data is one of the most far reaching decisions you will make with DB2 UDB EEE or Informix XPS. It's helpful to get it right from the beginning because changing your mind after the data is loaded involves a lot of work. Fortunately, there are guidelines that can help in making the decision.

- **How much raw data do you have in your database?**

  Data warehouses with up to 100 Gbytes of raw data (not including indexes and temporary tablespaces) are typically well suited to a single logical node. The additional administration associated with partitioned data is probably not worth the effort for a small data set.

- **How many CPUs do you have in your server?**

  Our experience suggests that for both UDB EEE and XPS the optimal number of CPUs per logical node is roughly between 4 and 12, although the number of concurrent users (more on this later) also affects this sizing. If you have 12 or more CPUs, it may be worth considering multiple nodes with 4 to 12 CPUs each. Choose a number of nodes that divides evenly into the number of CPUs you have; optimizers work best with nodes of the same size.

- **How much memory do you have in your server?**

  However much memory you have in your server, 32-bit databases will only be able to access 4 Gbytes. All databases running on versions of Solaris before Solaris 7 are 32-bit, and many implemented on Solaris 7 and later versions are also 32-bit, although 64-bit versions of both DB2 and XPS are available.

  The 4-Gbyte limit is associated with all applications and operating systems based on a 32-bit architecture. However, the limit is per process, not systemwide, so processes in each logical node can consume up to 4 Gbytes of memory. It is reasonable to configure between 512 Mbytes and 1 Gbyte per CPU to allow for buffer pool pages, sort heaps, and other application requirements.

  Many customers are likely to be satisfied with 4 Gbytes per logical node. If, however, you have substantially more memory than that in your server, you may want to configure more than one logical node.

- **Is your server likely to grow in the immediate future?**

  If you expect to add CPUs, it's worth thinking about the implications for your data layout. Adding more CPUs to a single logical node environment is simple, and no change to your data is required. When you run a query you will find that more CPUs can be configured to participate in its execution.

  The scenario can be a little more complicated with multiple logical nodes. If you have 12 CPUs, for example, with two logical nodes and you add another 6 CPUs, you will probably want to add an additional database partition. That means redistributing your data. DB2 and Informix provide utilities to help with this process, but it is worth being prepared for the additional system administration overhead.

  If your server is near its capacity, remember that logical nodes can grow beyond the biggest single server: physical and logical nodes can intermingle.

- **What is the relative importance of system administration and performance?**

  Partitioning data means splitting it before loading and possibly reorganizing it as your data or your environment changes. In general, system administration is more complicated with multiple logical nodes than with a single node. For large databases or large servers, though, you can probably squeeze more performance out of a partitioned installation.

  If performance is the major priority, go with multiple logical nodes for large systems. If your system administration resources are constrained, you will appreciate the relative simplicity of a single node and may still find performance quite satisfactory.

- **How many users will be querying your database concurrently?**

  Using multiple CPUs to speed the execution of a single query may be less important if you have a large number of users querying the database at the same time.

  It is worth remembering that with multiple logical nodes, a minimum of one subagent or thread will be active for each node involved in the query. So if your data is split across four nodes, a minimum of four CPUs will be active per user. In that sense, it is harder to restrict the degree of parallelism with multiple nodes than with a single node.

- **How easy is it to partition your data?**

  Deciding how to partition your data is usually no simple task. It isn't just a matter of evenly distributing your data across the partitions; it's also about facilitating evenly distributed access to your data across partitions, which may be a different matter entirely. Also, you want to avoid data shipping between partitions wherever possible. Colocated joins, where all the rows that are joined are resident in the same partition, are much more efficient than joins requiring access to data stored elsewhere. Unfortunately, it is rarely possible to split data in such a way that data shipping is avoided, especially for ad hoc queries. Colocated joins are discussed earlier in this chapter in "Massively Parallel Processor (MPP) Systems" on page 32 and in the DB2 tuning chapter in "The Data Shipping Problem" on page 410.

  Some data warehouses lend themselves to partitioning. For example, as discussed previously, deciding how to split an insurance database where much of the data revolves around an insurance ID could be fairly straightforward. It may be less easy with financial data.

  You may find you don't have to split your data at all. If you can't otherwise decide between single and multiple logical nodes, the ease of partitioning your data may help swing your decision one way or the other.

- **How well known are your queries?**

  If users will be running a relatively fixed set of predefined queries, you should take into account the join columns when partitioning the data.

Unfortunately, a successful data warehouse is likely to see greater use and often an increase in the number of ad hoc queries, many of which may not match the partitioning strategy.

- **How stable is your data?**

  The best-case scenario is that your partitioned data will stay reasonably well balanced as you add to and delete data from your warehouse. If that balance is difficult to achieve, you will find multiple nodes come with an ongoing system administration overhead that isn't there with a single node.

These guidelines highlight the issues to be considered in choosing a partitioning strategy with DB2 UDB and Informix XPS. The final decision is yours, based on your own unique requirements.

Choice is usually seen as a good thing, although sometimes it makes life more complicated. DB2 UDB and Informix XPS now offer you genuine choice in setting up your data warehouse. Choose carefully, and enjoy the benefits.

Part Two

Database
Architecture

- Introduction to Database Architecture
- Database Workloads
- The Role of the Buffer Cache
- The Role of the Database Optimizer
- Oracle Architecture
- Sybase Architecture
- Informix XPS Architecture
- DB2 for Solaris Architecture

5

INTRODUCTION TO DATABASE ARCHITECTURE

The implementation details of each Relational Database Management System (RDBMS) are unique, and different database suppliers use different terms to describe the behavior of their products. Nevertheless, the fundamental design of all relational databases is similar. In this chapter, we examine the architecture and process models of the major RDBMS products and also consider briefly the architecture and relevance of transaction monitors.

Architecture of Relational Databases

Relational databases consist of a number of common elements:

- **Data store** — Contains the data and is held on disk.

- **Database engine** — Provides the core functionality of the database system, including functions used by other components of the system.

- **Query optimizer** — Determines the most efficient access path to the data store when data is requested.

- **Shared memory** — Holds the database buffer cache as well as caches for other frequently used data. Facilitates interprocess communication.

- **Logger** — Records modifications to the data in a log file to preserve the integrity of the database in the event of a database or system crash.

- **Pagecleaners** (*Database Writers* in Oracle terms) — Flush modified pages from the database cache to disk.

- **Database recovery process** — After a database crash, restores the database to a consistent state and reapplies any transactions that were not written to database tables on disk.

- **Locking subsystem** — Allows concurrent access to the database while ensuring that data integrity is preserved.

- **System and process monitors** — Monitor all active processes in the system and provide for orderly shutdown of the system if any process fails.

Each of these components is under the control of the database system; users cannot gain direct access to them. Instead, the database system provides access to the database through the following mechanisms:

- **Interactive interface and batch interface** — Support execution of Structured Query Language (SQL) commands. SQL is the primary means of accessing data in a relational database.

- **Set of application programming interfaces** (APIs) — Allows database access by user applications. APIs provide access to SQL functionality from within other programming languages.

- **Performance monitoring tools** — Provide information about the efficiency of the database system.

We examine in turn each of the elements outlined above.

Data Store

Data in a relational database is held in *tables* (also referred to as *relations)*, as rows (or tuples), and columns (or attributes). Table data can be compared to the data held in a spreadsheet. Table data, however, might not be held in any particular sequence, and data is not guaranteed to be retrieved in any particular order unless an SQL command includes order by or group by clauses or the data is retrieved by an index.

System information about database files, tables, columns, and other objects in the database is also stored in tables (referred to as *system catalogs)*.

Indexes

Tables often have *indexes* to provide quick access to data rows by using keys. Indexes are stored as separate database objects, independently of the tables they reference. Quick access is achieved by storing pointers to the data rows along with the key values. Key values are stored in a form that supports fast and efficient searching. Once a specific key has been found, the data row can be retrieved with the stored pointer information.

A table typically has a *primary key*—a column whose values are used to uniquely identify the row—and an index associated with the primary key. Additional indexes using different columns can also be created for the same table.

Alternative index methods include the following:

- **B-tree indexes.** This index method is probably the most commonly used method. Key column data is stored in a tree structure after having been sorted by value. A B-tree index supports fast access on retrievals involving exact values (for example, the customer with a customer ID of 123456) or ranges of values (for example, all customers with zip codes between 94000 and 94050). The index is dynamic and will grow as the table grows. Finding the key value and its associated data row location could require more than one disk access; the larger the B-tree, the more branches of the tree (*nonleaf pages*) will be traversed to reach the final result (the *leaf pages*).

- **Hash indexes.** The location of the data page storing the index is determined by a hashing algorithm applied to the key column values. A hash index supports fast access on retrievals involving exact keys; hash structures are not suitable for range retrievals. Hash indexes can be stored in separate database objects, or the index can be eliminated altogether and the entire row stored directly in the hash page. The benefit of hash indexes is that the key value can often be reached with a single disk access.

- **Clustered indexes.** All table data, not just the key columns, is stored along with the index information, allowing efficient retrieval of table data once the index key has been located.

- **Bitmapped indexes.** Bitmaps are constructed for each unique value in a column and a single bit allocated for each row. The bit is turned on to indicate that the row contains that value. Bitmaps become more clumsy as the number of unique values in a table increases, since more space is required to store the bitmaps and the bits set in any specific bitmap become more sparse. Compressed bitmaps help to some degree, although they do reduce performance. An excellent candidate for a bitmapped index might be a Gender column containing one or other of the values M or F for each row.

  Bitmapped indexes allow for very efficient processing of predicates with OR and AND clauses using binary arithmetic.

Indexes can significantly improve the performance of queries, but they come at a cost. Apart from the additional disk storage requirement, the price of keeping indexes up-to-date must be paid every time table data is inserted or deleted: an insertion or deletion is required for every index associated with the table, and every update of a table column requires an update of every index with keys based on that column.

One of the benefits of the relational database model compared to older forms of data storage is that the application programmer need not understand the specifics of how data is retrieved from the database. Before relational databases, if access to a data file was achieved with a key, the programmer needed to declare a key variable and assign a value to it before retrieving data from the file. With the relational model, the programmer does not even need to know whether indexes are used at all. Adding a new index to a table may help query performance, but it does not require any change to the SQL code used to access the table data. In other words, logical and physical data structures are independent.

Database Pages

Table and index data within a relational database are stored in data blocks or *pages*, typically between 2 and 32 kilobytes in size. The page size determines the granularity of data access—each read or write to the database results in a minimum transfer of one page. If table data from a row 200 bytes in size is needed by an application program, a whole page (2 kilobytes or more) is read into shared memory, not just the 200 bytes required. If one byte is changed in the row, the entire page is flushed to disk, not just the byte that changed. Not surprisingly, the database page or block size also determines the size of pages in the shared memory buffer cache.

Online Transaction Processing (OLTP) applications typically use small page sizes, and Decision Support System (DSS) applications use large page sizes. Refer to "Influence of Page Size on Buffer Cache Effectiveness" on page 85 for more information about choosing the page size for a database.

Normalization

Many users follow Codd's rules of *normalization* in designing databases to ensure that duplication is avoided and the design is easy to understand and extend.

In particular, many users choose to store the data in *Third Normal Form* (3NF). A table is in Third Normal Form if:

- The intersection of each row and column in the table (or "relation") contains one and only one value (First Normal Form).
- Every nonprimary key attribute is fully functionally dependent on the primary key (Second Normal Form, provided First Normal Form is also true).
- No nonprimary key attribute is transitively dependent on the primary key.

As an example, let's look at what might happen if we put family details into a database.

Table 5-1 shows a family whose details are stored in a single family table.

Table 5-1 *Denormalized family table*

id	name	birth_date	death_date	spouse_name	children
1	John Smith	1 Jan 1961	NULL	Mary Jones	Fred Smith
					Anne Smith
					Harry Smith
2	Mary Jones	1 Apr 1962	NULL	John Smith	Fred Smith
					Anne Smith
					Harry Smith

Table 5-1 *Denormalized family table (Continued)*

id	name	birth_date	death_date	spouse_name	children
3	Fred Smith	10 Mar 1992	NULL	NULL	NULL
4	Anne Smith	20 Oct 1994	NULL	NULL	NULL
5	Harry Smith	7 Dec 1997	NULL	NULL	NULL

Since each parent has multiple children, the "children" column has multiple values for each row. This table is *denormalized*, or not normalized.

Holding multiple values in a single cell complicates processing of the data. A simple solution is to set up a separate row for each child, as shown in Table 5-2.

Table 5-2 *Family table in First Normal Form*

id	name	birth_date	death_date	spouse_name	child_name
1	John Smith	1 Jan 1961	NULL	Mary Jones	Fred Smith
1	John Smith	1 Jan 1961	NULL	Mary Jones	Anne Smith
1	John Smith	1 Jan 1961	NULL	Mary Jones	Harry Smith
2	Mary Jones	1 Apr 1962	NULL	John Smith	Fred Smith
2	Mary Jones	1 Apr 1962	NULL	John Smith	Anne Smith
2	Mary Jones	1 Apr 1962	NULL	John Smith	Harry Smith
3	Fred Smith	10 Mar 1992	NULL	NULL	NULL
4	Anne Smith	20 Oct 1994	NULL	NULL	NULL
5	Harry Smith	7 Dec 1997	NULL	NULL	NULL

This table, or relation, is now in First Normal Form. One unfortunate characteristic of the new Family Table is duplication of data. A death date for John Smith, for example, would need to be updated in three different rows. The solution is to reorganize the data into new tables in Second Normal Form, as in Tables 5-3, 5-4, and 5-5.

Table 5-3 *Family table in Second Normal Form*

id	name	birth_date	death_date
1	John Smith	1 Jan 1961	NULL
2	Mary Jones	1 Apr 1962	NULL
3	Fred Smith	10 Mar 1992	NULL
4	Anne Smith	20 Oct 1994	NULL
5	Harry Smith	7 Dec 1997	NULL

Table 5-4 *Spouse table in Second Normal Form*

id	name	spouse_id	spouse_name
1	John Smith	2	Mary Jones
2	Mary Jones	1	John Smith

Table 5-5 *Child table in Second Normal Form*

id	name	father_id	father_name	mother_id	mother_name
3	Fred Smith	1	John Smith	2	Mary Jones
4	Anne Smith	1	John Smith	2	Mary Jones
5	Harry Smith	1	John Smith	2	Mary Jones

The new Spouse and Child tables mean that only information directly relevant to the person needs to be held in the Family table. It is still possible to find out everything that was known before, but information is now concentrated in special-purpose tables.

There is still duplication of information, though. It isn't really necessary to hold both the Name and ID in the Spouse and Child tables. The ID is sufficient to allow the name and other details to be looked up.

The final step, Third Normal Form, leads to the final Spouse and Child tables shown in Tables 5-6 and 5-7.

Table 5-6 *Spouse table in Third Normal Form*

id	spouse_id
1	2
2	1

Table 5-7 *Child table in Third Normal Form*

id	father_id	mother_id
3	1	2
4	1	2
5	1	2

One of the implications of normalization is that table joins become necessary to answer questions. For example, to find out the names and birth dates of the children of John Smith, a join between the Child and the Family tables is required. In SQL it might look like this:

```
select a.name, a.birth_date
from family a, child b, family c
where c.name = 'John Smith' and c.id = father_id
and a.id = b.id;
```

Sometimes for performance reasons users choose to partly denormalize some tables. For example, the Second Normal Form Child table allows the names of the children of John Smith to be retrieved without a join. OLTP databases are usually normalized; DSS databases are sometimes denormalized, sacrificing maintainability for the sake of performance.

Database Engine

At the heart of a relational database is the code that provides the core resources needed to access the data store and maintain its integrity. The engine provides operating-system-specific code that interacts with the operating system, a data manager that accesses the data while preserving ACID properties (see below), and a lock manager that manages multiuser access to the data. The operating-system-specific layer ensures that the database takes advantage of the particular features of an operating system while preserving a consistent interface to users and programmers.

The lock manager acquires locks on tables or rows (and sometimes pages) on behalf of users to ensure that data is not lost or corrupted should simultaneous updates occur. Locks can also prevent access to uncommitted data or prevent update to protected data. The role of the lock manager is discussed in more detail in "Locking Subsystem" on page 55.

The data manager is responsible for retrieval and update of data in a manner that preserves the integrity of the data. The mechanism used by the data manager obeys the ACID model.

ACID properties refers to the database characteristics of atomicity, consistency, isolation, and durability, which are maintained for all database accesses.

Atomicity means that all modifications to the database either complete in full or not at all. So, for a transaction involving two or more data changes, either all the changes are committed or none are.

Consistency means that all changes to the database leave the database in a consistent state. In other words, a transaction leaves data in a valid state or, if a failure occurs, returns all data to its previous state.

Isolation means that a transaction not yet committed must remain isolated from all other transactions. So, each transaction behaves as though it is the only transaction running. Databases support multiple levels of isolation; usually DSS applications require lower isolation levels than OLTP applications. Even OLTP transactions might not require the highest isolation levels. A query reporting sales figures for the day, for example, may not require results with up-to-the-millisecond accuracy, so it may not matter if some of the data retrieved by the query is simultaneously being changed by another transaction.

Durability means that committed data is saved such that the database can survive the failure of a component after system restart and recovery. So, committed transactions are able to survive failures.

The programmer can take advantage of the ACID model simply by flagging SQL code with BEGIN at the start of a transaction and COMMIT at the end, or ROLLBACK if changes need to be backed out.

Query Optimizer

One of the attractions of relational databases is that the application developer need not know anything about the access path to the data. Deciding the best way to retrieve the data requested by a SQL query, either directly or by an index, for example, is left to the database *optimizer*. Modern query optimizers are becoming increasingly sophisticated; Chapter 8 describes the role and function of query optimizers.

Database Shared Memory

Each database sets aside a substantial area of *shared memory* accessible by all processes associated with the database. The shared memory includes the following components:

- A buffer cache to store recently used database pages or data blocks. Subsequent requests for the same pages can then be satisfied from the cache and the data need not be reread from the disks. The buffer cache stores pages of system catalog data as well as user table data.

  Modified data pages can also be held in the cache until they can conveniently be flushed to the disk. A data page can be modified more than once before being flushed, saving disk writes in the process.

- A cache to store prepared SQL statements. Each SQL statement is parsed and a query plan is generated before the statement can be executed. If an identical SQL statement is used later and recognized in the cache, it isn't necessary to parse it again and generate a new plan.

- A log buffer to store details of data modifications. When the log buffer is full or another triggering event occurs, the buffer is written to the log file.

- Message areas used in Interprocess Communication (IPC) between different database processes.

- Other database system-specific internal caches.

All database system processes attach to the shared memory, as do all user agent or shadow processes.

For 32-bit databases (all databases implemented on Solaris 2.6 or earlier, and still the most common option for Solaris 7 onward) the shared memory is limited to a maximum of around 3.75 Gbytes since the address space of processes is limited to 4 Gbytes. Only very large databases are likely to require more, in which case 64-bit databases on Solaris 7 or later allow huge shared memory segments.

Databases attach to shared memory with the SHM_SHARE_MMU flag, which invokes *intimate shared memory* (ISM), discussed further in "Intimate Shared Memory" on page 24. ISM brings a number of benefits:

- **"Pinned" or locked pages.** All shared memory pages are locked into memory and cannot be paged out by the operating system. Locking ISM pages ensures that crucial cache pages are always in memory. (It also means that oversized shared memory segments unnecessarily tie up physical memory, denying it to other processes.)

- **Shared address translation structures.** All processes attached to the shared memory share virtual-to-physical memory address translation structures pointing to the shared memory segment, avoiding duplication and saving considerable CPU time. The CPU savings translate to improved performance.

- **Large pages.** From Solaris 2.6 onward, large pages are used in the Memory Management Unit (MMU) to reduce the number of page table entries necessary to reference the shared memory. Large pages can map up to 4 Mbytes of memory with a single reference rather than the standard 8 Kbytes, a saving of 512 times! Large pages also reduce the overheads associated with Translation Lookaside Buffer (TLB) misses (the TLB is a cache of address translation information). The use of large pages can free up enough CPU to allow a throughput increase of several percent for some workloads.

- **Freed swap space.** From Solaris 2.6 onward, swap space is not required to back ISM segments. The swap space can be freed since the pages are locked in memory and therefore never need to be paged. The benefit here is a saving in disk space rather than any performance benefit.

Since ISM pages are locked in memory, a request to attach ISM segments will succeed only if enough contiguous physical memory is available to satisfy the request. If more ISM memory is requested than is available, one of two things will happen:

- The database will fail to start. In this case, the shared memory requirement must be reduced (for example, by reducing the size of the database buffer cache), and the database must be restarted.

- As a fall-back position, the database will request normal shared memory rather than ISM. This second request should always succeed provided enough swap space is available. On a heavily utilized system, though, performance may be noticeably impacted. If the user is not aware that ISM is not being used, the performance degradation may seem baffling.

  Oracle reports failed attempts to attach ISM segments in the `alert.log` file, and Sybase reports failed attempts in the Sybase error log.

The 1/01 release of Solaris 8 introduced a new form of intimate shared memory, called Dynamic ISM (DISM) or Pageable ISM, discussed further in "Dynamic Intimate Shared Memory" on page 27. DISM has the same behavior as ISM with two exceptions: pages are not locked automatically (that operation must be done independently with the `mlock(3C)` function call); DISM does not include large page support in the MMU. Further, because pages are not automatically locked, swap space must be allocated for the shared memory segment. On the other hand, DISM is not subject to failure due to lack of physical memory in the same way as ISM, so DISM segments will always enjoy shared page table support. Of course, an attempt to lock DISM pages may fail if physical memory is insufficient.

The key benefit of DISM is the ability to dynamically expand or reduce the size of the shared memory segment. A DISM segment is initially created large enough for the biggest active shared memory size anticipated. It is possible that the full size will not be required initially, in which case only a subset of the DISM segment will be locked and used. If more is required later, the additional memory can be locked and used. Conversely, memory can be unlocked if it is no longer required, thereby allowing a database to adjust its shared memory use in response to dynamic reconfiguration or other availability-related events. Oracle has included support for DISM as of the Oracle9i release, in the form of a dynamic or resizeable system global area (SGA). This feature is discussed in "Reconfiguring Oracle9i Dynamically" on page 344.

DISM is enabled programmatically with the `SHM_PAGEABLE` flag when attaching to a shared memory segment (with the `shmat(2)` system call) rather than the `SHM_SHARE_MMU` flag.

Logger

All modifications to the database are recorded in the database log. Once the modifications are successfully written to the log disk, the transaction is regarded as complete and the "commit" returns. The database tables on disk may not be updated until later.

In the event of a system crash, the information recorded in the database log can be used to ensure that all modifications to the database are applied to the data in the tables on disk.

The log file is not written to directly by database user processes. Instead, data intended for the log file is saved into an area of memory referred to as a log buffer. A *logger* process or thread writes the log data to the log file when the log buffer fills or when a user-specified time interval elapses. *Group commits*—commits from multiple transactions that are written from the log buffer to the log file in a single write—can increase the efficiency of the logger and help ensure that it does not become a bottleneck. For optimal performance, log files are located on raw devices.

Some databases use a fixed number of log files. When one is filled, the database switches to the next. When the last is filled, the first is reused. With this strategy, the logs are referred to as *circular logs*. DB2 for Solaris also has an alternative called *retained logs*: a new log file is created when the previous log is filled.

You may wonder how log data is preserved with circular logs. The answer is that log files are archived to disk or tape before being overwritten; most databases archive logs as soon as they are filled, when the log switch takes place.

Pagecleaners

As described above, modified pages are left in the buffer cache rather than being written immediately to database tables on the disks. The task of flushing modified or "dirty" data pages to disk is handled by the *pagecleaners* (*Database Writers* in Oracle terminology).

The pagecleaners wake up periodically and decide whether to flush dirty pages. The decision is typically based on factors like these:

- The percentage of data pages in the buffer cache that are dirty (modified).
- The percentage of free (unused) page buffers left in the buffer cache.
- The elapsed time since the oldest unflushed data page has been written to disk.

From time to time, most relational databases carry out a *checkpoint*, which is a point in time when the pages in the buffer cache are synchronized with the database pages on disk. The synchronization is achieved by the pagecleaners, which flush all dirty buffers from the buffer cache to disk. When the checkpoint has completed, a checkpoint record is written to the log file.

Database Recovery Process

After a system crash, the database recovery process or thread finds the most recent checkpoint record in the log file; recovery can begin from that point since the database pages on disk were up-to-date at the end of the checkpoint. The recovery process then begins a *roll-forward* phase: for each transaction in the log file after the checkpoint record, the relevant database pages are read from disk into the buffer cache and checked to see if they had been updated before the crash. If not, transaction changes are reapplied. At the end of the roll-forward, the database will have been recovered to almost the same state it was in immediately before the crash. Only *inflight transactions*—transactions that were only partially completed—will have been lost.

If the database crashes as a result of media failure, such as the failure of a disk drive, recovery is more complex. The database is recovered from the most recent full backup, and the database recovery process uses the logs (plus any archived logs) to reapply all changes made to the database since the full backup. Restore and recovery can be time consuming and for that reason many users like to keep an online disk copy of the last full backup.

Locking Subsystem

When more than one user wants to modify the same data page at the same time, the database system needs a way of ensuring that the changes do not interfere with each other. Database systems have sophisticated *locking* subsystems to implement the level of locking requested by the user.

Before a change is made, a lock is taken out on behalf of the user on either a database row, a database page (data block), or sometimes an entire table. Other users wishing to modify the same pages are forced to wait until the lock is available. The lock is released after the modifications are complete.

Different types of locks are used for different purposes. A *Share* lock flags a row or a table as being read by one application and available for read-only by other applications. An *Update* lock is similar to a Share lock, except that it shows an intent to update the row or table being locked. An *Exclusive* lock shows that the row or table is being changed by one application and is not available to other applications.

Isolation levels affect the types of locks acquired by an application; isolation levels can be set globally or per transaction. Isolation levels include those listed below.

- **Read stability.** Share row locks are held until the next commit or rollback. Read stability does not prevent new rows being added to the result set by insert or update, though, so the same query could return additional rows if repeated.

- **Repeatable read.** Share row locks are held until the next commit or rollback. Every row looked at will be locked, even if it isn't part of the result set. If the same query is repeated, it will not only return the same results, it will touch the same rows on the way to arriving at the results.

- **Cursor stability.** Share row locks are held only while a particular row is being processed. If multiple rows are returned in the result set, only the current row is locked. This isolation level improves concurrency and is often used for applications.

- **Uncommitted read (or dirty read).** Share row locks are not obtained when single rows are read or when read-only cursors are opened and fetched. (A *cursor* is used as a pointer to a particular row when multiple rows are returned). The Dirty Read isolation level improves performance, but at the price of data integrity risks.

Isolation levels apply only to reads. When rows are changed, an Exclusive lock must be acquired by the application.

Another important locking function carried out by the database is watching for *deadlocks*. Suppose, for example, that User 1 holds a lock on page 123 in Table A and is waiting for a lock to become available on page 987 in Table B. Meanwhile, User 2 holds the lock on page 987 in Table B and is waiting for User 1 to finish with and free the lock on page 123 in Table A. Both users will wait forever, causing a deadlock, or "deadly embrace." Databases have a process or thread, referred to as a *deadlock monitor*, watching for deadlocks; one of the user transactions will be aborted by the deadlock monitor, allowing the other to complete successfully. The user process must monitor the transaction return code, detect the deadlock, and retry the failed transaction.

System Monitor

A *system monitor* ensures that the database instance is shut down in a controlled fashion upon any kind of instance failure, such as the failure of a system process. A *process monitor* similarly ensures that the failure of a user process is managed in an orderly fashion, freeing any locks or other resources held by the user.

Command Interface

Most modern databases allow commands to be carried out either with a graphical user interface (GUI) or with a command-line interface (CLI). The GUI is most useful for interactive sessions; the CLI version is most useful for administrative tasks that can be coded into a script to be run as a batch job. Both the GUI and the CLI interfaces are primarily used for database administration.

APIs

Access to the database is typically achieved by application programs using one of the application programming interfaces (APIs) supported by the database. These include:

- JDBC (Java Database Connectivity) or SQLJ, both of which offer database interfaces suitable for use within Java programs.
- ODBC (Open Database Connect), Microsoft's de facto standard API for connecting applications to databases.
- Embedded native language interfaces, which support database access from languages as varied as C, Perl, and COBOL. Embedded languages typically add a precompilation phase to program compilation.

Commonly used applications like spreadsheets offer direct access to databases through APIs like ODBC. The access is usually achieved transparently—the user does not need any knowledge of the mechanism.

Database Monitoring

Eventually, databases may become self-monitoring and self-tuning. Some databases have already taken steps in that direction, but fully automated database tuning is still far from reality. Instead, most databases bundle sophisticated monitoring tools, often with easy-to-use GUIs, to allow the health and behavior of the database to be tracked. The database buffer cache hit rate, the frequency and rate of system wait events, and the distribution of read and write operations among the various database files are examples of the kind of monitoring typically carried out, either interactively or automatically with scripts.

Process Models

Although the database system appears as a single entity to the user, it is actually made up of a number of different components. The mapping of the various subsystems of an RDBMS to operating system processes is referred to as the *process model* of the database system. Two main process models are in use for database systems running on Solaris; they are broadly referred to as *2n architectures* and *multithreaded architectures*.

2n Architectures

The term *2n* refers to the fact that each user connection to the database is supported by two processes:

1. The application process that runs the application logic.
2. An *agent process* (*shadow process* in Oracle terminology) that connects to the database shared memory and accesses the data store on behalf of the user process.

The agent process runs on the database server system. The application process can run on the database server, a separate application server, or a user workstation. If both agent and application processes reside on the database server, they communicate with fast local Interprocess Communication (IPC) mechanisms like sockets and shared memory. If they reside on different systems, they communicate with a proprietary protocol, typically on top of TCP/IP.

Database access is achieved by a mechanism like this:

1. The application process passes SQL requests to the agent process.
2. The agent process parses the SQL and executes it.
3. The agent process returns the answer set to the application process.

Figure 5.1 illustrates the client connections in a 2n architecture.

Figure 5.1 *2n architecture client connections*

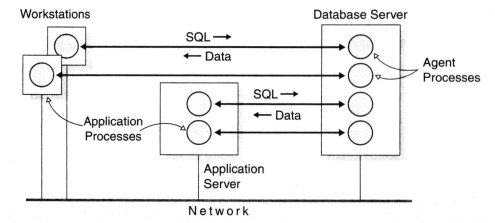

In fact, the model of SQL in and data out is somewhat simplified since other mechanisms, such as those listed below, are available.

- **Stored procedures.** A *stored procedure* is a function or procedure containing SQL and logic code that is compiled and becomes part of the database engine. A programmer can call the stored procedure instead of individually executing the SQL statements, reducing both the number of application-to-agent interactions and the overall execution time. Some kind of *call interface* API is typically available to a programming language to execute the stored procedure and capture the return status. Often, structures are used to send data to a stored procedure and receive the results of the queries carried out by the stored procedure.

- **Proprietary programming interfaces**. Some databases offer a non-SQL programming interface to the database. Oracle's OCI is an example.

Databases based on a 2n architecture (Oracle and DB2 for Solaris) also use separate processes for other key functions like the logger, pagecleaners, and process monitor.

Oracle also offers an optional connection mechanism called the Shared Server, previously known as the MultiThreaded Server (MTS). Shared Server is discussed in more detail in Chapter 9.

Multithreaded Architectures

Multithreaded architectures differ from 2n architectures in that there are no longer two processes for each user connection. The agent process is replaced by an agent thread in a multithreaded agent server. Each multithreaded server supports multiple agent connections, thereby significantly reducing the number of processes on the server and the memory requirements per user.

Each user connection to the database is supported by two things:

1. The application process that runs the application logic.

2. An *agent thread* running in a multithreaded server process. The server process connects to the database shared memory and accesses the data store on behalf of the user application.

The multithreaded server process runs on the database server system. As is the case for 2n architectures, the application process can run on the database server, a separate application server, or a user workstation. Database access is achieved by the same mechanisms for both architectures. Figure 5.2 illustrates the connections.

Figure 5.2 *Multithreaded architecture client connections*

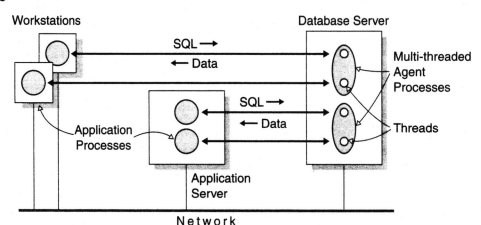

Databases based on a multithreaded architecture also typically use internal threads for other key functions like the logger, pagecleaners, and process monitor.

How does one multithreaded server process scale on an SMP system with multiple CPUs? The solution used by the database vendors has been to use one multithreaded server process on each CPU, thereby combining the benefits of a reduced process count with the scalability of an SMP system. Multithreaded server databases also tend to have lower Translation Lookaside Buffer (TLB) miss rates than databases based on 2n architectures.

Sybase, Informix, and Ingres are examples of multithreaded databases on Solaris.

It might seem logical for these databases to use Solaris threads to implement the multithreaded servers. In fact, each database uses its own internal threads libraries, both because portability between different Unix platforms is simplified and because the database vendors believe they can efficiently implement threads for a specific purpose.

Parallel Processing

With the ready availability of servers with multiple CPUs, database suppliers turned their attention to speeding tasks by parallel processing. By allowing multiple CPUs to participate in key database operations, vendors could reduce operation completion time, sometimes significantly. Today, many tasks can be parallelized, including:

- Database load and index creation.
- Bulk inserts and updates.
- Large query execution.
- Database backup and restore.

Distributed Databases

It is not always practical to store all data in one physical location. Accounting information might be stored at the head office location, production and manufacturing data at the manufacturing plant, and stock details at the warehouse. Sometimes data is held centrally, and access from other sites is achieved through wide area networks (WANs). Alternatively, data may be held at each site and subsets shipped to other sites as required. Another example is a college with teaching facilities spread across several different campuses. Rather than storing all student details centrally, the college can store student data at the campus the students most frequently attend.

Distributed databases were designed to solve the problem of providing access to data that may be split across more than one database. Taking the example of distributed college student records, suppose a student paid fees at a different campus from the one he or she normally attended. The payments received table would be updated at one campus and the student's personal record at another.

The challenge with distributed databases is making sure that both records are updated. You wouldn't want the local payment table update to succeed while the remote update to the student records failed because a communications line was down. Database vendors use *two-phase commit* (2PC) technology to avoid this kind of failure. Two-phase commits ensure that both records are updated or neither is.

Distributed databases have not proved popular. Unfortunately, they introduce multiple points of failure and the need to ensure that databases remain synchronized. Performance can also be a problem; two-phase commits involve a lot of network handshaking, often over wide area networks with high latencies. Although the technology is well established and reliable, the performance challenges and system and database administration overheads have deterred many potential users.

Replicated Databases

Databases can be so useful people sometimes decide to have two of them! A second copy of a database is often used for these purposes:

- As a backup to be called upon for disaster recovery. Sometimes the second copy is kept at a remote location to protect against a major disaster like an earthquake, a flood, or a hurricane.

- To provide a second copy of the data to be used for query access by power users. The query activity can then be offloaded from the live database.

Replication technology typically involves either shipping update transactions to the remote system or shipping log records. Log records can be shipped individually or as entire log files when log files are switched. Transactions can be shipped synchronously or asynchronously. In synchronous shipping, the replication transaction is processed immediately and the remote database is always up-to-date. In asynchronous shipping, the transaction can complete before the remote update takes place; therefore, updates to the remote database are always a little behind the primary database. When entire log files are shipped, the remote database is only as up-to-date as the last log file switch.

Full synchronous replication allows read and update access on both databases simultaneously. Conflicts can occur if the same data has been updated in both databases at once; sophisticated conflict resolution rules can be established to resolve them.

Standby databases are a variant of replicated databases. As the name suggests, standby databases provide a warm backup in case of failure of the primary database.

Transaction Monitors

Transaction monitors, or *TP monitors*, are used in Online Transaction Processing (OLTP) environments as an efficient mechanism for managing transactions and routing them within a network. (See Chapter 6 for a description of OLTP workloads.) TP monitors are often used in conjunction with databases, especially when heavy transaction loads must be supported.

Transaction monitors can significantly reduce the CPU resource required to process transactions, although they typically require the application developer to use the APIs associated with the transaction monitor. Examples of commercial transaction monitors include Tuxedo, supplied by BEA Systems, Transarc, Encina, Topend, and the IBM mainframe-based CICS.

Transactions and Ad Hoc Queries

Transaction monitors make most sense where transactions are stable and regularly executed. Both the inputs to a transaction and the results expected can be clearly defined. In addition, the transaction monitor can route transaction details to the appropriate database server, wherever it is located on the network, and return the results to the calling application.

Ad hoc queries, where the nature of the transaction is difficult to predict, are more easily handled with SQL directly.

User Multiplexing

One of the ways transaction monitors reduce CPU use is by multiplexing users (see Figure 5.3). User applications connect to the transaction monitor rather than directly to the database.

Figure 5.3 *User multiplexing with a transaction monitor*

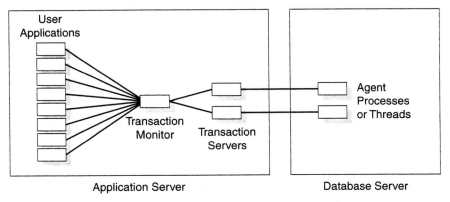

Applications execute transactions by calling the transaction monitor, passing the transaction data in a structure. The transaction monitor places the transaction request onto a queue. The request is picked up by one of the transaction servers that have registered with the transaction monitor. The transaction servers can run on either the application server or the database server. They are directly connected to the database through agent processes or threads and carry out any necessary SQL on behalf of the user, passing the results back to the user application from the transaction monitor.

User multiplexing can offer significant performance advantages compared with the standard approach shown in Figure 5.4.

Figure 5.4 *User connections with no transaction monitor*

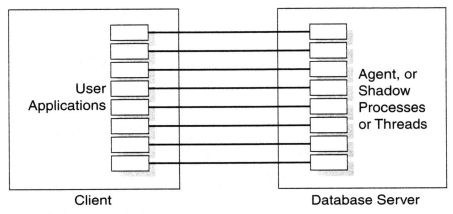

In particular, transaction monitors typically reduce the number of agent processes or threads required on the database server and also reduce network traffic. Peaks and troughs in both network traffic and requests to the database are also smoothed considerably by the use of queues.

Transaction Routing

In a complex network environment where data is spread across multiple databases in different geographic locations, transaction monitors can reduce programming complexity by offloading from the programmer the task of transaction routing. Transaction monitors are also able to manage two-phase commits in distributed databases. User applications at the client end and transaction servers at the server end simply connect to the transaction monitor and send or receive transactions. For example, a credit card transaction at a point of sale may be routed by a transaction monitor to the right banking institution.

These benefits are contingent upon the use of the APIs provided by the transaction monitor. Unfortunately, there are no industry-wide standards for such APIs, so it is difficult to change to a different transaction monitor once code has been written.

6

DATABASE WORKLOADS

Understanding the workload or workloads that run on your server is crucial to configuring it effectively and achieving optimal performance. A number of different workload types are well recognized; this chapter broadly defines the major workloads.

Many end-user environments have a mixture of workload types, sometimes coexisting on a single system. Also, some key activities, such as data extraction, transformation, and load, are not directly accounted for by any of the following characterizations.

Online Transaction Processing (OLTP)

Online Transaction Processing (OLTP) workloads are common since they have broad applicability in most commercial environments. Examples include inventory management and order entry systems, banking applications, airline reservation systems, service tracking systems, and general accounting applications including general ledger, accounts payable, and accounts receivable.

Anything from a few users to thousands of users can be supported by a single OLTP system, and the transactions can vary from simple to complex. Typical transactions complete in seconds rather than minutes.

End-user response times and consistent system performance during periods of peak load are key performance issues. The business-critical nature of OLTP applications makes system availability and recoverability very important.

Data access for OLTP applications typically shows skew; that is, some data is more frequently accessed than others, leading to efficient caching behavior, but also leading to contention for the "hot" data.

OLTP workloads can have the following characteristics:

- Many users executing transactions of varying complexity, mostly small.
- Mostly random I/Os.
- Usually 2-Kbyte, 4-Kbyte or 8-Kbyte disk accesses, depending on database block size.
- Typical read-to-write ratio between 1:1 and 3:1.
- Database caches that are important to performance. Refer to Chapter 7 for more detail about database buffer caches.
- Performance constrained by CPU capacity rather than I/O bandwidth. The number of I/Os per second (IOPS) that can be sustained might also be a performance issue.
- Heavy log I/O, mostly sequential synchronous writes.

Decision Support Systems (DSS)

Decision Support Systems are usually fed from OLTP databases and are used for applications like data warehousing, sales and market analysis, and product planning.

DSS queries may process large volumes of data and carry out complex multiple-table joins with aggregation and multiple predicates and sorts with order by and group by clauses. The result set from a substantial query can be quite small even when significant resources are consumed in arriving at the result.

Since most DSS operations can be parallelized, DSS workloads lend themselves well to parallelization for performance improvement. Some tables can be supported by multiple indexes to aid performance, adding significantly to the overall storage capacity requirements.

Although DSS queries may access a considerable volume of data, typically only a small proportion of the data held in the data store is touched regularly. Temporary tablespaces, used for sorts, may be heavily used, though, since many sorts will be too large to be executed in memory.

DSS can be subdivided into ad hoc environments, in which queries are unknown in advance and chaotic, and business reporting environments, in which queries are well understood. The latter have characteristics similar to those of OLAP (see below).

Query completion times and overall system throughput are the key performance issues. DSS systems are less likely to be mission critical than OLTP systems, although availability and recoverability may still be regarded as important.

An ad hoc DSS environment is characterized as follows:

- Relatively few users running large queries.

- Large individual I/Os (larger than 128 Kbytes).

- Many more reads than writes.

- Database caches that are not as useful as for OLTP.

- Performance that is influenced more by I/O bandwidth than by CPU capacity, although CPU requirements are also significant.

- Log I/O that involves heavy sequential writes during update and that is nonexistent during queries.

When queries are repeated frequently, you can reduce processing load by precalculating the results and storing them in *materialized views*. Views are stored SQL statements that can access multiple tables, evaluate multiple predicates, and carry out various forms of aggregation. Materialized views are views that have been precomputed, with the result set stored in a table. The optimizer can recognize a query that matches a materialized view and can retrieve the results without executing the query again. Oracle and DB2 for Solaris support materialized views.

Data Warehouses and Data Marts

A *data warehouse* is a collection of data that originated from other operational applications and possibly external systems. Sales information, for example, may be collated and stored in a data warehouse for later analysis and aggregation. Data may not be accurate up to the minute; typically, data is as accurate as the most recent update (possibly daily).

Data warehouses are subject oriented rather than transaction oriented. Data is likely to be organized into subject areas, such as sales data, rather than organized according to the source of the data. And since data may be integrated from different sources, with different product codes, for example, common coding rules must be used. Data is usually historical in nature, held at different levels of detail. Data warehouse data is typically read-only, apart from periodic updates.

After extraction from a data source, data is typically transformed into a more useful form before being loaded into a data warehouse. The usefulness of the data warehouse depends on the accuracy and integrity of the data, so *data cleansing* may be necessary to guarantee the trustworthiness of the final result.

Storing *metadata*, or data about data, facilitates understanding of the data and is a usual practice. Examples of metadata are acquisition metadata, used to describe data origins and algorithms used to summarize the data, transformation metadata, including a history of data transformations, and access metadata, providing navigation and graphical user interfaces to make access to the data more intuitive for a broad range of users.

Data warehouse tables are sometimes structured in a *star schema*. Star schemas use a central *fact table* and surrounding *dimension tables*. Figure 6.1 illustrates a star schema.

Figure 6.1 *Example of a star schema*

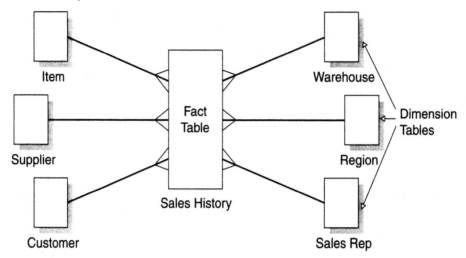

The central Fact Table in this example is a sales history table containing a large number of rows representing individual sales, with foreign keys in each row pointing to a number of smaller tables such as Item, Supplier, and Customer. The resulting schema probably bears little resemblance to the operational tables in the OLTP system from which the data was extracted, but this type of structure can prove better suited to data warehouse activity. For example, it can be more efficient to carry out joins on the dimension tables first and then retrieve the relevant rows from the fact table, rather than do joins directly on OLTP tables.

Data Marts

A *data mart* is a simple form of a database warehouse, typically smaller in size and more narrowly focused, usually on a single functional area. An organization may host a data warehouse, with subsets of the data extracted to data marts hosted by individual business groups within the organization.

Data marts are typically quicker to implement than data warehouses since their scope is more limited. Often data marts are constructed from existing data warehouses, though.

Operational Data Stores

An Operational Data Store (ODS) draws together information from disparate data sources to provide a consolidated view of specific categories of data. The integrated data is used to assist management in tactical decision making.

An ODS is typically a mixed OLTP and DSS environment, and both OLTP and DSS transactions can be carried out against it. Data is usually current rather than historical, and it is mostly held in relational, rather than multi-dimensional form. Some aggregation of OLTP data may have been carried out.

ODS transactions are typically read-only or read-mostly, though the data is continually being updated from the data sources. When data in an ODS is modified by user transactions, the changes are sometimes replicated back to the various systems the data originated from. The ODS can provide a convenient single source for all data related to a particular subject matter.

Data Mining

Data warehouses typically store a wealth of information, but a user's understanding about that information may be limited. For example, a sales organization may be well aware that holiday seasons are associated with increased sales activity, but many other potentially useful facts may never have been discovered. *Data mining* is the process of knowledge discovery, or finding previously unknown data dependencies or anomalies. An often quoted example is the discovery that in supermarkets men purchasing diapers often buy beer at the same time. Having learned this information, a supermarket may choose to locate beer near the diapers, or alternatively, locate beer within a line of sight of diapers, with other potentially interesting items positioned between them. The origins of this example are explored in an interesting presentation by Ronny Kohavi, available on the Web at http://robotics.stanford.edu/~ronnyk/chasm.pdf.

Another example is finding a relationship between patient data and medical diagnosis. I remember reading about a medical researcher in London in the Middle Ages who decided, on a hunch, to plot the home locations of victims of a recent plague outbreak. He discovered that almost all of them lived around a certain well. One elderly female victim, however, lived a considerable distance away. Upon investigation he learned that the woman particularly liked the water from that well and had it shipped to her regularly. His discovery saved many lives. Data mining is nothing new.

Today's data mining methods rely on sophisticated algorithms to derive relationships between groups of data. Techniques include neural nets, decision trees, nearest neighbors, genetic algorithms, and rule induction. For more information, refer to *Seven Methods for Transforming Corporate Data into Business Intelligence*, Vasant Dhar and Roger Stein, Prentice Hall, 1997. Automating the discovery of trends, behaviors, and previously unknown patterns can result in significant benefits to the organization involved.

Batch Workloads

Batch workloads are often run in the background during business hours and may be the primary workload when online users have logged off the system. Typical batch applications are periodic refresh or upload of data, period-end processing (such as end of day, week, month, quarter, or year), report generation, and indexing of table data. Administrative tasks such as table reorganization also fit into the category of batch workloads. Sometimes ad hoc queries that are found to be useful are turned into reports or batch jobs.

Often, large amounts of data are processed, sometimes in a single-threaded fashion, and locking and concurrency may not be an issue unless multiple batch jobs are in progress. Processing times may be long, and batch jobs may have a completion deadline.

Overall system throughput is the key performance issue. System availability and recoverability can be important, especially where the batch completion window is too small to allow jobs to be rerun.

Batch workloads are characterized as follows:

- One or more update or report streams run in the background.

- Read/write ratio is varied and may be dominated by read, write, or mixed I/O.

- I/O sizes can vary due to read-ahead, but probably will be mostly small.

- Database caches are unlikely to help performance much because little or no data is reused.

- Log I/O may be heavy (sequential writes) unless the batch workload is read-only.

Database administrators sometimes create ancillary structures like indexes, denormalized tables, or materialized views to improve the performance of batch jobs.

Online Analytical Processing (OLAP)

The need to perform ad hoc data analysis and provide multidimensional views of data has led to the availability of Online Analytical Processing (OLAP) products. OLAP variants include Relational OLAP (ROLAP), where data is presented in cubes with dimensions but is actually stored in a relational database, Multidimensional OLAP (MOLAP), where data is presented in a similar way but stored in a multidimensional database, and a hybrid form of ROLAP and MOLAP called HOLAP. Although I am using the generic term OLAP, my focus in this section is on MOLAP.

Unlike data warehouse queries, which may run for many minutes or even hours, OLAP servers typically return results in seconds or less. Fast response times are usually achieved by extensive precalculation of interesting results, although databases tend to become quite large in the process, especially when wide-ranging totals are produced for sparse data sets. As an example of a sparse data set, imagine you work for a multinational company selling sporting goods across a number of different geographies. You are likely to find that sales of scuba equipment are slow in central Australia and that very few snowboards are sold in the Bahamas. If you calculate totals for each item in each region, you will quickly find that some of the totals are of little interest. OLAP servers face a trade-off between performing full precalculation with its consequent database "explosion," and calculating totals on-the-fly, which is typically too slow.

OLAP products provide tools that allow users to easily carry out new ad hoc calculation, analysis, and reporting of data. A multidimensional view of the data is integral to OLAP servers, with hierarchies and multiple hierarchies supported.

Relational databases use two-dimensional tables (see Table 6-1 for an example).

Table 6-1 *Results held in a two-dimensional relational table*

Vehicle Type	Region	Sales Quantity
Cars	South	20
Cars	West	15
Cars	East	25
SUVs	South	30
SUVs	West	20
SUVs	East	25
Minivans	South	26
Minivans	West	34
Minivans	East	27

The same information can be presented in a different way with a matrix and preaggregated totals. Table 6-2 shows the matrix version of the same information with totals.

Table 6-2 *Results held in a two-dimensional matrix*

	South	West	East	Total
Cars	20	15	25	60
SUVs	30	20	25	75
Minivans	26	34	27	87
Total	76	69	77	222

These dimensions can be further broken down into hierarchies (such as cities within regions, models within vehicle types, or vehicle type within totals), and multiple additional dimensions added. Suppose an additional dimension, such as Sales Period, is introduced—each period is likely to have a full set of values for every combination of vehicle type and region. The result is a cube, as shown in Figure 6.2.

Figure 6.2 *Results held in a cube*

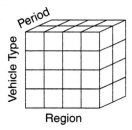

OLAP products allow you to focus on one layer, "slicing and dicing" the cube in different ways. Figure 6.3 gives an example.

Figure 6.3 *Slicing and dicing cube data*

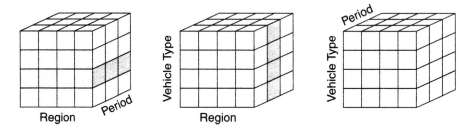

In the first cube, the second vehicle type is selected and held constant and results across multiple regions and periods are highlighted. In the second cube, vehicle types across regions are highlighted for the second period. In the third cube, vehicle types across different periods are highlighted for the second region. OLAP servers allow you to start looking at one dimension and then drill down to discover more detail.

Whereas OLTP workloads are typically transaction oriented, focused mainly on the present, dealing with business processes, and optimized for transaction processing, OLAP workloads typically deal simultaneously with many records and with data that is summarized, historical, oriented to subjects, and optimized for analysis.

OLAP is nontransactional, so there is no log. To update data, OLAP invalidates a page and appends new data to the database. Exports and imports eliminate the holes.

Cubes are almost always sparsely populated, so 100 Mbytes of base data can quickly explode into 20–30 Gbytes. This expansion is a function of the number of dimensions and the hierarchy imposed on the data.

OLAP workloads are characterized by the following aspects:

- A write-intensive load phase that is generally single threaded or minimally threaded and usually very fast. It is typically carried out weekly or monthly, rarely daily.

- A read/write intensive aggregation phase. Preaggregation, rollups, and precalculation may take 24–48 hours, so this phase is usually a weekend task.
- A read-only query phase.
- Queries mainly involving random reads.

A well-designed OLAP database can almost be reduced to cell retrievals even though OLAP software is quite complex.

For more information about OLAP, refer to *OLAP Solutions: Building Multidimensional Information Systems*, Eric Thomsen, John Wiley and Sons, 1997.

7

THE ROLE OF
THE BUFFER
CACHE

Although disk I/O is central to the operation of relational database systems, databases go to considerable lengths to avoid it. The reason has to do with disk access times. Access to CPU cache is significantly faster than access to main memory, which in turn is significantly faster than access to disk. So databases work more effectively with data that is a memory access away from the CPU, rather than a disk access away.

When a database operation needs a database block that is located on disk, the operation typically stalls while the page is read into memory. When data is written to the log file, the logger process stalls until the write is completed. The only database disk activity that does not routinely result in stalls is writing to database tables, since multiple pages are written asynchronously.

Overview of the Buffer Cache

One of the main tools used by databases to reduce disk I/O is the database buffer cache. The database acquires a segment of shared memory and typically sets aside the largest proportion of it to hold database blocks (also referred to as database pages). When a transaction requires a block, it reads the block from disk and stores it in the buffer cache; subsequent transactions requesting the same block can then retrieve it from memory rather than from disk.

In practice, there is rarely enough memory in the buffer cache to accommodate every database block required by transactions, so blocks cannot be held in memory indefinitely. Databases use a least recently used algorithm to retain the most frequently accessed blocks and replace blocks that have fewer accesses.

Some databases also provide alternative strategies to discriminate against or on behalf of blocks in selected tables. For example, there is little point in caching blocks from tables that are rarely reused; conversely, some small tables are so heavily accessed that they benefit from being cached permanently.

Although effective database buffer caches are crucial for efficient functioning of OLTP applications, not all database operations use the buffer cache. In DSS environments, for example, Oracle and Informix XPS bypass the cache for parallel queries on large tables. The reasoning is that table sizes are often so large compared to the cache size that a table scan would overwhelm the cache without any benefit. DB2 for Solaris does use the buffer cache for DSS table scans, although buffer caches do not need to be large since blocks are discarded quickly.

The buffer cache is most effective when data access is skewed. Access is skewed if some data is accessed more frequently than other data. Let me illustrate skewed access with a practical example. On a normal Saturday, my wife and I might complete a number of financial transactions. Between us we purchase food, gas, and other items, transfer money between accounts, and withdraw cash from an ATM. Since we are such busy shoppers, our account details will appear several times in the buffer cache of the accounts database at our credit union. Our credit card account will be accessed many times, our checking account might be accessed a couple of times, and our savings account probably won't be accessed at all. The account most likely to remain in the database buffer cache is the credit card account, since it is the most heavily accessed. In practice, of course, the volume of financial transactions on a Saturday is such that no individual's account is likely to be cached for long, but the example does illustrate skewed or nonuniform access to our three accounts.

In the same way, businesses often find that 80% of their business is done with 20% of their customers, with the result that some database rows are much more frequently accessed than others. The same principle has application in many database environments.

When access to data is uniform (that is, all rows are equally likely to be referred to), caching offers fewer benefits. When access to data is skewed, caching can greatly reduce the proportion of reads that require physical disk I/Os. Data skew is typical for OLTP applications and less typical for DSS applications.

Monitoring the Buffer Cache

Given that the buffer cache has a significant impact on the performance of OLTP applications, it should be no surprise that monitoring the effectiveness of the buffer cache is an important priority. The buffer cache hit rate is one of the main database metrics that you should monitor for OLTP workloads. The cache hit rate measures how many database blocks were found in the buffer cache rather than read from disk. Blocks read from disk are referred to as *physical reads*. Blocks retrieved either from disk or the buffer cache are referred to as *logical reads* (so physical disk reads are included in both metrics). The buffer cache hit rate is calculated in the following way:

$$BufferCacheHitRate = \langle 1 - (PhysicalReads)/(LogicalReads) \rangle \times 100$$

Not all databases supply the buffer cache hit rate in a convenient form; you might need to calculate it yourself. The chapters focusing on database tuning for Oracle, Sybase, Informix, and DB2 (Chapters 22 to 25) explain how to calculate this metric for each database.

Note that the buffer cache stores more than just table data. Index blocks are held in the buffer cache and tend to enjoy high cache hit rates since they are relatively compact and can store many index nodes per block. Since index blocks are frequently used, they are often given a more favorable weighting than data blocks so they will stay in the cache longer.

The data dictionary, which holds information about tables, columns, indexes, database files, and similar data, is held in database tables and therefore also finds its way into the buffer cache. Once the database has been running for a while, accesses to data dictionary blocks can usually be satisfied from the cache, leading to a high cache hit rate for these blocks (usually higher than for data table blocks).

An Acceptable Cache Hit Rate

What represents an acceptable buffer cache hit rate? Unfortunately, this question is not easy to answer.

I recently asked a database administrator about the cache hit rates on his Oracle instances. He told me they were within Oracle guidelines and added that they were over 90%.

If his answer was fuzzy, it certainly wasn't without foundation. I recently reviewed three Oracle8 tuning textbooks and discovered three different values for the minimum recommended buffer cache hit rate for OLTP applications: 70%, 95%, and 98%.

Unfortunately, achieving an acceptable buffer cache hit rate isn't as simple as setting an arbitrary value to aim for. As we will see, though, there are objective measures that you can use to evaluate your current hit rate. But first we need to consider the meaning and implications of the cache hit rate statistic.

The Cache Hit Rate Confusion

During training I have sometimes asked the following question: "If you were able to improve your cache hit rate from 90% to 95%, how much of a reduction will you see in your physical reads?"

Answers have ranged from "There will be a 5% reduction" to "You can't be sure." In fact you can be sure: the physical reads will be *halved*.

The confusion stems from the fact that the hit rate obscures the metric that we really care about: the *miss rate*. The miss rate is the number of I/O requests that cannot be satisfied from the cache and therefore result in a physical read. The miss rate is simple to compute: it is 100 minus the hit rate. So a 90% cache hit rate means a 10% cache miss rate, and a 95% hit rate means a 5% miss rate.

When the earlier question is expressed in terms of the miss rate, it becomes easier to answer: "If you were able to reduce your cache miss rate from 10% to 5%, how much of a reduction will you see in your physical reads?" Reducing the miss rate from 10% to 5% means that only half as many physical reads are required.

So the number of physical disk reads is halved when the buffer cache hit rate improves from 90% to 95%, and halved again from 95% to 97.5%.

With the implications of the cache hit rate clarified, which recommendation—70%, 95%, or 98%—is the optimal cache hit rate to aim for?

Cache Hit Rate Guidelines

There is no magic figure that represents the acceptable buffer cache hit rate for a particular database application or database system. There are, however, factors that you must consider in deciding whether your current hit rate is acceptable. The following list identifies the most important factors.

- **Available memory.** You typically increase the cache hit rate by expanding the size of the buffer cache. Such an expansion only makes sense if you have enough main memory to support it, though. If you put too much memory into the buffer cache and starve the applications as a result, you will cause application paging. Application paging is likely to lead to much worse performance problems than those you solved by increasing the size of the buffer cache.

  Occasionally you might actually find yourself decreasing the size of the buffer cache. For example, if the number of active users connected to the system increases, the demands on main memory will increase also. By decreasing the size of the buffer cache, you can expect to suffer an increase in the number of physical database reads. The lower cache hit rate will be worthwhile, though, if it helps you avoid application paging.

- **Disk utilization.** An increased cache hit rate means fewer physical reads, which means fewer I/Os on the data disks. Use the `iostat`, `sar`, or `statit` utilities to check the utilization of the relevant disks. If the utilization is high, reducing the number of disk reads might reduce the load on the disks sufficiently to reduce the disk response time. Reduced response times can translate into savings in transaction response times.

Remember that changes in cache hit rates have little effect on data disk writes. If, for example, you observe that half the disk I/Os are reads and half are writes, then halving the cache miss rate will only reduce disk I/Os by 25% since disk writes will stay constant.

If you are using UFS database files, then each physical read you eliminate means one less page the Solaris Operating Environment will need in the file system page cache (unless you are using Direct I/O, in which case UFS pages are not cached). The result is less kernel activity.

- **Application response times.** The transaction path length (that is, the number of machine code instructions executed) is shorter if a block is found in the buffer cache rather than if it is read from disk. Shorter path lengths mean lower CPU consumption, and freeing up CPU cycles can help improve transaction response times. If transaction response times are an issue, then a higher cache hit rate may help. Note, though, that many other factors contribute to transaction response times, so improvements resulting from caching effects may not prove to be significant.

A Worked Example

To illustrate the principles described above, let's consider a practical example. The following statistics, based on a real workload, were reported by the Oracle8 `utlbstat` and `utlestat` utilities (described in "The utlbstat and utlestat Scripts" on page 313):

```
consistent gets        52180045
db block gets          1675582
physical reads         1217906
physical writes        200263
```

We will flesh out the process by asking a number of questions.

- *What is the current cache hit rate?*

    As we see from "Calculating the Buffer Cache Hit Rate" on page 317, logical reads for Oracle8 are the total of `consistent gets` and `db block gets`, so the cache hit rate is:

    $$(1 - (1217906 \div (1675582 + 52180045))) \times 100 = 97.7\%$$

    According to two of the three Oracle8 tuning text books I referred to earlier, it's time to kick back and relax! We're almost at the 98% target suggested in the third book, too. So all appears to be well. However, there's still a lot we don't know, so we won't take a vacation just yet.

- *What is the physical read rate?*

We can see that we are doing more than a million physical reads, which sounds like a lot of I/O. Before we become too alarmed, though, we need to find out the duration of the measurement period. At the end of the report the measurement interval was reported as being one hour, from 17:53:06 to 18:53:06. So 1,217,906 physical reads in one hour means the rate was 338 reads per second.

- *What is the physical write rate?*

The report showed that in the same interval, 200,263 physical writes were completed, or 56 writes per second. The total I/Os per second to the Oracle data disks amounted to 394 (the sum of 338 and 56).

- *How many disks, and of what type, are used to store the data tables?*

In this case, I happen to know that the data tables were striped across eight old 5,400 rpm disks, each with a capacity of 2.1 Gbytes. These disks can reasonably be expected to sustain a peak of around 60 I/Os per second. Assuming the I/Os were evenly spread across the eight disks, we were averaging 49 I/Os per second, approximately 80% of the expected I/O capacity of the disks.

Most workloads are not uniform in the load they place on the system over the course of a one-hour period; peaks and troughs are more usual. So it is likely that I/O during peak periods will exceed 60 I/Os per second per disk. Increasing the cache hit rate could prove beneficial in this case, especially if the one-hour measurement interval does not represent a heavy workload period. If it proved impossible to improve the cache hit rate for some reason, it would be wise to use more than eight disks in the stripe.

- *How much free memory is available to expand the buffer cache?*

Before we decide to increase the size of the buffer cache to improve the cache hit rate, we need to be sure that we have enough free memory in the system to support an increase.

In this case, the buffer cache was tiny—only 40 Mbytes in size—and plenty of memory was available to increase it.

- *By what proportion can we increase the buffer cache?*

We also need to determine the percentage by which we can increase the buffer cache. In this case, the size of the buffer cache could have been quadrupled, and since the load on the disk was heavy, an expanded buffer cache might have been resulted in worthwhile benefits.

Unfortunately, the higher the cache hit rate, the more memory it takes to increase it further. Eventually a point is reached beyond which there is little improvement in the cache hit rate, no matter how much memory is added.

Suppose, for example, your cache is 512 Mbytes in size and your hit rate is 80%. You double the size of the cache by adding another 512 Mbytes and discover that your cache hit rate has increased to 90%. If you are hoping that a further 512 Mbytes will improve your cache hit rate by the same amount, bringing it close to 100%, you are likely to be sadly disappointed. It is more probable that you will need to double the cache again to achieve a significant improvement. The law of diminishing returns applies to cache sizing; we discuss this effect in more detail in the next section.

With a cache hit rate of 97.7%, we might have almost reached the upper limit. On the other hand, there could be further benefits to be enjoyed. The miss rate is 2.3%, and reducing it to 1.15% (representing a cache hit rate of 98.85%) would halve physical read I/Os. Only testing can reveal the possibilities.

In summary, the objective of monitoring the buffer cache hit rate is not simply to achieve some arbitrary number; it is to optimize database performance by finding a balance between memory consumption and disk I/O.

If your cache hit rate is 70%, you will probably find that even a modest increase in buffer cache size will reduce the rate of physical reads for an OLTP workload. If, however, you have little or no spare memory, your disk subsystem is comfortably coping with the load and your users are happy, you may not need to make any changes at all.

If your cache hit rate is 95%, you will probably need a substantial increase in buffer cache size to make much impact on the rate of physical reads. If your disks are overloaded and you have plenty of spare memory, though, it is worth the attempt.

The appropriate balance in your environment will depend on data skew, application response times, and, especially, the availability of memory and disk I/O capacity.

Sizing the Buffer Cache

Data skew and access patterns vary considerably between workloads, making it difficult to predict caching behavior. Consequently, sizing buffer caches is a challenging exercise. As a simple rule of thumb, some people suggest sizing the buffer cache as a proportion of the size of the database. I have read recommendations ranging from 1% to 20% of total database size; the variation in these recommendations highlights the degree of difficulty involved in such a sizing.

Some time ago, Performance and Availability Engineering conducted a study to better understand the relationship between cache sizes and hit rates and the impact of both on performance. As we will see, the optimal buffer cache size was between 10% and 15% of the database size for the workload used in the study.

The TPC-C schema and workload provided the test environment, and DB2 for Solaris was used as the test database.

The investigation was divided into two phases. In the first phase, the number of CPUs was held constant while the database size and the buffer cache size were varied. In the second phase, the number of CPUs was varied while the buffer cache size and database size were held constant.

Measurements were taken with buffer cache sizes ranging from 199 Mbytes to 3.1 Gbytes, and database scales of 100 (equivalent to 8.7 Gbytes), 250, 375, 425, and 525 (equivalent to 45.7 Gbytes).

The findings of the study included the observations outlined in the following sections.

Influence of Buffer Cache Size on Throughput

Transaction throughput is dependent on the ratio of the database size to the buffer cache size. When the buffer cache is small relative to the size of the database, throughput is far below the peak value achievable for the configuration. Figure 7.1 shows the relationship between the throughput and the size of the buffer cache.

Figure 7.1 *Throughput versus buffer cache size*

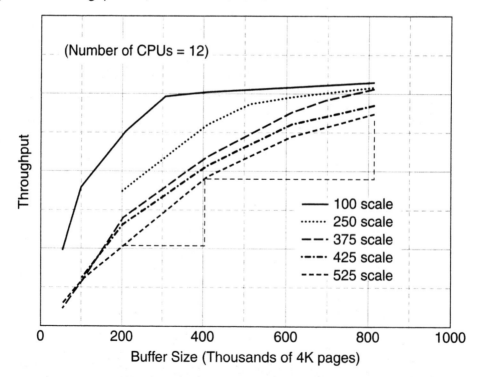

As the buffer cache is gradually increased in size, throughput rises steeply at first, then reaches a "knee point," after which it continues to increase, but at a greatly reduced rate. The 100 scale curve clearly shows this phenomenon: as the buffer cache increases from 50,000 to 300,000 pages, the throughput increases rapidly. Beyond that point, large increases in the size of the buffer cache only yield small gains in throughput. Larger databases (scale 250 and above) also exhibit this behavior.

The 525 scale result highlights another key characteristic: as buffer cache sizes grow, it takes more memory to achieve the same throughput increase. In this case, the throughput at 200,000 buffers doubled as the cache increased by another 200,000 buffers, but beyond 400,000 buffers, it took twice as much memory (400,000 buffers) to increase the throughput by the same amount again.

Figure 7.1 also clearly demonstrates that smaller databases benefit more than larger databases when a small buffer cache is increased in size. This behavior may seem counterintuitive, but it results from the fact that a high proportion of a small database can be cached quickly, whereas the same memory increase caches a small proportion of a large database. At the same time, the growth in the throughput slows much more quickly for small databases, whereas the benefits continue for larger databases. In every case, a point of diminishing returns is eventually reached, beyond which further increases in buffer cache size yield diminishing benefits.

The study demonstrated that, for this workload, the optimal buffer cache size is between 10% and 15% of the database size. Table 7-1 shows the buffer cache sizes required to reach the "knee point," the point beyond which further cache size increases result in diminishing returns.

Table 7-1 *Buffer size and data hit rate at knee points*

Scale	Buffer Size (Gbytes)	% of Database Size	Data Hit Rate
100	1.24	14.2	95.7%
150	1.59	12.2	96.7%
200	1.97	11.3	96.3%
250	2.19	10.1	96.3%

Results for larger database scales are not reported since the knee point was not reached (larger buffer caches would have been required). Note, too, that the cache hit rate shown in the table applies only to data pages (DB2 for Solaris separately reports cache hit rate statistics for data pages, index pages, and all pages).

As Table 7-1 shows, the smaller databases used slightly larger proportions of buffer cache memory to reach their knee points.

A more recent study on a different hardware platform with a different database suggested an optimal buffer cache size of between 5% and 10% of the database size. The difference between these results and those from the earlier study demonstrates that no single answer fits all situations.

Influence of Buffer Cache Size on Data Cache Hit Rate

Figure 7.2 shows the relationship between the data cache hit rate and the buffer cache size.

Figure 7.2 *Data cache hit rate versus buffer cache size*

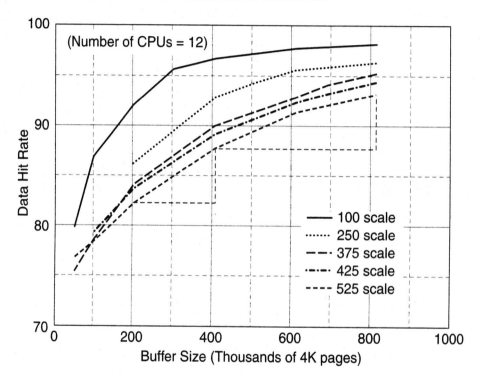

As with throughput, the data cache hit rate initially climbs steeply as the buffer cache increases in size, then reaches a knee point and gradually settles onto a plateau. As before, the 100 scale test illustrates the behavior most clearly, whereas the larger database sizes needed more memory to reach the cache hit rate upper limit.

The practical limit to the data cache hit rate for this workload was around 98%. The overall cache hit rate was higher, though; including the index cache hit rate in this figure would have increased the upper limit to around 99% since the index cache hit rate was consistently higher than the data cache hit rate.

Further tests confirmed that the behavior described for 12 CPUs also applied to 4 and 8 CPUs.

In concluding this discussion, it is worth noting that the memory capacities of Sun servers have increased significantly in recent years, a trend that is likely to continue. Although systems with 1 Gbyte of memory per CPU were typical in the past, current generation systems ship with 4 or 8 Gbytes per CPU. Larger memory configurations, combined with 64-bit databases on 64-bit Solaris, should allow buffer caches to be sized generously.

Influence of Page Size on Buffer Cache Effectiveness

Choosing the database page size (or block size) has important implications for performance of the database. Larger page sizes are usually chosen for DSS applications since they reduce overhead when large volumes of data are sequentially processed. Smaller page sizes are usually chosen for OLTP databases since I/O access tends to be random and row sizes relatively small.

One of the main reasons why the database page size impacts performance is due to its influence on the effectiveness of the database buffer cache. The page size determines both the size of pages in the buffer cache and the size of I/Os to and from the database tables on disk.

Consider a table with an average row length of 500 bytes: up to four rows can be accommodated in a 2-Kbyte page. The unit of database I/O is the page size, so every time a row is read into the buffer cache on behalf of an application, up to three other rows will accompany it. If the other three rows are required at the same time by that application or by other users, the buffer space is being used effectively and future I/Os will be saved. If the I/O access is random, though, then the other three rows are unlikely to be used.

The key issue here is *access locality*: locality of data access is high if data that is physically contiguous is accessed at or around the same time. Remember that in most cases, data is not stored in any particular order within a database table, so locality of access is hard to predict (although for some types of clustered index, data is stored in key sequence). When an entire table is scanned, such as for batch jobs or DSS queries, effective access locality is high since all rows will be processed within each page.

By contrast, up to 64 of the 500-byte rows can be accommodated in a 32-Kbyte page. If access locality is high and most or all of the other 63 rows can be used at the same time, many I/Os have been saved.

Large pages are the worst-case scenario, though, where data access is random and access locality is low. With 32-Kbyte pages, for example, each time a 500-byte row is read or written, a 32-Kbyte I/O must be completed. Worse still, for a buffer cache 2 Gbytes in size, the number of available 32-Kbyte buffers is only 65,536, compared to 1,048,576 buffers with 2-Kbyte pages. So fewer pages can be cached, while little benefit is derived from the large number of rows carried along with each page.

Very large buffer caches with 64-bit databases introduce other considerations. A 32-Gbyte buffer cache, for example, will support 16,777,216 pages 2 Kbytes in size and 1,048,576 pages 32 Kbytes in size. The overhead associated with managing the buffer cache increases as the number of pages increases. Consequently, a point will probably be reached beyond which it is more efficient to deal with fewer large pages.

To summarize, use smaller page sizes (2 to 8 Kbytes) for OLTP applications to maximize the effectiveness of the cache for randomly accessed data. Use larger page sizes for DSS applications to reduce the number of pages involved during access to large tables.

8

THE ROLE OF
THE DATABASE
OPTIMIZER

At the heart of a relational database system is the query optimizer. Most database systems provide ways of revealing query plans, although understanding the plans can be a daunting task if you don't understand how query optimizers work and how to interpret the jargon associated with them. This chapter attempts to demystify query optimization by looking at what query optimizers do, the methods they use, and the factors that influence them. Finally, we briefly consider various techniques used to reduce the amount of work query optimizers need to do.

Query Optimizers

The role of the query optimizer is to find the most efficient way of retrieving and processing the data necessary to satisfy a query. The approach decided on by the optimizer is variously called a *query plan* (QP), a *query execution plan* (QEP), or an *explain plan*. The effectiveness of the query plan chosen by the optimizer is important for Online Transaction Processing (OLTP) queries, which are typically lightweight, and crucial for Decision Support (DSS) queries, which can consume vast amounts of CPU and I/O resources.

An analogy might help illustrate the issues. You can get from California to New York by plane, bus, car, sea, bicycle, or on foot. If you want the fastest method you would fly, although that isn't likely to be the cheapest method. In the same way, different methods can be used to complete a query. The optimizer might decide to do a table scan (that is, read in the entire table and discard any rows that aren't needed) or retrieve the data with an index.

Some of your travel alternatives will consume fewer resources than others; for example, walking or cycling are not fast, but they use the least non-renewable resources. Some query plans use more system resources than others, too.

Some early database optimizers were *rule based*, that is, they used predetermined rules to determine a query plan. The rules usually favored the use of indexes if they were present and made assumptions about the nature of the data and the relative costs of different access methods. Modern *cost-based* query optimizers are more sophisticated: on the basis of detailed statistics about the content of table columns, a range of possible plans is evaluated, the expected cost of each is calculated, and the plan with the lowest cost is selected.

Whichever algorithm is used, predefined optimization strategies influence the choices made by database query optimizers. Sometimes databases allow users to influence these strategies by selecting the optimization level for queries. The optimization levels differ in the amount of effort they expend in trying to find the best possible query plan.

A query that needs to retrieve 5% of the rows in a table with 100,000 pages might help illustrate alternative query plans. If a suitable index is available, it might seem logical to use the index to identify the required rows and look them up in the table.

You might conclude that, based on index access to the table, 5,000 table pages will be needed plus a smaller number of pages from the index—many fewer pages than would be read with a table scan. The problem is that the query needs 5% of rows, not 5% of blocks. If the database page size is 16 Kbytes and the average row size for the table is 256 bytes, then each page will host an average of 64 rows and the table will have a total of 6,400,000 rows. Retrieving 5% of the rows will in fact involve random reads of 320,000 data rows through an index. Depending on caching effects, that could mean reading up to 320,000 data pages, plus index pages.

It may actually be more efficient, as well as faster, to simply retrieve all 100,000 pages with a table scan and throw away the rows that are not required. The optimizer must carry out the calculations and decide on the best alternative.

Query Compilation

Before SQL queries can be executed they must be compiled. The full query life cycle is a multistage process involving the following steps:

- **SQL statement parsing.** If syntax errors are found, an error report is issued and the query aborted; if no errors are found, the query is translated into an internal form meaningful to the optimizer.

- **Semantic expansion.** The query might involve a view or might reference a referential integrity constraint or trigger; the semantic implications of each must be taken into account.

- **Query optimization.** The most efficient access plan for the query must be chosen. Optimization might also involve rewriting the query into a functionally equivalent but more efficient form.
- **Code generation.** An internally executable form of the query is produced.

Finally, the database will execute the completed query plan to retrieve the data.

Query Optimization

The task of the query optimizer is to consider alternative query plans, model the expected behavior of CPU, I/O, and memory for each, and estimate the total cost of CPU, I/Os, and memory in each case. Taking into account its strategy and the cost estimates, the optimizer selects the appropriate plan with the cheapest cost.

Optimizers do not need to treat queries like the laws of the Medes and the Persians that could never be changed. Not all queries are crafted with equal care, so to improve efficiency, the optimizer might choose to rewrite the query into a semantically equivalent form. The value of rewriting queries is reinforced by the fact that SQL is often generated automatically and may not be coded efficiently.

Consider the following query:

```
select distinct phone_no, name from phone_book
```

If phone_no is the primary key of phone_book and forms a unique index, then the distinct keyword is redundant and can be ignored, eliminating one step from the query plan.

Another simple example of query rewriting is based on the following query with subselects:

```
select cust_id, name, address from customer
  where cust_id in
    (select cust_id from orders where order_id in
      (select order_id from order_lines
      where quantity > 200));
```

This query can be rewritten in the form shown below to give the optimizer more flexibility (although subquery-to-join rewrites are not always representable in SQL):

```
select distinct c.cust_id, name, address
  from customer c, orders o, order_lines l
  where c.cust_id = o.cust_id and o.order_id = l.order_id
  and quantity > 200;
```

Predicates can also be repositioned (pushed down or pulled up) to improve performance. Consider the following query based on a view:

```
create view credit_alert (zipcode, salesrep_id)
    as (select zipcode, salesrep_id from customer
    where balance_owed > credit_limit
    group by zipcode, salesrep_id);
select * from credit_alert
    where zipcode >= 94000 and zipcode < 95000;
```

The optimizer can internally rewrite the same view and query more efficiently in the following way:

```
create view credit_alert (zipcode, salesrep_id)
    as (select zipcode, salesrep_id from customer
    where balance_owed > credit_limit
    and zipcode > 94000 and zipcode < 95000
    group by zipcode, salesrep_id);
select * from credit_alert;
```

Now the `group by` can be carried out after, instead of before, the `zipcode` predicate has been applied, thereby reducing the amount of work.

Factors Affecting Query Optimization

Many factors affect query optimization, and effective query optimizers must take them into account in deciding on the best query plan. Apart from the obvious impact of hardware—such as the number and performance of CPUs and disks—on query performance, the following list highlights some of the important factors:

- **Data volume.** The greater the amount of data to be processed, the more important the query plan becomes, since inefficiencies can significantly stretch out query execution times. A poor query plan can increase the completion time for a query by orders of magnitude. Some of the factors considered by the optimizer include the number of pages in the table, the number of table pages that include rows, the number of leaf pages in an index, the number of levels in an index, and the density of index pages within an index.

- **Query complexity.** A query that involves subselects or joins of multiple tables increases the choices the optimizer must evaluate.

- **Data selectivity.** When a query predicate limits the data required from a table (for example, the where clause in `select name from customer where balance_owed >= credit_limit`), the optimizer needs to have some idea of what proportion of the rows in the table will be eliminated by the predicate. This effect is referred to as *selectivity*. High selectivity means fewer rows are returned (that is, the predicate is highly selective); low selectivity means more rows are returned. In multiple-table joins, selectivity helps the optimizer decide which tables to join first, since the fewer the number of rows carried forward to subsequent joins, the better.

- **Available memory.** The memory expected to be available affects the plan chosen by the query optimizer. Both memory in the shared buffer cache and local memory available for sorts and hash joins should be taken into account.
- **Degree of parallelism.** Where parallel queries are supported, the query optimizer must take into account the specified degree of parallelism in assigning the number of threads or processes to the query. In the same way, parallelism in disk activities depends on the number of I/Os per second and disk throughput supported by the disk spindles.

  Parallelism is not restricted to multiple subtasks, either. Access to data can proceed simultaneously and independently across multiple data partitions, and heterogeneous tasks can simultaneously process data as it is streamed from function to function (a pipeline effect).

- **Number of concurrent users.** The memory available for a query depends on the number of users executing queries at the same time. Where parallel queries are supported, the number of concurrent users affects the degree of parallelism that can be applied effectively to both CPUs and disk I/O.
- **Column statistics.** Databases collect statistics about the content of table columns to help with decisions about query plans. Examples of the kind of statistics collected include minimum and maximum values, histograms or quantiles to show the frequency of values (and therefore help predict how many rows will satisfy range predicates), and the number of unique values. For best query performance, make sure that statistics on your database are kept up-to-date.
- **Data skew.** Column statistics help identify *data skew*. Data skew occurs when some values appear much more frequently than others, leading to a nonuniform or skewed distribution. For example, the last names in the San Francisco phone book are skewed; there are a lot more Smiths than Higginbothams. Retail sales tend to be skewed, too; retail sales are greater in December than in February. Histograms are also useful in identifying data skew.
- **Available indexes.** Indexes provide paths to table data and sometimes offer the option of index scans (described later in this chapter).
- **Database-specific configuration parameters.** These include, for example, sort work area size, hash area size, degree of parallelism.

Optimization Methods

When the query optimizer chooses a query plan, it takes into account the methods available to it. It must decide how to access the table, the order in which tables should be joined, and what methods to use to carry out the join. In this section we consider each of these alternatives.

Note that optimizers may also consider data location, especially in shared-nothing environments. For example, can joins be performed locally (colocated joins), or does data need to be moved between nodes? The issues associated with colocated joins and data shipping are explored in "Massively Parallel Processor (MPP) Systems" on page 32.

Table Access

The simplest way of retrieving information from a table is to read the table data in its entirety. This operation is referred to as a *table scan*. Suppose, for example, you wanted to retrieve from an Employee table the names of all employees under 70 years of age. A table scan seems sensible—chances are you will need most rows in the table anyway. If you want to find all employees older than 70, though, most rows will be thrown away.

This example is more likely to apply to a data warehouse query; table scans are most often used in DSS environments. Table scans for anything other than very small tables are rare in OLTP environments and, from a performance perspective, usually a disaster. Since most transactions require only a small number of rows from a table, table scans are typically overkill and, consequently, performance hogs.

Table scans of large tables can consume a lot of CPU and disk resource if you use parallel query capabilities, and they take a lot of time if you do not. Even so, the optimizer might decide that a table scan is the most efficient way to get at the data you need.

Indexes, described in "Indexes" on page 46, consist of *nonleaf nodes* or *index nodes*, which hold information about the key values stored below them, and *leaf nodes*, which hold the actual key data (consisting of one or more columns) and a pointer to the rowid (RID) in the table. Figure 8.1 illustrates the structure of an index.

Figure 8.1 *Index structure*

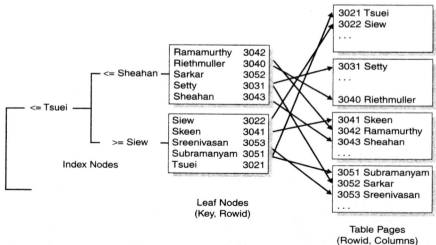

Since key column data is held in index leaf nodes, there are occasions when all the column information required from a table is held in an index. In that case, the optimizer won't need to refer to the base table at all; instead, an *index-only access* can be used.

One type of index-only access is an *index scan*, which is like a table scan except that it reads in an entire index rather than a table. The column values held in the leaf nodes are retained, and the index nodes are simply discarded.

Since an index is held in a sorted order, there may be occasions when a *range scan*, or *selective index scan*, can be used to reduce the amount of data read from the index. For example, a predicate specifying all invoices dated from January 2001 to June 2001 would lend itself to an index range scan if the date field has an index. Selective index scans can be used for index-only access or as a precursor to table access. Range scans can also be used on tables that have been partitioned appropriately. Range partitioning is discussed later in this chapter.

The most common use of an index in OLTP applications is to use a key value to provide *random access* into a table. Indexes are used for the same purpose in DSS queries. Index random access into a table may be less expensive on resources than a table or index scan if much of the scanned data is discarded. It is harder to parallelize index access, though, so it can take longer to complete the query. If random access with an index is going to retrieve more than 0.5% to 2% of a table, it may be more efficient to do a table scan on the table. Conversely, if the selectivity on a table is much less than 2%, you might improve query performance by creating an index if one does not already exist.

Table data is not stored in any particular sequence (except with some specialized table structures), so a table scan will return data unsorted. Compared to a table scan, all the index access methods described above have the advantage of returning data in key sequence. Depending on the query, that sometimes means that a sort can be avoided.

Another method used by some databases to optimize index access to tables is a *sorted rowid* fetch. In Figure 8.1, the index allows access to table pages, using the rowids found in the leaf nodes. The rowids accessed will be in order of the index: 3042, 3040, 3052, 3031, 3042, 3022, 3041, 3053, 3051, and 3021. That means the table pages will be accessed in the following order: third, second, fourth, second, third, first, third, fourth, fourth, and first. This simple example becomes much worse on large tables where data is more spread out. If the rowids are sorted, all the values in each table page can be processed at the same time (although the rows will not be returned in key sequence).

Table Join Order

When deciding the order in which to carry out joins of multiple tables, optimizers must decide on a search strategy to identify and evaluate the join alternatives. The fastest strategy (sometimes called *greedy join enumeration*) makes simplifications so it can be moderate in its space and time consumption. This strategy may miss the best plan, though. The most comprehensive strategy (sometimes called *dynamic join enumeration*) is exhaustive in its search for the best plan. This strategy can take a long time for complex joins, though, due to the large number of potential plans.

Query optimizers can also select from three table join strategies: left-deep, right-deep, and bushy tree. Deep trees have a leaf on all internal nodes, whereas bushy trees might not. All three types are illustrated in Figure 8.2.

Figure 8.2 *Left-deep, right-deep, and bushy trees*

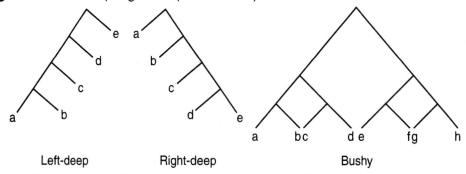

The letters a through h represent tables. The left-deep tree shown in Figure 8.2 may go through a join process as shown in the following steps, where t1 through t5 are temporary tables:

Step	Action
1	Scan a, Build t1
2	Scan b, Probe t1, Build t2
3	Scan c, Probe t2, Build t3
4	Scan d, Probe t3, Build t4
5	Scan e, Probe t4, Build t5

At each step, rows are scanned from the next table, predicates are applied, and the resulting rows are joined to the contents of the previous temporary table to create a new temporary table. The final result set is held in temporary table t5. Note, though, that not all join methods will require temporary tables for intermediate results.

The tables a to e can be joined in any order, and the number of plans the optimizer needs to check is $n!$, where n is the number of tables. So, the five tables represented here can be joined in 120 different ways.

The right-deep tree shown in Figure 8.2 will be handled quite differently, as illustrated in the following steps:

Step	Action
1	Scan a, Build t1
	Scan b, Build t2
	Scan c, Build t3
	Scan d, Build t4
2	Scan e, Probe t1, Probe t2, Probe t3, Probe t4, Build t5

The number of possible join combinations for right-deep trees can also be computed as $n!$, so once again the optimizer needs to consider 120 possible join orders for tables a to e. Depending on the join method, right-deep trees may require more temporary storage (and hence more memory) than do left-deep trees since all temporary tables are required until the final step. As the number of tables in the join and the number of rows to be joined increases, temporary storage requirements can increase significantly.

To illustrate the join process with a bushy tree join strategy, consider a subset of the bushy tree shown in Figure 8.2: specifically, the part of the tree involving tables a, b, c, and d. The join process could involve the following steps:

Step	Action
1	Scan a, Build t1
	Scan c, Build t2
2	Scan b, Probe t1, Build t3
	Scan d, Probe t2, Build t4
3	Probe t3, Probe t4, Build t5

An alternative join process is illustrated in the following steps:

Step	Action
1	Scan a, Build t1
	Scan b, Probe t1, Build t2
2	Scan c, Build t3
	Scan d, Probe t3, Build t4
3	Scan t4, Probe t2, Build t5

The biggest drawback of a bushy tree strategy is that it increases the complexity of the join possibilities. A bushy tree with only four tables gives rise to 120 possible query plans with only two join methods (join methods are described in the next section) and 960 possible plans with four join methods.

Many database optimizers do not implement bushy trees because of the level of complexity they add, and right-deep trees may be avoided where they require a lot of working storage during the join. Left-deep trees are commonly implemented.

Join Methods

When the optimizer has decided on the order in which to join the tables, the final step is to decide which join methods to use in each case. The major join methods are Cartesian joins, nested loop joins, sort merge joins, and hash joins. New join methods are also being used for joins involving star schema.

Cartesian Joins

The simplest join method is the *Cartesian join*, which must be used if no join predicates have been specified. Strictly speaking, a Cartesian join is not a join method—Cartesian joins can be carried out with a nested loop join method or even a sort merge join method (both described below).

To illustrate a Cartesian join, Figure 8.3 shows three sample tables: the `Region`, `Stock`, and `Sales` tables.

Figure 8.3 *Region, stock, and sales tables*

Product	Qty
Snowboards	20
Scuba Tanks	15
Sunblock SPF30+	92

Stock Table

Product	Region	QtySold
Snowboards	Arctic	3
Scuba Tanks	Bermuda	5
Sunblock SPF30+	Sahara	10
Sunblock SPF30+	Beruda	5
Sunblack SPF30+	Arctic	5

Sales Table

Region	SalesRep
Artic	Arnie
Bermuda	Billy
Sahara	Sally

Region Table

The following query will result in a Cartesian join:

```
select * from region, stock;
```

The result set shows the products available for sale in any region:

Region	SalesRep	Product	Quantity
Arctic	Arnie	Snowboards	20
Bermuda	Billy	Snowboards	20
Sahara	Sally	Snowboards	20
Arctic	Arnie	Scuba Tanks	15
Bermuda	Billy	Scuba Tanks	15
Sahara	Sally	Scuba Tanks	15
Arctic	Arnie	Sunblock SPF30+	92
Bermuda	Billy	Sunblock SPF30+	92
Sahara	Sally	Sunblock SPF30+	92

In the absence of a join predicate, the optimizer chooses a Cartesian join to form the result set. So, the number of rows resulting from a Cartesian join is the product of the number of rows in each table. Although the result set above is not especially meaningful, we can clearly see that every row from the `Region` table has been joined to every row from the `Stock` table.

Cartesian joins are usually expensive and are rarely chosen unless there is no other alternative.

Nested Loop Joins

A more efficient join method is the *nested loop join*. The optimizer chooses an outer table, which is the first table accessed and usually the smaller of the two tables, and an inner table, which is accessed last.

The following query could be processed with a nested loop join, thanks to the presence of a join predicate (specified in the where clause):

```
select r.region, product, qtysold, salesrep
    from region r, sales s
    where r.region = s.region;
```

The result set will contain the following rows:

Region	Product	QtySold	SalesRep
Arctic	Snowboards	3	Arnie
Arctic	Sunblock SPF30+	5	Arnie
Bermuda	Scuba Tanks	5	Billy
Bermuda	Sunblock SPF30+	5	Billy
Sahara	Sunblock SPF30+	10	Sally

For a nested loop join, the inner table is scanned once for each row of the outer table. So if the smaller table, the Region table, is chosen as the outer table, all rows in the Sales table (the inner table) will be searched to find those matching the first region, Arctic. If any rows match, they will be joined. Next, all rows in the Sales table matching the Bermuda region will be joined, and so on.

Nested loop joins are preferred when the tables are small, the predicates are highly selective (that is, only a small percentage of the data is selected), or when indexes are available on the join columns, allowing efficient random access to the base tables.

Sort Merge Joins

A *sort merge join* scans the rows from each table in turn, eliminating any that do not meet predicate constraints, and then sorts each result set on the join column before merging them. Consequently, the final result can be produced with only one pass through the inner table. The following query might be a candidate for a sort merge join:

```
select r.region, product, qtysold, salesrep
    from region r, sales s
    where r.region = s.region
    order by r.region;
```

The final result must be sorted by region, the join key. A sort merge join will present results in that order as a natural consequence of the sort merge process. Sort merge joins become more expensive as the data volumes increase due to the overhead of sorting.

Hash Joins

Although *hash joins* appeared after the other join methods in some query optimizers, they are often chosen because of their efficiency. Hash joins store the outer table rows that satisfy any predicate constraints in a hash table, using a hash function to determine the location. Each row from the inner table satisfying all of its predicates is then hashed with the same hash function and joined with any matching rows found in the hash table. The smaller table is usually chosen to build the hash table, and if enough memory is available, the hash table can fit entirely in memory, bringing significant benefits in processing time. Like sort merge joins, hash joins require only one pass through the inner table (although in practice a single pass is not necessarily guaranteed if the hash table cannot be held entirely in memory).

Hash joins are usually less expensive and faster than the other alternatives; they do not require both tables to be sorted as do sort merge joins, and they only require a single pass through the inner table, unlike nested loop joins.

Star Schema Joins

Star schema are described in "Data Warehouses and Data Marts" on page 67. Their special characteristics have offered database suppliers creative opportunities to optimize data access to them. For example, bitmaps can be built to indicate the presence of particular values in columns of the fact table. Where predicates are linked with AND clauses, binary arithmetic on the bitmaps can be used to eliminate rows that do not match the values specified. In a similar way, bitmaps can be used to process predicates joined by OR clauses.

Executing the Query Plan

Once the query optimizer has decided on the access method, the table join order, and the join method, the query can be executed. Joins typically involve up to four actions: scan, join, sort, and write. Some databases complete each action before moving on to the next. By contrast, other databases use pipelines to feed data to the next stage of the query plan while the previous step is still in process.

Reducing the Workload

Important as it is to efficiently access and process query data, it is even better if you can avoid doing the work in the first place. Most of the major database vendors have invested significant engineering effort to find ways of reducing the amount of data that needs to be processed and the amount of processing that is required. The main techniques for reducing the workload are discussed in this section.

Data Partitioning

One way of significantly reducing the volume of data to be processed is to partition or fragment the data so that the bulk of the data doesn't need to be accessed at all. For example, data often retrieved by date could be partitioned into different disk areas according to month. A query predicate specifying dates in the range July 2001 to September 2001 then becomes a signal to the optimizer to ignore disk partitions that do not contain data for those months. For queries with no date predicates, all disk partitions will be accessed.

Partitioning of this type is referred to as *range partitioning*. Range partitioning can be very beneficial, although its usefulness is limited by the static nature of the data partitions and by its restriction to a subset of queries.

Partitioning is discussed in more detail in "Shared-Nothing Databases on SMPs" on page 36, and some of the different data partitioning alternatives are discussed in "Fragmentation" on page 145.

Denormalization

Table joins are a significant consumer of CPU resource, so if joins can be eliminated, query performance should be improved. This potential improvement is one of the main reasons why users sometimes *denormalize* data warehouse tables. Denormalization means that duplicate data is held in a table to avoid a join with another table that would normally store the information. For example, a parts table may normally include a supplier ID column that is a foreign key pointing to the supplier table. To speed queries that join the parts and supplier tables to find the supplier name, the supplier name could be included directly in the parts table, thus avoiding the necessity for a join.

Although denormalization can speed up queries, it does have a negative performance impact on updates since data must be updated in more than one location. Denormalization also increases the size of tables and therefore results in more disk space being consumed.

Normalization is discussed in more detail in Chapter 5 in the section titled "Normalization" on page 48.

Concatenated Indexes

If all columns needed by a query can be found in an index, an optimizer is likely to choose an index scan to avoid accessing the base table altogether. *Concatenated indexes* take advantage of this behavior by including additional columns at the end of the index key that are not necessary for indexing purposes. Carefully chosen concatenated indexes allow some queries to be fully satisfied from the index.

Earlier I suggested that creating an index might improve query performance if query predicates are selective enough to filter out all but 0.5% to 2%

of a table. This restriction does not apply to concatenated indexes that allow the query to bypass the base table, since an index scan will almost always be more efficient than a table scan.

I have seen the use of concatenated indexes taken to bizarre lengths during benchmarking, but they are nonetheless useful tools when used appropriately. Changes to the columns referenced in the index necessitate changes to the index, so update performance is negatively affected by the use of concatenated indexes.

Exotic Optimizations

Competitive benchmarking encourages strange innovations, some of which prove useful to end users and some not. Two such innovations, join indexes and materialized views, were largely responsible for the demise of the Transaction Processing Performance Council's TPC-D benchmark, described in Chapter 27.

Join Indexes

The purpose of *join indexes* is to eliminate joins by building indexes with columns from more than one table. Like concatenated indexes, join indexes can obviate the need to access the base table by inclusion of additional columns in the index. But they go farther than concatenated indexes by incorporating columns from more than one table. In effect, join indexes carry out a prejoin of the tables and store the results in the index.

The cost of avoiding the join is a complex and highly specialized index. Like all indexes, join indexes must be updated whenever data changes in the base table columns it references, so update completion times increase with join indexes.

Materialized Views

A database view is simply stored SQL code that presents a virtual table and its columns. A view often simplifies more complex underlying code, including multiple-table joins and aggregation. Although the view appears to be referencing a real database table, the "table" referenced by the view does not actually exist.

Materialized views change the nature of views by executing them and storing the results permanently, just as for normal tables. As the name suggests, the view results are instantiated or materialized.

Complex views and queries on large tables can take a long time to execute. By precomputing the result set, materialized views overcome this problem. As long as the optimizer is aware of the materialized view, queries that require the columns stored in it can be satisfied by a simple table lookup rather than a lengthy query execution.

Materialized views typically benefit a limited subset of queries, and like join indexes, they incur an update performance penalty. Changes to the table columns on which they are based will require updates to the materialized view data.

Since materialized views can store prejoined and aggregated data, they can be regarded as another step by traditional relational databases in the direction of Online Analytical Processing (OLAP).

Given that materialized views are still relatively new arrivals on the database scene, it remains to be seen whether they become widely adopted by end users.

Expert Intervention

"When the database optimizer lets you down, you can always force it to do the right thing."

This view has held sway for a long time in some data warehouse environments, although query optimizers have been improving significantly in recent years. The comment makes sense for databases that permit the user to provide hints to the optimizer.

For example, Oracle allows a variety of hints, including those in the following list:

- Ignore indexes and perform a full table scan.
- Use an index scan for the specified table.
- Perform a hash join.
- Perform a nested loop join.
- Perform a sort merge join.
- Join tables in the order specified in the FROM clause.

Not all databases allow hints—DB2 for Solaris does not, for example. I heard a senior IBM employee express the view that the user only needs to supply hints if the optimizer is broken, in which case the best solution is to enhance the optimizer, not to offer a hint capability. This view may be debatable, but we certainly all look forward to the day when none of the query optimizers need assistance.

9

ORACLE ARCHITECTURE

Oracle continues to be a key product on the Sun platform; Oracle's dominant database market share in the Unix marketplace translates to a large customer base on Sun systems. In this chapter we examine the architecture of Oracle, focusing on the process model, memory management, and data storage. We also consider parallel processing issues.

Process Model

The Oracle process model is organized around an *instance*, which consists of shared memory and a group of database system processes. Only one database can be opened by an instance, although an instance can be started initially without any database being mounted or opened at all. Real Application Clusters (RAC) technology (previously known as Oracle Parallel Server, or OPS) actually allows multiple instances to open the same database, allowing clustered systems to share a single database. Each instance has a unique instance ID, set with the ORACLE_SID environment variable, and the characteristics of an instance are determined by the contents of a parameter file, usually called init{$ORACLE_SID}.ora.

The shared memory belonging to an instance is called the *system global area* (SGA). It is allocated when the instance is started and deallocated when the instance is shut down. The SGA is described in "Memory Management" on page 108.

A number of Oracle database system processes are started when the instance is started. The following list identifies them:

- **SMON.** The System Monitor performs instance recovery. It is also used at instance startup after an instance crash to roll forward changes that appear in the redo log file but not in the database blocks. SMON is responsible for cleaning up and reclaiming unused temporary segments. Only one System Monitor process runs per instance.

- **PMON.** The Process Monitor performs the recovery after failure of a user process and any necessary transaction rollback. PMON is responsible for releasing locks and cleaning up any cache memory used by the process. Only one Process Monitor process runs per instance.

- **DBWR.** The Database Writer process (or processes, since multiple Database Writer processes can be started as of Oracle8) is used to flush dirty (that is, modified) buffers from the SGA's buffer cache to database pages on disk. This process operates asynchronously; in other words, writes are deferred (a) to allow flushing to be scheduled efficiently, (b) to piggyback the writes (that is, reduce the number of write I/Os by allowing multiple transactions to modify the block before it is written), and (c) to keep the most frequently accessed data in memory (flushing of dirty buffers focuses on least recently used blocks).

  The Database Writer performs checkpoints as prompted by the CKPT process, flushing dirty blocks to disk to synchronize the contents of the buffer cache with the tables held on disk.

  Effective flushing of dirty blocks is essential to good performance because it ensures that clean blocks are available for new transactions. If the supply of clean blocks is inadequate, transactions will be forced to block while the Database Writer cleans more.

  As of Oracle8, Database Writers use the notation DBWn, reflecting the fact that multiple Database Writers are supported. In update-intensive environments with large buffer caches, multiple Database Writers allow Oracle to keep up with the demand for clean buffers.

- **LGWR.** The Log Writer process writes redo entries from the redo log buffer in the SGA to the redo logs on disk. This process is also important to performance since transaction commits do not complete until the log record has been successfully written to disk. The Log Writer attempts to piggyback commits to achieve an average of less than one write I/O per commit. Only one Log Writer process runs per instance.

- **RECO.** The Distributed Transaction Recovery process resolves transaction failures in a distributed database. Only one Recovery process runs per instance.

- **CKPT.** The Checkpoint process updates the control files and data file headers with checkpoint information after a checkpoint. Checkpoints occur when a redo log file switch takes place, the checkpoint interval expires, or a database administrator manually requests a checkpoint. In Oracle7, the Checkpoint process was optional (it was enabled by setting the `checkpoint_process` parameter to `true` in the Oracle parameter file—generally referred to as `init.ora`); in its absence the Log Writer managed checkpoints. The CKPT process was created to free the Log Writer to concentrate on its primary task of writing redo log records. Only one Checkpoint process runs per instance.

Oracle8i introduced the concept of incremental, or continuous check-pointing to reduce the impact of checkpoints. Oracle also allows you to set your preferred recovery time. These issues are explored in more detail in "Recovering Oracle" on page 346.

- **ARCH.** The Archiver process, active when `ARCHIVELOG` mode is set for the database, archives the last active redo log file when a log switch takes place. The redo logs operate on a round-robin basis, that is, the first log is reused when the last is filled. The Archiver process is needed to ensure that no data is irretrievably lost when redo logs are overwritten. In the event of a disk crash, backups must be restored and a roll-forward carried out from the redo logs. Archived logs provide access to old log data that has since been overwritten in the redo logs.

- **D***nnn***.** The Dispatcher processes are used when the Oracle Shared Server (previously known as the MultiThreaded Server, or MTS) is enabled. User processes connect to a shared dispatcher process, which routes requests to the next available Shared Server process (described immediately below). One or more dispatcher processes can be assigned to each connection protocol.

- **S***nnn***.** The Shared Server processes also are used only when Shared Server is in use. Shared Server allows many users to share a smaller number of Shared Server processes, thereby minimizing memory and system resources as the number of user connections increases.

- **LMD0.** The Distributed Lock Manager Daemon is a process specific to Real Application Clusters (RAC). It manages locking of resources such as data blocks, rollback segments, and data dictionary entries between instances. It receives resource requests, sends resource notifications, and tracks ownership of resources.

- **LCK***n***.** The Lock processes (LCK0 to LCK9) are also RAC-specific processes that manage locks used by an instance and coordinate requests for locks from other instances. Lock processes communicate with the Distributed Lock Manager.

These process names appear in a `/usr/bin/ps` list prepended with `ora_` and appended with `_{$ORACLE_SID}`. The following `ps` listing shows the processes for a running Oracle8 instance with the instance ID set to `live`:

```
oracle% ps -aef | grep ora
   oracle 13888 13835  0  Apr 11 pts/21   0:00 -csh
   oracle  7015 13888  0 13:16:18 pts/21   0:00 grep ora
   oracle  1322     1  0  Apr 02 ?        0:00 ora_pmon_live
   oracle  1324     1  0  Apr 02 ?        0:00 ora_dbw0_live
```

```
oracle  1326    1  0    Apr 02 ?          0:00 ora_lgwr_live
oracle  1328    1  0    Apr 02 ?          1:12 ora_ckpt_live
oracle  1330    1  0    Apr 02 ?          0:01 ora_smon_live
oracle  1332    1  0    Apr 02 ?          0:00 ora_reco_live
oracle  1334    1  0    Apr 02 ?          0:00 ora_s000_live
oracle  1336    1  0    Apr 02 ?          0:00 ora_d000_live
oracle%
```

Oracle is based on a 2n architecture (described in Chapter 5 in the section titled "2n Architectures" on page 58). In addition to the Oracle system processes, each user connection has a dedicated *shadow process*, or *server process*, that connects to the SGA and reads from the database files on behalf of the user's application. Each shadow process also has its own private memory area called the *program global area* (PGA). Figure 9.1 shows the 2n architecture on a single server; client applications could also be run on separate client systems.

Figure 9.1   *Oracle's 2n process architecture*

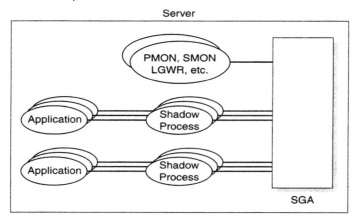

Application processes connect to shadow processes, which in turn attach to the SGA. When application processes running on a remote client system connect to Oracle, the connection request is processed by a *listener* process. The listener starts the shadow process on the client's behalf. Some users set up a single listener to handle multiple instances, some users set up a separate listener for each instance (running on a different port), and some users establish multiple listeners for a single instance (if the connection rate is high).

The Shared Server offers an alternative way for user applications to connect to Oracle. Note that Shared Server was referred to as MultiThreaded Server (MTS) until the Oracle9i release. It was first introduced in Oracle7. Instead of a dedicated shadow process being forked for each user application, each user application is allocated by a listener process to one of a number of dispatcher processes. After allocating a dispatcher, the listener plays no further part. The dispatcher places the user's SQL requests on a request queue in the SGA. Shared Server uses a pool of server processes to process the entries in the request queue on behalf of user connections and to place the results in a response queue.

The Shared Server process model is illustrated in Figure 9.2.

Figure 9.2 *Shared Server process architecture*

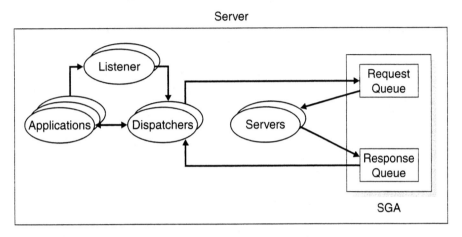

Shadow processes store user session information in process local memory called the program global area (PGA). This approach is not practical with Shared Server, though, since any available server in the pool can act on behalf of a user. For this reason, user session information is made more generally accessible by being placed in shared memory and, specifically, in the shared pool, which is part of the SGA. In the same way, a special sort area is established in the SGA for use by Shared Servers in place of the application sort areas normally located in the PGA. The large_pool_size parameter in init.ora controls the size of this sort area.

In spite of its original name (MultiThreaded Server), Shared Server is not a multithreaded server; it is more accurately a queue-based streamlining of the same 2n architecture. Nonetheless, it does significantly reduce per-user memory requirements, and DBE tests have suggested that, with careful configuration, performance close to that experienced with dedicated shadow processes can be achieved. If you decide to use Shared Server, make sure that you increase the size of the shared pool (by increasing the shared_pool_size parameter in init.ora, described in the next section) to accommodate user session data.

One of the most efficient ways of achieving connection pooling is to use a Transaction Processing (TP) monitor (described in "Transaction Monitors" on page 62).

Memory Management

Oracle makes use of a dedicated memory area shared by Oracle system processes and shadow processes, as well as private memory areas used by individual shadow processes.

System Global Area (SGA)

The database shared memory area plays a key role in the operation of the Oracle instance. It provides a storage area so that commonly used objects such as database blocks and optimized SQL statements can be cached for use by other processes. It also facilitates the communication between Oracle system processes (for example, sharing locking information). Oracle refers to this shared memory area as the *system global area* (SGA).

The SGA consists of the following major components:

- **Data block buffer cache**. The buffer cache provides one of the most important elements of a well-performing Oracle instance. It caches data and index blocks, rollback segment blocks, and temporary tablespace blocks, allowing frequently used database blocks to be readily accessed by other applications without recourse to disk I/O. The size of the buffer cache is controlled by the db_block_buffers parameter in init.ora (the parameter relates to the number of blocks, not the number of bytes, so it depends on the number of bytes in db_block_size). As of Oracle9i, a new parameter was introduced: db_cache_size, the number of bytes in the buffer cache. Oracle9i also supports tablespaces with different block sizes, so a new set of buffer cache parameters was also introduced (db_2k_cache_size for tablespaces with 2-Kbyte blocks, for example). Refer to "Setting Tunable Parameters for OLTP Workloads" on page 336 for more details.

  Although Oracle does not provide dedicated caches for tables or tablespaces, Oracle8 introduced two new buffer pools: the *keep* and *recycle* pools, controlled by the buffer_pool_keep and buffer_pool_recycle parameters in init.ora. These parameters specify the number of db_block_buffers blocks that should be dedicated to the keep and recycle pools, respectively. The size of the main buffer cache is therefore reduced by the total of buffer_pool_keep and buffer_pool_recycle.

  The normal caching policy of the buffer pool is based on a least recently used (LRU) algorithm, which means that older buffers are flushed first. By contrast, buffers in the keep pool are never flushed, so the pool is useful for small, heavily accessed tables that should remain in memory at all times. Buffers in the recycle pool are instantly flushed, eliminating the need to maintain an LRU list and reducing time spent waiting for buffers. The recycle pool is useful for data that is rarely reused.

Tables can be associated with the keep or recycle pools when they are created, or subsequently with the `alter table` statement. An example is given in "Setting Tunable Parameters for OLTP Workloads" on page 336.

- **Shared pool.** This pool is usually the second-largest consumer of SGA memory after the buffer cache. It holds the library cache, or shared SQL area, which contains SQL statement text and parsed SQL statements, the dictionary cache, and session information when Shared Server is active. The library cache also holds stored procedure and trigger code. The size of the shared pool is managed by the `shared_pool_size` parameter (the unit is bytes) in the `init.ora` file.

- **Dictionary cache.** This cache stores data dictionary information, covering all objects in the database, including users, tables, indexes, and storage objects like tablespaces and segments. The information is accessed every time an SQL statement is parsed and again when it is executed, so the cache can be heavily utilized, especially in OLTP environments. As of Oracle7, this cache is located in the shared pool and therefore does not need to be separately tuned.

- **Session data.** User context information is usually held in the program global area (in process local memory) rather than in shared memory. Session data is, however, stored in shared memory (in the shared pool) if the Shared Server is active.

- **Redo log buffer.** This buffer holds current redo log records that are ready to be written to the redo log files. By buffering log records, the Log Writer typically reduces log writes to less than one per commit. When the redo log buffer fills, it is flushed to the redo log file, resulting in excessive log file I/O if the buffer is too small. The size of the log buffer is managed by the `log_buffer` parameter (the unit is bytes) in `init.ora`.

- **Distributed lock area.** This SGA area is only used when Real Application Clusters is installed. It holds parallel cache management (PCM) locks, which coordinate access to resources, such as data blocks and rollback segments, across multiple RAC instances.

The SGA also holds integrity information, such as locks and latches (cheap locks used to protect internal Oracle data structures).

Figure 9.3 shows the SGA, the Oracle system processes, and their interactions with the database files and redo logs.

Figure 9.3 *Interactions between the Oracle instance and database files*

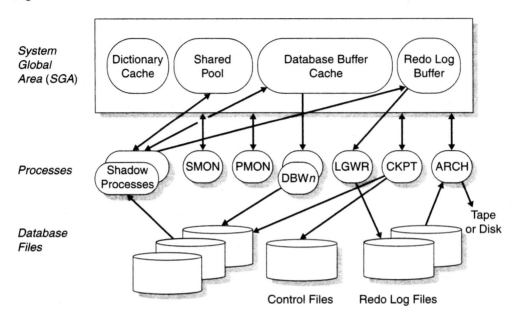

Program Global Area (PGA)

The program global area (PGA) is private memory used by shadow processes associated with Oracle applications. It contains cursor status information and a working storage area for sorts (the size of which is controlled by the sort_area_size parameter in init.ora), as well as application-specific database information. Before Oracle7, it also contained the SQL statement text and parsed SQL statement; these statements are now held in the library cache, part of the SGA shared pool.

If Shared Server is active, the information normally held in the PGA is held in the SGA's shared pool.

Physical Data Storage

Oracle databases for both OLTP and DSS applications are implemented as a single data store; Oracle does not use a shared-nothing architecture. Tablespace files store database blocks (data, index, rollback segments, and temporary storage), and log information is held in redo log files. Status information about database files is held in control files. This section examines each of these file types.

Tablespaces

Data is held in *tablespaces* that span one or more data files. Tablespace data files can be either file system files or raw devices (that is, raw disk partitions or raw volumes created by a volume manager such as Solaris Volume Manager or Veritas). Raw devices typically offer better performance, although file system files have the advantage that they can be automatically extended by Oracle if free space is exhausted.

Oracle allocates extents (see "Extents" on page 113) across underlying data files in a round-robin fashion. This behavior provides a simple form of striping (the value assigned to the NEXT extent storage parameter acts as the stripe width).

Redo Log Files

Modifications to database blocks are recorded in the *redo log files*. The log records in the redo log files include row change records written by user shadow processes (showing the row before and after the change), transaction commit records, and checkpoint records. Checkpoint records flag a point in time when the system synchronized the buffer cache with the tablespace files by writing to disk any modified blocks in the buffer cache.

The information held in the redo log files preserves the integrity of the data. If a database or system crash takes place, log records are rolled forward from the last checkpoint to ensure that data pages are up-to-date. If a disk failure occurs, tablespace file backups can be restored and the log files rolled forward to reinstate database changes made since the backup. Finally, the redo log information allows a transaction to be rolled back if it has not been committed.

The redo logs are circular, which means that when the last file is filled, the first is reused. To prevent loss of data as a result, Oracle's Archiver system process can be used to back up a redo log immediately after Oracle switches to the next log file. Roll-forward recovery after media failure automatically makes use of archived redo log files if necessary. A checkpoint is triggered whenever Oracle switches log files.

Multiple redo log files can be used, but a minimum of two redo log files is required to ensure that database activity does not block during a checkpoint. While one redo log is being processed, data can be logged to the other.

Redo log files can be located on the same disk since Oracle only writes to one at a time.

Control Files

The control files are created during database creation. They contain information about each database file and redo log file, including timestamps and the database ID. Without the control files a database cannot be successfully opened.

Oracle supports and recommends the use of multiple control files (whose location is listed in the `init.ora` file). Since the control files are crucial, it is wise to keep mirrored copies as insurance against media failure.

Logical Data Storage

Oracle tablespace data is stored in segments, and within segments in extents. Extents are made up of blocks, which form the basic unit of access to and from the SGA and disks.

Segments

Oracle uses four types of segments: data segments, index segments, temporary segments, and rollback segments. A tablespace can hold one or more segments, including segments of all four types and multiple segments of one type, and each segment is wholly contained within a single tablespace. When a segment is dropped, free space becomes available within the tablespace (possibly also leading to fragmentation of data within the tablespace).

Data segments store tables and table data. Clusters are a special kind of data segment where rows are stored within the cluster in sorted order of the column designated as the cluster key. Hash clusters use a hash key to determine the physical location of the row. Clusters are most likely to be suitable for static tables; you incur performance overheads when you place dynamically changing tables in clusters.

Index segments store indexes. Index segments can coexist with data segments in a tablespace, although separate tablespaces are often created for indexes.

Temporary segments are used when sorts run out of memory and spill to disk. Sorts are associated with SQL statements, for example, with `group by` and `order by` clauses, and with substantial operations like index creation. Oracle lets you create dedicated temporary tablespaces and assign users to them; dedicated temporary tablespaces are a good idea for performance reasons.

Rollback segments store transaction before-image information (information about the contents of a row before it was modified by a transaction). Thanks to this information, Oracle can roll back uncommitted transactions to their previous state. Rollback segments also allow Oracle to maintain read consistency for long-running transactions referring to blocks that have changed since the transaction began. Rollback segment entries are also written to the redo logs, so even after a system crash, an active transaction can be rolled back. When a rollback entry is no longer required, its space is reused by another rollback entry. Rollback segments are created explicitly with the `create rollback segment` command.

Extents

Within a segment, data is stored in *extents*. An extent is a logical unit of database storage space consisting of a number of contiguous data blocks (blocks are described in the next section). A segment consists of one or more extents. When segment free space is exhausted, Oracle allocates a new extent for the segment.

Default extent sizes can be specified for each tablespace; these defaults will be used for the objects in the tablespace (tables, indexes, or clusters) unless you override them by setting new values for each object.

Three storage parameters can be set as tablespace defaults. For each object: initial determines the size of the object's first extent, next determines the size of the second extent, and pctincrease is applied to next cumulatively to determine the size of the third and subsequent objects. For example, initial 1M next 100K pctincrease 10 results in a first extent 1 Mbyte in size, a second extent 100 Kbytes in size, a third extent 110 Kbytes in size (100 Kbytes + 10%), a fourth extent 121 Kbytes in size (110 Kbytes + 10%), and so on. Setting pctincrease greater than 0 means that extent sizes can increase dramatically; it is usually safer to set pctincrease to 0 and allow the tablespace to grow in size linearly.

A minimum number of extents can be enforced with the minextents keyword, and the maximum number of extents can be limited with the maxextents keyword. A new extent will be created whenever the previous extents are full, provided the tablespace has sufficient free space and maxextents is not exceeded. As of Oracle8, maxextents unlimited is supported.

For tables likely to be table-scanned in DSS environments, initial should be set to a multiple of the amount of data read during a multiblock read (to calculate the amount of data read during a multiblock read, multiply db_file_multiblock_read_count by db_block_size).

Temporary extents are created and dropped regularly, so for temporary tablespaces it is wise to set initial equal to next, and pctincrease to 0, to avoid complications arising from fragmentation. Set initial equal to next for rollback segments also.

Blocks

Within extents, data is stored in *blocks* (extent sizes are always rounded up to a whole number of blocks). The block size, or database page size, is the minimum unit of database access. So for a block size of 2048 bytes, all database reads and writes will transfer 2 Kbytes (except for special cases like multiblock read-ahead, where multiple blocks are read at one time). Blocks can be 2, 4, 8, or 16 Kbytes in size.

Blocks are not usually filled with data. For each table you can specify with the pctfree parameter how much free space should be reserved within each block. When updates are carried out, free space allows a column to be increased in size while still remaining within the same block. The alternative, spreading the row across multiple blocks (row chaining), leads to poor performance. Once pctfree has been exceeded, new rows cannot be added to the block. Setting pctfree too high means that blocks will only be partially populated and you will need to read more blocks during a table scan.

The pctused table parameter regulates the packing density of data blocks. If the percentage of data in the block drops below pctused because of deletes, the row becomes available to receive new row inserts. Keeping blocks reasonably densely packed means that fewer blocks are read during table scans (important for DSS and batch applications).

Partitions

As of Oracle8, horizontal partitioning is supported for tables. Horizontal partitioning means that tables can be split across multiple tablespaces, and rows placed in one of the tablespaces according to the value of one or more of the columns. Even though each partition can be directly referenced and administered independently, Oracle is still able to transparently treat the table as a single object. When executing a query, Oracle's optimizer automatically either references the entire table or ignores partitions that do not contain data pertinent to the query. Oracle's implementation of horizontal partitioning uses partitions based on data ranges (range partitioning).

Consider a simple table with sales data held by month, for example. The table can be partitioned with a command like the following table creation command:

```
create table sales (product_id varchar2(20) primary key,
    customer_id number(10), quantity number(8),
    unit_price number(10,2), month_no number(2))
    partition by range (month_no, region)
    (partition jan values less than (2, 'C')
        tablespace ts_01,
    partition feb values less than (3, 'E')
        tablespace ts_02,
    ...,
    partition dec values less than (maxvalues, maxvalues)
        tablespace ts_12);
```

The tablespaces ts_01 to ts_12 could each be striped across the available disks, ensuring that all disks will be active even if most of the tablespaces are eliminated by the optimizer for a query.

System Tablespace

The SYSTEM tablespace stores Oracle's internal data dictionary tables, which contain information about data files, tablespaces, tables, indexes, clusters, rollback segments, views, synonyms, users, grants, stored procedures, triggers, and other such data. At a minimum, every database has a SYSTEM tablespace, although usually other tablespaces are created and user data is kept out of the SYSTEM tablespace. User tables must be explicitly placed in other tablespaces, or their location defaults to the SYSTEM tablespace.

Temporary tablespaces and rollback segments, already discussed in this chapter, are other objects directly related to system rather than user activities.

Parallel Processing

To assist with the processing of large amounts of data, Oracle provides parallel processing features that break tasks into smaller units of work capable of being executed concurrently. These features are of particular relevance to DSS environments. The following database activities can be parallelized:

- Queries (select statements, including subqueries within delete, update, and insert statements, and create table as select). This feature is known as the *Parallel Query Option* (PQO).

- Data Manipulation Language (DML) operations (as of Oracle8). Run the alter session parallel dml command to enable parallel DML.

- Database load (SQL*Loader Direct Path).

- create index and rebuild index operations.

- Database recovery.

- Index scans (as of Oracle8).

The architecture of the PQO is explored in the next section; a similar architecture applies to the other parallel capabilities listed above.

The Parallel Query Option (PQO)

Before the advent of the PQO, all work was carried out on behalf of an application process by its shadow process. The result was that only one CPU participated in executing the query, resulting in very long query execution times for queries retrieving large data sets.

The major significance of the PQO is that it allows multiple CPUs to be used to execute a single query, also increasing I/O parallelism in the process. PQO achieves this parallelism by delegating the task of reading data to multiple *query slaves*.

Although this discussion does not focus on Real Application Clusters (previously referred to as Oracle Parallel Server, or OPS), let us note here that RAC allows parallelism to be further extended to multiple systems by additionally delegating parallel activities to instances running on different servers and attaching to the same database.

Table Scans

The simplest case of query parallelism is a table scan, which retrieves all rows from a table. A single table scan might satisfy the requirements of a simple query; a complex query might use a table scan as just one step in the query plan.

For example, suppose a user executes the following SQL statement:

```
select * from CUSTOMER;
```

The result would be a full table scan of the CUSTOMER table. Figure 9.4 illustrates the process model used by the PQO for a table scan with a degree of parallelism of 4.

Figure 9.4 *The PQO process model for a table scan*

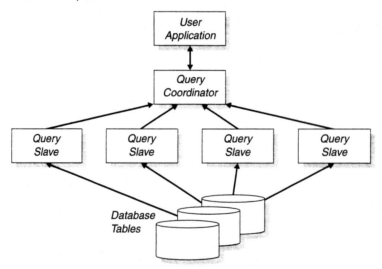

When a PQO query is executed by a user application, the shadow process acts as a *query coordinator*, dynamically calling upon multiple query slaves to each retrieve a subset of the data blocks from the database tables. As well as reading the data, the query slaves evaluate any relevant query predicates to eliminate unnecessary rows before passing the result set to the query coordinator. The query coordinator assembles the data retrieved from each query slave and carries out any necessary final processing before passing the results to the user application.

The number of query slaves assigned to a query is determined by the degree of parallelism for the query. The degree of parallelism can be set for each table as shown in the following example:

```
alter table CUSTOMER parallel (degree 12);
```

Query parallelism can be disabled for a table, as shown in the following command:

```
alter table REGION noparallel;
```

Any table settings can be overridden with the PARALLEL query hint, for example:

```
select /*+ PARALLEL(customer, 12) */
    NAME, ADDRESS, BALANCE_OWING
    from CUSTOMER;
```

Alternatively, parallelism can be disabled (for example, if the table is too small to benefit from parallelism) as in the following example:

```
select /*+ NOPARALLselect /*+ NOPARALLEL(region) */
    * from REGION;
```

If parallelism has not been specified either at the table level or by a hint, Oracle selects a degree of parallelism based on factors like the number of CPUs on the server, the size of the table, and the number of database files used by the tablespace in which the table lives. Where multiple tables are accessed in a query, the degree of parallelism is determined for each and the highest value is then used for the query.

Note that Oracle8 supports limited query parallelism within a partition (partitions are described in "Partitions" on page 114). For inserts, updates, and deletes, if a query accesses a single data partition, only one query slave will be used, and if four partitions are accessed, a maximum of four query slaves will be used. Query parallelism within a partition is supported for selects.

Starting new query slave processes is expensive. Oracle avoids the penalty of process startup and shutdown costs for each query by maintaining a pool of processes for use as query slave processes. When an instance is started, the initial size of the query pool is determined by the parallel_min_servers parameter in init.ora. As more query slaves are needed, the number of processes in the query pool can grow to a limit set by the init.ora parallel_max_servers parameter. When processes in the query pool remain idle for parallel_server_idle_time minutes, some are terminated until only parallel_min_servers processes remain in the pool.

The parallel_max_servers parameter also determines the maximum possible degree of parallelism for a single query.

You can mandate the minimum number of query slaves that must be available before a query is allowed to run by using the optional init.ora parameter parallel_min_percent. For example, suppose the degree of parallelism for a query is set to 12 with the PARALLEL query hint and parallel_min_percent is set to 25: the query will run if four or more query slaves are available and will otherwise abort with an error.

Table Scans with Sorts

If the Oracle optimizer decides on a table scan, the number of query slave processes used to retrieve the data will be $n+1$, where 1 refers to the query coordinator process and n is the actual degree of parallelism (which may differ from the requested degree of parallelism for the reasons given in the previous section).

If the table scan is followed by a sort, though, the number of query slave processes used will be $2n+1$.

For example, consider the following SQL statement:

```
select * from CUSTOMER order by CUST_NAME;
```

The result would be a full table scan of the CUSTOMER table followed by a sort. Figure 9.5 illustrates the process model used by the PQO for a table scan and sort with a degree of parallelism of 4.

Figure 9.5 *The PQO process model for a table scan with sort*

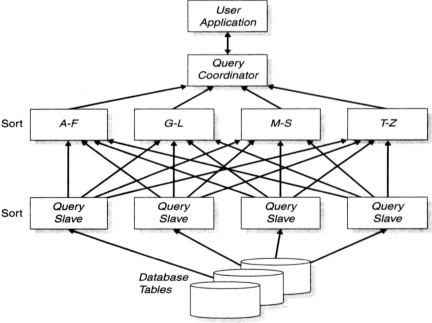

The sorts are carried out by an additional group of query slaves. Even though the degree of parallelism was 4, four slaves are allocated for sorts and another four for scans. Each scan process must communicate with every sort process; the table data is not stored in any particular order, and each scan process will retrieve data destined for all sort processes. All nine processes can potentially run on a different CPU, so it is possible to consume a lot more CPUs than the degree of parallelism might suggest.

Other Parallel Capabilities

Queries are not the only database operations that benefit from being parallelized. Data loads, index creation, and execution of Data Manipulation Language (DML) statements like `update` and `delete` are all examples of operations that can benefit from being broken up into multiple concurrent units of work. The benefit is seen in the form of reduced completion times, especially when the data sets are very large.

Table Creation

Table creation can be parallelized, with the query coordinator delegating the creation task to multiple slave processes. Note that if the table storage clause specifies a `minextents` value of 2, normally two extents will be created with the table. With parallel table creation, *each* slave process will create two extents. The result can be the allocation of more space than expected. Parallelism can be achieved for `create table as select` commands, both for the query (as of Oracle7.1) and the insert (as of Oracle7.2).

Index Creation

Oracle parallelizes index creation by dedicating the table scan phase to multiple query slaves and dedicating the sort phase to a second set of query slaves. The results are merged and the index is written by the query coordinator. The following command illustrates the syntax necessary for parallel index creation:

```
create index CUSTOMER_INDEX1 on CUSTOMER (CUST_ID, REGION)
    parallel(degree 12);
```

Note that `UNIQUE` and `PRIMARY KEY` constraints must be disabled until index creation has completed.

DML Statements

Parallel DML can be enabled with the following command:

```
alter session enable parallel dml;
```

Hints can then be applied, as shown in the following example:

```
insert /* parallel(customer, 12) */ into customer
    select * from temp_table;
```

Database Load

The SQL*Loader command can be run in parallel with the `DIRECT=TRUE` `PARALLEL=TRUE` options. Each SQL*Loader session runs independently, bypassing the buffer cache and writing data directly to tables. Indexes must first be dropped, and primary key and unique constraints disabled. Indexes can be recreated and constraints reenabled after the load has completed. Each session will allocate a new extent in the table, and preallocated space will not be used. An optimal load procedure is outlined in "Optimizing Oracle Load Performance" on page 341.

Database Recovery

Finally, you can use multiple processes during database recovery by setting the `recovery_parallelism` parameter in `init.ora`. Although a single Oracle system process reads the redo log files, the information is passed to multiple recovery processes.

10

SYBASE
ARCHITECTURE

Sybase Adaptive Server Enterprise (ASE) is widely used on Sun systems, especially in OLTP environments. In this chapter we discuss the process model, memory management, and data storage characteristics of ASE. We also examine the system databases and the parallel query capabilities of Sybase ASE 11.5 onwards. Finally, we explore the architecture of Sybase Adaptive Server IQ with Multiplex.

Process Model

Sybase ASE uses a multithreaded architecture to make efficient use of CPU and memory resources. The multithreaded Sybase kernel, which uses Sybase's own threading model rather than Solaris threads, handles scheduling and dispatching of user threads and internal database threads. See "Multithreaded Architectures" on page 59 for more information on multithreaded database architectures.

Symmetrical multiprocessing support for ASE is provided by Sybase's Virtual Server Architecture (VSA) which supports multiple database engines. The database engines run as cooperating processes communicating through shared memory and accessing common databases and memory data structures. The engines provide a fully symmetrical environment for executing user tasks: each engine is capable of carrying out all functions, including disk I/O, locking, and network I/O. The use of multiple engines to execute user tasks is transparent—users see only a single service.

Sybase ASE is typically configured on Sun servers with one engine per CPU (assuming Sybase is the only workload). On large systems with very heavy workloads, engines might not be assigned to every CPU; one or more CPUs might be set aside to handle disk and network I/O interrupts.

ASE also provides a fully symmetrical environment for user task execution, using a feature of ASE called Multiple Network Engine (MNE). Before the ASE 11.9.x release, there was one exception to the full symmetry of task execution: for the sake of simplicity, all incoming user logins were handled by the first engine (engine 0). Once a user session established a login session, including authentication and establishment of the environment, the connection was moved to one of the other engines. Since ASE 11.9.x, only the `select` call is handled by engine 0; all processing associated with establishing the connection and login is now assigned to an engine according to load.

The engine selected for the connection is the one with the least number of connections currently assigned. This strategy provides a crude form of load balancing across the multiple engines. However, the load from each connection is not known at time of the assignment, leading to load imbalance if some tasks generate more load than others.

Once a user connection has been assigned to an engine, the engine creates a user task and places it on a sleep queue. Once every clock tick the engine checks for incoming commands for that task. When a command is received for the task, the task is awakened and put on the run queue. When it reaches the head of the queue, the next available engine schedules the task and begins execution. If the task needs to wait for an I/O, the task is returned to the sleep queue pending I/O completion. Whenever it enters the scheduler, the engine runs its I/O service routine to determine if an I/O request has been completed. When the I/O returns, the task is again placed on the run queue to be scheduled on the next available engine.

When the task needs to send data back to the client, it makes a network I/O request. Until ASE 12.0, the engine currently executing the task first stored the details for the pending network I/O and then placed the request on the pending network I/O list for the engine originally assigned to the user connection. The I/O service task issued a network "send" request to the Solaris networking layer. The task was then put back on the run queue to continue execution on an engine. Since ASE 12.0, when an engine wants to send the data to the client, it does so directly.

Multiple Network Engine greatly increases the ability of ASE to handle a large number of concurrent users and the ability to scale network performance with additional engines.

Figure 10.1 illustrates the thread model of Sybase ASE.

Figure 10.1   *Sybase ASE task management in an SMP environment*

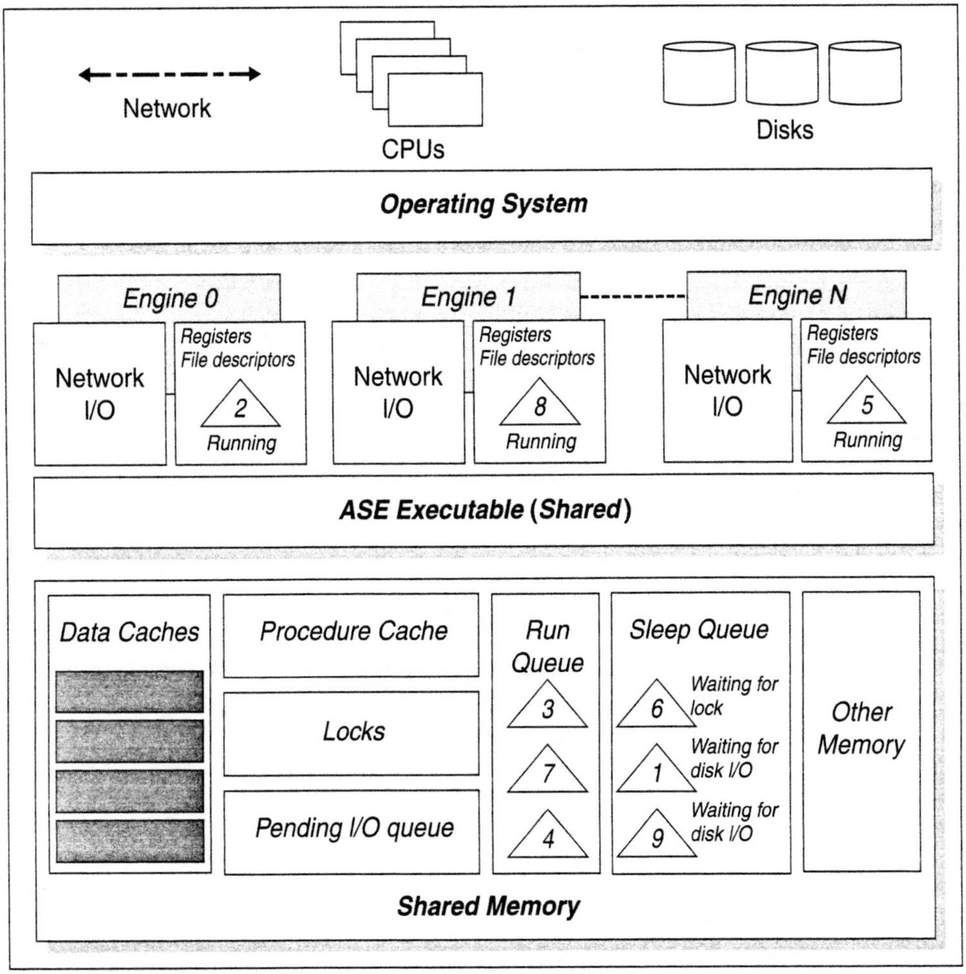

In the example, three threads are running on the engines and three more threads are waiting on the global run queue. Three threads have previously run and are now waiting on the sleep queue for I/O to complete or for a lock.

Since ASE 11.9.x, in addition to a global run queue, run queues are maintained for each engine. Each task has soft affinity to an engine: when a task runs, it acquires an affinity to the engine it is running on, and after yielding the CPU, it will tend to be placed back on the run queue for that same engine.

Each task has an associated priority that ASE can increase if the task is holding a critical resource or has been waiting a long time for a resource. You can also assign priorities to logins, procedures, or applications with sp_bindexeclass and related system procedures. You can also create engine groups with sp_addengine, and you can bind execution objects to an engine group; the effect is analogous to Solaris processor sets (described in "Processor Sets" on page 210).

Each engine checks its own high-priority queue and the global high-priority queue, and it can steal tasks from the queues of other engines if it has no work to be done.

Memory Management

Memory is managed within Sybase ASE by the Buffer Manager. ASE uses shared memory to hold the data cache, the procedure cache, and Sybase kernel data structures such as the run and sleep queues and lock chains.

Before ASE 12.5, changes to parameters affecting the size of shared memory did not take effect until a Sybase reboot. ASE 12.5 allows these parameters to be changed dynamically. For more detail, refer to "Dynamic Memory Tuning" on page 361.

Data Cache

Effective algorithms for caching data are critical for performance—when data is found in the cache, a physical read is avoided. The Buffer Manager's job is to minimize the number of physical I/Os needed to execute any task. An effective Buffer Manager strategy combined with adequate memory will deliver the highest possible cache-hit rate for data and index pages requested by user tasks.

The Buffer Manager features for ASE include support for multiple named caches, efficient page cleaning strategies, and multiple buffer pools within a named cache.

Named Caches

The logical memory manager is capable of maintaining multiple caches, referred to as *named caches*. Each named cache can be reserved for specific databases or database objects such as tables and indexes. This mapping allows frequently accessed objects such as indexes to be kept in memory longer by directing pages for other objects into different caches. Memory-hungry data types, such as images and tables with low levels of data reuse, can be restricted to separate caches to prevent them from filling the entire data cache. Although named caches can only be changed by a database reboot, cache assignments can be changed dynamically.

The default cache and named caches can also be split into partitions to reduce spinlock contention. The number of partitions that can be assigned per cache can be any of 1, 2, 4, 8, 16, 32, or 64.

Page Cleaning

Each cache maintains data in buffers that are linked in a most recently used - least recently used (MRU-LRU) chain as shown in Figure 10.2.

Figure 10.2   *Sybase ASE page cleaning strategy*

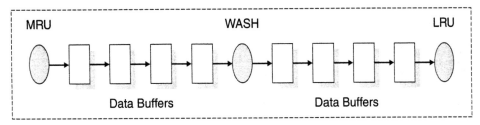

The chain has a *wash marker,* a point in the chain beyond which dirty (modified) buffers will be flushed to disk automatically. Each buffer pool has its own MRU-LRU chain. The default wash size is 20% of the buffers in the memory pool for pools less than 300 Mbytes, and 20% of 300 Mbytes for larger pools. The larger the wash setting, the more vigorous the cleaning of dirty buffers, thereby reducing the amount of work to be done during a check-point. On the other hand, setting the wash marker too high can cause frequently accessed pages to be flushed more often than necessary.

ASE reduces the number of pages to flush during a checkpoint with a *housekeeper thread* that flushes dirty pages during periods of inactivity. Pages flushed by the housekeeper are referred to as *free writes*. The house-keeper behavior can be controlled with sp_configure by modification of the housekeeper free write percent configuration parameter, introduced in System 11. A value of 20 means that the housekeeper thread is permitted to increase I/O by 20% by flushing dirty pages to disk; a value of 100 means the housekeeper thread is constantly active, regardless of the performance implications.

Fetch-and-Discard Strategy

Usually the MRU-LRU chain enforces a first-in, first-out (FIFO) replacement strategy on the data buffers. In some instances, however, this policy isn't desirable. When it is known that the data being accessed is not needed again, there is no value in caching the data. To address this issue, ASE offers a fetch-and-discard buffer replacement strategy. Data pages can be placed toward the LRU end of the chain to keep them in the cache for a much shorter time than with a FIFO policy.

Large I/O and Multiple Buffer Pools

Even though ASE (before version 12.5) uses a fixed page size of 2 Kbytes, I/O can be carried out in other block sizes: 4, 8, and 16 Kbytes. Larger block sizes are more efficient when contiguous blocks are being read (for example, table scans) or written (for example, log file I/O).

For I/O to be performed in large block sizes, the cache must be configured with buffer pools of the appropriate size. For example, a named cache can be created with its available memory divided between a 2-Kbyte buffer pool and an 8-Kbyte buffer pool, each with its own MRU-LRU chain. Each cache can support buffer pools for all four (2, 4, 8, and 16 Kbyte) block sizes. When more than one buffer pool is available in a named cache, the Query Optimizer determines the optimal block size for each query and uses the appropriate buffer pool.

ASE 12.5 introduced page sizes of 4, 8, and 16 Kbytes as well as 2 Kbytes. Up to four buffer pools can be configured for larger page sizes also. With a 16-Kbyte page size, for example, buffer pools of 16, 32, 64, and 128 Kbytes can be configured. Consequently, 128-Kbyte I/Os can be carried out with a 16-Kbyte page size, offering significant performance benefits in DSS and some batch environments. Some of the issues to be considered in choosing a page size are discussed in "Influence of Page Size on Buffer Cache Effectiveness" on page 85.

Procedure Cache

The procedure cache provides a memory-based repository for stored procedures and triggers. Both user-written stored procedures and system procedures are accommodated. Once a stored procedure is saved in the cache, its compiled query plan is available for use by other users, saving a disk access and procedure compilation.

Physical Data Storage

ASE can use both raw disk devices and UNIX files for data storage, although Sybase recommends the use of raw devices for data storage in production environments.

ASE initializes each disk device and maps virtual page numbers onto the device. When a database is allocated space on a device, the added space becomes a *device fragment* in the database. Before ASE 12.0, each database supported a maximum of 128 device fragments. Hence, the maximum size of a single database was 128 × <max_device_size_supported>. The largest supported device size on Solaris was 2 Gbytes until the introduction of 64-bit kernel asynchronous I/O (KAIO) in Solaris 2.5.1. Since the ASE 12.0 release, an unlimited number of device fragments has been supported.

Sybase provides RAID 0 (mirroring) capability natively. This feature mirrors disk devices within ASE without any additional software or hardware at the Solaris or disk subsystem level. However, for enhanced performance and more sophisticated forms of RAID, such as RAID 0, 0+1, and 5, operating system or hardware RAID is necessary. Refer to "Introduction to RAID" on page 232 for more information on RAID.

Logical Data Storage

The basic unit of storage in ASE is a *page*. The size of a page before ASE 12.5 was fixed at 2 Kbytes on most platforms, including Solaris. ASE 12.5 builds the master device with the `dataserver` rather than the `buildmaster` binary and extends the number of supported page sizes to include 4-, 8-, and 16-Kbyte pages.

Up to 44 bytes at the start of a page are occupied by header data, with pointers to previous and next pages in the page chain and the object ID of the database object the page belongs to, leaving the remaining bytes in the page available for data.

Pages are grouped in units of eight, called *extents*. Allocation and deallocation of space for tables and indexes is done one page at a time, except for data loads, which carry out large page allocations—one extent at a time (that is, 16 Kbytes for 2-Kbyte pages).

The next level up in the data storage hierarchy is an *allocation unit*. An allocation unit consists of 32 extents or 256 pages (512 Kbytes). When a disk device is initialized by ASE (`disk init`), space allocation is created in allocation units. The first page in an allocation unit consists of an allocation page for the remaining pages in the allocation unit. The allocation page contains a structure for each of the 32 extents within that allocation unit. Each extent structure includes an allocation map and the ID of the object the extent is allocated to.

Each table and index has one or more *Object Allocation Map (OAM)* pages, which identify the allocation pages with extents that belong to the table or index. OAM pages also hold summary information about used and unused pages and the number of rows in the table. The OAM pages allow ASE to quickly locate pages available for use by a table or an index.

Disk space in Sybase is partitioned into *segments*, which are mapped onto one or more disk files or partitions. When a database is created, three segments are automatically created: a `default` segment for tables and indexes; a `system` segment, for system tables; and a `logsegment`, a segment for storing the `syslog`. It is not necessary to make further use of segments, although some users choose to do so. User-defined segments offer control over the placement and size of database objects, and with control over placement comes control over I/O performance.

The relationship between segments and devices is many-to-many; a segment can be spread across multiple Sybase devices, and a single device can host multiple segments.

The following example illustrates the mapping between segments, devices, and objects, assuming that `dev1`, `dev2`, `dev3`, and `dev4` have previously been initialized. Suppose we create a database as follows:

```
use master
go
create database salesdb
 on dev1 = 250, dev2 = 250, dev3 = 250
 log on dev4 = 100
go
```

The default and system segments will map to dev1, dev2, and dev3, and the logsegment to dev4. Suppose we next create a customer table with the following commands:

```
use salesdb
go
create table customer
  cust_id integer,
  cust_name char(40),
  cust_address char(60))
go
```

We have no control over the location of the table; it could be placed on either dev1, dev2, or dev3.

Suppose we now create a segment with the following command:

```
sp_addsegment Myseg, salesdb, dev3
```

The new segment is located on dev3, which could be a volume created by a volume manager, a raw partition, or a UFS file. We can place a sales_history table on this device with the following (abbreviated) command:

```
create table sales_history
(...) on Newseg
```

Since we had control over the choice of device used for Newseg, we could choose where the sales_history table was located. We could later extend the Newseg segment to dev1, one of the devices originally used to host the salesdb database. The following command could be used:

```
sp_extendsegment Newseg, salesdb, dev1
```

The Newseg segment is now mapped to storage space on dev3 and dev1. So dev1 hosts three segments: default, system, and part of the Newseg segment.

Just as segments can be spread across multiple devices, database objects can be spread across multiple segments. For example, we could decide to insert new customer table rows into the Newseg segment, with sp_placeobject, as shown in the following command:

```
sp_placeobject Newseg, customer
```

Existing customer table rows will be located in the default segment; future rows will be located in the Newseg segment.

Segments offer considerable flexibility. Since objects cannot grow beyond their segment, you can control the size of fast-growing tables by placing them in separate segments. You can also manage the I/O performance of the trans-action logs independently of other database objects with a dedicated segment. At the same time, the examples above should help illustrate why tight administrative controls are necessary to ensure that segments remain manageable.

Tables and Indexes

As with any relational database, data is stored in tables. Each data page consists of one or more rows of data. In the past, ASE limited the maximum supported row size to 1,962 bytes; this limit was lifted in ASE 12.0. A row cannot span data pages except for *text* and *image* columns.

Indexes are used for quick access to data rows within a table. ASE provides two types of indexes: clustered and nonclustered. In a clustered index, the leaf pages of the index are also the data pages, whereas in nonclustered indexes, the leaf pages are pointers to the data pages. Each table can support a maximum of 1 clustered index and up to 249 nonclustered indexes.

Nonclustered indexes exist as separate objects and do not affect the table structures or application logic. They can be created, modified, and dropped as warranted. Clustered indexes affect table structure in two ways: first, the index determines the sort order of the table; second, if the index is placed in a particular segment, the table will be moved to the disk or disks on which the segment is located.

Clustered indexes can help index performance. Without a clustered index, all `insert` and "out of place" `update` statements go to the last table page, making lock contention prohibitive in environments with high transaction rates. Indexes help `select` performance and hurt `insert` performance. Too many indexes can hurt performance in update-intensive environments.

Table Partitioning

Tables can be partitioned to allow for parallel query processing and to reduce lock contention. Partitioning creates multiple page chains for a table, greatly improving the performance of inserts and parallel query processes, as well as allowing for parallel load and `dbcc`. Older versions of ASE only allow heap tables to be partitioned, but as of ASE 11.5 you can create clustered indexes on partitioned tables. You might consider partitioning a table for the following reasons:

- To create multiple insertion points for a heap table.
- To distribute a table's I/O across multiple devices.
- To speed database loads.
- To improve performance of parallel queries (each worker process in a scan can read a separate partition).

Partitioning is not guaranteed to improve performance; the right tables must be selected for partitioning, and they must be partitioned correctly. To identify likely candidates for partitioning, consider the following suggestions:

- Use `sp_sysmon` to find heap tables with last-page lock contention. Partitioning heap tables creates multiple insertion points so that more concurrent inserts can be supported.

- Look for tables with low (< 90%) cache hit rates. If the data is already in cache, partitioning the table may not help performance (although some queries might still benefit from the use of multiple threads).

Queries that scan fewer than 20 of a table's data pages will not be executed in parallel. If you are enabling parallel query processing, consider partitioning read-only or read-mostly tables only if they are likely to have more than 20 data pages read in a single query.

Partitioning can create performance problems if not correctly implemented and monitored. Partitioning frequently inserted tables can result in partition skew (unevenly filled partitions) in tables with clustered indexes. Small amounts of skew can do surprising damage to performance, particularly if devices are not striped. Heap tables are usually not subject to skew.

You can rebalance partitions by dropping and recreating the clustered index. Make sure you allow enough space to do regular index builds on tables that are subject to skew.

The following list offers some partitioning rules of thumb:

- The number of partitions for a table should be less than or equal to the number of devices.

- Each partition should reside on its own device, and the devices should be spread across as many disks as possible. The optimizer does not take partition layout into account, and placing multiple table partitions on a single spindle can create I/O problems rather than alleviate them, particularly in parallel processing situations.

- Partitions increase I/O parallelism at the cost of consuming more CPU resources. Consequently, adding partitions only helps until the CPU is saturated. After that, increasing the degree of parallelism will degrade performance.

System Databases

When ASE is initially installed, a minimum of four system databases are created: the `master` database, the `model` database, the system procedures database, referred to as `sybsystemsprocs`, and the database `tempdb` for temporary tables. A number of optional databases can also be installed: the auditing database `sybsecurity`, sample databases `pubs2` and `pubs3`, the `dbcc` management database, referred to as `dbccdb`, and a syntax database called `sybsyntax`, which provides syntax help for Transact-SQL commands. ASE 11.5 also introduced a new database called `sybsystemdb`, used to track two-phase commits. User databases are then created in addition to these system databases.

The `master` database is central to the operation of ASE. It stores information about all user databases and their associated devices, keeps track of metadata such as user logins, remote servers and users, configuration variables, ongoing processes, storage allocation, and locks. Since the master database is critical to the operation of ASE, you are advised to place it on its own device and protect it against failure either by mirroring it or, at the least, by regularly backing it up.

The `model` database provides a template or prototype for creating new user databases. When a new user database is created, the `model` database is copied into the new database, enabling database administrators to enforce default policies on databases.

Sybase provides several system procedures to administer and maintain ASE databases. These system stored procedures are placed in the syb-systemprocs database.

ASE requires scratch space for its temporary working storage. The scratch space is provided by the `tempdb` database. Index creation and queries with `group by` or `order by` clauses all require sorts, and sorts use `tempdb`. By default, `tempdb` is 2 Mbytes in size and resides on the master device. However, when large sorts or numerous sorts are common, it may be advisable to increase `tempdb` by extending it onto its own device or devices.

Parallel Processing

As of ASE 11.5, Sybase supports Intra-Query Parallelism (IQP). Previous versions of Sybase allowed multiple queries to run in parallel, but ASE 11.5 allows the work of an individual query to be divided among multiple threads called *worker processes*. This multithreading is especially useful for complex DSS queries that require table scans, although more memory is consumed, both for the worker processes and for the procedure cache.

When enabling IQP, the database administrator specifies the number of worker processes, thereby determining the maximum number of concurrent parallel tasks. Each worker process consumes roughly the same amount of memory as a user connection. When the optimizer decides to run a query in parallel, it determines the optimum degree of parallelism within the system limits. For example, a query running with 8-way parallelism requires eight worker processes and one coordinating process to execute the query. This group is called a *process family*. Each worker process handles all aspects of its portion of the query, and the coordinating process merges the results and returns them to the client process.

If ASE is configured to allow parallel processing, the optimizer will consider whether query completion time can be reduced by running part or all of the query in parallel. Parallel queries are optimized for speed rather than cost, since running a query in parallel involves more overhead than does a single-threaded query. Because of this overhead, the optimizer will not perform parallel scans on a table if fewer than 20 data pages will be read.

The optimizer does not consider the number of available engines, location, and layout of partitions, or the ratio of the number of engines to CPUs when computing cost. The onus is on the database administrator to be sure the system and database are properly configured before enabling parallelism.

Parallel processing requires planning and testing to determine the optimum degree of parallelism, the correct number of worker processes to configure, the tables which should be partitioned and the number of partitions to create, and the physical disk layout that will best support I/O-intensive operations.

The Parallel Query implementation in ASE 11.5 allows individual queries to be parallelized and their load split among multiple tasks and engines. IQP speeds large, complex queries at the cost of some additional overhead in memory, engine usage, and disk I/O.

Adaptive Server IQ with Multiplex

The challenge of efficiently processing large volumes of data has led to increasing sophistication in relational database system optimizers. Optimizer improvements have been accompanied by new methods of reducing the amount of work to be done, such as range partitioning, concatenated indexes, and more exotic technologies like join indexes and materialized views. These subjects are discussed in Chapter 8.

Sybase Adaptive Server IQ with Multiplex (IQ-M) takes a very different approach to solving this problem. Instead of storing data in rows, IQ-M stores data in columns. The full set of data for a column is stored in a single entity called a *column vector*.

Column Storage

With IQ-M, the column vector is itself an index containing the raw data, so every column has at least one index. The default index is referred to as a *fast projection* (FP) index, and IQ-M selects from a range of FP indexing mechanisms depending on the number of unique values in the column (the column cardinality) and whether the column values are constrained by a UNIQUE clause.

To illustrate the potential benefits of storing data by columns, consider a customer table with 20 million rows and 50 columns, with a total row length of around 1,000 bytes. A conventional relational database will store the table as a single entity, with a total size of 20 Gbytes. By contrast, IQ-M will store the columns separately as 50 column vectors. Suppose a user executes a query listing the customer name, sales region, and balance owing for all customers with an outstanding balance of more than $100,000. The conventional database will most likely do a table scan to retrieve the data, resulting in 20 Gbytes of I/O. IQ-M, though, will only need to retrieve the three columns. If the column lengths for the three columns total 60 bytes, it will only be necessary for IQ-M to retrieve 20 million × 60 bytes, or 1.2 Gbytes. In fact, it would probably be less, given that the size of the column vectors will probably be halved by compression.

Since the values in a column are all of the same type, column vectors can be efficiently compressed.

The worst-case scenario for IQ-M compared to a conventional database is the retrieval of all columns of a single row. A conventional database will only require a single I/O to return a row of the `customer` table, compared to 50 for IQ-M. Full column retrievals from a single row, though, are not representative of most data warehouse table accesses.

Indexing

Sybase recommends aggressive indexing. As we saw, every column has at least a default index; as many as three indexes could be created. Even so, Sybase expects that the total size of data plus indexes will be no more than the original size of the raw data. This capacity requirement compares favorably with conventional databases in which the final database size usually balloons out to between three and five times the original size of the raw data.

Sybase IQ-M supports multiple index types, including bitmapped indexes, bitwise indexes (a patented proprietary technology), and B-tree indexes. Bitmapped indexes are used when a column has low cardinality (in this context, low cardinality means a small number of unique values). Bitwise indexes are used for low- and high-cardinality columns when aggregation and range searches are important, and B-tree indexes are used to index a group of columns, often when some are low cardinality and some are high cardinality.

Some indexes are more suitable for some purposes than others. For example, B-tree and bitwise indexes are better suited for retrieving ranges of values than are bitmapped indexes. Sometimes IQ-M query performance benefits when multiple indexes are maintained for a single column.

I/O and Caches

In addition to the memory requirements of the IQ-M server process, IQ-M uses two memory caches: the IQ-M Main Cache and the IQ-M Temporary Cache. The Main Cache stores data pages and the Temporary Cache handles joins, sorts, subqueries, and temporary tables. If the Temporary Cache is too small for an operation, the Temporary Store on disk is used as an overflow area.

During data load, the Main Cache stores data for all but one of the index types (which is instead managed out of the Temporary Cache). If the Main Cache is too large, data pages will be cached and not flushed until the load finishes, slowing down the load operation as a result. If the Main Cache is too small, the load will fail.

Note that to improve I/O efficiency, IQ-M automatically stripes data across the devices belonging to the database, although this feature can be disabled. When devices are already striped, either with a volume manager or hardware RAID, the default data layout will be data-striped across striped devices.

Parallelism

Relational databases achieve parallelism by breaking queries into multiple units of work; the increased concurrency helps reduce query completion times. IQ-M aims to promote parallelism in a different way: IQ-M reduces the amount of work required to complete a query, and so multiple concurrent users can be supported. Sybase IQ-M specifically targets environments with large numbers of users running ad hoc queries.

IQ-M automatically supports parallelism during some phases of data load; multiple concurrent load processes are therefore unnecessary.

IQ Multiplex

The multiplex capability of IQ enables multiple SMP nodes to access the database within a single IQ environment. Only one node can manage and write to the database; other nodes have read-only access. As a result, there is no need to lock records and no contention between the read-only instances. If a node fails for some reason, users can be switched to another node.

During database update, only the master node sees the changes while the updates are proceeding. Read-only instances do not see the updates until they are completed.

This behavior also applies to a single node; query users do not see updates until the update process has finished. Although query users see data that may be slightly out of date, the benefit is that locking is not required to preserve data integrity during concurrent access to the database.

Interfaces

Sybase IQ-M supports SQL and Java interfaces, including Java support for stored procedures and user-defined functions.

Sybase IQ first appeared in 1996, initially only on Sun servers and later on multiple platforms. The current version is a mature product that offers strong support for multiple users running ad hoc queries on large data sets.

11

INFORMIX XPS ARCHITECTURE

Informix offers—or rather offered, since IBM has now completed its takeover of Informix's database business—a broad range of database products. The major enterprise database products are Informix Dynamic Server and Extended Parallel Server.

Informix Dynamic Server (IDS)—at the time of this writing, the current version was IDS 2000 Version 9.2—is targeted primarily at Online Transaction Processing (OLTP) applications, web environments, and applications requiring object-relational capabilities. Support is also provided for small-scale Decision Support Systems (DSS). The object-relational features of IDS include support for user-defined data types, user-defined routines, and inheritance of tables and types. IDS 2000 Version 9.2 is a merge of the code base from Informix Dynamic Server 7.2 and the Universal Server product originally developed by Illustra. A follow-up version of IDS 7.2—Informix Dynamic Server 7.3—was also released.

Extended Parallel Server (XPS) is primarily targeted at complex DSS environments, although it can also be used for workloads involving some elements of batch and OLTP. Extended Parallel Server Version 8.3 is the successor to Informix Dynamic Server with Advanced Decision Support and Extended Parallel Options Version 8.2, also referred to as Dynamic Server with AD and XP Options. The 8.2 release was itself the successor to Informix Online XPS Version 8.1. The first 64-bit version of XPS on Solaris became available with Version 8.3.

The Informix database product range also includes the Informix Red Brick Decision Server and a number of products acquired from other sources.

IBM's buyout of the Informix database business does not spell immediate doom for Informix technology, since IBM has publicly committed to continuing to sell, support, and enhance the major products. Realistically, though, it seems reasonable to suppose that the future for Informix products as independent entities is hazy, at best.

Informix's change of fortunes also influenced the content of this chapter and Chapter 24 (Monitoring and Tuning Informix). I originally intended to cover both IDS and XPS but decided instead to narrow the focus to XPS, since it has attracted the most interest on the Solaris platform.

In this chapter we discuss the process model, memory management, and physical and logical storage characteristics of XPS, briefly describe the system database, and consider query parallelism. The primary focus is on DSS environments.

Process Model

An XPS database consists of one or more cooperating instances called coservers. The database server processes that actually do the work are called virtual processors since they behave somewhat like CPUs in scheduling multiple threads to service user applications.

Coservers

The processing hub in Informix XPS is the *coserver*, an entity consisting of one or more CPUs, shared memory, and disk space. A coserver can run in a physical node, such as a server in a cluster, or as a logical node in a large SMP system. In this section we consider the characteristics of a coserver, the architectural model on which it is based, and the way users connect to coservers.

Coserver Instances

The single database image presented to the end user by XPS is actually delivered by one or more coservers. Each coserver runs as an independent instance, managing its own buffer cache, logging, locking, and recovery. Coservers are not really independent, though, since they perform database operations in cooperation with other coservers located on the same server (in the case of an SMP system) or on other servers (in the case of networked servers or a cluster). Coservers can be thought of as instances of Informix joined at the hip.

Each coserver has its own shared memory segments and dedicated processes. Although coservers on an SMP have physical access to disks owned by other coservers, they have no need to access them.

Figure 11.1 illustrates a 16-CPU SMP system subdivided into four logical nodes or coservers, each with four CPUs.

Figure 11.1   *XPS coservers in an SMP system*

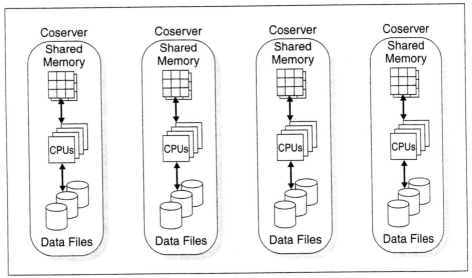

Shared-Nothing Model

Although coservers communicate with each other to carry out database operations cooperatively, they use a *shared-nothing* model, meaning that the
coservers do not share memory or disks. Coservers in an SMP system, however, communicate through shared memory, providing efficient interprocess
communication. When coservers are deployed in a cluster, the cluster interconnect carries traffic between the coservers; when they are deployed on servers loosely connected by a network, the network carries the traffic.
Communication between coservers is discussed in more detail in "Tuning
Inter-Coserver Communication" on page 397.

Thanks to coservers, even 32-bit versions of Informix XPS and the Solaris
Operating Environment can overcome the 4-Gbyte address space limit. Since
the 4-Gbyte limit is per process, not systemwide, each coserver and its associated processes can consume its own unique set of shared memory segments
totalling close to 4 Gbytes. In this way, large amounts of memory can be used
effectively even in 32-bit environments.

Shared-nothing databases introduce a number of issues, though. Data
must be split (that is, partitioned) among the logical nodes (coservers), and
decisions must be made about how many CPUs to include in each coserver.
Any decision about the optimal number of CPUs per coserver must take into
account the query performance and scalability that can be achieved within a
single coserver compared to that achievable between coservers. These issues
are explored in detail in "Shared-Nothing Databases on SMPs" on page 36.
Scalability within a single coserver can be increased with the 64-bit version of

XPS, allowing larger SMP systems to be used effectively before it becomes necessary to fragment the database.

XPS began life on MPP systems (described in "Massively Parallel Processor (MPP) Systems" on page 32); Version 8.11 was the first to support SMP systems. Large SMP systems with adequate interconnect bandwidth are good choices for shared-nothing databases, though. Coservers in an SMP system should always outperform clusters or networked systems because SMP interconnect bandwidths are greater and latencies lower than for cluster interconnects or networks. This chapter focuses on the features of Version 8.2 and later releases.

With large SMP systems, Database Engineering has found that assigning all available CPUs to a single coserver does not always offer the best scalability. Instead, the optimal number of CPUs per coserver is in the range of 4 to 12. Multiple coservers improve overall scalability at the cost of requiring data to be split among coservers. Splitting data introduces a communication overhead as data and commands are transmitted between coservers. This overhead can be significant, especially for ad hoc queries.

Cogroups

Coservers are grouped together to simplify administration. A group of coservers is called a *cogroup*. When the database is initialized, XPS creates a cogroup called `cogroup_all` from all configured coservers. Other cogroups can be created by the database administrator.

User Connections

Users can connect to different coservers. Once a user connection is established, the host coserver is known as a *connection coserver*. A user query may require access to data held on another coserver or coservers—they are referred to as *participating coservers*. The connection coserver generates a plan for the query, with subplans for each participating coserver. The subplans are then executed simultaneously on all the affected coservers.

Virtual Processors

The XPS server processes that run inside coservers are referred to as *virtual processors* (VPs). VPs are multithreaded processes with connections to the same shared memory segments. For more information on the multithreaded database architecture, refer to "Multithreaded Architectures" on page 59.

VPs run various threads, including *user threads* that process SQL commands from user applications and *internal threads* that carry out various internal database functions, such as logging, flushing modified pages to disk, and recovery.

XPS uses a number of different classes of VP, including those in the following list:

- **CPU:** The most important VP. CPU VPs run all threads necessary to carry out query processing on behalf of user applications, and they also run some system threads.

  CPU VPs run threads that carry out Kernel Asynchronous I/O (KAIO) when database tables are located on raw devices. CPU VPs also carry out I/O to the physical-log and logical-log files if they are located on raw devices.

  One CPU VP is typically assigned for each CPU in the server.

- **LIO:** A disk I/O VP that writes to the logical-log file if it is located in a file system file.

- **PIO:** A disk I/O VP that writes to the physical-log file if it is located in a file system file.

- **SHM:** A network VP that performs shared memory communication.

- **TLI:** A network VP that performs network communication by using the Transport Layer Interface (TLI).

CPU VPs run non-preemptable threads that yield the CPU only when they have to wait on I/O or have no further work to do. Even within a single CPU VP, each DSS query will be assigned multiple threads, with each thread managing one part of the query. Thread creation and switching is based on the Informix threads library rather than on Solaris threads.

Memory Management

Informix XPS shared memory includes internal tables, buffers, session data, thread data, the dictionary cache, and various memory pools. The main consumers of XPS shared memory within a coserver are the buffer pool and the DS memory pool. In this section we explore both of these memory pools and examine the way in which XPS dynamically allocates shared memory.

Buffer Pool

Apart from pages read during a DSS query, database pages are read into the Informix buffer pool, which uses a configurable number of least recently used (LRU) queues. Two types of LRU queues are maintained by XPS:

- A free least recently used (FLRU) list, which identifies unmodified pages in the buffer pool.

- A modified least recently used (MLRU) list, which identifies modified pages in the buffer pool.

When buffer pool free space is exhausted, a user thread randomly selects one of the FLRU queues and removes the page at the least recently used end of the queue. Once the user thread has finished with the page, it is placed back on the most recently used end of the MLRU queue if it has been modified, or on the most recently used end of the FLRU queue if it has not.

Dirty (that is, modified) pages are flushed periodically from the MLRU queue.

DS Memory

OLTP queries and DSS index accesses use the buffer pool, but in DSS table scans the buffer pool is bypassed. Instead, threads scan data directly into a special shared memory area called DS memory, using *light scan* threads that have been optimized to read sequential data efficiently with large block transfers. One thread is assigned to each table fragment that is being scanned (fragmentation is discussed in "Fragmentation" on page 145).

DS memory is scratch memory that is dedicated to a particular query. XPS uses DS memory for scans and sorts. Although DS memory lives in a shared memory segment, only the threads associated with a single query share access to it. If a query runs out of DS memory, it either will overflow to disk or will fail if no temporary disk storage has been established.

Dynamic Memory Allocation

The initial shared memory segment allocated by XPS is not necessarily the final demand made on shared memory resources. XPS can allocate further segments as required, up to the system limit. In a multiuser environment, a user can configure the maximum amount of memory available to a single query. For more information about how shared memory is allocated, refer to "Shared Memory Allocation" on page 392.

Page Cleaning

Database shared memory pages that have been modified by user threads and marked as dirty are regularly flushed to disk by pagecleaner threads. XPS runs at least one pagecleaner thread, and if multiple threads have been configured, the LRU queues are divided equally among them to improve efficiency.

XPS flushes the following buffers:

- **Buffer pool.** Pagecleaner threads flush the buffer pool under the following circumstances: when user threads have been trying without success to find an unmodified buffer, when the number of buffers in an MLRU queue reaches a specified limit, and when checkpointing is occurring.

- **Physical-log buffer.** The physical log is described in "Logical and Physical Logs" on page 145. The buffer is flushed when it is full, during a checkpoint, and before a related modified page in shared memory can be flushed.

- **Logical-log buffer.** The logical log is described in "Logical and Physical Logs" on page 145. Some of the events that will cause the buffer to be flushed are the buffer becoming full, a checkpoint, and a transaction being committed in a database with unbuffered logging. "Unbuffered logging" refers to traditional database behavior—data integrity is guaranteed during all phases of transaction activity.

Physical Data Storage

The smallest unit of physical storage used by XPS is the *chunk*. A chunk can be either a raw device (including volume manager devices and LUNs from storage arrays) or a file system file (such as a UFS file). Informix recommends using raw devices for optimal performance.

Chunks are created with the name of the raw device or file (or a symlink to it), a size, and an offset. The offset means that more than one chunk can be placed in a single raw device or file, although this strategy is not recommended.

XPS also supports mirroring of chunks. Data is copied from the *primary chunk* to the *mirror chunk*. In the event of a physical disk failure, the mirror chunk will be brought online automatically.

A fixed amount of disk space is allocated when a chunk is created. If the database needs to expand, more chunks can be added. Chunk sizes and offsets of up to 4 Gbytes are supported on the 32-bit version of XPS, and significantly larger sizes are supported on the 64-bit version.

Logical Data Storage

XPS manages and accesses its physical storage by using several logical units of storage, including pages, extents, and dbspaces. Database objects created by users, such as tables and indexes, build on these logical storage units.

Pages

The unit of XPS access to physical disk is the *page*. The page size is configured with a parameter in the onconfig configuration file (the onconfig file is described in "Changing Informix XPS Tunable Parameters" on page 381). The page size parameter, PAGESIZE, can be set to 2, 4, or 8 Kbytes, with a default of 4 Kbytes. Once the page size has been set, it cannot be changed unless the database is unloaded and reloaded.

Extents

When a table is created, the database server allocates a fixed number of contiguous pages for table data. When that space is exhausted, more contiguous pages are allocated by XPS. The unit of allocation in each case is called an *extent*, and the initial and subsequent extent sizes are determined by the `initial-extent` and `next-extent` clauses of the `create table` and `alter table` statements.

An individual extent cannot cross chunk boundaries, although extents for a single table can be located in more than one chunk.

Dbspaces

Just as the chunk is the primary unit of XPS physical data storage, the primary unit of logical data storage is the *dbspace*. Dbspaces are used to map database objects to disk space.

Every dbspace is created with at least one chunk assigned to it, and more can be added later as required. The database determines data placement within dbspaces; for dbspaces with more than one chunk, though, the user cannot direct data to a specific chunk.

Figure 11.2 illustrates how tables map to dbspaces and how dbspaces map to chunks.

Figure 11.2   *Mapping between tables, dbspaces, and chunks*

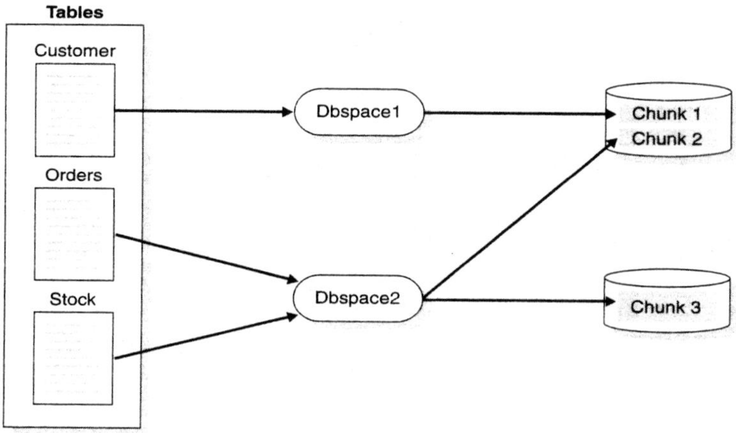

A special dbspace called the *root dbspace* is created by the database server to store internal tables with information about physical and logical units of storage. An initial chunk (and its mirror if one is specified) is created when the disk space is initialized. Other chunks can later be added to the root dbspace. A number of parameters in the `onconfig` file, including `ROOTPATH`, `ROOTSIZE`, and `ROOTOFFSET`, define the initial chunk of the root dbspace.

The root dbspace is the default location for new databases established with the `create database` command.

Temporary dbspaces are another special type of dbspace; they are used as scratch space for temporary tables. XPS also uses temporary space for overflow of scan data from DS memory and for working storage during index building. Although temporary dbspaces are themselves permanent entities, their contents do not survive a database reboot.

Temporary tables can also be placed in other dbspaces, although temporary tables created implicitly by XPS are not usually placed in the root dbspace. The reason is that the `DBSPACETEMP` configuration parameter defaults to `NOTCRITICAL` (that is, place temporary tables only in noncritical dbspaces).

Logical and physical logging is not performed for temporary dbspaces, improving performance and reducing recovery times. Temporary dbspaces are not backed up during a full system backup.

Dbslices

So that parallel access across coservers can be achieved, data chunks are declared on each coserver and grouped into dbspaces. To simplify management, dbspaces are combined into a *dbslice*, a named set of dbspaces spread across coservers that can be managed as a single storage object. The optimizer takes into account the mapping between coservers and chunks when generating query plans.

Dbslices are created with the `onutil` utility. The following example illustrates the syntax for creating a dbslice:

```
create dbslice custdbs from cogroup cogroup_all
    chunk "/data/custdbs1.%c" size 500000;
```

The `custdbs` dbslice will have one chunk for each coserver in `cogroup_all`. The default unit of size is `KBYTES`; `MBYTES` and `GBYTES` can also be specified.

Tables and indexes can be created in the dbslice, thanks to extensions to the `create table` command.

XPS creates a number of its own dbslices. The `rootslice` provides the root dbspace of each coserver and is created when XPS is first initialized. The optional `physslice` and `logslice` are used for the physical and logical logs, respectively.

Decisions about dbslice layout on disk must take into account data skew in table data; otherwise, disk loading can be unbalanced. Balanced distribution of data across coservers does not always imply balanced access to that data.

As we saw in the previous section on dbspaces, the temporary dbspace location is defined with the `DBSPACETEMP` parameter in the `onconfig` file.

You can use dbslices for temporary dbspaces, as shown in the following example:

```
DBSPACETEMP                     tempdbs # Default temp dbspaces
```

In this example, `tempdbs` could be a dbslice spread across four coservers, as illustrated in the following command:

```
create temp dbslice tempdbs from
 cogroup cogroup_all chunk "/data/tdbs1.%c" size 2000000,
 cogroup cogroup_all chunk "/data/tdbs2.%c" size 2000000,
 cogroup cogroup_all chunk "/data/tdbs3.%c" size 2000000;
```

In this case 12 dbspaces will be created—one for each of 12 chunks. The `%c` will be expanded by `onutil` with the coserver number, and three similar dbspaces will be created on each coserver. During query processing XPS will assign a separate scan thread to each dbspace.

Tables and Indexes

Each XPS table lives in the dbspace in which it was created, although tables can also be partitioned across dbspaces by means of fragmentation (discussed later in this chapter).

Informix has introduced the concept of table types. Tables can be dynamically changed from one type to another with the `alter table` command. Permanent tables can be any of the types shown in the following list:

- **Raw:** Used to specify nonlogging tables with *light appends* (that is, fast appends to the end of a table that bypass the buffer pool and are not logged). Raw tables are good choices for initial loading of data but are not suitable for normal operation since they do not log updates, inserts, or deletes and do not support indexes.

- **Static:** Used for nonlogging tables that contain index and referential integrity constraints. They do not support inserts, updates, or deletes, though. They are good choices for *light scans* (scans that bypass the buffer pool), and since they are read-only, the server need not acquire locks.

- **Operational:** Used for logging tables with light appends. Inserts, updates, and deletes are logged, but light appends are not. Light appends are allowed only if the table has no indexes or constraints. Such tables are not recoverable after a crash.

- **Standard:** Used for logging tables that allow rollback, recovery, and restoration from archives. Light appends are not supported. This is the default table type.

- **External:** Used to load and unload data.

XPS also supports two temporary table types: scratch and temp. Scratch and temp tables support bulk operations such as light appends. They are dropped when a user session ends and do not survive a database reboot.

Logical and Physical Logs

Informix XPS maintains two sets of logs. The *logical log* stores details of all transactions in case they are needed for transaction rollback or fast recovery after a database crash. Informix requires a minimum of three logical-log files in the logical log. Logical-log files can be reused only after they are archived to tape or disk.

The *physical log* stores before-image pages—copies of database pages before they were modified by a transaction. Physical-log records are used for fast recovery after database failure. Modified data pages are first restored to their state at the last checkpoint; the logical log is then used to roll transactions forward up to the point of the failure. The physical log is also used in database server backup.

Fragmentation

A central feature of the Informix architecture is data fragmentation: the ability to split or partition tables within a coserver into multiple storage areas. The optimizer takes into account fragmentation in determining a query plan, so effective fragmentation and data placement are crucial to efficient parallel processing of queries.

One of the key benefits of fragmentation is the capability it provides of eliminating unnecessary fragments from the query plan (known as *fragment elimination*). For example, if data has been fragmented according to the contents of a month table column, a query requesting data for the first quarter of a calendar year can ignore the fragments containing data for April through December.

Fragmentation needs to be carefully planned, since the degree of parallelism for a table scan is determined by the number of dbspaces remaining after fragment elimination. If too many fragments are eliminated, parallel query performance may suffer. The solution is to configure enough dbspaces for each dbslice; the number of dbspaces remaining after fragment elimination will determine the number of scan threads and hence the degree of parallelism.

XPS also supports fragmentation across coservers to further increase parallelism. The benefit of sharing the workload among multiple coservers must be balanced against the disadvantages associated with data shipping, discussed further in "Colocated Joins" on page 150.

Informix XPS supports the following fragmentation mechanisms:

* **Round-robin fragmentation.** Data is assigned to each coserver in turn. This strategy is not recommended since it does not allow fragment elimination. With round-robin partitioning, XPS cannot determine which coserver hosts a particular row—all rows on all coservers must be scanned.

* **Range fragmentation.** Values are distributed among coservers in accordance with the values of a particular column. As a result, entire

coservers can be eliminated during a table scan, leading to imbalance in access to system resources.

- **Expression-based fragmentation.** Data is inserted into a dbslice according to a user-defined rule—often a range expression. The range expression determines the coserver into which the data will be placed. This mechanism can result in data skew between coservers and hence uneven parallelism.

- **Hash fragmentation.** An internal hashing algorithm is used on the specified columns to distribute rows. Fragment elimination is not possible with hash fragmentation, but hashing does allow even distribution of rows among coservers and hence balanced parallelism. A hash distribution is a good choice for tables that do not lend themselves to fragment elimination. It is also important for colocated joins (described later in this chapter).

The following example illustrates the syntax used for table creation based on hash partitioning:

```
create table customer (
    c_id integer,
    c_name varchar(50),
    c_address varchar(50),
    c_account_balance decimal(12,2)
) fragment by hash (c_id) in dbother
lock mode table;
```

In this example, the hashing algorithm is applied to values in the `c_id` column, with the result determining which coserver the data will be located in.

- **Hybrid fragmentation.** This approach to fragmentation takes advantage of both hash and range fragmentation techniques. Different columns are specified for the hash fragmentation and the range fragmentation phases. Fragments can be eliminated on the basis of the range key, provided the elimination proceeds on all coservers simultaneously. An example is given below.

```
create table order (
    o_id integer,
    o_total_value decimal(12,2),
    o_order_date date
) fragment by hybrid(o_id) expression
o_order_date < '2001-04-01' in o_qtr1,
o_order_date >= '2001-04-01'
    and o_order_date < '2001-07-01' in o_qtr2,
o_order_date >= '2001-07-01'
    and o_order_date < '2001-10-01' in o_qtr3,
o_order_date >= '2001-10-01'
    and o_order_date <= '2001-12-31' in o_qtr4
lock mode table;
```

In this example, the hashing algorithm is applied to values in the o_id column, with the result determining which coserver the data will be located in. The coserver having been determined, a second key, o_order_date, is used to further fragment the data within that coserver. Dates across the entire year range will be located in each coserver, and only one-quarter of the dates will appear in each fragment.

Indexes can also be fragmented and are not restricted to the same slice as the table they reference. The same fragmentation strategies—round-robin, range, expression-based, hash, and hybrid—are also available for indexes.

Tblspaces

The pages and extents that make up a table are together referred to as a *tblspace*. Tblspaces allow a database administrator to track all the disk space allocated to a particular table or table fragment (if the table is fragmented). Index pages reside in a separate tblspace in the same dbspace. Once extents have been allocated to a tblspace, they remain part of that tblspace, even if the data is deleted and the extents become empty.

A tblspace does not correspond to a particular region of disk—extents for a particular table can be scattered throughout multiple dbspaces. Extents for a particular table can be interleaved in a dbspace with extents for other tables.

The partn column of the sysfragments system catalog table shows the tblspace ID for a table fragment.

System Database

The sysmaster database, established when XPS is initialized, provides access to database statistics with standard SQL. It is presented as a read-only database with a number of tables, although the tables are in fact pseudo-tables that reside in memory as internal database structures.

The sysmaster database contains a number of system monitoring interface (SMI) tables that provide information about the state of the database server. For example, you can monitor resource usage, locks, session information, extents, and VP CPU usage.

The following tables are examples of those available in the sysmaster database:

- syschunks — Chunk information and statistics.
- syscogroup — Information about cogroups.
- sysconfig — Configuration information.
- sysdbspaces — Dbspace information and statistics.
- sysdatabases — Database information.
- sysextents — Extent allocation.
- syslocks — Lock information.

- `syssessions` — User session information.
- `systabnames` — Table information.
- `sysvpprof` — CPU utilization for each virtual processor.

The `sysmaster` database also stores catalog tables related to archive and backup.

Parallel Processing

XPS supports parallelism for a number of SQL operations, including scans, joins, sorts, aggregation, group-bys, loads, inserts, and index builds. In the final section we consider the query parallelism supported by XPS and look at colocated joins—one of the challenges of parallel query processing that is based on a shared-nothing model.

Query Parallelism

The Parallel Database Query (PDQ) feature of XPS improves the performance of individual queries. PDQ allows the database to carry out parallel scans of fragments in a single coserver or fragments spread across multiple coservers. A query plan is first broken up into subplans to speed execution. The subplans are then allocated to a number of threads and processed in parallel.

XPS uses SQL *operators* and *exchanges* to break up a query plan into subplans. An SQL operator is a thread that accepts a stream of rows from one or two data tables and carries out a predefined action on the data. An exchange consolidates the data processed by one or more operators and sends it to the operators involved in carrying out the next phase of the query plan. This model is referred to as the *iterator model*.

Some of the SQL operators and their actions are outlined in the following list:

- **SCAN:** Sequentially reads fragmented data from a local table, unfragmented table, or index data.

- **NESTED LOOP JOIN:** Carries out a nested loop join. Refer to "Nested Loop Joins" on page 97 for more information.

- **HASH JOIN:** Carries out a hash join. Refer to "Hash Joins" on page 98 for more information.

- **GROUP:** Groups data and computes aggregates according to an SQL `GROUP BY` clause.

- **SORT:** Sorts data according to an SQL `ORDER BY` clause or for internal database purposes.

- **REMOTE:** Sequentially reads remote data.

For a simple analogy, consider the actions that take place inside a post office. The "scan operators" are postal employees who collect mail in their vans and bring it to the post office. The action of consolidating the mail and feeding it into the sorting machines represents the first "exchange." The sorting process represents "sort operators." The sorted mail is then gathered and put into mail bags (another exchange process) for delivery to the various destination post offices.

Consider the following SQL query:

```
select sales_area, sum(invoice_total)
      from customer a, orders b
      where a.cust_id = b.cust_id
      group by sales_area order by sum(invoice_total)
```

Figure 11.3 illustrates a possible configuration of operators and exchanges that might be established to process this query.

Figure 11.3 *XPS query operators and exchanges*

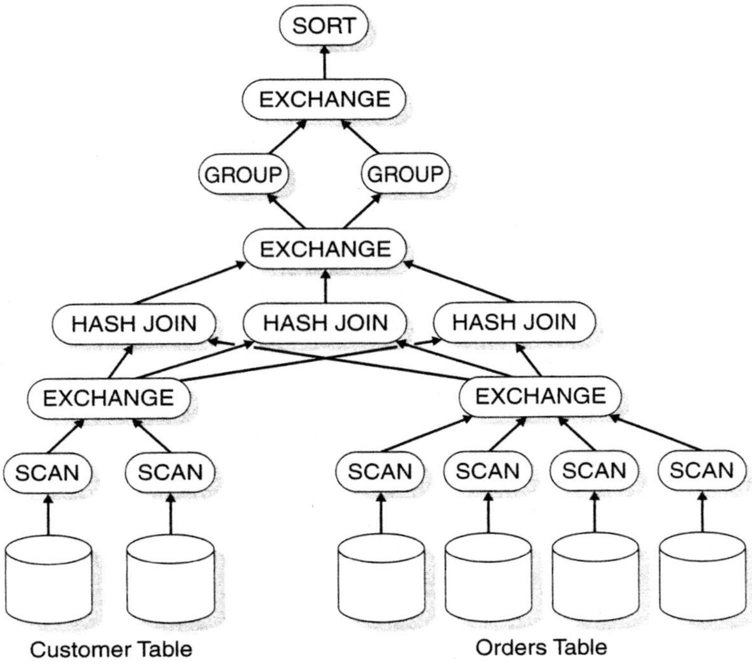

The steps in this process are described below.

- Two coservers each scan a fragment of the customer table.

- Simultaneously, four coservers each scan a fragment of the orders table.

- Two exchanges assign the scanned rows to three hash join operators, according to the join key.

- An exchange combines the results from the join operators and distributes the results to two group operators.

- An exchange consolidates the results from the group operators and sends them to another coserver for sorting.

- The sort operator carries out the final step in the query. The results are passed to the user application.

Sorts are made parallel with a number of sort iterators; data is passed to them in a round-robin fashion. The exchange following the sort phase carries out an ordered merge. Group-bys are handled in a similar manner.

For hash joins, a hash table is built for the first table and the hash table is then probed with the join column values from the second table.

The Data Flow Manager (DFM) manages the movement of data through exchanges to SQL operators.

Colocated Joins

When data is physically fragmented across multiple coservers, it often becomes necessary to ship data between coservers to complete a query. This operation is expensive in resources and can be time consuming.

Colocated joins are joins where the scan and join phases of a query take place within each coserver without the need to ship rows. Colocated joins become possible if the same attribute or column was used to fragment both tables and if that attribute is the join attribute for the query. Unfortunately, a fragmentation attribute that proves ideal for one query may cause a lot of data shipping in another query.

For an explanation and an example of the issues associated with colocated joins, refer to "Massively Parallel Processor (MPP) Systems" on page 32. Refer also to "The Data Shipping Problem" on page 410. The latter discussion is based on DB2, so you will need to substitute "coserver" where you see the terms "node," "partition," or "logical partition," and substitute "fragmentation" in place of data "splitting" or "partitioning."

Since data can only be fragmented across coservers according to one fragmentation strategy, the choice of strategy and fragmentation column is important. The best choice will take into account queries that have most impact on system resources either because they are run frequently or because they process a lot of data.

Monitoring XMF traffic (for more information refer to "Monitoring XMF Traffic" on page 399) can provide some indication of the degree of data shipping required by queries.

12

DB2 FOR SOLARIS ARCHITECTURE

DB2 Universal Database for the Solaris Operating Environment (DB2 UDB) is possibly less well known than some other databases, having not been available on the Sun platform for as long. In this chapter we examine the architecture of DB2 UDB, its process model, memory management, and physical data storage characteristics.

Process Model

Each DB2 Universal Database for Solaris database is associated with an *instance*. An instance belongs to a specific user and may contain more than one database, all of which share the same instance characteristics. When DB2 is started, only the instance is established, involving a small amount of shared memory and a number of DB2 system processes. The database is only started when the first user connects to it. At that time, all the database shared memory segments are allocated and the processes specific to the database are started, including the logger, the pagecleaners, the prefetchers, and an agent process for the connected user. Conversely, when the last user disconnects from the database, the DB2 system processes are removed and the shared memory segment released.

Setting up and tearing down shared memory segments and processes is expensive. In view of this, DB2 allows the user to activate a database (db2 activate database *dbname*) to establish the processes and shared memory before they are needed. An initial pool of agent processes can be created in advance to reduce the startup time for new user connections, and a pool can be maintained to retain processes when users terminate their connections.

DB2 Universal Database for Solaris uses a 2n architecture (described in "2n Architectures" on page 58), which means that for each user application an *agent* process is started on the server. Separate application and agent processes are used whether the user application is running on the server or is connected to the server remotely, such as from a PC, a UNIX workstation, or a separate application server. DB2 UDB transparently supports application connectivity over local area networks (LANs) or wide area networks (WANs). In other words, once the system is configured, the user doesn't need to know or care how the connection takes place or where the database server is located. Figure 12.1 shows a DB2 UDB database with clients connecting remotely over a network.

Figure 12.1 *Database partition on a server with remote clients*

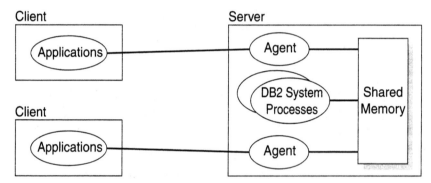

The DB2 agents shown in Figure 12.1 interact with the database and with DB2 system processes by connecting to shared memory and by using Interprocess Communication primitives, like semaphores and message queues within the database server, and sockets to connect with remote applications. DB2 system processes include the following: *pagecleaners*, which ensure that changes made to data cached in the bufferpool (database page buffer cache) are flushed to the database tables on disk; *prefetchers*, which anticipate data requirements during sequential access and preload the data pages into the bufferpool; a *logger* that writes update information to the log files; and several other processes that monitor and maintain the instance and any active databases.

The prefetchers are heavily used in Decision Support System (DSS) environments where table and index scans take place.

Memory Management

The shared memory contains everything necessary to manage shared access to data between multiple users and also provides working storage (buffers) for database operations. The most important buffers in the shared memory are the page buffers, called the *bufferpool*, and the sort heap (or sort heaps—DB2 will allocate as many as required). DB2 typically allocates three shared memory segments for a single database and instance.

Bufferpools

DB2 UDB supports multiple bufferpools—an enhancement over DB2 Version 2, which allowed only one. UDB stores data in tablespaces, and each tablespace can be allocated to one of the bufferpools, which means that all data retrieved from the tablespace will be cached in that bufferpool. More than one tablespace can be assigned to a single bufferpool. By default, DB2 creates a single bufferpool, called IBMDEFAULTBP; this bufferpool is used as the sole buffer cache if no other bufferpools are explicitly created and tablespaces assigned to them.

Bufferpool Management

Index and table data is read from disk into bufferpool pages and updated in the bufferpool. Dirty (that is, modified) bufferpool pages are flushed to disk by the pagecleaners. This flushing achieves two main purposes:

1. Recovery time is reduced in the event of a crash.
2. A supply of clean bufferpool pages is maintained for the benefit of agents needing to bring new data pages into the bufferpools.

Pagecleaner behavior is influenced by the number of pagecleaners (set with the NUM_IOCLEANERS parameter) and the changed pages threshold (the CHNGPGS_THRESH parameter). The changed pages threshold represents a percentage of dirty pages in each bufferpool. When this threshold is reached within a bufferpool, the pagecleaners will be activated for that bufferpool. The changed pages threshold parameter is set per database, not per bufferpool.

Although cleaning bufferpool pages is the primary responsibility of the pagecleaners, agents are also able to clean pages. If a DB2 agent is unable to find a clean buffer, it will clean one itself rather than stalling. (In the same way, agents are able to read pages into the bufferpool even when prefetchers are active.) This behavior is not expected to be the norm, though.

Unlike other major databases, DB2 UDB does not use checkpoints. Instead, DB2 uses a write-ahead logging protocol to guarantee recovery. This protocol uses "soft" checkpoints to write least recently used (LRU) bufferpool pages to disk, independently of transaction commit. However, enough log information to redo or undo the change to a database page is committed to disk before the bufferpool page itself is written. This protocol therefore renders checkpoints unnecessary for DB2 UDB.

Nonetheless, there is a need to ensure that dirty bufferpool pages are regularly flushed to disk to facilitate recovery time. A parameter (SOFTMAX, the percentage of a single log file reclaimed before a soft checkpoint) is set to determine the point at which pagecleaner behavior changes from flushing the least recently used pages to flushing the oldest pages. The larger this setting, the longer the pages are cached before being flushed, and therefore the longer the recovery time.

Physical Data Storage

DB2 databases can be established as a single data store or physically split across multiple nodes. Where data is split, the nodes may be different servers networked together or multiple database partitions on a single server. On a single server, these partitions are referred to as logical database partitions (LDPs). LDPs are, in effect, virtual shared-nothing nodes, coexisting inside the same server rather than on separate systems. Whether the nodes are real or virtual, the data is split according to a partitioning key and the whole data set is only visible if all partitions are queried. Fortunately, DB2 accesses the partitions transparently; the user does not need to know which data is located in which partition. LDPs are discussed in more detail in "Parallel Processing" on page 156, and the concepts associated with implementing shared-nothing databases on SMPs and NUMA systems are discussed in "Shared-Nothing Databases on SMPs" on page 36.

Tablespaces

DB2 databases store data in *tablespaces*. Each tablespace can consist of one or more storage objects called *containers*. A container is either a file system file or a raw device.

Each table lives in one and only one tablespace on a node, although the indexes for a table may be placed in a special index tablespace (indexes for a table must all live in one tablespace—either the same tablespace as the table itself or a nominated index tablespace). Apart from data and index tablespaces, there are two other types of tablespaces: LOB tablespaces, which store large objects, and temporary tablespaces, which are used when sorts overflow from memory to disk.

Two different storage strategies are used for tablespaces. System-managed-storage (SMS) tablespaces grow dynamically as the tablespace becomes filled. SMS tablespaces are implemented with UFS files. The DB2 system catalogs are typically stored in an SMS tablespace. Database-managed-storage (DMS) tablespaces are preallocated according to a size parameter specified at tablespace creation time and are implemented on either UFS files or raw devices. All tablespaces are created by user choice as either SMS or DMS.

DMS tablespaces almost always offer the best performance on Solaris systems. SMS tablespaces are good choices for temporary tablespaces with OLTP workloads, though, since it can be difficult to determine in advance the appropriate preallocation size for temporary tablespaces. For DSS workloads, DMS tablespaces offer performance advantages.

DMS tablespaces are typically extended by the addition of one or more containers. When data is loaded into a tablespace, it is automatically striped across all available containers. Consequently, when new containers are added to a tablespace, DB2 forces a rebalance (or restriping) of the data. Rebalancing is time consuming, and the tablespace is locked against access while rebalancing completes.

For these reasons, it is wise to create each tablespace at its final size if at all possible. An alternative is to later unload the data, recreate the tablespace with more containers, and then reload the data. Note, too, that Version 7.1 introduced support for resizing of DMS containers. If the container is a raw device that can be extended (with a volume manager, for example), you can notify DB2 of the new size. DB2 will take advantage of the extra space, avoiding the need to rebalance the data.

Since DB2 automatically stripes data, volume managers are only needed for UDB if mirroring or software RAID 5 is required. Note that for performance reasons, software RAID 5 is not recommended. RAID 5 is only recommended on storage arrays that offer hardware RAID 5 support (such as the Sun StorEdge T3 or A1000). RAID levels are discussed in "Introduction to RAID" on page 232.

Log Files

Log files can be configured as either *circular*, which means a fixed number are created and used in turn, the first being reused when the last is full, or in *log-retain* mode, which means new log files will be created as old log files are filled. If circular logs are used, log files can be automatically archived with *user exits* (user-supplied programs or scripts) once they are filled.

Log files can be placed on either file system files or raw devices for both circular logs and logs in log-retain mode. Sample user exits are also provided that can extract and archive log extents from a raw log device. Best performance is achieved with raw log files.

Logical Data Storage

Within a container, DB2 organizes data in *extents*, and within an extent in *pages*, which can be either 4, 8, 16 or 32 Kbytes in size. An extent consists of a user-specified number of pages (the default is 32). Note that before DB2 UDB Version 5.2, only 4-Kbyte pages were supported; support for 8- and 16-Kbyte pages was added in Version 5.2, and support for 32-Kbyte pages was added in Version 6.1.

A page is the lowest level of DB2 addressable data. When DB2 retrieves a row from a table on behalf of a user, the process involves reading at least one page from disk into the buffer cache in memory. When modified rows are flushed to disk by the pagecleaners, each I/O will write an entire page (a minimum of 4 Kbytes).

When data is read sequentially, as during a table scan or index scan, the prefetchers each read one extent rather than one page at a time. Consequently, a single read can retrieve 512 Kbytes of data with 16-Kbyte page sizes and an extent size of 32.

System Tablespaces

The DB2 system catalogs and their views are stored in an SMS tablespace, called SYSCATSPACE, created when the database is created. A new database is also created with two other SMS tablespaces: USERSPACE1 (for user data) and TEMPSPACE1 (a temporary tablespace).

Each database must have at least one temporary tablespace. Temporary tablespaces are used when sorts overflow from memory to disk. SQL queries with group by or order by clauses, for example, result in sorts, as do index create operations.

Parallel Processing

DB2 UDB introduced support for parallel processing in stages. In this section we examine the building blocks on which the current versions of DB2 UDB are built.

DB2 Universal Database Enterprise Edition (EE)

DB2 UDB Enterprise Edition (EE) shipped in September 1997. For the first time, DB2 for Solaris users were able to use intraquery parallelism, an essential component in deploying data warehouse applications. Intraquery parallelism is achieved within a single database partition by means of multiple CPUs to execute the query plans selected by the optimizer.

Figure 12.2 shows resource usage without intraquery parallelism.

Figure 12.2 *Resources used with no query parallelism*

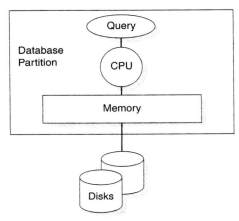

Without query parallelism, only a single CPU can be used by the agent process for each query. As the amount of data to be processed increases, the single processing thread becomes a severe limitation. The ability to support intraquery parallelism within a single database partition is called *intrapartition parallelism*.

DB2 achieves intrapartition parallelism by assigning subagents to act on behalf of a database agent. Because each subagent can potentially consume a single CPU, all available CPUs can be used for any query. For example, on an 8-CPU server, all eight CPUs can be used to satisfy an individual query. Figure 12.3 illustrates the resources that might be used to execute a single query with intrapartition parallelism on a 4-CPU server.

Figure 12.3 *Resources used with intrapartition parallelism*

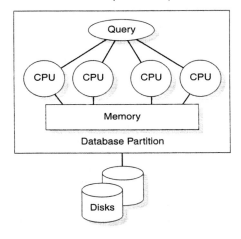

DB2 Universal Database Enterprise-Extended Edition (EEE)

In the first quarter of 1998, a new version of DB2 UDB for Solaris became available: Enterprise-Extended Edition (EEE). DB2 UDB EEE extended the configuration options for decision support users. Symmetrical multiprocessing (SMP) clusters, including high availability (HA) functionality, were supported for the first time. The ability to support multiple database partitions in a single large SMP server was also provided. Figure 12.4 shows multiple logical database partitions (nodes) in a single SMP system.

Figure 12.4   *Interpartition parallelism on a single SMP system*

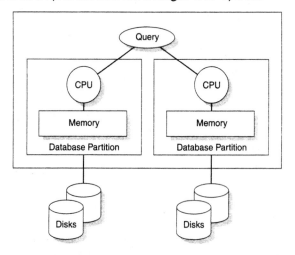

For example, on a 16-CPU server, 16 logical database partitions could be configured. In this case, each database table is spread across some or all of the database partitions, although this underlying layout is transparent to the user—when a query is executed the data is automatically retrieved from the partition or partitions in which it resides. The design factors to be considered in choosing between a single large database partition or multiple logical database partitions are discussed in "Shared-Nothing Databases on SMPs" on page 36.

Using logical database partitions is a little like running a massively parallel processing (MPP) system in a single SMP server. The advantage compared to an MPP system, though, is that interpartition communication uses shared memory and fast IPC mechanisms rather than an external interconnect. Consequently, throughput is higher and latencies lower, typically by more than an order of magnitude in each case.

Figure 12.5 shows a combination of interpartition parallelism within and between SMP systems.

Figure 12.5 *Interpartition parallelism on an SMP cluster*

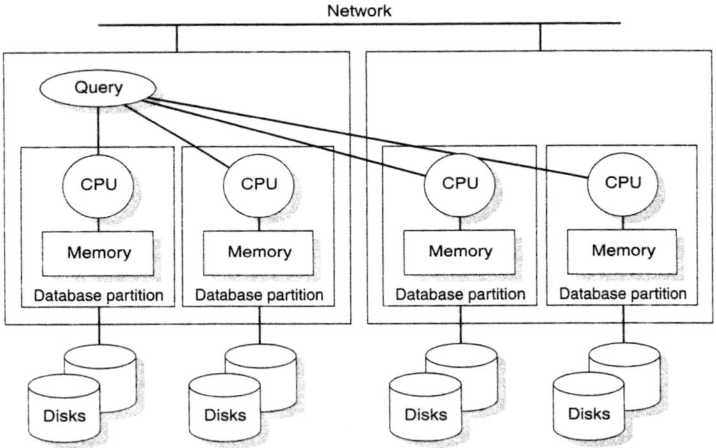

Enterprise-Extended Edition also supports clusters, so multiple SMP systems can be connected and the database tables split across them. DB2 provides the db2split tool to simplify the splitting of data. In the example shown in Figure 12.5, the database tables could be spread across two logical database partitions in each of two 2-CPU servers clustered together.

Combining Inter- and Intrapartition Parallelism

As of the release of DB2 Universal Database EEE Version 5.2, DB2 UDB combined the functionality of EE and EEE. The new version allowed both interpartition parallelism and intrapartition parallelism to be used together. Multiple logical database partitions can be configured in a single SMP server, each partition with multiple subagents and hence taking advantage of more than one CPU when executing queries as for EE. Multiple SMP servers can be clustered, each partitioned into multiple logical database partitions, as for EEE but with each partition using multiple CPUs. Database tables would be spread across some or all of these partitions.

The partition subdivisions are logical, not physical, and have meaning only to the DB2 database management system. There is no need to use hardware or operating system mechanisms (such as the domain capability first made available on the Enterprise 10000) to separate them, although a different processor set could be used for each partition (processor sets are provided by the Solaris Operating Environment as of Solaris 2.6).

Figure 12.6 illustrates how interpartition plus intrapartition parallelism might look in practice.

Figure 12.6   *Interpartition and intrapartition parallelism combined*

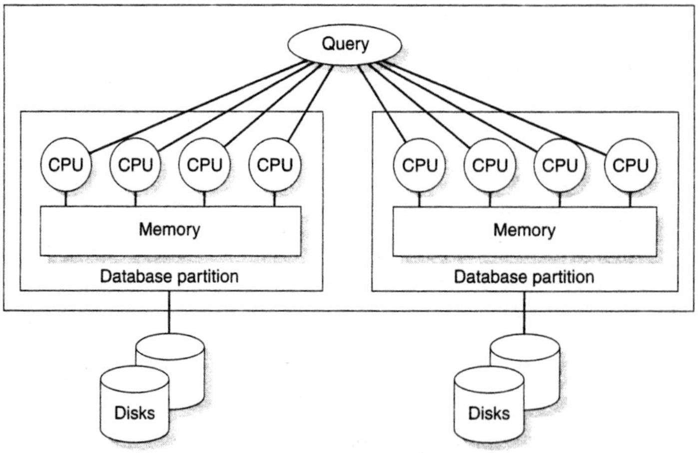

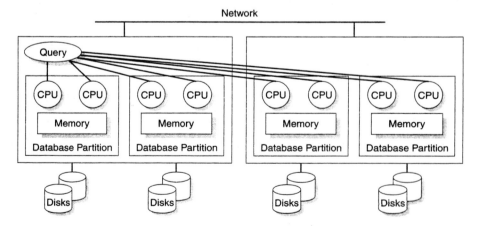

For example, a 48-CPU server could be subdivided into six logical database partitions with eight CPUs available to each. In very large SMP systems, such as Starfire or large Sun Fire servers, this approach will probably yield the best query performance.

Clustering is still possible, too, allowing a single database to be further extended beyond a single SMP system. Figure 12.7 illustrates clustering.

Figure 12.7 *Interpartition & intrapartition parallelism on an SMP cluster*

Other DB2-Related Products

The following list outlines other IBM-supplied products related to DB2.

- DB2 Connect, a communication product allowing users to connect to any database server implementing the Distributed Relational Database Architecture (DRDA) protocol, including all DB2 server products.

- DB2 Extenders, specialized data types and functions for managing, storing, and retrieving objects beyond the scope of regular data. Extenders focus on data such as text, images, video, or audio.

- DB2 DataJoiner, a gateway product enabling users to transparently interact with data from a variety of other relational database systems, including Oracle, Sybase, Microsoft SQL Server, and Informix as well as nonrelational systems such as IMS and VSAM.

- Data Propagator, a replication product allowing data changes to be captured on one DB2 database and applied on other.

- Tivoli Storage Manager (TSM), a network-based backup and restore capability. TSM manages the backup copies as well as creating them.

- Intelligent Miner, a data mining tool capable of retrieving data from DB2 databases.

- DB2 OLAP Server, essentially the Essbase OLAP product from Arbor integrated into the DB2 environment.

Part Three

Sizing and Configuring Sun DBMS Servers

- Sizing Servers for Databases
- Configuring Systems
- Configuring CPU
- Configuring the Network
- Data Layout

13

SIZING SYSTEMS FOR DATABASES

"How big a system do I need?"

Sun account representatives are regularly asked to prepare system configuration quotations on behalf of customers. Generating a quote is not difficult. But coming up with an accurate system sizing is extremely challenging. By "sizing" I mean deciding on the number of CPUs, the memory capacity, the number of disks and disk controllers, and the number of networks of each type to include in the configuration.

Sometimes a customer will specify exactly the configuration to be quoted. But often the account representative is expected to provide some assistance in sizing.

The worst-case scenario is something like this: "I need to support 250 users and I need 300 Gbytes of disk. How many CPUs and how much memory will I need? Oh, and by the way, can you please guarantee one-second response times?"

Even if the question is fuzzy, it is still important to provide the best sizing possible given the information supplied. Sun has invested a lot of engineering effort to help its field organization quantify the answers to sizing questions.

Payback for the effort is considerable. Some cynics believe hardware vendors deliberately oversize systems to increase the value of sales. In fact, there is considerable incentive to configure systems accurately. Oversized systems are also overpriced systems; in our competitive environment, price blowouts can easily cost a vendor business. Even if the sale is made, the end result may be a dissatisfied customer. The converse—undersized systems—almost invariably leads to customer dissatisfaction.

165

This chapter examines the principles behind the sizing process and concludes with a detailed account of the development of a sizing tool that embodies those principles.

Basis of a Sizing Estimate

You may expect application suppliers or RDBMS suppliers to be able to offer meaningful sizing guidelines with their own products. But unfortunately, that's not always the case. Suppliers can be experts in their own product without having detailed knowledge of all the hardware platforms on which the product may be deployed.

Systems integrators and major consulting practices typically have specialist staff who can help with the sizing process. (Sun does, too: SunPS—the Sun professional services group.) If your sizing is based more on guesswork than concrete data, it's probably a good time to call in consultants. Sometimes a little expenditure up front can avoid major pain later.

However you arrive at your estimate, it is important to understand how much confidence you can place in it. Not all sizing estimates are equal; here is my personal hierarchy, from best to worst:

1. **Estimates based on application migration.**
   The best estimates are based on detailed knowledge of an existing application. If an existing workload is being transferred to a new system, you should be able to first profile the resource requirements of the applications and then use the results as the basis of the sizing. Confidence in the estimate is reduced if the following complications arise:

   - The target environment changes. For example, more users will lead to a consequent increase in the transaction rate.

     You might assume that 50% more CPU and memory will support a 50% increase in user load, but it isn't always that simple. Every commuter knows that getting more people to work cannot simply be achieved just by adding more cars; to avoid delays, the freeway system may first require an upgrade. In the same way, hardware or software limitations may prevent a workload from scaling perfectly.

   - The architecture of the target system changes. Each generation of server hardware tends to come with a different bus architecture and CPUs with a different clock speed. CPU clock speed alone is not always a reliable indicator of relative performance.

   - A change is made from one hardware vendor to another. As well as differences in the hardware architecture and CPUs, there may be differences in the efficiency of the operating system, system services, and third-party applications.

2. **Estimates based on an application benchmark.**
   You can simulate the final user environment on the target system by using a remote terminal emulator or remote browser emulator to place a

load on the system. Remote terminal emulators are described in more detail in Chapter 27, "Benchmarking."

For the estimate to be meaningful, use the user's own application and data and ensure that the emulated users operate exactly as the real users operate.

One of the main challenges is to avoid discrepancies between the emulation and reality, especially in the way emulated users operate. Such discrepancies can significantly compromise the usefulness of the end result. Beware the temptation of believing that the accuracy of an estimate is directly proportional to the amount of effort expended creating it! Application benchmarks typically require abundant time and heroic effort. I have seen application benchmarks compromised, though, by inaccurate assumptions about the way real users operate. For example, if think times (delays used to simulate pauses in user activity) are too short, the benchmark system will be driven too hard, leading to oversizing.

3. Estimates based on similar configurations.
   Sometimes you can find a similar application elsewhere running on a system similar to the proposed target system. Of course, you must factor in the inevitable differences, thereby reducing the confidence in the end result. Nonetheless, the result is probably much better than a guess.

4. Estimates based on models.
   In the absence of detailed real-world information (sometimes because an application has not yet been developed), you can sometimes relate expected application behavior to a known workload and extrapolate accordingly. Treat such results with significant caution, but realize that model-based estimates are still better than the final alternative.

5. Guesstimates.
   Guessing is free and easy and defers the pain until later!

Minimum Requirements

As an absolute minimum, you need two things to carry out system sizing:

- A knowledge of the type and number of business transactions to be processed in a given period of time. Business transactions can be as varied as OLTP transactions, batch reports, or DSS queries, depending on the application.

- Some understanding of the system resources (CPU, memory, disk, and network) required to complete the business transactions.

The same metrics are explored in detail in Chapter 26 in the context of performance monitoring, but the principles apply in sizing and capacity planning also. The application of these metrics in a sizing model is also discussed in "A General-Purpose OLTP Sizing Tool" on page 188.

Limitations of Estimates

As I suggested earlier, a sizing estimate based on a benchmark using deployed applications, a realistic workload profile, and actual transaction data can still result in a grossly inaccurate estimate.

Why? Often guesses are made about the following:

- User think time (the amount of time a user is not directly using the system). Think time is often underestimated, resulting in oversizing.

- Acceptable response time. This can also be underestimated, again resulting in oversizing.

Mistakes don't always favor oversizing, though. It is easy to underestimate the total amount of disk space required. Data and indexes may be sized accurately, but overhead such as rollback, temporary tablespaces, logs, etc., may be undersized. To save money, people may be tempted to underconfigure the number of disks.

The more limited the information available, such as the number of users and the amount of disk space, the more your estimate becomes a guesstimate.

Data from one user survey revealed that many Sun users run servers that appear to be significantly oversized.

The Right Questions

The more detail available, the better the chances of meaningful sizing estimates. But you need the right kind of detail. So, we'll start by looking at the questions that need to be answered when you are sizing and configuring database systems in a meaningful way.

What type of workload is it?

Workload types have already been discussed in Chapter 6. Our discussion here focuses on the sizing implications of four of the major database workloads. Many customer environments are complicated by having a mixture of workload types, sometimes coexisting on a single system. All workloads must be taken into account in sizing estimates; it is often easier to size each workload independently and then estimate the impact of consolidating them on a single server if that is the intention.

- **Online Transaction Processing (OLTP) workloads.**

  High CPU requirements. Throughput is typically CPU bound (that is, CPU limited) rather than I/O bound.

  Average I/O requirements. I/Os are mostly random and of small size (usually 2 Kbytes to 8 Kbytes). The number of writes is typically significant, although often less than the number of reads. Disk drives rated at 7200 rpm can support roughly 75 I/Os per second, and 10,000 rpm disks around 100 I/Os per second. The current generation of disk controllers is usually able to handle the required IOPS, provided enough disk drives are available.

High memory requirements. The database buffer cache is likely to be important because it reduces disk I/O and therefore saves CPU time.

Varying network requirements. In wide area networks, network performance can be an important issue. Local area networks are usually well able to cope with OLTP workloads, even quite large ones.

- **Decision Support System (DSS) workloads.** Ad hoc DSS environments can be characterized as follows:

  Medium CPU requirements. Much of the CPU requirement relates to I/O processing. A 400 MHz CPU can process about 30 Gbyte/sec using large I/Os during a table or index scan; this information may help you size enough CPUs to ensure that your I/O throughput is not constrained by CPU capacity. CPU requirements vary greatly, depending on the type of query, of course. For example, aggregations and joins will increase CPU requirements while slowing down the I/O rate.

  High I/O requirements. Ad hoc queries typically involve sequential reading of large amounts of data, so disk throughput is paramount. The number of disk controllers is important, as is the number of disk spindles. Writes are significant only during database update or reload.

  High memory requirements. Instead of the shared database buffer cache, memory is typically used for local sort areas for processes and, in the case of Oracle, for local hash-join work areas. It is difficult to make use of the cache since the volume of data access means that data is rarely reused and the cache contents change rapidly.

  Low network requirements. DSS applications are usually run directly on the server. Even if the access is remote, relatively little data is transferred over the network. For example, a query initiated remotely may process 300 Gbytes of data and eventually spit out half a page of results. Typically, it is only the results that are transferred over the network.

- **Batch workloads.** Batch workloads are often an integral part of OLTP or DSS workloads rather than independent workloads.

  Medium-to-high CPU requirements. Batch workloads are more likely to be I/O-bound rather than CPU-bound.

  High I/O requirements. Large amounts of data are accessed, often sequentially but with small I/Os. Batch applications can be read-only, as with reports, or write intensive, as with batch updates.

  High memory requirements. Batch workloads make heavy use of the database buffer cache but are rarely able to take advantage of caching since they rarely reuse the same data pages.

  Low network requirements. Batch workloads are typically run directly on the server, even if associated with OLTP client/server applications.

- **OLAP (Online Analytical Processing)**

  The particular variant of OLAP referred to here is MOLAP. See "Online Analytical Processing (OLAP)" on page 70 for more details.

  Medium-to-high CPU requirements. Preaggregation, rollup, and precalculation are CPU intensive. Queries can become CPU-bound.

  Low I/O requirements. The load phase is write intensive and is typically carried out weekly or monthly. The aggregation phase is read/write intensive. Queries are read-only and somewhat similar to OLTP transactions involving random reads.

  High memory requirements. The database buffer cache is critical, as for OLTP systems, and process local memory is important, as for DSS applications.

  Medium network requirements. OLAP workloads may support relatively large numbers of users connected remotely, in which case remote area networks need to be sized appropriately. Local area networks are capable of supporting large OLAP systems.

This list of workloads is not exhaustive. Some workloads combine the characteristics of the workloads described. For example, operational data stores combine elements of OLTP and DSS workloads. OLAP variants have different characteristics from those described above under OLAP.

What is the status of the application?

As already discussed, it is vastly easier to size an existing application than one that has not yet been implemented.

If the application has already been implemented, ask the following questions.

Are existing system statistics available?   Existing system statistics should allow a much better estimate of the CPU, I/O, and memory resources required, although it may be necessary to estimate the relative performance of a different range of Sun or competitive hardware. Sun systems engineers have access to internal comparisons based on an internal set of M-values that provide the Sun Constant Performance Metric. When comparing a Sun system with a competitive system, as in the case of an upgrade to a Sun system, published results like TPC-C throughput or even SPECrate may provide a crude basis of comparison (don't expect this kind of comparison to be accurate, though).

Are more users being added?   An increase in the number of users suggests a relatively simple scaling exercise, assuming the user proportion for each shift remains the same. At first appearance it might seem logical, for example, that doubling CPU capacity should allow twice as many users to be supported. Unexpected software or hardware bottlenecks may be exposed as the workload increases, however, preventing linear scaling. In the worst case, a point may be reached beyond which no increase in transaction throughput is possible no matter how much additional CPU resource is added. It may be necessary, for example, to tune key applications and add more disks and memory as well as CPUs before the additional user load can be supported.

Is new functionality being implemented? The sizing implications of nnew application functionality is likely to be more difficult to estimate unless the new applications have been extensively profiled.

If the application has not yet been implemented, the following questions should be asked.

Has the application already been written or developed? If the development has not started, the task is considerably more difficult than if an already working product is to be implemented. If an existing application is to be redeployed on another platform, then you can monitor the current system to assess resource requirements.

Sometimes the redeployment also involves a change in the workload. If the application is not instrumented, estimating the new resource requirements will not be straightforward. An "instrumented" application is one that captures transaction statistics such as transaction count and transaction response time. Unfortunately, many applications are either poorly instrumented or not instrumented at all. Application monitoring is discussed in more detail in Chapter 26.

If not, how can the application be profiled? You can profile performance with modeling tools, for example, SES/Workbench and Strategizer, which only run on the Windows operating system (refer to http://www.hyperformix.com). Software Performance Engineering (SPE) techniques can also help you to evaluate progress against performance goals throughout the project's entire life cycle (refer to the SPE*ED modeling tool, described at http://www.perfeng.com).

If the applications do not exist and no modeling is being carried out, no one can make definite statements about sizing. The other information here may give an indication, but all estimates will probably prove inadequate when the application goes live.

Is a software package sizing guide available? Many software packages (for example, from SAP, Peoplesoft) have sizing guides or consultants to help quantify hardware requirements.

How many users?

This question is better asked as two separate questions:

- How many users will be connected?

- How many users will be concurrently active?

Connected users can be either idle or active. Active users are referred to as *concurrent users*. Connected users that are not active consume little more than swap space. When they become active, they cause a temporary burst of CPU, disk, and memory activity.

What do *active* and *idle* mean in this context? I am not limiting the definition to users actually touching the keyboard or waiting for the system to respond to their last keystrokes. Under my definition, users still count as active if they are currently pausing to sip their coffee or to think. If they have not been engaged in some kind of system-related activity for longer than one minute, they can reasonably be regarded as idle.

The number of concurrent users gives a broad indication of the processing requirements of the workload. However, there are many different types of users, including the following:

- **Casual OLTP users.** Examples are users performing occasional queries or entering batch requests. Casual usage results in relatively light load except for requests for batch jobs or reports that are often run in the background and therefore regarded as batch jobs.

- **Heavy OLTP users.** Data entry users are good examples. Heavy usage can consume a lot of CPU and cause substantial small, random read/write I/O activity.

- **Data warehouse users.** Data warehouse applications typically support a few power users executing a small number of queries that can result in very heavy I/O activity.

Clearly "200 users" can generate *very* different loads depending on the situation.

Some time ago, Tim Read, a senior consultant with Sun UK, put together a user sizing chart, shown in Table 13-1.

Table 13-1 *A sizing estimate example: concurrent OLTP users*

Server Type	No. of Disk Spindles	--Timeshare--		--Client/Server--	
		Memory Needed (MB)	No. of Concurrent Users	Memory Needed (MB)	No. of Concurrent Users
Enterprise 450 (4 x 300 MHz 2MB E$)	60	2048	510	1600	790
Enterprise x000 (2 x 336 MHz, 4MB E$)	32	1152	280	896	420
Enterprise x000 (4 x 336 MHz, 4MB E$)	60	2048	510	1600	790
Enterprise x000 (10 x 336 MHz, 4MB E$)	125	3968	990	3328	1650
Enterprise Server 6500 (24 x 336 MHz, 4MB E$)	210	5824	1450	5568	2770
Enterprise Server 10000 (32 x 250 MHz, 4MB E$)	235	6208	1536	6208	3084

Tim's sizings—now dated—were based on a specific Oracle Financials General Ledger environment and may not be applicable to any other environment. I have included it more as an example than as a recommendation.

Tim analyzed a mass of data and summarized it in an understandable form. Analyzing data is one of the key processes in producing sizing estimates. The beauty of documenting the results in a concrete fashion like this is that the document becomes a reference point for the future. It can evolve if reality proves significantly different from the estimates or if the workload's processing characteristics change over time.

Do processing requirements vary with work shifts?

Many user environments involve markedly different processing characteristics at different times of the day. From the perspective of resource requirements, there may be a morning shift, an afternoon shift, and an evening shift.

Different shifts will often involve a different user mix and different workload types. For example, the morning shift may be characterized by a mixture of heavy OLTP and light OLTP users. Additional light OLTP users may join the afternoon shift along with a light batch load. The evening shift may be almost exclusively batch.

The key questions become:

- Which shift consumes the most of each type of system resource?

- Which shift should form the basis of the sizing? Is it the heaviest shift or is some other factor more important? For example, the batch workload from the evening shift may be the heaviest, but user response times during the daytime shifts may be regarded as more crucial.

How are users connected to the database server?

If users connect to applications running on the same server as the database, the database server sizing must take into account the processing requirements of the applications as well as the database. Servers running both database and application software are described as running in *timeshare* mode (see Figure 13.1).

Figure 13.1 *Timeshare configuration*

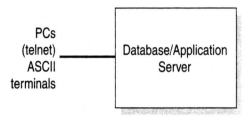

Although a PC may provide a window in which the application runs (through telnet, for example), in this case the application is still running on the remote server, not the PC. The PC is simply emulating an ASCII terminal and does not relieve the server of any application processing.

One of the characteristics of database applications is that they can readily be run in *client/server* mode, with the client application hosted on a different workstation or server connected by a network to some kind of server process that accesses the database on the application's behalf. Figure 13.2 shows a server running in client/server mode.

Figure 13.2 *Two-tier client/server configuration*

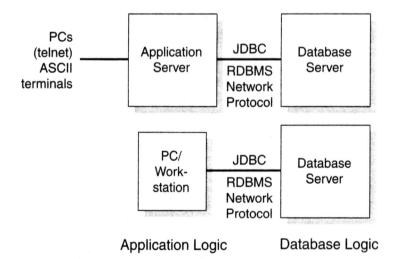

When the application is run on a separate system, the database server workload can typically be reduced by one-third to one-half. In the case of SAP and other Enterprise Resource Planning (ERP) products, the savings are even more significant since the database server component is a smaller part of the workload than the application component. Client/server configurations, therefore, can be used to reduce the size of the database server. The trend toward client-side resource consumption is likely to continue and increase.

Remember that if client/server connectivity is used, you must size networks accordingly and take into consideration the server CPU resources that will be consumed in processing network traffic.

Is ODBC or JDBC in use?   ODBC provides a standard mechanism for applications to connect to databases and is often used by PC applications. JDBC offers equivalent functionality from a Java program.

If ODBC or JDBC is used, PCs or other intelligent clients may be involved and therefore the client load may not be on the database server. If the application software generates the SQL automatically, it may be poorly constructed, with implications for performance.

JDBC can be implemented with a native driver to connect to the database or with an ODBC driver using a JDBC/ODBC bridge, as shown in Figure 13.3.

Figure 13.3 *JDBC-to-database communication mechanism*

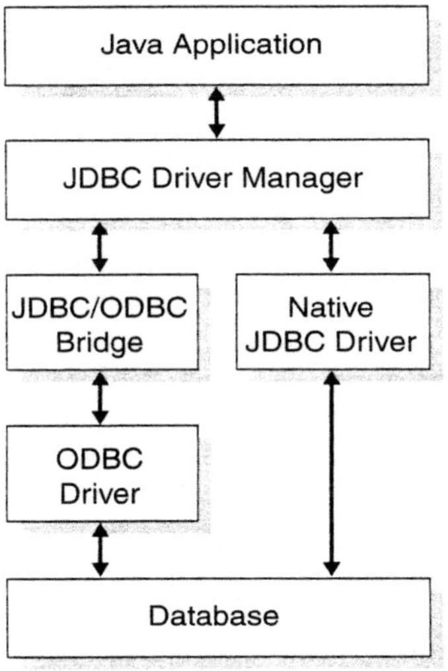

Are WANs involved or only LANs?   Sizing local area networks (LANs) is relatively straightforward since the available bandwidth is very considerable (100BaseT Ethernet networks are widely deployed and Gigabit Ethernet networks are readily available), latencies are quite low, and cost is modest. By contrast, wide area networks (WANs) are still relatively expensive, and both bandwidth and latency are likely to be factors that you must carefully consider when sizing a system.

Is database connectivity achieved by use of web-based applications?
Client/server configurations can be more complex when web-based access is involved. In addition to database applications talking to database servers,

web servers talk to applications. See Figure 13.4 for an example of three-tier client/server configurations.

Remember to size the web server for content delivery and also to size any Java servlets or CGI applications called from it.

Figure 13.4 *Three-tier client/server configurations*

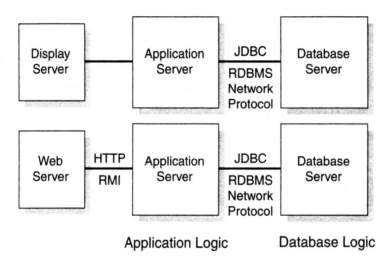

Are CORBA, RMI, EJB, or TP monitors being used?   The use of specialized protocols such as CORBA or RMI introduces further performance considerations that you should explore. The client communication to the application server is frequently RMI over IIOP or XML over HTTP, each with different bandwidth requirements. See "Other Related Technologies" on page 476 for more information.

What are the response time expectations?

If a definite response time expectation has been defined, some other questions must be asked.

Do response times relate to a business transaction or per field?   The TPC-C benchmark (described in Chapter 27), for example, specifies response time as the total time taken to complete a transaction (for example, commit a new order transaction or complete an inquiry) once all keystrokes are completed.

Some users are interested in the maximum response time at the data field. Forms applications may do processing (including database access) upon entry or exit from a field. The accumulated processing can result in substantial processing times for an entire business transaction.

What percentage of users are casual vs. professional data entry users?
Casual users typically intersperse their keystrokes with frequent pauses, whereas professional data entry staff may enter and commit data very rapidly.

Has anyone studied the think time patterns?   What is the transaction submission rate? Even professional data entry staff have substantial think time, when the keyboard is not in use. The reasons can be as simple as pausing to stamp the last piece of paper and pick up the next. Nobody is capable of sustaining uninterrupted data entry for hours on end.

Do users expect consistent response times?   Peak workload periods or a heavy background batch workload can cause normally consistent response times to increase. Users may not readily tolerate such variations. Whether you base your sizing on periods of peak load or normal load, the final decision is likely to have implications for user satisfaction.

What I/O capacity and throughput are required?

For I/O capacity, remember that final database size can be three to five (or more) times the size of the raw data, due to indexes, temporary tablespaces, and logs. Disk availability requirements will add more: double in the case of mirroring, 25% for RAID 5 if a 4+1 configuration is used (see "RAID 5: Striping with Distributed Parity" on page 238 for more information, and refer to Chapter 17 for a general discussion of the issues related to disk layout). Consider the following factors.

Adequate disk capacity.   Deciding on the required disk capacity for a computer system is usually the easiest part of sizing disk storage. Most end users can say with a reasonable degree of accuracy how much capacity they require. But it is much more difficult to decide how many disk spindles and controllers will be required to achieve sufficient I/O operations per second (IOPS) and throughput (typically measured in megabytes per second (Mbyte/sec).

Having adequate capacity without adequate IOPS and throughput is like building a passenger jet with the seating capacity of two jumbo jets and the power of a Lear jet. It would never get off the runway. You don't want your storage subsystem to suffer an equivalent fate.

Number of disk spindles.   The simple solution is "The more the better." Having too many spindles (disk drives) will never hurt performance, although it could complicate system administration. Cost inevitably plays a major role in determining the number of spindles available for a given application.

A good question is "What is the minimum number of spindles I need for sufficient IOPS, throughput and low enough latency to ensure that my applications are not disk bound?"

This is not a simple question to answer. Here are some of the reasons why I/O can be wrongly sized:

- Transaction rates and data capacities supplied by the end user are incomplete. In my experience this has been the most common scenario.

- Transaction rates and data capacities supplied by the end user are inaccurate. Bad information results in bad sizing: the well-known "garbage-in, garbage-out" scenario. I have personally been involved in situations where customers supplied detailed information in good faith, believing it to be accurate, yet they subsequently found the data contained significant inaccuracies.

- Transaction rates and data capacity details are available and accurate, but the disk capacity and throughput requirements of the applications are not accurately known. Knowing the storage requirements of the application allows the disk capacity to be calculated. But some understanding of the I/O access for each application is also needed before the required spindles and controllers can be determined.

It is difficult to predict the disk capacity required for a given configuration because each company's business requirements vary greatly. The collection of this sizing information must be the primary responsibility of the end user.

Typical utilization patterns.   Once you determine disk capacity, you can make some high-level observations.

Research carried out at Sun has suggested that customer disk subsystems typically average about one I/O per Gbyte of disk per second, corresponding to an 18%–20% utilization (a little less than 18 I/Os per second) for 18-Gbyte disks. Obviously, there will be considerable variation depending on the application, the average size of I/Os, the time of day, seasonal variations, and the particulars of any given installation. OLTP applications may not drive disks as hard as do data warehouse queries, for example, although they are likely to result in a more consistent load pattern. But the view from 20,000 feet suggests that many sites will find that 18-Gbyte disks offer an adequate storage strategy with respect to both performance and price performance. And there should still be spare I/O capacity for peak periods. Be aware that 72-Gbyte disks—now readily available—offer four times the capacity of an 18-Gbyte disk but not four times the throughput and I/Os per second (IOPS).

Small, heavily accessed databases may require more disks. For example, trying to locate an entire database plus logs on a single 18-Gbyte disk is not ideal either for performance or availability.

Single disk capabilities.   OLTP access tends to involve a mixture of read and write I/Os of 2 to 8 Kbytes in size. A rule of thumb based on experience is that 18-Gbyte 7200 rpm disks supporting OLTP-style access can sustain a consistent workload of 75 I/Os per second when the entire disk is used (at a disk utilization of a little over 70%) as long as service times are not excessive (less than 30 msecs is desirable). 10,000 rpm disks are good for at least 100 IOPS (the rpm is more significant than the capacity).

Data warehouse access will most likely drive the disks harder. I/Os will be fewer in number but larger in size (typically a minimum of 128 Kbytes) and disk utilization may increase beyond 70% while service times may stretch beyond 30 msecs. Use this information to estimate the total number of IOPS available for a given disk configuration.

When sizing disks, bear in mind that the I/O activity associated with typical workloads includes peaks and troughs and that even a consistent disk load can increase significantly during database checkpoints. Figure 13.5 shows the disk response times for a data disk running a write and update intensive workload.

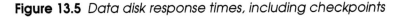

Figure 13.5 *Data disk response times, including checkpoints*

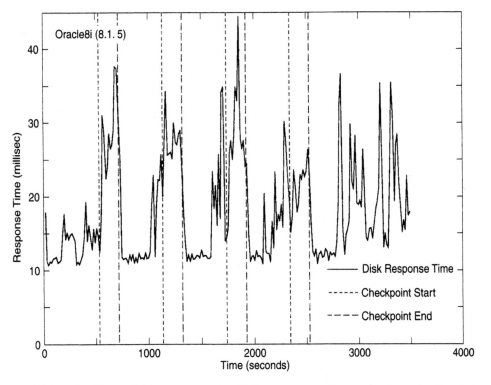

Note the three-fold increase in disk response times during checkpoints (due to the additional write activity). Later versions of Oracle flush buffers more proactively to reduce the impact of checkpoints on the system.

Figure 13.6 shows the load on one of the other data disks during the same period of time.

Figure 13.6 *Data disk read and write activity, including checkpoints*

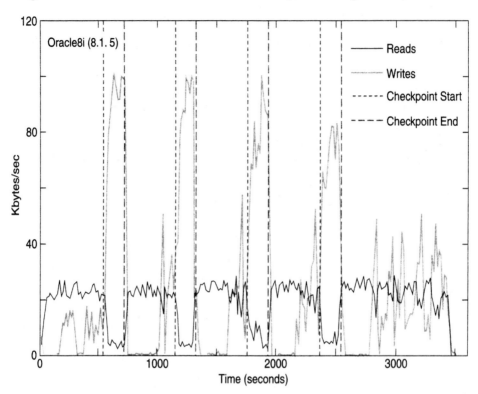

Notice the four-fold increase in write activity during checkpoints. The drop-off in read activity during checkpoints suggests this disk was overloaded at that time.

Both graphs were prepared with data collected with the `iostat` utility.

The right number of disks. The problems associated with configuring too few spindles often become most obvious with small databases. It may be possible to configure enough capacity for a small database with a single 36-Gbyte disk, but more spindles may be needed if many users are doing a lot of I/O on the database. You need to consider the number of IOPS per Gbyte as well as the price per Gbyte.

In our benchmarks at Sun, we typically configure a lot of disks for our benchmarks, many more than the capacity requirements demand. Our usage is not typical, though—we operate on a model where costs are not the primary constraint and systems are driven to the limit. TPC-C, an OLTP benchmark (see "Introduction to TPC-C" on page 449), for example, mandates the configuring and pricing of a significant amount of extra storage for database growth, so there is no real price penalty for overconfiguring disks during benchmarking. We need most of the excess capacity in the final priced configuration anyway.

For most real-world users with large databases (hundreds of gigabytes), configuring the appropriate number of 18- or 36-Gbyte disks for the required capacity is likely to be a reasonable starting point. If the budget is available, configure 30% more disks than the capacity demands. That will give some spare capacity for growth as well as a lot more flexibility in laying out the data for best performance.

Number of controllers.   Our experience within Database Engineering at Sun has demonstrated that controller bandwidth is less an issue for OLTP workloads than for DSS workloads. In fact, we have been able to avoid controller bottlenecks in our TPC-C benchmarking, even when all disks on a controller are heavily used. By contrast, our TPC-D benchmarking on SPARCstorage Arrays (SSA) showed that the controller capacity of an SSA was easily exceeded during heavy sequential I/O activity (for example, executing a query involving a large table scan). The practical limit for sequential reads from an SSA was around 17 Mbyte/sec. This limit could be reached with a little more than half of the 30 disks supported in the smallest SSA.

The good news is that the current generation of disk arrays from Sun (the Sun StorEdge product range) boast significantly increased bandwidth compared to the previous generation (SPARCstorage Arrays). Current arrays such as the A5100 and A5200 are capable of throughput of 90 Mbyte/sec on a single loop, four to five times the bandwidth of the older SPARCstorage Arrays.

Nevertheless, none of the arrays have the bandwidth to sustain the full throughput off each disk in a fully configured array. A "plaid" approach can boost throughput: striping across controllers as well as disks (see Figure 17.11 on page 249 for an illustration).

In conclusion, don't worry too much about controllers when configuring for OLTP applications. When configuring for DSS workloads, use A5200, A5100, or T3 arrays when heavy I/O is required. If older arrays are being deployed, try to avoid concurrently accessing all the disks in an array during heavy sequential read activity.

Backplane (bus) bandwidth.   It is very unlikely that your database application will consume all the available bus bandwidth on current Sun systems. Sun has been able to achieve world-record TPC-C and TPC-D/TPC-H performance on the older Enterprise 6500 and Starfire (Enterprise 10000) servers without exceeding the capacity of the system bus.

How is this possible, since CPUs keep getting faster and I/O throughput demands keep increasing, placing more load on the system bus in the process? The reason is that each new generation of Sun servers comes with significantly increased bus bandwidth. The system bus bandwidth has been increased again on the Sun Fire server range. That trend will definitely continue.

I/O bottlenecks.   In conclusion, I/O bottlenecks can occur in a number of places: at the disk, at the disk controller, which may be located in a disk array or in the server, in the peripheral bus on the server, or in the system backplane bus within the server. The dashed lines in Figure 13.7 illustrate these points of bottleneck.

Figure 13.7 *Potential I/O bottlenecks*

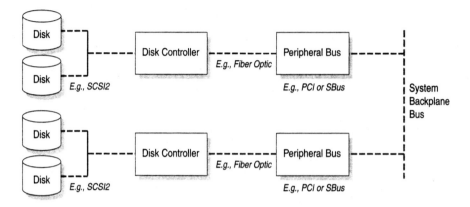

Each component has its own limit for both disk operations per second and throughput. If each disk supports throughput of 16 Mbyte/sec, for example, and the SCSI bus supports 25 Mbyte/sec, two disks may be able to saturate the SCSI bus. The fiber optic connection to the peripheral bus may be capable of supporting 90 Mbyte/sec, so multiple disk controllers could share the fiber without reaching limits. The disk controllers connect to the server through an SBus or PCI, each of which has its own limitations (110 Mbyte/sec per SBus, higher for PCI). Finally, the backplane bus also has a maximum capacity. You must account for these potential limitations when sizing systems.

How much memory is required?

Memory on a database server is consumed in several different ways.

The database cache. Database Engineering research suggests best performance comes with a cache that is between 5% and 15% of the database size for OLTP applications (refer to "Sizing the Buffer Cache" on page 81 for more information). This sizing assumes, though, that your data is skewed and therefore can take advantage of caching. As an example of data skew, consider a manufacturer of garden supplies. Eighty percent of orders may be shipped to a small number of warehouses for large stores like Wal-Mart and Kmart, while the other 20% go to a large number of smaller stores. You would expect to find Wal-Mart's account details regularly accessed and therefore in the database buffer cache, whereas account details for Joe's Corner Hardware Store may need to be retrieved from disk.

For DSS applications, cache requirements are usually very small, although significant amounts of memory can often be used in other ways (for example, private sort areas and, for Oracle, private hash areas). DSS benchmarks published by Sun have used well over 1 Gbyte per CPU in total, almost none of it used as database cache. Most databases avoid the cache for DSS queries since there is little opportunity for data sharing and tables are usually too large to fully cache. The result is that the cache can get in the way of performance.

Database application overhead.   As a rough rule of thumb, allow between 32 Mbytes and 64 Mbytes for initial memory requirements on the database server.

User applications.   Memory sizing for user applications is very application dependent. If no information is available, try allowing between 2 and 4 Mbytes per user on the client (much more—as much as 10 to 16 Mbytes—for ERP applications) and between 1 and 2 Mbytes per user on the database server for OLTP users. Add these figures together if client/server is not being used.

The file system cache (for file-system-based database files).   Don't try to size for the file system page cache—let the database do the caching since it can most effectively decide what to cache. If raw devices or Direct I/O is used, file system cache memory will not be consumed by database files. If database files are placed on UFS, additional demand will be placed on memory and an additional CPU overhead will be incurred (refer to "Raw Devices vs. UFS" on page 242 for more information).

The OS kernel.   OS memory reservations depend on the amount of memory in the system, but allow between 32 Mbytes and 64 Mbytes plus other OS overheads.

What is the expected system growth rate?

Once a system has been purchased, it probably will not be upgraded for some months at least. Don't forget to allow for growth during that period in your initial sizing.

Not all growth necessitates additional capacity: revenue can be increased without an increase in volume if each sales item increases in price, for example. But usually an increase in revenue implies additional capacity requirements.

The effects of even modest growth become significant over time. For example, if overall growth is expected to be 20% compounded per annum, then capacity requirements will double in 4 years.

Guess at your growth rate, allow a little extra as a margin for error, then calculate the total growth over the duration of your purchasing cycle.

Users and applications.   Will the number of users increase over time? Will further applications be deployed in the future? If so, expect implications for CPU, memory, disk, and network requirements.

Processing and disk requirements.   How much is disk capacity expected to grow over time, and how much are processing capacity requirements expected to grow?

Using Published TPC Results for Sizing

Given the availability of published TPC (Transaction Processing Performance Council) benchmarks, it is tempting to use them for sizing. TPC benchmarks are discussed in detail in Chapter 27; if you are not familiar with the details of TPC benchmarks, it might be worth briefly visiting that discussion before reading on.

Using TPC-C to Size Real-World OLTP Servers

If you are brave enough to use TPC-C results for sizing, here are a few steps to arrive at a rough estimate (the emphasis is on rough!):

1. Double the reported transactions per minute to include all transactions, not just new-order transactions (the reported TPC-C throughput includes only new-order transactions).
2. If you're not using a TP monitor, halve the result.
3. Divide the result by 3 if your applications use forms software, or by 1.5 if they use lightweight screen handling (curses, for example).
4. If your applications and SQL are not highly tuned, halve the result.
   By "highly tuned," I mean applications use stored procedures wherever appropriate, and all source code and SQL has been carefully analyzed to determine the optimal data access paths.
5. If you run batch jobs or reports concurrently, halve the result.

The result is a crude estimate of the real-world transaction rate that can be supported by the hardware configuration in question.

This sizing is only for the database server. You will size client applications differently. Don't forget that TPC-C applications are extremely lightweight—you may need several times more processing power on the client side.

The preceding estimation steps assume you are deploying on exactly the same platform. If not, don't forget to also account for differences in the following:

- **Number and speed of disk spindles.** Disks usually do not affect performance directly as long as I/O access is well balanced; the number and speed of disks does affect the total available IOPS and throughput, though.

- **Bus speed.** For example, a system with a 150 MHz bus will feature higher throughput and lower latencies than a system with a 100 MHz bus.

- **CPU clock speed.** Doubling clock speed will not result in twice the transaction throughput unless the bus speed also doubles. If bus speed does not change, the benefit will be less than the clock speed may suggest.

- **CPU secondary cache size.** Doubling cache size usually translates to a transaction throughput increase of between 5% and 10%.

Finally, TPC-C carefully defines user delays (think time and keying time) as well as acceptable response times (the specification is available at the TPC website: http://www.tpc.org). Make sure you know the number of expected connected and active users for your site and the expected response times and think times.

If this all seems too hard, then at least you're properly warned!

Using TPC-D or TPC-R to Size Real-World DSS Servers

My reaction is simple: Don't try it!

There are a number of reasons why it is unwise to attempt sizing based on old TPC-D or current TPC-R results:

- As described in Chapter 27, TPC-D and TPC-R are very highly optimized and irrelevant to most data warehouse users.

- TPC-D results have not been stable over time. It is hard to compare early results with recent results because new database features have caused power metrics to increase exponentially, well beyond any improvement in hardware and operating system performance. The same is likely to hold for TPC-R as results emerge. It is more a test of software technologies than of server systems.

- As for TPC-C, key system and database metrics are not revealed in the TPC-D/TPC-R Full Disclosure Reports (FDRs) required by the TPC. More importantly, query plans are not revealed. These omissions make it very difficult to compare results.

- TPC-D/TPC-R (and TPC-H) metrics are not intuitive since they use geometric means (a geometric mean of n values is the nth root of the product of those values). Therefore, it is difficult to understand what the metrics mean for real-world environments. For example, if a TPC-D query run time improved from 1,000 seconds to 300 seconds, a welcome speedup, the power metric improved by 7.3%. The nature of a geometric mean is such that a query improvement from 1 second to 0.3 seconds would result in the same power metric improvement, even though it makes little practical difference to an end user. The TPC-R/TPC-H metrics are even more difficult to visualize since they involve geometric means of geometric means.

- The TPC-D throughput metric tended to discourage multistream benchmarks. Most users ran 1 TB database benchmarks with no more than 3 to 10 concurrent users. This low user count is increased with TPC-H, but not significantly. TPC-R is easier to run with more users since it does so much less work. Some DSS environments do involve a handful of power users, but many others are not well represented by the limited user load of TPC-D and TPC-H.

Using TPC-H to Size Real-World DSS Servers

TPC-H does provide engineering data relevant to system sizing for DSS servers along with completion times for each query. Unfortunately, though, the usefulness of this information depends on access to details like query plans and system utilization statistics. Since the TPC-H specification does not require vendors to disclose any of those details, it is extremely difficult to draw useful sizing guidelines from published TPC-H results.

The historical results for some individual TPC-D/TPC-H queries can still yield some useful sizing information for those with access to the necessary background information. Query 1, which has not changed from TPC-D to TPC-H, does illustrate the behavior of a substantial, single-table tablescan with aggregation. Query 1 performance was greatly affected by materialized views toward the end of the TPC-D era, so only TPC-H and early TPC-D results are useful. Query 9, also unchanged in TPC-H, gives some indication of the performance of a complex six-table join. Other queries are of limited usefulness, in my opinion, mainly because their performance was affected over time by the introduction of technologies like concatenated indexes, partition elimination, join indexes, and materialized views. These issues are discussed further in Chapter 27.

The inside information necessary to arrive at a meaningful interpretation of Queries 1 and 9, though, amounts to a hurdle that few are likely to leap. So, as for TPC-R, my advice is "Don't try this at home, folks!"

Using Remote Terminal Emulators

Remote terminal emulators (RTE) are software applications that emulate real user activity, typically on PCs, browsers, or ASCII terminals. Rather than find enough hardware and real users to stress-test an application, it is easier to use an RTE. A number of sophisticated products are available on the market (for example, preVue from Rational). The HandsOff Remote Terminal Emulator, a character-based RTE is available on the book website for both the SPARC and x86 Solaris platforms. Web-based emulators, referred to as Remote Browser Emulators, are becoming available.

Although RTEs are commonly used for benchmarking, they are also useful for profiling applications as they are developed. It is always better to expose bottlenecks before an application goes live. Application profiling or characterization is also used for regression testing (ensuring that functionality and performance are not degraded by a new release of software or hardware). Most large ERP applications (for example, those from SAP and Peoplesoft) have benchmark suites associated with them. These suites have been extremely useful in identifying and fixing bottlenecks before users have discovered them. Unfortunately, many major applications go live without thorough multiuser testing.

If you are developing applications, plan stress tests and regression tests, using an RTE as part of the regular development cycle.

Summary of Rules of Thumb

Some of the rules of thumb presented in this chapter are summarized below.

- Configure 30% more disk capacity than your requirements demand. This additional capacity will allow both for growth and for flexibility in disk layout.

- Disk activity across the full seek range of a 7200 rpm 9-Gbyte disk will allow approximately 75 I/Os per second (IOPS) with seek times of around 30 msec and throughput of around 8.5 Mbyte/sec. Current 18- and 36-Gbyte 10000 rpm disks support in excess of 100 IOPS and 12 to 20 Mbyte/sec, even when the entire disk capacity is in use. These estimates assume small I/Os (2 to 8 Kbytes in size).

- SPARCstorage Arrays can support throughput of around 17 Mbyte/sec. StorEdge A5100 Arrays can support around 90 Mbyte/sec on a single loop. T3 arrays can support up to 100 Mbyte/sec.

- A single SBus is capable of supporting throughput of around 110 Mbyte/sec.

- 400 MHz UltraSPARC CPUs can process around 30 Gbyte/sec through a database by using large I/Os (128 Kbytes or greater).

- The final database size may be three to five times the size of new data, attributable to indexes, temporary tablespace, and logs.

- Configuring required capacity using 18- or 36-Gbyte disks will probably provide adequate performance and price performance for many environments.

- Planning for high availability increases disk capacity requirements by 100% for RAID 1 (mirroring) and by 25% for 4+1 RAID 5 configurations.

- Using client/server to offload applications onto separate systems can reduce CPU requirements on the database server by one-third to one-half. In the case of SAP and other ERP applications, the reduction is much greater.

- Allow 32 to 64 Mbytes for initial database server requirements.
- Allow 32 to 64 Mbytes for initial operating system overheads.
- Allow 2 to 4 Mbytes per user on the client (much more—as much as 10 to 16 Mbytes—for ERP applications) and 1 to 2 Mbytes per user on the database server for OLTP workloads if no better information is available. Add these requirements if using a timeshare configuration.
- Configure buffer cache memory equivalent to 5% to 15% of your database size.
- Avoid using TPC benchmark results for system sizing.

A General-Purpose OLTP Sizing Tool

To illustrate the principles outlined in this chapter, I am including a description of the development of a general-purpose OLTP sizing tool used within Sun to assist systems engineers and sales representatives with OLTP database server sizing. The material that follows is drawn from a paper titled "Developing a General-Purpose OLTP Sizing Tool" (Allan Packer and Brian Wong) delivered at the Computer Measurement Group (CMG) International Conference in Orlando, Florida, in December 2000. The paper is used with the permission of the CMG.

The rationale behind developing an OTLP server sizing tool was simple: sizing is a difficult task, as we have seen, and much useful data gathered within the Sun engineering organization had not found its way to Sun's field organization in a useful format. The issues faced in developing the tool are much the same as those faced by an end user carry out sizing for capacity planning.

Background

In spite of the growing maturity of the open systems community, very little effective capacity planning methodology or knowledge appears to have filtered down to end users. While sizing is recognized as an crucial element in equipment purchase, it is usually left to major independent software vendors (ISVs) to supply some kind of sizing questionnaire or spreadsheet. Even where a sizing method is available, many end users are unable to provide accurate answers to the detailed questions on which the sizing is based. The awful truth is that much open systems server sizing involves far more art than science, with guesswork filling in most of the blanks.

At first glance, the notion of developing a generic sizing tool seems very attractive. Even an estimate with an accuracy of ±30% would be a vast improvement over the "wet finger in the air" alternatives. On the other hand, who wants to steer through treacherous waters already littered with the wrecks of previous explorers? Overambitious goals, false assumptions, inaccurate or incomplete baseline data, and unrealistically complicated models have all contributed to previous failures. Unfortunately, too, some users seem to believe that the reliability of a tool's output is directly proportional to its apparent degree of sophistication and the attractiveness of its user interface. Not surprisingly, expectations are higher when people are given an answer than when they make a guess.

Such risks notwithstanding, we decided to make the attempt. The business risks of inaccurate sizing are such that even a vaguely accurate estimate is better than a guess.

Establishing Metrics

Just as any serious voyage of discovery begins with a review of the known facts and a careful study of the legacy of previous explorers, this project leveraged off the efforts of others. In particular, Brian Wong [Wong 98] developed a set of metrics for describing the utilization of an open system. Some of these metrics, including quanta consumption, relative I/O content, DASD (disk) skew, access density, processing density and data remoteness, were in turn borrowed from a larger set discussed by [Major 91] and [Major 95] in the context of MVS workload characterization. The most important of these terms are briefly described below.

Processing capacity is measured by:

- Quanta consumption, Q, the units of computational power consumed by a given workload. Quanta is not simply a measure of raw CPU power (such as MIPS, for example); it is intended to measure processing power consumed by workloads that exercise the system as a whole. The measurement of quanta is only broadly useful if a method exists (such as a comparative performance table) to uniformly express the processing potential of all systems under investigation.

- Processing potential, M, the processing capability of a system (also known as the M-value). Quanta consumption can be expressed as that proportion of M consumed by a workload ($Q = M \times$ utilization). For example, if a dual-processor 300 MHz system has $M = 6{,}150$, where the units of M are quanta, then the same system running at 72% utilization can be said to be consuming $Q = 6150 \times 0.72 = 4428$ quanta.

Disk I/O is measured using:

- The relative I/O content, a measure of the amount of DASD I/O associated with each part of the workload ($R = S \div Q$, where S is the global number of disk I/Os per second).

- DASD skew, a measure of the imbalance of access across a DASD farm ($Sk = umax \div uaverage$, where u is the utilization of disks, that is, actuators or RAID disk groups).

Further insights are gained by measuring the following:

- Access density, the ratio of I/O activity to the amount of online DASD storage ($AD = S \div NC$, where NC is the net allocated storage capacity in Gbytes).

- Processing density, the ratio of processor activity to DASD net capacity ($PD = Q \div NC$).

- Data remoteness, the relative proportion of host memory to DASD capacity ($DRF = NC \div m$, where m is main memory size in Gbytes).

To these, [Wong 98] added several measures:

- DASD throughput content ($DT = Tdisk \div Q$, where $Tdisk$ is the global DASD I/O bandwidth consumed by the workload).

- Relative network content ($N = P \div Q$, where P is the systemwide sum of transmitted and received packets on all physical network interfaces).

- Network throughput content ($NT = Tnet \div Q$, where $Tnet$ is the global network bandwidth consumed, measured in Kbytes per second).

We decided to use these metrics as the starting point in measuring workload behavior.

The Search for Simplifying Assumptions

There are many ways to try to model workloads. Taking a view from 20,000 feet, if you know a typical value for processing density for a given workload, you can predict CPU requirements from the disk storage requirements. At the other extreme, if you know the detailed CPU and I/O footprint of each individual business transaction on the system to be sized, you can start to build up a picture for a workload as a whole.

There may, of course, be big differences in nature and scope between a business transaction and a database transaction. A complex Online Transaction Processing (OLTP) business transaction such as a sales order, for example, can involve many database transactions. One simplification expresses business transactions in terms of their CPU requirements and the number and type of logical I/Os for each type of database transaction (for example, update, insert, select, and delete).

Another possibility builds a baseline by analyzing the transactions for a known workload, such as the Transaction Processing Performance Council's industry-standard OLTP workload,[1] TPC-C, then attempting to relate each transaction in the new workload to one of the known TPC-C transactions. With this in mind, we analyzed in detail the logical I/O behavior for each TPC-C transaction during the exploratory stages of this project and verified our analysis by using data collected during several TPC-C benchmarks.

---

1. See http://www.tpc.org. The TPC-C specification is also available at this site (http://www.tpc.org/cspec.html). TPC-C is a registered trademark of the Transaction Processing Performance Council (TPC).

The greatest difficulty of a complex model, though, is that considerable detail is required to use it. Many end users are unable to supply the logical I/O and CPU breakdown for their business transactions; a surprising number are unable even to supply a detailed count of business transactions processed during a given time period. The likelihood that end users will lack detailed information prompted the decision to work with a model based on a fairly simple set of assumptions.

Gathering the Raw Data

Before a sizing model can be built, two types of raw data are needed to underpin it. First, the capacity and performance characteristics of systems and key system components must be identified. This means the number of CPUs supported by a particular server must be known, along with the clock speed and external cache size of all available processors. In addition, for each type of storage array, the capacity, throughput, and number of I/Os per second (IOPS) must be known for both the disks and the storage array as a whole. Where multiple arrays can be shared on a single controller, the scalability of IOPS and throughput also must be taken into account.

Brian Wong went further than merely describing a set of metrics; he compiled an exhaustive table of *M*-values both for current and older Sun systems in use at customer sites. This was not a trivial exercise. Processing potential depends on a number of factors, ranging from the operating system release to the backplane bus characteristics in addition to the obvious effect of the number and speed of CPUs. Furthermore, workload scalability as CPUs are added depends on the nature of the workload as well as the capabilities of the hardware, so no single model of scalability applies to all workloads. This necessitated finding a reasonable approximation given the kind of workloads typical for Sun servers. The result was the computation of an *M*-value for every unique combination of the following factors:

- Sun system family (for example, Ultra10™ desktop, Enterprise 450™ server, Enterprise 10000™ server)
- Type of CPU (including clock speed and external cache size)
- Number of CPUs
- Operating system release

M-values have achieved sufficient acceptance within Sun to ensure they will be maintained as new hardware and operating system releases become available.

The availability of *M*-values for every Sun system removed one significant hurdle in the path of a sizing tool: finding a consistent way of ranking the processing capabilities of different systems. Disk performance characteristics proved more challenging. Although a wealth of information was available, much of it was unsuitable for sizing purposes and further research proved necessary. The specific data finally collated comprises the following metrics:

- Number of disks and formatted (usable) disk capacity in Gbytes for each array type.
- IOPS, based on full-stroke random reads and writes of small block sizes, and throughput capacity, based on sequential reads and writes of larger block sizes, for each type of disk. "Full stroke" refers to I/O access that spans the entire disk surface, thus exercising the entire seek range of the disk.
- IOPS and throughput capacity for each type of array.
- Scalability for IOPS and throughput for each type of array as multiple arrays are added to the same controller.
- Hardware RAID support for each type of disk array.

A second type of data is needed before a model can be established: detailed transaction workload data showing both transaction rates and the system load associated with the transactions. A sizing tool intended to be generally applicable for OLTP workloads should draw upon reference data from a number of different workloads. As a first step, we calculated the metrics discussed above, using workload data from several sources:

- A large number of TPC-C results on different Sun hardware platforms and different databases over a period of years.
- The results of internal workloads based on real-world financials applications and data.
- A small number of customer sites that had provided detailed data.

In each case, we needed access to hardware configuration details in addition to detailed system utilization and transaction throughput data.

Asking the Right Questions

One of the first pieces of sizing information typically offered by customers is the number of users to be supported. While the user count might seem an obvious foundation on which to build a sizing model, there are a number of problems with it:

- A "user" can be an executive making occasional inquiries, a data entry clerk using the system constantly, or a power user firing off resource-hogging batch jobs.
- Not all customers understand the distinction between connected and concurrent users. The definition of "concurrent" also varies widely.
- A user session can involve more than one stream of execution if multiple active application connections have been established.
- Even if all types of users can be profiled accurately, seasonal business activity can result in fluctuations in the productivity, and hence system resource requirements, of some or all users.

For all these reasons, we decided that the transaction rate offered a more interesting measure of user-generated load. The transaction rate finally settled on was business transactions rather than lower-level alternatives such as database transactions. Business transactions are more likely to be counted and understood by end users.

Building a Model

Once we decided to use the transaction rate as the foundation of the sizing model, the next step was to examine the data from the available workloads to characterize their behavior. The *M*-value for each system configuration was combined with the known CPU utilization (either at a point of sustained peak throughput or averaged over a period of steady-state processing) to calculate *Q*, the quanta consumed. The quanta consumed per transaction was calculated next, leading to a new metric:

- Quanta consumed per TPM ($Qt = Q \div TPM$, where *TPM* is transactions per minute)

The *Qt* calculated for the TPC-C results proved reasonably consistent across time, hardware platforms, and databases (within ±15%, apart from one outlier). Nevertheless, the real-world workload data showed quanta consumption per transaction two orders of magnitude greater than that for TPC-C.

The magnitude of the difference between real-world and TPC-C transactions may be significant, but the fact that a difference existed is not surprising since business transactions vary greatly in their resource consumption. We decided to include as an input to the sizing process a percentage breakdown between lightweight, middleweight, and heavyweight transactions. These classifications were intended as a simple way of breaking down the range of transactions represented by our sample; the choice of thresholds was arbitrary. A workload investigated later in the study included transactions off the scale of our original classification, necessitating the addition of a very heavyweight category. While this approach is far from precise, the reality in many cases is that the greater the detail in the questions, the more guesswork goes into answering them, undermining any appearance of greater accuracy.

This led to the following equation to calculate the quanta required:

- $Q = TPM \times (Light\%*cpuL + Medium\%*cpuM + Heavy\%*cpuH + Very\text{-}Heavy\%*cpuV)$

where

  cpuL = CPU load factor for lightweight transactions

  cpuM = CPU load factor for middleweight transactions

  cpuH = CPU load factor for heavyweight transactions

  cpuV = CPU load factor for very heavyweight transactions

***Equation 1.* Simple calculation for predicted quanta requirements**

The CPU load factor determinations were based on the available workload data.

To illustrate the coarse granularity of the model, based on a detailed analysis of logical I/Os, we characterized TPC-C transactions as 96% lightweight and 4% middleweight (the stock-level transaction). Note that the TPC-C benchmark contains no heavyweight or very heavyweight transactions by our criteria.

We used a similar approach in developing equations for the following:

- S, the global I/Os per second.

- $Tdisk$, the global disk throughput in Kbytes per second.

- m, the main memory in Gbytes.

Additional metrics became necessary to assist in the process of understanding the workload data:

- St, the global disk I/Os per transaction
  $(St = S \times 60 \div TPM)$

- Ts, the global disk I/O bandwidth consumed per disk I/O
  $(Ts = Tdisk \div S)$

- Rwt, the read/write throughput ratio
  $(Rwt = Tdisk(Read) \div Tdisk(Write))$

- Rws, the read/write global disk I/O ratio
  $(Rws = S(Read) \div S(Write))$

- mt, the main memory per transaction
  $(mt = m \div TPM)$

Given the discrepancy between the CPU cost per transaction for TPC-C and real-world workloads, it is not surprising that St, the global disk I/Os per transaction, was significantly lower for TPC-C than for real-world workloads. TPC-C still manages to consume large systems—it compensates for the lightweight nature of its transactions by huge increases in the transaction rate.

Over a period of time the complexity of the model gradually increased to take into account the following additional elements:

- The level of application optimization (low, medium, or high). This parameter was necessary to account for the differing amounts of effort applied to optimizing workloads. TPC-C, for example, is an example of a highly optimized workload, whereas many customer workloads are poorly optimized. ISV applications are often somewhere in the middle.

- The use of forms software in application design. Commercial forms software requires considerably more CPU and memory resource per seat than does a lightweight library like curses. TPC-C is even more lightweight, with its block-mode approach to terminal input.

- Client/server-based deployment of applications (applications run on separate client systems) versus timeshare (applications run on the database server).

- The use of transaction monitors. Transaction monitors allow users to be multiplexed via queues, thereby considerably reducing the server-side CPU and memory resource requirement.

- The deployment of database files on Unix file systems or raw devices.

- The background batch workload, if any, classified as either none, light, medium, heavy, or very heavy.

- The desired maximum CPU utilization.

- The expected growth in the workload prior to the next hardware upgrade.

Each of these elements acquired an associated CPU load factor and, in some cases, an IOPS, throughput, or memory load factor as well. So the final equation for predicted quanta requirements looked something like this:

- $Q = TPM \times$
  $(Light\%*cpuL + Medium\%*cpuM + Heavy\%*cpuH + VeryHeavy\%*cpuV)$
  $\times (Element1*LoadFactor1) + (Element2*LoadFactor2) + ...$
  $+ (ElementN*LoadFactorN))$

Equation 2. Final calculation for predicted quanta requirements

Deriving the load factors for each of these elements was only possible by individually characterizing their impact on workload performance. We achieved this characterization by using benchmarks designed to vary only the element under consideration. In some cases workload data was already available, in some cases it became available during the course of developing the model, and in other cases it was necessary to carry out research.

The number of users is requested but does not play a significant role in the sizing calculation. Metrics added to account for users were:

- CU, the number of connected users.

- Qu, the quanta consumed per connected user ($Qu = Q \div CU$).

- $TPMu$, the transaction rate per connected user ($TPMu = TPM \div CU$). This value provided a reality check by giving feedback about whether the supplied transaction rate per user was low, high, or average.

- Su, the global disk I/Os per connected user ($Su = S \div CU$).

The disk storage capacity increase from indexes, temporary tablespaces, logs, rollback segments, and growth requirements was modeled along with the impact of using RAID technologies. If RAID is implemented in hardware, additional I/Os and throughput are seen by the storage array but not by the operating system. By contrast, software RAID results in the additional load being seen by both the operating system and the storage array. These effects were researched and taken into account in the model.

Memory consumption proved the most difficult to model. Although actual CPU consumption, disk I/O, and throughput statistics were available, accurate memory consumption statistics were not—only the total amount of main memory in the system. It is likely that in at least some cases more memory had been installed than was actually necessary, making it difficult to arrive at a model that predicted memory requirements matching the main memory found in the systems. The database size, where available, was one of the factors eventually used in estimating main memory size requirements.

Validating the Model

Having built a detailed model, it was important to validate it against the known data points. For each workload the known requirements were compared to the calculated requirements for each of the following:

- Quanta (processing requirement).
- Global I/Os per second.
- Global disk throughput per second.
- Main memory.

The comparison showed occasional outliers, but the bulk of the predicted results fell within −5% to +30% of the actual results for Q and ±20% for global I/Os per second. This result was better than expected. Most global throughput and main memory calculations were better than ±30%, an informal boundary for acceptable results set at the start of the exercise. Rather than evenly spreading Q estimation errors, we deliberately designed the model to push Q errors into the positive range, meaning that recommended values for Q were overstated rather than understated compared to actual values. We thought a slightly oversized system was preferable to any kind of undersized system.

As a reality check, we visited a live installation and fed its workload data into the model to compare predicted versus actual results. This comparison necessitated some adjustment of the factors, but the basic approach worked. Further work is required to validate and tune the model more fully. The estimation errors for some of the data points are plotted in Figure 1.

Figure 1   *Estimation errors for the OLTP sizing model*

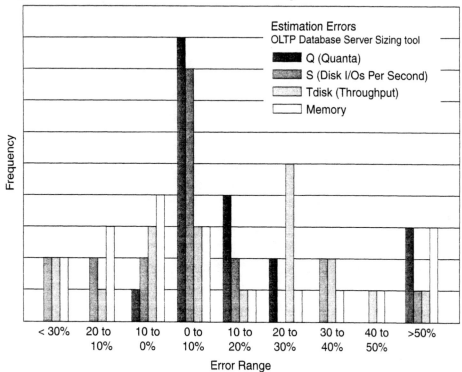

The Resulting Tool

We built a tool by using an HTML user interface with CGI scripts on the back end. The *M*-values were stored in a database; once the required quanta was calculated using the model described above, a small number of systems with equal or greater processing potential could easily be retrieved as recommendations.

To further enhance the tool, we later wrote a disk-sizing module, using the CLIPS expert system language, and called it from the CGI script. The disk-sizing module took as inputs the required IOPS and throughput, information about workload characteristics (used to determine the relative importance of IOPS and throughput), any hardware RAID requirements, and the importance of price. The module used knowledge about available Sun storage arrays to recommend the solutions that best fit the requirements.

No attempt was made to enforce system configuration rules; we assumed any selection from the suggested systems and storage arrays would be validated by existing configuration tools.

We later enhanced the tool outputs with disk layout recommendations tailored to the specified environment and suggested `init.ora` settings for Oracle users. A further enhancement was to build a Java applet version of the tool with the Swing library, which offered a more user friendly interface. The ability to print or email the results was included in the Java version. Initial user feedback has been positive. The introductory screen of the tool is shown in Figure 2.

One critical objective was to fully document the data supplied by the user, the assumptions made by the tool, and the tool's recommendations. Documenting the inputs and assumptions does not resolve the classic Garbage In / Garbage Out problem, but it does at least provide a reference point for the future if the model estimates are shown to be misleading.

Figure 2   *The introductory screen of the OLTP sizing tool*

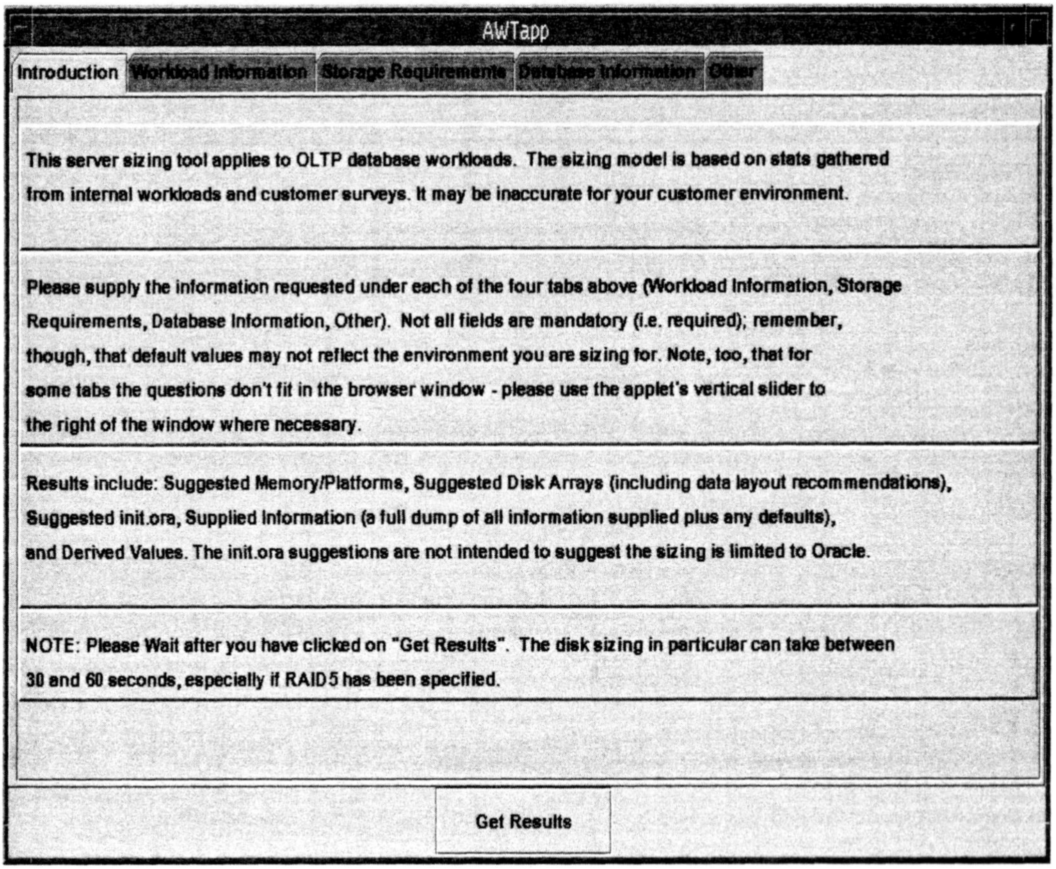

Conclusions

The process of developing a general-purpose OLTP sizing tool proved as complex as expected. The validation phase showed better than expected results, although the outliers suggest that any sizing recommendation could still prove to be significantly inaccurate. Of course, any margin of error in the tool's recommendations may well be small compared to inaccuracies in the information supplied to the tool. The users of the tool will be the ultimate judges as to its usefulness.

One key challenge is to follow sizing recommendations through to implementation. Such a feedback loop would provide the best validation, not just of the tool, but of the accuracy of the input data.

In conclusion, it is to be expected that as the open systems market matures, more sophisticated methods for system sizing than this tool will quickly become available.

Bibliography

[Wong 98] Wong, Brian, "Characterizing Open Systems Workloads and Comparing Them With MVS," *Proceedings of the Computer Measurement Group*, 1998.

[Major 91] Major, J. B., "Resource Usage Metrics and Trends: Host Systems," *Proceedings of the Computer Measurement Group*, p. 76, 1991.

[Major 95] Major, J. B., "Mainframe Resource Usage Relationships Evolution," *Proceedings of the Computer Measurement Group*, p. 242, 1994.

14

CONFIGURING SYSTEMS

It is a mistake to think you can buy a computer system, install and populate a database, and magically achieve optimal performance. Given the capabilities of modern computer systems, you might reasonably expect efficient performance out of the box. While that is the goal, we're not there yet.

The Solaris Operating Environment is not the main culprit for the configuration workload; in fact, we will see that very little Solaris configuration is necessary. The main issue is efficient data layout, although there are a number of other items on the checklist.

The next few chapters address in turn the technologies and techniques available for:

- Configuring the Solaris Operating Environment
- Configuring memory
- Configuring CPUs
- Configuring networks
- Effective data layout strategies

201

Solaris Configuration

As we have seen in Chapter 3, the Solaris Operating Environment offers many features that help database performance, including Kernel Asynchronous I/O (KAIO), `pread` and `pwrite`, preemption control, and intimate shared memory (ISM). However, all of the major databases already take advantage of all or most of these capabilities on Solaris. Apart from the CPU, memory, and data layout issues already discussed, tuning Solaris for database servers simply involves the following actions:

- Setting appropriate shared memory, semaphore, and message queue parameters in `/etc/system`.

- Ensuring that the Starfire dispatch table for the TimeShare scheduling class is enabled. This issue is discussed under "The TS Class" on page 220.

The default Solaris shared memory, semaphore, and message queue parameters need to be changed before any of the major databases can be used. Most of these parameters do not impact performance. Instead, they are necessary to ensure that Solaris does not run out of key shared memory, semaphores, and message queue resources. If these resources are not available, it is often impossible even to start the database. In most cases, it is advisable to simply set the parameters high.

For DSS applications, it is useful to be able to do large I/Os. Oracle8.0 supports reads of up to 512 Kbytes, and Oracle8i supports 1-Mbyte reads. To enable Solaris to support 1-Mbyte reads, use the following in `/etc/system`:

```
set maxphys = 1048576
```

Where Veritas Volume Manager is installed, it is important to set `vxio:vol_maxio` to `2048` to allow 1-Mbyte asynchronous I/Os and to prevent large asynchronous I/Os from being turned into synchronous I/Os.

Figure 14.1 shows a sample `/etc/system` file.

Figure 14.1 *Sample /etc/system file*

```
* Remove the following 2 lines for UFS database files
set tune_t_fsflushr = 50
set autoup = 300

* Increase the default no. of ptys (requires a "boot -r")
set pt_cnt=1024

* Message queue parameters (needed by DB2)
set msgsys:msginfo_msgmax = 65535
set msgsys:msginfo_msgmnb = 65535
set msgsys:msginfo_msgmap = 3002
set msgsys:msginfo_msgmni = 2000
```

```
set msgsys:msginfo_msgssz = 16
set msgsys:msginfo_msgtql = 8192
set msgsys:msginfo_msgseg = 16384

* Semaphore parameters
set semsys:seminfo_semmap = 1026
set semsys:seminfo_semmsl = 300
set semsys:seminfo_semmns = 2500
set semsys:seminfo_semmnu = 2500
set semsys:seminfo_semume = 2500
set semsys:seminfo_semmni = 2500
set semsys:seminfo_semopm = 150

* Shared memory parameters
set shmsys:shminfo_shmmax=0xFFFFFFFF
set shmsys:shminfo_shmmni=1024
set shmsys:shminfo_shmseg=48

* Solaris max I/O size (in bytes)
set maxphys = 1048576

* Veritas max I/O size (in 512-byte blocks)
set vxio:vol_maxio=2048

* Switch on priority paging (pre-Solaris 8)
* (Only for Solaris 2.5.1, 2.6 and 7)
set priority_paging=1

* The following lines are automatically
* inserted by SVM and Veritas
* Begin MDD database info (do not edit)
set md:mddb_bootlist1="ssd:3552:16 ssd:3056:16 ssd:3032:16"
* End MDD database info (do not edit)

* vxvm_START (do not remove)
forceload: drv/vxdmp
forceload: drv/vxio
forceload: drv/vxspec
* vxvm_END (do not remove)
```

Priority paging prevents application pages being displaced to free up room for UFS cache pages. It is especially important to protect application pages when database files are placed on Unix file systems because available memory is in demand as UFS pages are constantly brought into the UFS buffer cache in main memory. OS patches are available to add priority paging for Solaris 2.5.1 and Solaris 2.6. Priority paging ships as standard as of Solaris 7, but you must explicitly enable it. From Solaris 8 onward, changes to the Solaris virtual memory subsystem render priority paging unnecessary, so don't enable it. Refer to "Optimal Performance on File Systems" on page 245 for more information on priority paging.

The `tune_t_fsflushr` and `autoup` parameters reduce the rate at which the fsflush daemon checks and flushes memory. If you use raw devices for database files, you can increase these parameters from the defaults (the example above shows values that are 10 times the default).

The `pt_cnt` parameter increases the number of ptys (and hence telnet sessions) beyond the default of 48. A reboot with the `-r` parameter is necessary before any change takes effect since the /devices tree is affected. It is not necessary to set this parameter for Solaris 8 and later releases.

Representative shared memory, semaphore, and message queue parameters are shown in the preceding example. Most databases will boot and run with these settings. Note that there is no memory penalty for setting `shmmax` to its maximum possible setting. The `shmmax` parameter should be further increased for 64-bit systems.

Finally, Solaris Volume Manager and Veritas Volume Manager parameters will appear in the `/etc/system` file, as shown, if these volume managers are in use—do not edit these variables!

In conclusion, Solaris tunables are relatively simple to manage. Once set, they rarely need to be revisited.

Memory Interleaving

For optimal performance, memory should be interleaved as much as possible. Interleaving in this context refers to the system carrying out a single physical memory access using more than one memory bank. It is a memory equivalent of disk striping and, like disk striping, can boost overall system performance. Memory striping can enhance performance by a small percentage, and the benefit increases as the number of memory banks and the memory capacity increase.

Memory interleaving typically requires memory banks to be filled with memory of the same density. A system with a mix of memory densities is still able to use interleaving by linking only those banks filled with memory of the same density. The end result, though, is likely to be a lower level of interleaving than can be achieved with memory of uniform density.

A single system board typically supports more than one memory bank, and hence interleaving is possible even within the same board.

The Starfire (Enterprise 10000) automatically uses either 2-way or 4-way interleaving on system boards, depending on the memory density. Interleaving memory across boards provides no performance benefit on the Starfire and is not supported because of the limitations it would place on dynamic reconfiguration (DR).

The Enterprise 3x00 to 6x00 range of servers supports up to 2-way interleaving within a system board, and the more recent Sun Fire server range supports up to 16-way interleaving within a system board. For these servers, too, the use of memory interleaving precludes DR operations. Where DR is needed, its benefits will outweigh the performance penalty associated with the loss of memory interleaving.

Benefits of Memory Interleaving

When DR is not required, a performance benefit is available through memory interleaving. As the amount of physical memory increases, the benefits of interleaving also increase. Tests within Database Engineering on Enterprise servers have shown increases in throughput ranging from around 5% at 4 CPUs with 4 Gbytes of memory (4-way interleaving) up to 14% at 24 CPUs with 24 Gbytes of memory (16-way and 8-way interleaving) compared to no interleaving at all.

Evaluation of Interleaving

Use /usr/platform/`arch -k`/sbin/prtdiag to check interleaving.

Figure 14.2 shows the best memory interleaving achievable with three banks of memory on an Enterprise 3500 server.

Figure 14.2 *Memory interleaving on an E3500 with 3 Gbytes of memory*

```
========================= Memory =========================


                                                  Intrlv. Intrlv.

 Brd   Bank   MB    Status   Condition  Speed     Factor   With

 ---   ----   ----  -------  ---------- -----     -------   ----

   5    0    1024   Active      OK      60 ns     2-way      A

   7    0    1024   Active      OK      60 ns     2-way      A

   7    1    1024   Active      OK      60 ns     1-way
```

If more system boards were available, then either low density SIMMs or more memory would allow better interleaving (up to 8-way with four system boards). Note that interleaving is possible even within one system board, provided the memory in each bank is the same density.

Up to 16-way is achievable across eight system boards. Figure 14.3 shows an example based on an Enterprise 6500.

Figure 14.3 *Memory interleaving on an E6500 with 24 Gbytes of memory*

```
========================= Memory =========================

                                                 Intrlv.  Intrlv.
  Brd   Bank   MB    Status   Condition  Speed    Factor    With
  ---   ----   ----  -------  ---------- -----    -------   ----
   0     0     1024  Active      OK      60 ns    16-way     A
   0     1     1024  Active      OK      60 ns    16-way     A
   2     0     1024  Active      OK      60 ns    16-way     A
   2     1     1024  Active      OK      60 ns    16-way     A
   4     0     1024  Active      OK      60 ns    16-way     A
   4     1     1024  Active      OK      60 ns    16-way     A
   6     0     1024  Active      OK      60 ns    16-way     A
   6     1     1024  Active      OK      60 ns    16-way     A
   8     0     1024  Active      OK      60 ns    16-way     A
   8     1     1024  Active      OK      60 ns     8-way     B
   9     0     1024  Active      OK      60 ns    16-way     A
   9     1     1024  Active      OK      60 ns     8-way     B
  10     0     1024  Active      OK      60 ns    16-way     A
  10     1     1024  Active      OK      60 ns     8-way     B
  11     0     1024  Active      OK      60 ns    16-way     A
  11     1     1024  Active      OK      60 ns     8-way     B
  12     0     1024  Active      OK      60 ns    16-way     A
  12     1     1024  Active      OK      60 ns     8-way     B
  13     0     1024  Active      OK      60 ns    16-way     A
  13     1     1024  Active      OK      60 ns     8-way     B
  14     0     1024  Active      OK      60 ns    16-way     A
  14     1     1024  Active      OK      60 ns     8-way     B
  15     0     1024  Active      OK      60 ns    16-way     A
  15     1     1024  Active      OK      60 ns     8-way     B
```

An EEPROM setting determines whether memory interleaving should be used on an Enterprise 3x00 to 6x00 server. Use `eeprom -v` to check the `interleave-memory` setting. A value of `max` means that memory interleaving across system boards will be used; `min` means it will not.

Finally, Figure 14.4 shows memory interleaving on a Sun Fire 3800 with 4 Gbytes of memory.

Figure 14.4 *Memory interleaving on an F3800 with 4 Gbytes of memory*

```
======================== Memory Configuration ====================

             Logical Logical Logical
             Port Bank  Bank    Bank     DIMM Interleave Interleave
FRU Name      ID  Num   Size   Status    Size   Factor    Segment
-------------  ---  ---  ------ ------   -----  ------    -------
/N0/SB2/P0/B0   8    0   512 MB  pass   256 MB  8-way        0
/N0/SB2/P0/B0   8    2   512 MB  pass   256 MB  8-way        0
/N0/SB2/P1/B0   9    0   512 MB  pass   256 MB  8-way        0
/N0/SB2/P1/B0   9    2   512 MB  pass   256 MB  8-way        0
/N0/SB2/P2/B0  10    0   512 MB  pass   256 MB  8-way        0
/N0/SB2/P2/B0  10    2   512 MB  pass   256 MB  8-way        0
/N0/SB2/P3/B0  11    0   512 MB  pass   256 MB  8-way        0
/N0/SB2/P3/B0  11    2   512 MB  pass   256 MB  8-way        0
```

The example shows 8-way interleaving within a single Sun Fire board (up to 16-way interleaving can be achieved).

15

CONFIGURING CPU

The Solaris Operating Environment effectively manages database workloads running on multiple CPUs without the need for system administrator intervention.

But for those willing to do some exploration, there may be low-hanging fruit ripe for the plucking in the area of configuring CPUs for performance. And sophisticated technologies are now available to help in the task of workload management.

Managing Workloads

In this section we discuss aspects of managing workloads: domains, processor sets, and resource management (with Solaris Resource Manager).

Domains

The ability to partition the Starfire (Enterprise 10000) into separate systems, or domains, was undoubtedly one of the features contributing to the remarkable success of that server. The domain capability has since made its way onto the next generation of Sun servers, the Sun Fire family.

A domain functions like a separate server in that it runs its own operating system instance and sees only the memory and disks within the domain. It is even electrically isolated from other domains. Thanks to dynamic reconfiguration, though, CPUs, memory, disks, and networks can be moved from one domain to another, adding a degree of flexibility not available on separate servers. Dynamic reconfiguration allows system administrators to manage processing peaks more efficiently by temporarily transferring system resources from a less critical or underutilized domain, such as training.

Domains are often used to separate workloads of different types, such as OLTP and DSS, or to support independent development, testing, training, and production systems on the same server.

Processor Sets

Processor sets are much simpler than domains and allow a system to be actively partitioned with respect to CPU usage only. On a six-CPU system, for example, a processor set with four CPUs can be created for online applications while the remaining two CPUs are left for batch applications. Application processes bound to a particular processor set will be restricted to consuming CPU resources belonging to that set. Child processes inherit the processor set binding and so remain within the same processor set. Separating the OLTP workload allows the response times of online users to be protected by preventing the batch workload, which has no think time, from consuming all available CPU.

You might expect that partitioning CPU resources alone would provide only a partial solution. The system load caused by batch applications, for example, often has as much to do with the considerable disk I/O generated as with application CPU utilization. Processor sets can prove surprisingly effective, though, as we will see.

It is very simple to dynamically reconfigure processor sets, so CPUs can be almost instantly transferred between processor sets, or new processor sets can be created as application resource requirements change. On the other hand, CPU resources may be poorly utilized unless processor sets are monitored and reconfigured as required. There is little value in having one processor set running at full CPU capacity while another is idle. Solaris Resource Manager (SRM), discussed later, does a better job at dynamically managing the CPU requirements of changing workloads.

Processor sets are created and managed with the psrset(1M) command. Only the superuser can create processor sets. All CPUs except one can be assigned to a processor set. So to set up two equal-sized processor sets for an eight-CPU system, it is simplest to create one processor set with four CPUs and allow the other four to remain as a "virtual" processor set.

Unlike domains, processor sets do not allow total partitioning of applications. Applications generate interrupts (for example, to handle disk and network I/O) that may be handled in another processor set. This behavior occurs because the I/O driver for each device (such as a disk or an Ethernet controller) is bound automatically by the OS to a CPU at boot time. This binding may not be permanent, either, since the drivers are rebalanced automatically across available CPUs whenever CPUs are turned on or off, for example, by psradm.

For this reason an application may indirectly consume CPU time in another processor set if it requires I/O on devices whose drivers are bound to CPUs in other processor sets.

As of Solaris 7, interrupts can be turned off for a given processor set. The -f option of the psrset command is used to disable interrupts, with the -n option enabling interrupts again. This allows applications to be isolated more effectively than if the CPUs in a processor set were also required to process interrupts. Before turning off interrupts on a large scale, though, bear in mind that some CPUs still need to be available to carry out interrupt processing.

Another key difference between domains and processor sets is that a single OS image is shared across all processor sets. Consequently, kernel CPU activity is carried out on behalf of all active processes and as such cannot be distributed among processor sets.

Nonetheless, processor sets are very effective at partitioning application workloads. The following example is based on the combined TPC-C / TPC-D benchmark published by Sun in November 1997. Both TPC-C and TPC-D (described in Chapter 27) were run on the same system at the same time (the system was an E6000 with 16 CPUs running Solaris 2.6)—a first in the industry and an achievement that has never been repeated (up to the time this book went to press at least). Each workload used eight CPUs and 5 Gbytes of memory. The CPUs were allocated as two processor sets of eight CPUs each: one processor set was created with eight CPUs and the remaining eight CPUs formed a "virtual" processor set. The TPC-C applications were bound to the created processor set, and the TPC-D applications ran in the remaining CPUs.

TPC-C in particular requires consistent throughput during the steady-state period. The CPUs servicing disk interrupts on behalf of the TPC-C workload were identified during a warm-up run by use of mpstat to monitor the interrupts. These CPUs (seven of them as it turned out) were then allocated to the TPC-C processor set. As a result, the entire TPC-C workload, including related disk interrupts, ran inside one processor set. When TPC-D was started, it turned out that a small proportion of the disk interrupts from the TPC-D workload were also serviced by CPUs inside the TPC-C processor set, but the impact was not noticeable.

The TPC-C throughput graph for the published run is shown in Figure 15.1, followed by a TPC-C throughput graph for a similar run without using processor sets (Figure 15.2).

Figure 15.1 *TPC-C throughput, with TPC-D in another processor set*

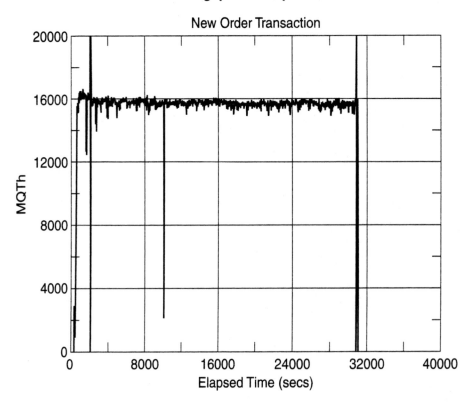

The dip in the graph at around 10,000 seconds was due to a disk error (a recoverable error, thankfully!).

Figure 15.2 *TPC-C throughput, with TPC-D running but no processor sets*

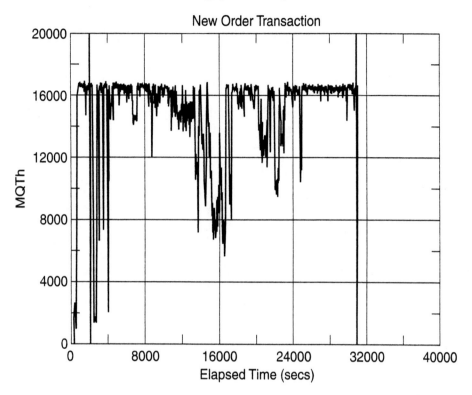

Throughput vs. Elapsed Time

With no processor sets, TPC-C throughput was not protected from the peaks and troughs in the CPU consumption of the TPC-D workload (unlike the case with TPC-C, CPU usage by TPC-D was not uniform). The result was unpredictable behavior. The TPC-C throughput was higher for much of the time but dipped dramatically at other times, sometimes for considerable periods. Significantly degraded response times were associated with the dips in throughput.

Resource Management

Until Solaris 9, Solaris Resource Manager (SRM) 1.x offers the most effective method of dynamically dividing CPU resources among users and applications.

Note: Solaris 2.6 requires SRM 1.0, Solaris 7 requires SRM 1.1, and Solaris 8 requires SRM 1.2.

Each user in the /etc/passwd file (plus active users connected by NIS or other means) is assigned an *lnode*. The lnode extends the properties associated with a user by adding resource allocations for CPU, virtual memory, and the number of active processes.

The virtual memory allocation and number of active processes for an lnode can only be controlled by an upper limit that is set. The virtual memory limit prevents applications with memory leaks from consuming all available swap space. Use virtual memory limits with caution, though; a limit set too low could prevent a well-behaved application from functioning. In a database environment, this functionality could prove to be a problem. If a database for some reason exceeds its allocation, it is likely to crash, and the cause of the crash may not be immediately obvious. We strongly advise users to avoid using virtual memory limits with databases. The same caution applies to setting limits on the number of active processes.

Increased Flexibility with Groups and Users

CPU resource management is more flexible: *shares* are allocated to each lnode, representing the amount of CPU resource available to the user if required. The share is a proportion rather than a percentage, since the total number of shares allocated does not have to equal 100.

You manage shares in groups by setting up a hierarchical structure of lnodes. For example, staff members reporting to a manager can have their lnodes grouped under the lnode of the manager. Figure 15.3 illustrates a hierarchical lnode structure with a manager and three employees.

Figure 15.3 *A hierarchical lnode structure*

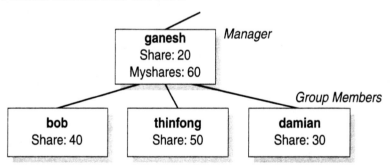

In this example, the CPU allocation for the whole group is determined by the 20 shares assigned to Ganesh's lnode. Within the group, members each have their own share, and since the group lnode might also have active processes, a *myshare* setting is used to determine Ganesh's share relative to the other group members. The total shares within the group are 60 + 40 + 50 + 30 = 180, and the *myshare* setting entitles Ganesh to 60/180, or one-third, of the allocation for the group.

To determine the effective proportion of Ganesh's 20 shares compared to other users on the system, the shares of all other groups or users would need to be considered. This calculation can become quite challenging to perform with a multilevel hierarchy.

A GUI tool, `srmtool`, is available on the book website. The tool includes pie charts showing the effective percentage of total CPU to which a group and its users are entitled, and also plots the actual CPU used by currently active users. The tool works with SRM 1.x and generally simplifies the use and administration of SRM.

Management of Multiple Database Instances

There are occasions when multiple applications share the same UNIX user ID (for example, multiple database instances). You can start the first instance with one share allocation and start the second under the same user ID with a different share allocation by attaching it to a different lnode, using the `srmuser` command. The result is that the two instances are managed independently by SRM.

To illustrate the use of SRM with databases, consider an example where a database administrator wants to start two Oracle instances under the same `oracle` user, but give different resource allocations to each instance.

One possible solution is to start the first `oracle` instance under the `oracle` user lnode, then start the other instance using the lnode and associated shares of a second user. For the second user we will use `otheruser`, where `otheruser` can either be a real user or a virtual user set up specifically for this purpose. In either event, `otheruser` should have a valid entry in the `/etc/passwd` file.

The first step is to make sure that the `oracle` user has permission to start applications under the `otheruser` lnode. You do this by carrying out the following steps (as superuser).

- Make `oracle` the scheduling group parent of `otheruser` by attaching the `otheruser` lnode to the `oracle` lnode:

    ```
    oracle% limadm set sgroup=oracle otheruser
    ```

- Give the `oracle` user permission to launch applications under other lnodes within its group:

    ```
    oracle% limadm set flag.admin=set oracle
    ```

Suppose the `oracle` instances are to be started with scripts called `oracle_start_script1` and `oracle_start_script2`. Start the first instance in the following way:

```
oracle% oracle_start_script1
```

Start the second instance under `otheruser`'s lnode:

```
oracle% srmuser otheruser oracle_start_script2
```

In this case, though, any later `sqlplus` session launched from the `oracle` user and connected to the second instance will still use the `oracle` lnode and the shares associated with it. The reason for this behavior is that the `sqlplus` session is forked from a shell owned by the `oracle` user and running under its lnode, not by an Oracle system process running under the `otheruser` lnode. The shadow process is forked by the new `sqlplus` process and so it will also run under the `oracle` lnode, even though the shadow process is owned by `otheruser`. You can ensure that an `sqlplus` session and its shadow process also run under `otheruser` in the following way:

```
oracle% srmuser otheruser sqlplus scott/tiger
```

Another simple way of starting both `oracle` and subsequent `sqlplus` sessions using a different lnode is with the following steps:

```
oracle% srmuser otheruser /bin/csh
oracle% oracle_start_script2
oracle% sqlplus scott/tiger
```

Anything started under the new `csh` will inherit the lnode settings for `otheruser`.

Users connecting remotely under Oracle Net will inherit whichever lnode was used to start the listener (`lsnrctl`). To run remote users under the `otheruser` lnode, simply start the listener as follows:

```
oracle% srmuser otheruser lsnrctl start
```

If multiple instances are being used under different lnodes, a separate listener must also be started under each lnode to ensure that incoming sessions share the same lnode and associated shares as the instance.

Note that SRM 1.x is not supported with Oracle's Database Resource Manager capability, first released with Oracle8i. Oracle supports the use of SRM 1.x with Oracle provided all processes within the same `oracle` instance share the same lnode (changing the relative priorities of some processes within a single instance can have unpredictable results).

Benefits of SRM Share Allocations

Share allocations guarantee users a minimum amount of CPU if the system is busy. If other users are not busy, though, active users can "steal" CPU resources from other users within or outside their group.

The benefit of SRM compared to processor sets is that an application group can take more than its share if other share groups are not using their full allocation. For example, batch applications often need to be restricted to prevent them from dominating system resources at the expense of active online users. If other groups are utilizing their full shares, a batch application can be restricted to the shares allocated to it. If unused CPU capacity is available, though, the batch application can make use of the idle resource.

Management of CPU Resources

Once shares have been established with the SRM `limadm` command, SRM uses its own scheduler (a BSD-style scheduler rather than the standard Solaris scheduler) to manage access by processes to CPU resources. Processes are scheduled according to their priorities, and processes lose access to the CPU when their quanta expire, when they block for I/O, or when they are preempted, as is normally the case.

What is different is that every few seconds (4 seconds by default) the SRM daemon wakes up and examines the CPU usage of processes under its control to see how the relative CPU consumption compares with that specified by the lnodes to which they are attached. If necessary, SRM adjusts process priorities by using nice(2) to increase the resource consumption of one group of processes at the expense of others. Note that SRM's use of nice(2) still honors any priority assigned by a user to a process with the nice(1) command.

The end result is that the relative CPU consumption of processes is not deterministic but tends toward that specified by the lnode share. In other words, the shares specified by the user are not guaranteed. Database Engineering testing suggests, though, that SRM does a good job for most share allocations (for example, 50/50 and 66/33). Corner cases (for example, 95/5) may not exactly result in the requested split if each workload is consistently active (the workload with a low share setting may receive more CPU than it should).

Performance Implications of SRM

Use of SRM can involve a performance penalty, although our tests suggest that for most workloads the worst-case performance degradation is no more than around 5% even with 24 fully utilized CPUs. In some cases we observed a performance improvement with SRM that appeared to be due to SRM's use of a larger per process quantum (110 msec) than the high-priority quantum default (20 msec) used with the normal Solaris TimeShare dispatch table used on Enterprise E3x00 to E6x00 systems. The Solaris TimeShare dispatch table is discussed more fully in "The Starfire TS Dispatch Table" on page 221.

In general, the more processes active, the more CPU cycles consumed by the SRM daemon in managing CPU resources. Increasing levels of SRM lnode hierarchy will also increase the overhead incurred by the SRM daemon.

A New Resource Management Framework

An entirely new and more powerful resource management framework has been developed under Solaris 9. This release builds on the concept of a *project* introduced in Solaris 8, allowing the same kind of control—including permissions, monitoring, and accounting—that is currently possible for a user. *Tasks* can be associated with a project, where a task can be a group of processes such as a database instance. Resource management, including CPU and physical memory management, can be carried out at the project level, not just the user (or lnode) level as for SRM 1.x.

The extended accounting features in Solaris 9 include projects as well as accounting at the user, process, and system level, offering much more flexibility.

CPU Performance

In this section we consider ways of improving the effectiveness of CPUs by taking advantage of the Solaris scheduling classes and by binding processes to CPUs.

Process Binding

Just as processes can be bound to processor sets, processes can be bound to a single CPU with the pbind(1M) command. Once bound, a process can only run on that CPU, even if the CPU is busy and others are idle.

Binding is not usually recommended for optimal performance for the following reasons:

- Binding is rigid and any given binding policy may not always be equally effective.

- If more than one process is bound to each CPU, there may be periods when CPU load is not balanced.

Solaris has a sophisticated scheduler that is almost always able to do an excellent job at scheduling work among available CPUs.

Binding can work well in some situations, however. Sybase engines and Informix virtual processors perform best when bound to a CPU. In this case, only one process is bound to each CPU. Sybase and Informix are both multi-threaded applications (based on internal threads libraries rather than Solaris threads) and carry out their own internal load balancing between available engines/coservers. Binding does offer a small performance benefit, thanks to improved cache warmth and reduced context switching.

There can also be benefit in binding Oracle's Log Writer and Database Writers for optimal performance; this binding can prove useful for workloads with high throughput and heavy CPU utilization. Placing the Database Writers in a dedicated processor set has proved to be a better option, though, on very large servers.

In some cases, we have even seen benefits by binding Oracle shadow processes to other CPUs on a round-robin basis. While this type of binding may work well for workloads like TPC-C, where the workload is unusually uniform, it could cause performance problems in typical user environments because of uneven CPU utilization.

Note that process binding differs from processor sets in that the operating system may choose to schedule unbound processes onto a CPU with bound processes. This behavior may be an advantage on a lightly loaded system and a disadvantage on a system where the CPUs with bound processes are heavily utilized.

The pbind command can be used by any user to bind a process the user owns. It should be used with care.

Solaris Scheduling Classes

Each process belongs to a scheduling class, used by Solaris to determine priorities for sharing access to the CPUs. The standard processor classes are shown in Figure 15.4.

Figure 15.4 *Solaris scheduling classes*

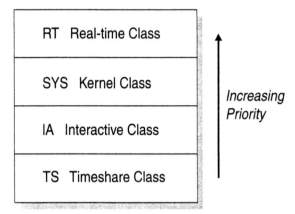

Kernel daemons run in the SYS class and user processes run in the TS class. The IA class is used for desktop applications to guarantee priority to the current window with input focus. You can view class assignments for processes by using the ps command with the -c flag. For example, ps -aefc lists all processes and includes a column for the scheduling class.

Processes running in lower-priority scheduling classes will only receive CPU time left over by higher-priority scheduling classes.

The RT Class

The real-time (RT) class offers top-priority access to the CPUs. As the name suggests, it is intended for processes that require real-time or deterministic access to CPU resources.

The characteristics of the RT class are:

- Processes running in the RT class can only be interrupted by other RT processes running at a higher priority.

- Multiple processes running at the same RT priority will be allocated CPU time on a round-robin basis, unlike the more complex dispatch table approach used by Solaris to schedule TS processes.

Processes can be launched in one scheduling class and later changed to another scheduling class. The priocntl(1) command is used for both purposes. Only the superuser can place processes into the RT class; the priocntl command can be run by any user to modify the TS class scheduling properties of processes owned by that user.

It doesn't take much imagination to conclude that application performance might be boosted by promoting processes into the real-time (RT) class.

Unfortunately, there are downsides. Real-time processes operate at a higher priority than kernel processes and therefore cannot be interrupted by them. Imagine the consequences if kernel daemons never get any CPU time. Worst-case scenarios can range from inexplicable system slowdowns to total system lockouts when rogue processes hog all available CPU. I have personal experience of accidentally locking up the system while playing with the RT class; a system reboot was necessary to resolve the problem.

We strongly recommend against running database systems in the RT class. When using the RT class for benchmarking, do so with caution and remember that results may not be repeatable in normal real-world environments where RT is not used.

The TS Class

For database systems, a safer alternative than RT is the TS class, which can also be modified to improve performance where necessary.

User processes normally run in the timeshare (TS) class. The TS class uses a dispatch table to determine the way process priorities should change over time. To view this table, use the dispadmin -c TS -g command. The first line in the table shows the resolution of the quanta used in the table. By default, the resolution is 1000, indicating that the quanta are in milliseconds (1 / 1000 seconds).

There is one row in the table for each of 60 priority levels, 0 to 59, where 59 is the highest priority. Each row has an associated *quantum* (ts_quantum) and various columns indicating the next priority level at which a process at this level should run, depending on the circumstances.

The TS Scheduler   All processes running in the TS scheduling class (the norm for user processes on a server) have an associated TS priority (not to be confused with a user-supplied nice priority). In conjunction with the TS dispatch table, this priority is used by the Solaris scheduler to determine the order in which processes should next be scheduled to run and how much CPU time (the quantum) they should be allocated when they do run.

Put simply, the scheduler works as follows: When processes are preempted (interrupted by the scheduler) before they have used up their allocated quantum, their priority is increased (as per the ts_lwait column). When processes are able to complete their quantum, their priority is decreased (as specified by the ts_tqexp column). Processes waking up after sleeping have their priorities set according to ts_slprtn. Higher priorities are associated with lower quanta. So, as the priority of a process increases, its quantum decreases, making it more likely that the process will complete its quantum before being preempted.

The same TS dispatch table is not common to all Sun platforms. The dispatch table used on the Starfire is different from the table used on other Sun systems, including the Enterprise and Sun Fire midrange systems. The dispatch table can be viewed or changed with the dispadmin command.

The Starfire TS Dispatch Table   For heavily utilized server systems with large numbers of database users, you can almost always expect performance benefits by using the Starfire dispatch table rather than the standard Solaris table, both for benchmarks and in customer environments. This dispatch table was originally introduced by Cray on the SPARC-based CS6400, the predecessor of the Starfire. The Starfire dispatch table is included on the book website.

It can be loaded as follows:

```
aussie# dispadmin -c TS -s dispatch.starfire
```

This assignment needs to be carried out after each reboot. To do it automatically, you could set up a file in /etc/rc2.d, as shown in Figure 15.5.

Figure 15.5 *Loading a dispatch table automatically upon reboot*

```
aussie# cat /etc/rc2.d/S99dispatchtable
#!/bin/sh
/usr/sbin/dispadmin -c TS -s /export/home/dispatch.starfire
aussie# ls -l /etc/rc2.d/S99dispatchtable
-rwxr-xr-x   1 root     sys      66 Feb 22 15:58 S99dispatchtable
```

On Solaris 7 (but not on later releases), look for a script called /etc/rc2.d/S99tsquantum. This script handles the task automatically on Starfire platforms, and it is also present on other platforms (although the dispatch table it uses, /usr/lib/class/TS/TSbigquanta, is only present on the Starfire).

Elevating Process Priorities   It is also possible to permanently guarantee some processes a higher priority than other processes without using the RT class. The method involves artificially promoting the priority of these processes so that they always run at priority 59 (the highest possible priority), and modifying the dispatch table such that other processes are never admitted to priority 59. The processes that always run at priority 59 will be scheduled on a round-robin basis, as for the RT class, and will always receive first access to an available CPU. Unlike the RT class, however, kernel daemons will never be locked out, since user processes still run in the TS class.

A Dispatch Mods script, embedded in a tar file called dispmod.tar available on the book website, offers a simple way to carry out this procedure. It includes a shell script that does the following:

- Installs a modified TS dispatch table that isolates priority 59 and gives it a quantum of 300 (up from 20 on non-Starfire systems).

- Accepts a string as an argument and promotes the priority of all processes listed in ps that match the string. Any valid egrep string can be used as an argument, so multiple patterns can be used, separated by the pipe symbol (|).

The same kind of approach can also be used to isolate processes at the bottom of the dispatch table, with the result that they only run if other processes leave idle CPU.

Although Database Engineering has made good use of elevated process priorities along with a specially modified TS dispatch table for benchmarks, be careful before implementing it. It is possible that rogue processes (by which I mean processes that never do any I/O and so never need to yield the CPU) could cause a system to effectively lock up if they are running with this kind of enhanced priority, provided there are at least as many of them as there are CPUs. Although kernel processes will not be affected, other user processes will never be scheduled to run, so the system administrator may also be locked out. While this scenario is unlikely, I have experienced it on rare occasions. For user production environments, the safest alternative is to simply implement the Starfire dispatch table, which offers most of the same benefits without the risks.

How the Starfire TS Dispatch Table Helps   Why does the Starfire dispatch table improve performance on heavily loaded database servers? Experiments indicate that the main benefit from using the Starfire dispatch table for database server applications is that the time quantum available to a process is increased compared to the standard Solaris dispatch table (from 20 msec to 340 msec at priority 59). Increasing the quantum can noticeably reduce context switching. Figure 15.6 shows the end of the standard Solaris dispatch table.

Figure 15.6 *The last 10 entries in the standard Solaris dispatch table*

#ts_quantum	ts_tqexp	ts_slpret	ts_maxwait	ts_lwait	PRIORITY	LEVEL
40	40	58	0	59	#	50
40	41	58	0	59	#	51
40	42	58	0	59	#	52
40	43	58	0	59	#	53
40	44	58	0	59	#	54
40	45	58	0	59	#	55
40	46	58	0	59	#	56
40	47	58	0	59	#	57
40	48	58	0	59	#	58
20	49	59	32000	59	#	59

The quantum for the standard Solaris dispatch table drops from 200 msecs at priority 0 to 20 msecs at priority 59. These quanta usually result in good process behavior in a workstation environment, but suboptimal behavior in a database server environment.

Compare this with Figure 15.7, which shows the last 10 entries in the Starfire dispatch table.

Figure 15.7 *The last 10 entries in the Starfire dispatch table*

#ts_quantum	ts_tqexp	ts_slpret	ts_maxwait	ts_lwait	PRIORITY	LEVEL
340	40	51	2	51	#	50
340	41	52	2	52	#	51
340	42	53	2	53	#	52
340	43	54	2	54	#	53
340	44	55	2	55	#	54
340	45	56	2	56	#	55
340	46	57	2	57	#	56
340	47	58	2	58	#	57
340	48	59	2	59	#	58
340	49	59	2	59	#	59

By contrast, the quantum for the Starfire table begins at 400 msecs for priority 0 and gently reduces to 340 msecs for priority 59.

Consider the case when the time quantum of a process expires while the process is holding a critical database latch (a database-specific mutex, or mutual exclusion lock, that reserves access to a critical section of code or a structure). If the process is context-switched (that is, taken off the CPU) while still holding the latch, other processes requesting the same latch will spin whenever the operating system schedules them to run. By *spin*, I mean burn CPU cycles by executing unproductive loop instructions. The idea is to stay on the CPU in the hope that the process with the latch will run on another CPU and release the latch shortly. Spinning may sound wasteful, but in a multi-CPU environment it is typically more efficient to waste a little CPU and try again rather than to go to sleep, release the CPU, and pay the overhead costs of a context switch.

It is much more efficient to allow the process holding the latch to complete its work and release the latch *before* being preempted, freeing both the latch and the CPU for useful work by other processes.

Tests carried out by Database Engineering have suggested that for some applications the optimal quantum value is around 300 msec for processes at priority 59 when the modified dispatch table is used in conjunction with altered process priorities.

This problem is greatly reduced when databases use one of the preemption control primitives available in Solaris releases since Solaris 2.6. Preemption control allows a process to indicate to the operating system that it is holding a critical resource and should not be preempted, thus preventing the kind of unproductive thrashing described earlier. Oracle has implemented preemption control as of Oracle 8i (Solaris 2.6 or later is also required). Preemption control is discussed under "Preemption Control" on page 20.

16

CONFIGURING THE NETWORK

When configuring a network for use by a database server, you should mainly consider network bandwidth and network latency.

Network bandwidth is crucial since performance will inevitably suffer if the network is unable to sustain the packet rate generated by the applications. Studies have suggested that user network bandwidth requirements are quadrupling every three years.

Network latency is equally important since it affects response time. Having unlimited bandwidth doesn't help if the latency is unacceptable. It's like having an eight-lane freeway with choked access roads. Even though traffic on the freeway may be flowing freely, the time taken to get on and off the freeway makes the overall experience a nightmare.

Performance Considerations

In Database Engineering we have been able to sustain more than 30,000 TPC-C transactions (of all types) per minute (corresponding to around 24,000 users executing very lightweight transactions) on a single 100BaseT Ethernet subnet. Even though most of these transactions use stored procedures, which greatly reduce network traffic, our experience suggests that most end users will be able to comfortably deploy substantial client/server solutions based on a single Fast Ethernet LAN.

TPC-C network traffic tends to be relatively stable, however, whereas most real-world workloads are more likely to be bursty. Research with an Oracle Financials workload showed that, although one 10BaseT subnet should have been able to support 1,000 users given the packet traffic, 300 users was more realistic because periods of peak traffic increased the number of collisions. The results are shown in Table 16-1.

Table 16-1 *One-hour packet traffic for 10 Oracle Financials users*

	No. of Packets	Av. Packet Size (bytes)	Rate (bytes/sec)
Sent from client	41,011	208	2,369
Sent from server	38,365	103	1,097
Total	79,376	157	3,461

Note that although the number of packets from client and server was similar, the average packet size and therefore the throughput from the client was more than double that from the server.

Packet sizes are application dependent. Keystrokes and file transfers result in widely varying packet sizes. The Solaris network drivers also affect the effective packet size, both by the choice of packet size and by the coalescence of packets to improve efficiency. The packet size used on a 100-Mbit Ethernet is likely to be considerably smaller than that used on an ATM network, for example. If the packet rate is greater on the 100-Mbit Ethernet, you might easily draw the wrong conclusion about bandwidth requirements. For that reason it is important to consider the packet size as well as the number of packets in sizing networks.

Sizing wide area networks requires more caution than does sizing local area networks since WANs typically involve lower bandwidth, higher latency, and significantly higher cost. Remember that network latency and bandwidth are poor performers compared to disk or memory latency and bandwidth. And don't forget that server CPU resources are required to process network traffic.

When network access is key to the success of a project, be sure to carry out a detailed study before committing yourself to any particular network topology. Consider involving SunPS or a similar systems integrator if appropriate.

Availability Considerations

Network planning should take availability requirements into account. For example, a decision to install a single Gigabit Ethernet connection to a server rather than multiple 100-BaseT Ethernet subnets should take into account redundancy as well as performance. Single points of failure reduce the resilience of a network.

17

DATA LAYOUT

The need for adequate disk capacity is so obvious it often overshadows the equally important need for adequate disk I/O throughput and an effective data layout strategy.

A simple analogy might help clarify the issues. When shopping at a supermarket, you expect to find everything you need in stock and carefully laid out on the shelves. But you also expect to get out of the store without waiting in line too long. The supermarket needs efficient checkout operators and enough checkouts to cope with peak shopping periods. And if your shopping cart is full, you don't want to find half the checkouts are empty express lanes while the lines for the regular lanes stretch halfway around the store.

In the same way, it isn't good enough to simply cram all your data onto online storage. You also need to be able to get it off the disks efficiently, and you don't want some of your disks fully utilized while others are idle.

When installing the disk arrays for a database server, you need a pre-planned data layout that will support optimal performance while achieving the desired level of availability. In this chapter we discuss the following data layout technologies and strategies:

- Storage subsystems.
- Data layout tools.
- RAID and other data layout and performance technologies.
- Data layout strategies.
- High availability.
- Storage cocktails.

The chapter concludes with recommendations.

227

Storage Subsystems

Storage subsystems have grown in variety and complexity in recent years. Before we examine data layout issues, we briefly consider some of the primary ways in which storage is delivered to end users.

Individually Addressable Disks

The simplest storage configuration consists of disks that are individually addressable by the operating system. Such disks are usually located in racks or individual storage cabinets, and the host-based storage adapter that connects the disks to the server is usually based on Fiber Channel or Small Computer System Interface (SCSI) technology. Modern disks have SCSI or Fiber Channel controllers embedded on the drive itself. Sun product offerings of this type include MultiPacks, StorEdge D1000 arrays, and StorEdge A5x00 arrays.

The system administrator can take advantage of a high degree of flexibility in deciding how to configure data on individually addressed disks. Unfortunately, this flexibility includes the ability to make data layout choices that deliver poor availability and poor performance.

The acronym JBOD—Just a Bunch of Disks—is sometimes used loosely to describe this type of disk configuration, although the acronym is also used to refer to a collection of disks that are combined into larger logical volumes without the use of any form of RAID (RAID is described in "Introduction to RAID" on page 232).

RAID-Based Arrays

Rather than presenting individual disks to the operating system, a RAID-based array combines the disks into volumes referred to as Logical Unit Numbers (LUNs). The details of the disk configuration underlying a LUN are not visible to the operating system.

RAID-based arrays usually present fewer LUNs than there are disk drives, so a LUN may exceed the capacity and throughput of a single disk. For practical purposes, LUNs can be treated like disk drives, often with larger capacities, higher performance, and improved availability characteristics. The StorEdge A1000 and T3 arrays are examples of Sun RAID-based storage arrays.

Sometimes host-based controllers are used to provide a RAID front end to an array of otherwise individually addressable disks. An example is the StorEdge SRC/P Controller that can be combined with MultiPacks on Enterprise 240 and 440 servers.

Storage Area Networks (SANs)

Storage areas networks (SANs) are networks dedicated to providing storage. As well as providing physical connections, a SAN manages the connections and storage devices to provide reliable and efficient data transfer. Servers connect to the storage indirectly with switches and hubs, typically using Fiber Channel technology. One of the advantages of SANs is the ability to make many-to-many connections between multiple servers and multiple storage subsystems. The SAN solution sold by Sun is the StorEdge 99x0 range, made by Hitachi Data Systems (HDS).

Figure 17.1 illustrates the topology of a SAN.

Figure 17.1   *SAN topology*

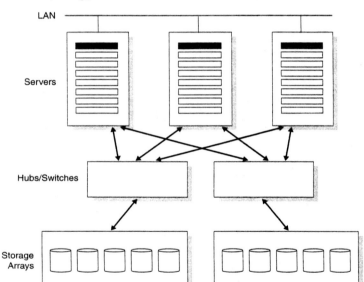

Network Attached Storage (NAS)

Network Attached Storage (NAS) provides access to file services, such as Network File System (NFS) or Common Internet File System (CIFS) files. Serving files across a network is certainly not new—Sun servers have done it for many years. NAS takes a "black box" approach to file serving by integrating the necessary hardware and software within a dedicated product. Sun supplies a NAS solution: the StorEdge N8x00 Filer range.

Figure 17.2 illustrates a NAS environment.

Figure 17.2 *NAS system serving files*

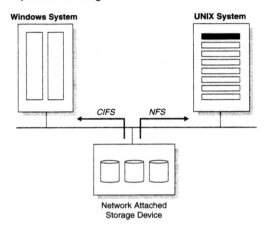

Volume Managers

The Solaris Operating Environment does not provide all the tools necessary to achieve an optimal data layout. But fortunately, the missing pieces are readily available in the form of the Veritas Volume Manager (Veritas) and Solaris Volume Manager (SVM, previously referred to Logical Volume Manager, and before that as Solstice DiskSuite). Both are widely used within the Sun user community.

Veritas and SVM are volume managers that provide specialized help in both laying out data and achieving highly available disk subsystems. They do this by implementing various levels of RAID in software.

RAID can also be implemented directly by hardware devices, thereby relieving the server of the processing associated with disk accesses to RAID devices. With hardware RAID, volume management is delivered in the form of disk subsystems consisting of storage arrays and intelligent controllers, usually accompanied by server-based software that provides access to the capabilities of the storage arrays. Sun's StorEdge A1000 array and StorEdge T3 array are examples of this type of storage device. The Raid Manager (RM6) software supports the A1000, and Component Manager supports the T3 array. It is also possible to log in directly to T3 arrays and configure devices by using command-line utilities.

The various levels of RAID and their implications for data layout and availability are discussed later in this chapter.

Veritas Volume Manager (Veritas)

Veritas Volume Manager—often abbreviated to VxVM, although I will use simply Veritas—supports RAID, hot spares, hot relocation, dirty region logging, online volume and file system expansion, a journaling file system

(Veritas supplies the optional VxFS at additional cost), dynamic multipathing (DMP), and performance monitoring, among other features. Volumes can be moved on a live system (hot relocation), and mirrored volumes can be relocated automatically in the event of a disk failure.

Typically, Veritas takes over a disk: partition 3 stores housekeeping information (the private region), and partition 4 stores the volumes that hold user data.

One benefit of this approach is that Veritas can recognize a disk even if it has been physically moved to another controller or if the controller number has changed for some reason (for example, a Solaris upgrade or replacement of a failed controller). Another benefit is that Veritas is not limited to the number of partitions on a disk—an almost limitless number of volumes can be created.

Veritas is a powerful tool that is suitable for use in enterprise-level environments.

Solaris Volume Manager (SVM)

SVM supports RAID, hot spares, dirty region logging, online volume and file system expansion, a journaling file system, and performance monitoring. Hot relocation and dynamic multipathing are not supported.

SVM has the benefit of simplicity in that it sits directly on top of Solaris disk partitions. Before the SVM 4.2.1 release, no SVM information is stored on the disk, since all necessary SVM housekeeping data is kept in separate *metastate databases*. Each SVM metapartition maps directly to a Solaris partition (or multiple partitions in the case of RAID). The downside of this mapping is that only seven partitions per disk are possible.

The SVM 4.2.1 release introduced soft partitioning to resolve this limitation. This release does store SVM information on individual disks.

Changes to controller numbers are not automatically detected by SVM, resulting in extra administrative work (if not disaster!) after an OS upgrade or controller replacement. This limitation is expected to be addressed in a future release. Disksets, part of the cluster version of SVM, include functionality to overcome this problem.

RAID Manager (RM6)

RM6, in conjunction with the hardware RAID devices it supports, provides RAID, hot spares, and performance monitoring, among other features. Dirty region logging, online volume and file system expansion, a journaling file system, hot relocation, and dynamic multipathing are not supported.

RM6 is used to manage StorEdge A1000 arrays and the older A3000 and A3500 storage arrays.

Component Manager

Component Manager is a software tool that can be used to monitor and manage StorEdge A5x00 arrays (A5000, A5100, and A5200) and T3 arrays. In the case of T3 arrays, it can be used to create and manage LUNs. T3 LUNs consist of disks aggregated together using one of a number of supported types of RAID (stripes, striped mirrors, and RAID 5 are all supported). T3 arrays also support hot spare disks.

GUI Administration

All of these volume manager tools offer a GUI interface. GUI administration offers significant benefits in ease of use, but it becomes increasingly impractical as the number of disks grows beyond about one hundred. Command-line alternatives allow repetitive administration tasks to be automated with scripts, something that isn't possible with GUIs. Within Database Engineering, we use command-line utilities encapsulated within scripts for disk administration.

Relative Performance

Performance tests at Database Engineering have shown similar performance with either Veritas or SVM used for mirroring. Any volume manager typically introduces a performance overhead, reducing by a few percent the maximum throughput that can be achieved on a server. The costs are outweighed, though, by the benefits.

Data Layout Technologies

We begin with an outline of the tools and technologies available to the end user for effective data layout. In doing so, we cover the major levels of RAID, including striping, mirroring and RAID 5, write caches, and the storage alternatives for database files (file systems and raw devices).

We describe the technology rather than provide recommendations. The following section, "Data Layout Strategies" on page 242," looks in detail at the performance implications of the various alternatives and offers recommendations.

Introduction to RAID

"RAID," an acronym for "Redundant Arrays of Inexpensive Disks," describes a variety of technologies that have become closely associated with data layout and performance. The term suggests a hardware device, but in fact RAID can be equally well implemented in software. The "array of disks" can be physical, virtual, or a combination of both.

When RAID levels are implemented in hardware—an approach sometimes referred to as controller-based RAID—the processing is usually carried out by a dedicated controller, often within a separate disk array unit.

Software RAID provides the same functionality within the host system by using software device drivers. Software RAID is typically less expensive but does not perform as well as hardware RAID, especially for RAID 5.

Since hardware RAID devices contain their own embedded CPU and some form of operating system, it could be argued that hardware RAID is really software RAID implemented on an independent device. Hardware RAID devices do often contain a hardware XOR engine, though, to accelerate RAID-5 parity calculation (more on this later).

Concatenation

The simplest way to spread large amounts of data across multiple disks is to successively fill the disks. This approach, called *concatenation*, is the normal method used by Sybase and Informix databases to store data.

In Figure 17.3, the first disk would be filled before data was written to the second, and so on.

Figure 17.3   *Concatenation across multiple disks*

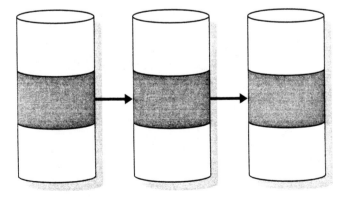

Concatenation offers few benefits for database performance, although it can act as a crude method of balancing disk input/output (I/O) in OLTP environments. Avoid concatenation.

RAID 0: Striping

A much better alternative is *striping*, also known as RAID 0. DB2 for Solaris and Ingres stripe tablespaces automatically across all supplied data files, and Oracle allocates extents to underlying data files in a round-robin fashion, which achieves the same effect. Striping is often implemented by Veritas, SVM, or RM6. T3 arrays also support striping.

The *stripe width* (or *interlace*) is the amount of data placed on each disk before a move to the next one. In Figure 17.4, if the stripe was created with a stripe width of 64 Kbytes, a single 256-Kbyte read operation would involve all four disks. This approach can offer significant performance advantages when the system is carrying out large I/Os.

Figure 17.4 *Striping across multiple disks*

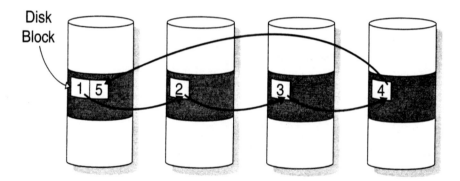

Both concatenation and striping are susceptible to data loss if any of the disks fail—there is no data protection through parity or redundancy. For this reason RAID 0 is usually used in conjunction with RAID 1 (mirroring).

RAID 1: Mirroring

Mirroring is used to ensure data integrity and availability in the event of a disk failure. All data is automatically duplicated, and the loss of a disk does not interrupt data access. To recover from a disk failure, the data from the surviving disk must be duplicated on a replacement disk.

Volume writes (see Figure 17.5) are replicated automatically to all mirrored devices (there may be more than two images). Volume reads (see Figure 17.6) can either come from a specified device or alternate between all participating mirrors in a round-robin fashion. Round-robin reading spreads I/O across more disks.

Figure 17.5 *Writing to mirrored disks*

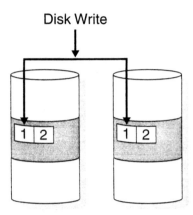

Figure 17.6 *Reading from mirrored disks*

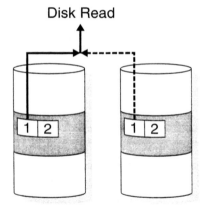

The performance impact of mirroring is relatively small for most disk operations (the maximum possible throughput is typically reduced by a few percent). The capacity cost, however, is substantial since twice the amount of disk space is required.

RAID 0+1: Striping Plus Mirroring

RAID 0 and RAID 1 together can be used to achieve the following benefits:

- Single-volume capacity greater than that of a single disk.
- The performance benefits of striping.
- The increased reliability of mirrored data.

As with all RAID 1 solutions, the penalty is a doubling of disk requirements.

RAID 0+1 striping is not affected by the failure of a single disk, as illustrated in Figure 17.7.

Figure 17.7   *Striping plus mirroring*

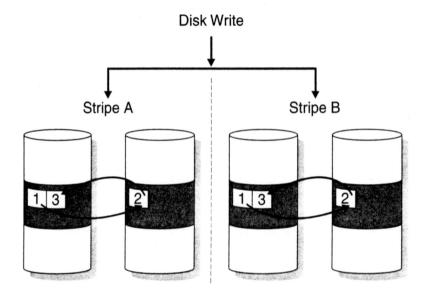

Failure of a second disk in the surviving stripe will result in lost data.
Recovery after a single disk failure involves update of an entire stripe.

Veritas before Version 3.1.1 implements combined striping and mirroring
in this fashion.

RAID 1+0: Mirroring and Striping

An alternative method of combining striping and mirroring is RAID 1+0 where mirrored pairs of disks are striped to form a larger volume, as shown in Figure 17.8.

Figure 17.8 *Striping plus mirroring*

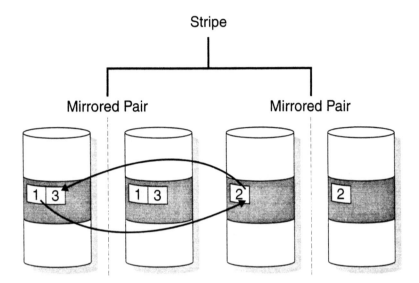

This configuration offers all the benefits of RAID 0+1 plus increased availability, since only one pair of disks is affected by failure of a single disk, not a whole stripe. Data will only be lost after a second disk failure if the same mirrored pair is affected.

Recovery after a disk failure only involves update of a single disk.

As with all RAID 1 solutions, the penalty is a doubling of disk requirements.

SVM and RM6 implement combined striping and mirroring in this fashion, and Veritas is able to achieve it from Version 3.1.1. T3 arrays also support striping of mirrored pairs of disks.

RAID 3: Striping with Dedicated Parity Disk

RAID 3 and RAID 5 offer a unique approach to disk storage, especially with respect to high availability. Data is grouped in chunks (typically three or more chunks per group) with an additional chunk for parity. The parity is calculated by an XOR operation on the data in the data chunks. Each of the chunks is stored on a separate disk. If one of the disks fails, the parity information can be used to recover the missing information. Figure 17.9 illustrates the configuration.

Figure 17.9 *RAID 3 disk layout (3 + 1)*

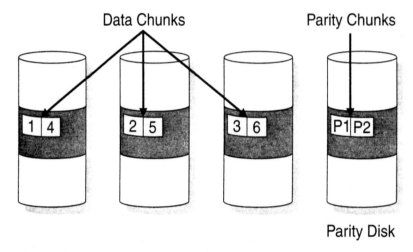

RAID 3 sets aside a dedicated disk for the parity chunks. In this example, a parity chunk is used for every three data chunks.

Because an additional parity chunk is written along with the data chunks, RAID 3 disk space requirements are increased by 100/N percent, where N is the number of data chunks per parity chunk.

RAID 5: Striping with Distributed Parity

RAID 5 is much more popular than RAID 3. It is similar to RAID 3, except that parity chunks are spread across all disks rather than concentrated on a dedicated disk. This layout prevents the parity disk from becoming a performance bottleneck during writes. Figure 17.10 illustrates the configuration.

Figure 17.10 *RAID 5 disk layout (3+1)*

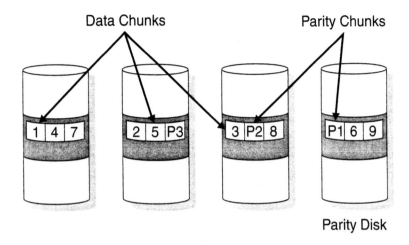

As with RAID 3, because an additional parity chunk is written along with the data chunks, RAID 5 disk space requirements are increased by 100/N percent, where N is the number of data chunks per parity chunk.

The main attraction for RAID 5 is that it offers high availability without the need for mirroring and the consequent doubling of disk requirements.

The major downside of RAID 5 is write performance. RAID 5 can be implemented on the host, typically with software, or by a controller, usually within the RAID unit. RAID 5 controllers use a combination of specialized RAID 5 hardware and write caches to improve write performance. Controller-based RAID 5 implementations typically outperform host-based RAID 5 implementations and also consume less CPU resource per I/O.

Veritas and SVM implement RAID 5 with software, and T3 arrays and RM6-based arrays (the A1000 and older A3500 arrays) support hardware controller-based RAID 5.

Summary of RAID Technology

The most commonly used levels of RAID are RAID 0 (striping), RAID 1, usually combined with striping (RAID 0+1), and RAID 5. For performance reasons, software-only RAID 5 implementations are best avoided. Mirroring can be effectively implemented in software, and if the mirrored devices are located on different controllers, redundancy is provided against disk, array, and controller failure.

Refer to Chapter 7 of Brian Wong's *Configuration and Capacity Planning for Sun Servers* (Sun Press) for a comprehensive treatment of all levels of RAID.

Database Files on UFS

In spite of the performance implications, many users prefer to place database files on Unix File System (UFS) files. The major reason is that system administration is simpler with UFS files than with raw devices. A secondary reason is that some database vendor Systems Engineers recommend the use of file systems (often without offering a clear justification).

File systems and the files they contain are visible by means of standard UNIX tools like ls and df, and the precise size of a database file can be easily determined with ls -l.

It is true that some backup utilities expect to work with UFS files, although the widely used Veritas Netbackup has optional database add-on modules capable of backing up raw devices. It is also true that a system administrator could accidentally create a UFS partition on top of a raw database partition. However, effective administrative procedures should be able to overcome such problems.

File systems can host multiple database files, and spare file system capacity can be used by allowing database files to be expanded dynamically or by adding new files.

File systems require consistency checks when the system is booted. For this reason you should turn on file system logging (described under "UFS Logging" on page 23) for database files on UFS (only supported as of Solaris 7).

UFS is a viable alternative for storing database files. UFS files are supported by all databases, including Sybase, which for many years only supported the use of raw devices. The performance implications of using UFS files for databases is discussed later in this chapter under "Raw Devices vs. UFS" on page 242.

Database Files on Raw Devices

You can also place database files on raw devices by specifying the name of the raw device instead of a regular file (remember to make sure your database user has access permissions). This approach can be used for raw disk partitions, Veritas raw devices (volumes beginning with /dev/vx/rdsk/), SVM raw devices (beginning with /dev/md/rdsk/), and Logical Unit Numbers, or LUNs.

Unlike the case with file systems, only one database file can be placed in each raw device (although Informix XPS is an exception). Tablespaces are typically grown by addition of raw devices. If the database file is smaller than the raw device in which it is placed, the extra space is usually wasted, although some databases do offer support for extending database files on raw devices. Raw devices can be extended if they are based on volume manager volumes.

It is not easy to discover the size of a database file by using operating system utilities, although volume managers provide a simple way of determining the exact size when the raw devices are volumes. Oracle also provides the `dbfsize` utility—when passed a file name (including the path), it displays the file type and size in blocks.

Raw devices require no special recovery when the system is restarted.

Once database files have been placed on raw devices, it can be awkward to move the data since the name of the raw device changes in the process. A simple solution is to use symbolic links from the beginning. Symlinks are discussed in more detail in "Database File Naming Using Symlinks" on page 258.

Write Caches

Write caches are memory-based disk front ends that speed disk access by temporarily storing disk writes in memory to be flushed to disk later. Since memory access is much faster than disk access, writes complete more quickly. Once a block destined for disk is stored in the cache memory, the write operation completes, allowing the application to go on with other things. The cache manager is then responsible to flush the block to disk.

Write caches can be implemented in a number of ways:

- Within the host system (for example, the StorEdge Fast Write Cache).

- Within the disk controller (usually inside a disk array). Examples include the T3, A1000, and the older A3500 StorEdge Arrays and SPARCstorage Arrays.

- On the disk itself. Most disks have small caches, but Sun typically ships them with the write cache disabled to avoid the risk of data corruption.

For preservation of data integrity in the event of a power failure or a system crash, host and controller write caches are normally battery backed. The battery backup allows dirty pages in the cache to be flushed when the system starts up again.

Battery-backed cache depends on power being restored before the batteries are exhausted; otherwise, data can be lost. An Uninterruptible Power Supply (UPS) can help in this case. That may sound strange, since a UPS typically provides minutes of power rather than the many hours of backup power provided by the cache battery. However, a UPS does more than just preserve cache memory, it allows systems to continue to operate briefly. Cache controllers typically flush dirty pages automatically after a specified period (usually about 1 minute). So, a UPS can allow dirty pages to be flushed from the cache to the disk before the system shuts down.

If the write cache is physically located within a disk array, a UPS can be provided for the disk array. If the write cache is within a host system, then the entire host system including its disk would need to be UPS protected.

The performance implications of write caches are discussed in "Write Caches for Improved Performance" on page 251.

Data Layout Strategies

The main objective of data layout is to avoid disk bottlenecks by spreading disk I/O evenly across all available disks. You need to avoid one disk being fully utilized while others are idle. Never lose sight of this objective and always refer back to it!

At the same time you need to make sure you achieve the desired level of availability. Fortunately, taking availability into account does not undermine any of the principles involved in planning an effective data layout strategy.

Efficient Data Layout

Efficient data layout must take into account many factors:

- How to spread data across multiple disks (for example, concatenation, striping, RAID 5).
- Where to place different types of data (raw data, indexes, temporary work areas, logs).

  Where to locate data on an individual disk.

It is also important to make informed choices—such as whether to implement data files on raw devices or Unix File System (UFS) files and where it makes sense to use write caches—between technologies that affect performance.

Raw Devices vs. UFS

A good place to start planning for efficient data layout is with one of the most basic decisions about data storage: the choice between raw devices and UFS (Unix File System) files.

When should you use UFS files for database files and when should you use raw devices? The answer is fairly simple: if you care about performance, always use raw devices. This simple rule of thumb is true for database files generally, but especially important for database logs. The biggest performance gains are achieved by moving UFS log files to raw devices (or Direct I/O files), even if other database files are left on UFS. I would go so far as to say that UFS files should never be used for database logs except perhaps for small databases where performance is unimportant—raw devices or Direct I/O files are much better choices.

Placing database files on raw devices offers the best all-around database performance for these reasons:

- All major databases use asynchronous I/O to access database pages (although not all of them use asynchronous I/O exclusively). When asynchronous I/O is performed on raw devices, Solaris automatically invokes Kernel Asynchronous I/O (KAIO). KAIO reduces the number of instructions needed to complete an I/O and eliminates the interaction between the kernel and the user mode `libaio` library. As a result, I/Os complete more quickly and less CPU is consumed in the process. This behavior translates into a performance win. Asynchronous I/O is supported for file systems, but it is implemented with a user library, `libaio`; KAIO is not available with UFS files, even when asynchronous I/O is used.

KAIO is further described in "Kernel Asynchronous I/O" on page 21.

- The code path within the Solaris kernel is much shorter (that is, fewer instructions are required to complete an I/O) with raw devices than with UFS files because of the UNIX-level caching carried out by the kernel on behalf of UFS files. This shorter code path means that not only does a raw I/O complete more quickly, but it consumes less CPU in the process.

- The UFS file system page cache can interfere with performance, especially for insert- or update-intensive batch jobs.

- File systems must be checked for consistency (with the `fsck` utility) when a system boots, increasing recovery time after a failure. UFS logging, though, supported as of Solaris 7, significantly reduces the file system recovery time. See "UFS Logging" on page 23 for more information.

  While the UNIX file system page cache can behave as an effective read cache, an adequately sized database buffer cache delivers a more efficient caching strategy than does the second-level cache offered by the operating system. The same observation is true for caching writes. Sometimes a 64-bit database might be needed to size buffer caches appropriately on systems with large amounts of memory.

- Some applications such as large batch jobs gain little or no benefit from caching pages, yet the use of UFS means each page must be brought into the UNIX cache before it can be used. Once all free pages have been used, the page daemon is forced into action to find clean pages for the application to use. If clean pages are not available, dirty pages must be flushed to disk before pages are ready for consumption by the application. When this point is reached, performance can dip dramatically, especially if the application is constantly dirtying pages itself. The DBMS can more efficiently handle this page management process directly with raw devices.

- UFS file access sometimes involves double reading. Pages are read into the database buffer cache through the file system page cache. If the page in the database buffer cache is modified, it may be some time before it is written to disk since that operation is carried out independently by the pagecleaners.

  By the time the page is flushed to disk, the memory set aside for it in the file system page cache may have been stolen and used by another page. In that case, the original page must be reread from disk into the file system page cache (displacing another page in the process) before it can be updated from the database buffer cache and written to disk. The end result is two reads for one write.

- Multiple writes to a UFS file are constrained by the single UFS writer lock (mandated by POSIX), which prevents any other process from reading from or writing to the file when a process is already writing to it. This limitation can have a major impact when heavy database I/O is directed to a single UFS file. As of the Solaris 8 1/01 release, using UFS file systems in combination with Direct I/O (the `forcedirectio` flag in `/etc/vfsstab`) overcomes the single writer lock problem. This issue is discussed further in "Unix File System Enhancements" on page 21.

- Even though the database block size may be 2 Kbytes in size, all UFS database I/Os become 8-Kbyte I/Os (since the files are opened with the `O_DSYNC` flag). The result can be an increase of up to four times in read throughput if most reads are random in nature. Equally, all 2-Kbyte writes become 8-Kbyte writes; if the 8-Kbyte page is not currently in memory, the write must first be preceded by an 8-Kbyte read.

  Log writes are often larger than 8 Kbytes in size. With UFS database log files, though, larger writes are broken up into 8-Kbyte writes (a side effect of the fact that the files are opened with the `O_DSYNC` flag).

Raw devices also deliver slightly more bytes of usable storage. UFS partitions carry an overhead of superblock and inode information and, for performance reasons, typically reserve a further 1% (10% in older versions of Solaris) of the available storage only accessible to the superuser.

Occasionally, UFS files can be demonstrated to offer better performance than that of raw devices. For example, read-only workloads where the database is carrying out 2K sequential reads may sometimes benefit from UFS read-ahead, although the database will usually do read-ahead automatically where appropriate. Equally, if the database cache is too small, file system page buffering can save I/Os. But in the vast majority of cases, a well-tuned system with raw devices will outperform UFS files.

File systems may offer an advantage where considerably more than 4 gigabytes of memory are available but the database cache is limited to 3.75 gigabytes because of 32-bit limitations in the database or Solaris. In this case, read-based workloads may be able to use the file system page cache to avoid disk reads. The availability of 64-bit database versions as of Solaris 7 make this less of an issue, though.

File System Alternatives

If you decide to implement database files on file systems, you can choose from a number of alternative UFS-style implementations:

- **Standard UFS (as implemented by Solaris).** All access to UFS pages is managed through the Solaris file system page cache. We considered the characteristics of UFS files in the previous section.

- **Direct I/O.** As of Solaris 2.6, file systems can be mounted with the `forcedirectio` option. Disk accesses to files on such file systems will bypass the Solaris file system page cache. KAIO (Kernel Asynchronous

I/O) is not used, however, when asynchronous I/Os are issued on Direct I/O-enabled files. If log files are not placed on raw devices, they should be placed on file systems mounted with Direct I/O support.

As of the 1/01 release of Solaris 8, a number of improvements have been made to Direct I/O that benefit database workloads considerably. Testing at Sun has suggested that database throughput with Direct I/O database files approaches 90% of raw performance.

For a more detailed discussion of Direct I/O, refer to "Unix File System Enhancements" on page 21). For information about using Direct I/O with Oracle, refer to "Using Oracle with File Systems" on page 340.

- **VxFS.** This optional Veritas file system (available for additional cost) can be used as an alternative to the standard UFS file system.

- **VxFS with Database Option (Quick I/O).** This optional VxFS add-on allows files to be simultaneously treated like file system files and also to be opened and accessed by databases as raw volumes, thus bypassing the buffer cache and allowing the use of KAIO. Performance tests using the TPC-C workload at Database Engineering at Sun have shown that VxFS Quick I/O is able to achieve performance similar to the performance achievable with Direct I/O and close to that of raw devices. Note that before you deploy VxFS, it is important to check whether the current Veritas-recommended version is supported by Sun Enterprise Services.

Optimal Performance on File Systems

For optimal performance, use the following (in order of preference):

1. Raw devices.

2. Direct I/O as of the Solaris 8 1/01 release, or VxFS with Quick I/O.

3. Solaris Direct I/O (as of Solaris 2.6).

4. UFS.

If you use UFS files for databases, it is important to avoid using a small number of very large files striped across multiple disks. Such usage can result in reader/writer lock contention at the inode level because of the single UFS writer lock referred to earlier in this chapter. It is better to use multiple files, even on the same file system. Direct I/O as of the 1/01 release of Solaris 8 does not have this limitation.

Priority paging (a standard feature in Solaris 7 and available from a patch in Solaris 2.5.1 and Solaris 2.6) should *always* be enabled when standard UFS is used prior to Solaris 8 (where it is superseded and not recommended). Priority paging avoids application memory starvation by causing Solaris to target pages in the file system page cache when memory is required.

Set priority paging by using the following line in /etc/system:

```
set priority_paging = 1
```

Significant changes to the Solaris VM system in Solaris 8 have resulted in much greater efficiency for UFS-based systems. In all previous releases, when the memory was required, the page daemon would search the whole of memory for suitable pages. As of Solaris 8, pages in the file system page cache are separately accounted for. This means free memory can still be used to cache file system pages, but old file system pages can be released for application use without the intervention of the page daemon. This technique frees CPU cycles, delivers free memory more quickly, and prevents the page daemon from becoming a bottleneck on systems with very large amounts of memory.

Further information on the implications of UFS in monitoring databases is provided starting with "Normal Paging Behavior Prior to Solaris 8" on page 284.

The Right and Wrong Way to Stripe

We have seen that data striping, also referred to as RAID 0, refers to the practice of spreading data across multiple disks by a round-robin distribution pattern.

The stripe width is the amount of data the system places on each disk before moving to the next one. For example, if 10 Mbytes are striped with a stripe width of 128 Kbytes across eight disks, then the first 128 Kbytes will be written to disk one, the second 128 Kbytes to disk two, and so on. After the eighth 128 Kbytes have been written to disk eight, the ninth will start at disk one again. Thus, 10 Mbytes would be written in ten full stripes of 1 Mbyte. Each disk would contain a total of 1280 Kbytes.

The disk transfer time to read 1 Mbyte from a single 36-Gbyte disk is 33 msecs at best, assuming the disk is capable of delivering data at 30 Mbytes/sec. When 1 Mbyte is read in a single operation from the stripe described above, all eight disks would be involved, each contributing 128 Kbytes. The disk transfer time for 128 Kbytes is 4 msec for each disk. Both the 128 Kbyte and 1 Mbyte reads should require similar seek times. So a single striped read should complete much faster, although at the cost of a small additional CPU overhead to reassemble the data. This is the reason for striping I/O for Decision Support Systems (DSS) applications.

Splitting a Single I/O Across Multiple Disks

It's easy to understand the benefits of spreading large I/Os across multiple disks. Unfortunately, some people think the same logic applies to small I/Os. For example, why not stripe each 4-Kbyte page across four disks in 1-Kbyte chunks to speed up 4-Kbyte reads?

Imagine you live in a village with a water supply consisting of four wells. If a lot of water is needed in a hurry (someone's house is burning down, for example), it makes sense to send buckets to all four wells at once. On the other hand, when filling a small cooking pot with water for dinner, would you send four people to four wells to get a quarter pot of water each? With everyone in the village lining up for water, this strategy won't make you popular.

In the same way, using a stripe size of 1 Kbyte or 2 Kbytes to split small (for example, 4-Kbyte) I/Os is a poor strategy. Considerably more data than that is stored on a typical disk cylinder, so 4 Kbytes can be read quickly and efficiently without head movement. Splitting 4-Kbyte I/Os across four disks simply quadruples the number of disk operations for no benefit at all. Further, the I/O is not complete until the slowest of the disks completes its transfer. When hundreds of users are doing such I/Os concurrently, that's a great way of slowing down the system.

Applying the Theory to the Real World

We've seen that it's a lot faster to read 1 Mbyte from eight disks at once than from a single disk. However, the theory is often more straightforward than the real world, and this simple example quickly becomes complicated in real life. It's rare to find only one application process running on a server. What if eight application processes are all reading 1 Mbyte at the same time? Is it better to have each application read from a single disk without interference or to have each contend for all eight disks at once to complete their reads? And what if there are sometimes eight, sometimes five, and sometimes twenty concurrent applications running, some doing 2-Kbyte and others 1-Mbyte disk accesses?

Establishing Two Fundamental Principles of Striping

To bring order to the chaos, let's establish some guiding principles:

1. *Large I/Os should be split across multiple disks.*

   For applications typically retrieving large chunks of data at a time (for example, data warehouse applications), use striping to involve multiple disks in a single disk operation. By a large I/O, I mean more than 128 Kbytes in a single access (although this value is somewhat arbitrary). Whether the disks are being accessed by one user or by ten, a stripe size of 128 Kbytes or more will ensure that all will participate.

   Suppose multiple 1-Mbyte reads take place concurrently, though. Rather than striping across eight disks, wouldn't it be more efficient to use a stripe size of 1 Mbyte, thereby ensuring that each read is satisfied from a single disk? Provided each read uses a different disk, the answer is "yes." Unfortunately, though, it is very difficult to ensure that the I/Os are evenly spread. If two 1-Mbyte reads target the same disk, the second will have to wait a minimum of 33 msecs (assuming the disk delivers data at 30 Mbyte/sec) plus seek time before even starting. If two reads are already on the disk queue, a third read will take more than one second to complete. If other disks are not equally busy, queuing is inefficient.

   Given that our main data layout objective is to avoid disk bottlenecks by spreading disk I/O evenly across all available disks, it is better to stripe large reads across multiple disks.

2. *Small I/Os should not be split across multiple disks.*

OLTP applications usually retrieve small chunks of data in a single disk access (often 2, 4, or 8 Kbytes at a time). I/Os less than 128 Kbytes in size can be regarded as small I/Os. Use striping with a stripe size of 64 or 128 Kbytes to balance disk access across all available disks while making sure a single disk operation is satisfied from a single disk.

The purpose of striping data for OLTP applications is not to split individual I/Os but to balance disk access. If the access to OLTP data is random, as is usually the case, striping the data means that all disks host roughly the same amount of data. As the number of disk accesses increases, the randomness of access means that access will be distributed throughout the striped data and hence all disks will be equally busy. In practice, some segments of a table may be hotter than others, causing localized hot spots. A small stripe size (32–64 Kbytes, for example) can help spread hot spots across multiple disks.

I suggest a stripe size lower limit of 32 Kbytes for OLTP applications. I have used 32, 64, and 128 Kbytes with a variety of databases and not seen significant performance differences between them. For DSS applications, a minimum of 128 Kbytes is a good starting point.

It is worth noting that striping may result in more disk accesses than expected. For example, if a stripe width of 128 Kbytes is used, a 128-Kbyte read will require two accesses rather than one unless the starting point of the read is perfectly aligned with the starting point of the stripe on the disk. If the read begins halfway through the striped data, then half the data will be read from the stripe on the first disk and the other half from the stripe on the next disk. In the same way, reading 1 Mbyte from a disk stripe that is 128 Kbytes wide may require nine disk operations.

Finally, when laying out disks for striping with DSS applications, it is useful to stripe across disks on different controllers (sometimes referred to as "plaiding") rather than striping across all the disks on one controller and then moving to the next controller. For OLTP workloads, plaiding is less of an issue, since controller I/O limitations are harder to exceed.

A plaid layout is well worth considering for optimum throughput, especially with large sequential reads. Accessing disks across controllers helps prevent controller bandwidth limitations from becoming a bottleneck. Figure 17.11 illustrates a plaid layout.

Figure 17.11 *A plaid layout—striping across controllers*

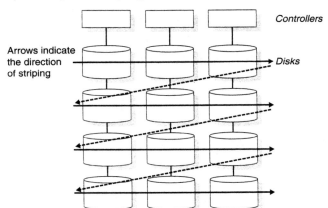

Deciding How Broad to Make a Single Stripe

Given that it is wise to stripe all data types across all disks, should each database file be striped across every available disk? The answer depends on the number of disks. If you have just a few disks (fewer than 20, say), then it makes sense to stripe each database file across all disks.

With one hundred disks, though, striping each file is probably overkill. All data types can be striped across all disks without striping every file across all disks. If, for example, the customer tablespace has five data files containing equal amounts of data, each could be striped across 20 disks, thereby striping the customer tablespace across all the disks and balancing I/O in the process.

Database Engineering studied the memory requirements of the Veritas Volume Manager with several hundred disks. The study showed that striping each database file across all disks consumed hundreds of megabytes more kernel memory than striping each file across 45 disks. Striping a single volume across 500 disks caused Veritas to consume over 1 Mbyte of kernel memory. Striping the same volume over 45 disks required only 0.1 Mbyte of kernel memory. It seems intuitive, too, to limit the complexity of the volume manager environment by restricting the number of objects the volume manager needs to manage.

Striping with LUNs

In our discussions about striping so far, we have assumed each disk is individually addressable by the operating system. Disks of this type are often referred to by the acronym JBODs (Just a Bunch of Disks).

Many disks, though, are configured in storage arrays where individual disks are not directly accessible. The Sun StorEdge T3, A1000, and the older A3000 and A3500 storage arrays are examples of this type of array. Instead of presenting individual disks, these storage arrays use Logical Unit Numbers

(LUNs). Intelligent disk controllers within the storage arrays map the LUNs to the physical disks that underlie them.

LUNs use the same naming convention as individual disks (that is, /dev/[r]dsk/cntndnsn), but each LUN typically represents several striped disks (RAID 0) or several disks in a RAID 5 configuration.

For practical purposes LUNs can be regarded as high-capacity disks with substantial throughput and IOPS capabilities. Here are two simple rules of thumb for striping with LUNs:

- Don't mix LUNs and individual disks in the same stripe. Creating a stripe with disks of significantly different performance characteristics will result in uneven disk utilization.

- Think of a LUN as a stripe of the disks that underlie it. If the LUN is a RAID 0 device, count the number of disks in the stripe. If it is a RAID 5 device, count the number of disks for reads; write performance is more difficult to calculate. A write cache helps RAID 5 write performance significantly, though.

Placing Data and Indexes

Raw data is just one consumer of database disk capacity. Indexes, temporary tablespaces, and database logs also require considerable disk space, IOPS, and throughput resources.

There are two main alternatives for layout:

- Place data on one set of disks, indexes on another, and temporary tablespaces on a third.

- Spread all types of data across all available disks.

The first alternative used to be recommended so that indexed access to data would be certain to involve separate data and index disks without head contention. However, Database Engineering has used the second approach for several years.

Different database operations place different demands on database files. Consider index creation, for example. A table scan phase first reads table data, a sort phase then intensively accesses the temporary tablespaces, and finally, a write phase puts index pages into the index data files. The only way to make all disks active during all phases is to stripe all types of tablespaces across all disks.

Where there are a very large number of disks, it isn't necessary to stripe every database file across every disk. But it is still worth striping all types of tablespaces across all disks.

Keep database logs on their own disk or disks if possible, and ensure that the logs are protected against disk failure by using either mirroring or RAID 5 (mirroring is preferred, since a disk failure in a RAID 5 stripe will impact stripe performance, even though data is still protected). If only a small number of disks are available, logs can be placed with the main data, provided the layout prevents a disk failure from destroying the integrity of both the data and the logs.

There is no perfect layout strategy for all environments. The complex disk access patterns of real-world workloads are rarely as straightforward as just described, but it remains true that the simplest way to balance disk activity is to use broad stripes, laying out raw data, index data, and temporary tablespaces on the same disks. This recommendation may not always be perfect, but it is usually the best starting point as well the simplest to implement.

Laying Out Data on a Single Disk

In the 1970s we used to place the most heavily accessed data in the center of a disk and the least frequently accessed data at the beginning and the end. The aim was to reduce head movement by concentrating head movement around the center of the disk. Since each cylinder contained the same amount of data, this approach made good sense.

Modern disks, though, use zone bit recording (ZBR) to pack more information on the larger outer cylinders of the disk. The result is throughput on the outside of the disk that is around 50% greater than on the inside. So, for performance reasons it is best to locate the most heavily accessed data on cylinder 0 (usually partition 0 in the format utility). Database Engineering has long taken advantage of this behavior in competitive benchmarks.

The best-case scenario is to fill the inner cylinders with lightly accessed data and keep head movement centered around the outer cylinders. This approach reduces the seek time and therefore the I/O response time.

Write Caches for Improved Performance

Write caches, described in "Write Caches" on page 241, can offer a performance benefit for the following database workloads:

- Database loads, since I/O completion time is so significant in load performance.

- Index creation.

- Large sorts that overflow to temporary tablespaces on disk.

- I/O-intensive activity that bypasses the database buffer cache.

- Workloads where small (for example, 2-Kbyte) writes can be coalesced into large (up to 2-Mbyte) writes (as supported by the StorEdge Fast Write Cache). Software RAID 5 implementations can be helped by this technique.

- Writes to the log subsystem.

In general, write caches benefit small synchronous writes the most. Completion times for small sequential and random writes can be speeded considerably, provided the cache does not fill up.

Write caches can significantly help database performance when used for database logs, especially on systems with heavy throughput. Only use write caches for database logs in combination with a UPS or, at the very least, an effective battery-backed cache (see the discussion below for more detail).

Write caches typically will *not* benefit the following workloads:

- Read-only or read-mostly workloads like DSS (Decision Support Systems).

- OLTP data writes (because data write performance is usually not crucial to throughput).

- Workloads that can overwhelm the cache. If the cache is too small to keep up with the volume of writes, the cache becomes a bottleneck.

- Workloads with large writes.

Why is it that using write caches for data disks with OLTP workloads typically doesn't help performance? Disk writes are carried out asynchronously from the transactions that give rise to them.

For a transaction to commit, all that is necessary is for details of all changes to be successfully written to the log file. Data page modifications are reflected in the database buffer cache but need not be flushed to disk immediately. That task is carried out asynchronously (that is, independently, or not in synch) by the pagecleaners at an opportune time, taking into consideration the frequency with which the page is being accessed and the period of time since the page was last flushed. So, the completion of a transaction is not dependent on the time taken to complete a write to disk. Since the writes are carried out with asynchronous I/O and therefore multiple I/Os can be done in parallel, write caches do not usually help OLTP workloads, although it may be possible to use them to reduce the number of disks required.

Write caches can hinder performance when the cache is too small to keep up with the I/O rate. If writes are forced to stall while a cache page is flushed to disk and freed, application performance can suffer. Bulk updates and large write-intensive batch jobs are examples of workloads that could overwhelm a write cache.

Making Effective Use of Write Caches

The fastest write cache strategies (with respect to latency) are, in order of preference:

- Host-based write caches (for example, the StorEdge Fast Write Cache card).

- Controller-based write caches (usually inside a disk array).

- Disk-based write caches.

Host-based write caches will complete I/Os faster than will controller-based caches, since it is not necessary to go to the disk controller to complete the I/O and hence the latency of the write is lower. Similarly, disk-based write caches have the longest latency since the host, controller, and disk cache are all involved before the write reaches the cache. So, the closer the cache is to the host, the faster the write is able to complete.

On the other hand, once writes are in a host-based cache and therefore "completed," the disk pages still have to be sent to disk, requiring further CPU activity on the host. CPU cycles therefore will not be freed up by a host-based write cache unless multiple writes to the same page can be piggy-backed. Host-based caches are also likely to be smaller than controller-based caches.

Sun has released a second-generation, host-based write cache (the first-generation product was the PrestoServe SBus card, which was primarily targeted at NFS environments). It is referred to as the StorEdge Fast Write Cache, available in both SBus and PCI card format. The write cache is battery backed and can be internally mirrored across two cards for redundancy.

Preserving Data Integrity with Write Caches

If I use a write cache with my data disks, is there any possibility that my data could become corrupted, for example, in the event of a power failure? This question often bothers people and in my experience has been a subject of considerable and often confused debate. Our discussion is confined to DBMS systems, although write caches are also useful for other applications, such as NFS.

The problem is that database pages updated or "dirtied" in the buffer cache are not necessarily written to disk immediately after a transaction is committed. Dirty pages are flushed to disk later, maybe much later if they are frequently accessed. This delay is possible because all changes must first be successfully written to the log file before a commit is allowed to complete.

Consequently, the key to DBMS recoverability is the database log. Since all modifications to database pages are recorded in the log, the log can be used after a failure to reapply changes that didn't make it to disk. Partially completed transactions appearing at the end of a database log can also be backed out (rolled back) in a manner that leaves the database consistent.

In the event of a power failure, the DBMS performs a roll-forward recovery after power is restored and the database restarted. The recovery manager checks that all changes recorded in the log are reflected in the database pages on disk. If for some reason a page on disk is out of date, the changes are applied. When the recovery process has completed, the pages on disk have been synchronized with the log file. Clearly, the log and any log archives need to be large enough to hold all the data necessary for recovery.

Suppose a write cache is in use with the data disks. A power failure that outlasts the batteries supporting the write cache in the controller or host will cause the loss of any data not flushed to the data disks. But it doesn't matter; the logs preserve the integrity of the data.

Unlikely as it may be, there is still a tiny window in which data could be irretrievably lost. During a checkpoint, dirty data pages are flushed from the database buffer cache to disk. When all of these writes have completed (which merely means written to the write cache in this case), a checkpoint record is written to the log indicating that all data pages are up-to-date.

All of the following must apply before data can be lost:

- Power is lost immediately after the log checkpoint record is written.

- Not all disk information has been flushed from the disk write cache to disk.

- Power is not restored until after the write cache batteries are exhausted (or the batteries fail).

During recovery, the roll-forward process will start from the most recent checkpoint. The recovery manager will wrongly believe that all data pages on disk were up-to-date as of that point. The result is an inconsistent database.

You can eliminate this potential problem by ensuring that all disks that use write caches are connected to UPS devices and that the write cache manager is configured to automatically flush the write cache after a small delay (typically one minute). UPS devices typically provide power for several minutes at least, thereby allowing adequate time for the disk write caches to be completely flushed to disk. If the write cache is host based, then the host must also use a UPS.

The worst-case scenario with write caches is a situation where only part of a database block (for example, the first two 512-byte sectors of a 2-Kbyte block) is successfully written to disk before the power fails. If the cache is not battery backed, the rest of the data is lost, and the data block is now corrupted. This is the reason Sun ships storage with only the read cache, and not the write cache, enabled at the disk level.

Using Write Caches for Database Logs

Given that successful recovery is totally dependent on the database logs, nothing can be allowed to compromise their integrity. This means log disks should be mirrored and located on disk devices that either do not use write caches or use write caches supported by UPS devices. The write cache manager must also be capable of automatically flushing the write cache before the UPS power expires.

Host-based write caches can undermine the effect of mirroring logs unless they are also internally mirrored (a feature that is supported on the StorEdge Fast Write Cache product). A single point of failure has been introduced if a single cache supports both log disk mirrors. For the same reason, it is wise to mirror log disks across different controllers.

As for performance, I have seen write caches with database logs significantly benefit OLTP performance and have sometimes seen them make no difference to throughput, even though the disk response times did improve noticeably.

So, using write caches with database logs will probably help performance and could possibly help it significantly. But don't be disappointed if it makes no difference in your environment.

At the very least, a write cache could mask poor log disk layout. Log disks should be striped for high throughput environments or when monitoring of the log disks reveals high response times or heavy disk utilization. A write cache can also help when UFS files are used for the logs.

In one case, we used write caches for raw logs and saw response times on the log disks of around 3 msecs. After we switched off the write cache, response times climbed to around 13 msecs.

The 10-msec discrepancy translates to extra latency in completing the transaction since a commit cannot complete until the log has been written. For a transaction response time of 0.1 second, this discrepancy corresponds to a 10% increase in transaction response time. If the transaction response time is 1.0 second, the increase is just 1%.

So, applications that depend upon commit latency will be most affected. Examples are single-threaded batch jobs where the application stalls each time a commit takes place. One of the reasons why OLTP workloads may not always be affected as much is that the extra latency can be hidden by the effect of multiple transactions sharing the log buffer and being written to disk together (referred to as *group commits*).

High Availability

An organization's high availability strategy is a unique expression of its needs and expectations and will not necessarily be similar to that of other organizations. Some general principles apply, though.

Planning for disk high availability is planning for disk failure. And disk failure is inevitable.

It's all a matter of statistics. I remember one of my undergraduate professors telling us he refused to fly Qantas. His reason: Qantas had (and still has) a safety record second to none, being the longest operating airline never to have never suffered a jetliner crash. He argued that one day statistics would strike back and wipe out the entire Qantas fleet at the same time!

Thankfully, total catastrophic failure of your disk farm is unlikely. Unfortunately, a disk farm with Qantas reliability is also unlikely.

Disk Failure Planning

Disks can have a Mean Time Between Failure (MTBF) of better than 200,000 hours (23 years), even when used 24 hours a day, and the MTBF of more recent disks is significantly longer. It sounds impressive, but that is an average, not a guaranteed lifetime. Disks have an expected service life that is limited, too, often in the range of five years. With 100 disks in use, a disk with an MTBF of 200,000 hours can be expected to fail on average every 2,000 hours

(3 months). With 500 disks, expect a failure every 17 days, and with 1,000 disks, almost every week. Refer to Table 17-1 for details.

Table 17-1 *Disk MTBF scenarios*

No. of Disks	1	100	500	1,000
Disk MTBF (hours)	200,000	200,000	200,000	200,000
Hours between failures	200,000	2,000	400	200
Days	8,333.33	83.33	16.67	8.33
Months	277.78	2.78	0.56	0.28
Years	22.83	0.23	0.05	0.02

Clearly, the more disks that are used, the more frequently failures can be expected. Many database users with 500 disks probably won't tolerate a crash every 17 days, with the resulting downtime for disk replacement and database restore and roll-forward. We use very large disk configurations in our benchmarking and see these statistics at work. Consequently, we learned a long time ago to maintain adequate online backups to minimize downtime.

To protect against data loss:

- Use mirroring or RAID 5 wherever possible.

- Use hot spares.

- Don't mirror to the same disk. It sounds impossibly stupid, but I've seen it done. I've also observed that people only tend to do it once!

- Use alternate pathing.

You can enhance availability by combining mirroring with the use of *hot spares*, disks set aside to "step in" after a disk failure and take over the role of the failed disk. Since only half the mirror is unavailable, the good copy can be used to synchronize the hot spare, thus restoring a fully working mirror set. Both Veritas and SVM offer a hot spare capability. Even without hot spares defined, Veritas will do this task automatically through the relocation daemon (vxrelocd).

RAID 5 and mirroring protect against disk failure but not controller failure (unless disks are also mirrored across controllers). Alternate pathing uses the ability of Sun disk arrays to support two controller connections, allowing an alternate route to the disks to be defined by another controller. If one controller fails, the other can be used without interruption to applications

Alternate pathing is supported on the Starfire and on Enterprise Exx00 servers as of Solaris 2.6. This functionality is also essential to the Dynamic Reconfiguration capability offered on the Starfire, Enterprise Ex500, and Sun Fire systems. System boards cannot be removed without disruption to data access unless an alternate path to the disks has already been defined.

Performance Implications of Mirroring

The use of mirrors means that every write operation has to be repeated on two disks and that the operation is not complete until both writes have completed. This sounds like it would double the write time, but in fact the writes are issued in parallel. Our benchmarks have demonstrated a relatively small performance degradation due to mirroring—typically no more than a few percent for either of Veritas or SVM.

One option associated with mirroring is round-robin reading. The idea is to take advantage of the two copies of the data on separate disks by automatically alternating reads between them. In both SVM and Veritas, this is the default behavior. In Veritas, you can disable round-robin reading by nominating a plex as the primary read device, using the `vxvol rdpol prefer` syntax.

Our benchmarks within Database Engineering have shown mixed results from round-robin reading. It can improve performance; for example, if controller throughput has become a bottleneck, reading from the mirrors may be able to spread the I/O and relieve the bottleneck.

Elimination of Single Points of Failure

Which elements of the disk subsystem should be protected with RAID 5 or mirroring? Here are some suggestions:

- **Log disks.** Essential. Log disks are vital to the integrity of data in a database.

- **Root, swap, and /usr.** Highly recommended. A disk failure in any of these areas will be very time consuming to recover from (swap may not be as bad).

- **Data disks.** Recommended. Data integrity is preserved by backups plus the log disks. The decision to mirror or apply RAID 5 to data disks depends on the length of time taken to restore and roll forward the database if a data disk fails.

- **Index disks.** Recommended. Indexes can be restored or recreated from data. Once again, the time taken to do this is the crucial factor.

- **Temporary disks.** Recommended. It is usually easiest to recover from a temporary tablespace disk failure since the temporary tablespaces are only used for temporary internal database operations. Recovery can be complicated, though, and needs to be properly documented and tested if temporary disks are not protected by RAID 5 or mirroring.

- **Application disks.** Less essential. Applications can usually be quickly and easily restored from backups.

Other Data Layout Issues

To conclude the data layout discussion we examine symlinks, RAID performance with databases, and some of the pros and cons of Veritas and Solaris Volume Manager.

Database File Naming Using Symlinks

Whether raw devices or file system files are used for database files, it can prove inconvenient to move a file to a different location since file names are hardcoded at the time tablespaces are created. A simple and elegant solution to this problem is to create tablespaces using symlinks rather than direct file names.

For example, suppose the customer table consists of three database files placed on Veritas raw volumes: /dev/vx/rdsk/ourdata/vol23a, /dev/vx/rdsk/ourdata/vol34, and /dev/vx/rdsk/ourdata/vol16. Rather than hardcode these pathnames, you could create a directory and place the links in it:

```
aussie# mkdir /links
aussie# ln -s /dev/vx/rdsk/ourdata/vol23a /links/customer01
aussie# ln -s /dev/vx/rdsk/ourdata/vol34 /links/customer02
aussie# ln -s /dev/vx/rdsk/ourdata/vol16 /links/customer03
```

Relocating a customer data file to another location on disk is now a simple matter of copying the file and rebuilding its symlink (having first shut down the database).

The same approach also works for Veritas, SVM, RM6, and UFS files. I always use symbolic links rather than direct file names, both for raw devices and for UFS database files.

Migration Between Raw Devices and File Systems

A little-known fact is that database files located on file systems can be moved to raw devices, and vice versa, without the tablespace requiring a rebuild. Once the database is shut down, the dd utility can be used to copy the file. If symlinks are used, the pathname known to the database can be redirected to the new location and the database restarted.

Copying a database file from a UFS file to a raw devices is simple, since the dd will complete when the necessary number of bytes has been copied. Copying a database file from a raw device to a UFS file can be a little more complex, since the exact size of the database file may not be known (a raw device is usually larger than the database file it hosts). At worst, the end result may be a UFS file that is larger than necessary. Note that you can use the dbfsize utility with Oracle to determine the exact size of a raw device.

RAID 5 Performance with Databases

The important question for this discussion is "What place does RAID 5 have with database workloads?"

Database Engineering at Sun compared hardware and software RAID, using Oracle7 and the TPC-C OLTP workload on a heavily loaded but not fully utilized server. The aim was to see how different levels of RAID affected throughput, CPU utilization, and disk utilization.

The test system consisted of two CPU E4000 servers running Solaris 2.6. The software RAID tests used eighty-four 4-Gbyte disks in two RSM214s with fast writes enabled. The hardware RAID tests used seventy 4-Gbyte disks in two StorEdge A3000s. The RAID 5 LUNs on the A3000 used a typical layout: four data plus one parity.

The results demonstrated two things:

1. RAID 5 performs poorly compared to RAID 0+1 when both are implemented with software RAID.

2. For all levels of RAID, hardware RAID is less demanding on server CPU resources than is software RAID.

The Implications of RAID for Database Optimizers

Sophisticated database optimizers know how many disks are available to the database and use this information in deciding on query plans. Some optimizers also use lower-level information such as disk seek time and throughput.

When you use RAID 0, 3, or 5, there is no longer a one-to-one relationship between physical and logical disks. In other words, a single RAID 0 or RAID 5 "disk device" actually involves multiple physical disks. The same is true for arrays like the T3 and A1000 where LUNs hide the underlying disk layout. Database optimizers can be fooled by this apparent shortage of devices into assuming that disk throughput is limited and thus could become a bottleneck. The result could be suboptimal query plans, especially for DSS queries.

There is no way for a database to determine the underlying disk topology for all the RAID devices that exist on a server. Sometimes, the choices made by the optimizer are important for the performance of your applications. This is especially true for DSS applications where efficient query plans are one of the key factors determining query completion times.

In such cases, you may need to help out the database optimizer. How? Here are some suggestions for DSS environments:

- Use a volume manager to create multiple volumes on RAID devices or LUNs, up to the same number of volumes as there are disks underlying the logical device. For example, if there are five physical disks in a LUN or stripe, you could create five logical volumes on it. Otherwise, the database optimizer might wrongly conclude that the "single disk" will cause a disk bottleneck and favor a plan that minimizes access to it.

- Don't overdo the number of multiple logical volumes you create on the same physical disk. Be aware that the database optimizer might assume that every logical volume is a single disk.

- Avoid creating multiple logical volumes on the same disk for the same tablespace. The database optimizer might assume that the tablespace is actually spread across multiple disks.

There is probably no way to totally compensate for every aspect of this complexity, and not all database optimizers are equally sophisticated. Simply be aware that some database optimizers will make assumptions about how many disks are available to execute a query plan. These assumptions are typically based on the number of database files or devices used by each tablespace affected by the plan.

Volume Manager Pros and Cons

If faced with a choice between the Solaris Volume Manager (SVM) and the Solaris Enterprise Volume Manager (Veritas) volume managers, how do you decide which to use? Because their features and behavior are not identical, one may be more suitable than the other in some situations. The comments below are based on my experience—they are observations rather than recommendations.

Disk Layout

Perhaps the main attraction of Solaris Volume Manager before the advent of soft partitions is its simplicity. Apart from the metastate databases, which are specially created on separate partitions, SVM does not use any disk space for its own administration. For example, suppose a mirrored UFS partition, d10, is built from two simple metapartitions, d11 and d12, where d11 is defined as a normal Solaris disk partition /dev/dsk/c2t1d0s3 and d12 as /dev/dsk/c3t2d0s3. If the metapartitions are removed by metaclear, it is still possible to mount either /dev/dsk/c2t1d0s3 or /dev/dsk/c3t2d0s3 directly from Solaris since no special SVM information has been written to the disk. This opportunity does not exist for more complex metapartitions like stripes, of course.

One element of SVM's simplicity is that SVM sits directly on top of Solaris disk partitions. Each SVM metapartition maps directly to a Solaris disk partition (or to multiple partitions in the case of striping or RAID 5). This direct mapping makes SVM simple to set up and makes it easy for you to visualize where the data actually lives. On the other hand, it also means that only seven partitions per disk can be used by SVM, since Solaris only supports seven partitions per disk (0 to 7, not counting partition 2, which represents the whole disk). Veritas, on the other hand, allows as many volumes as the user requires since it manages the disk space itself.

By contrast, Veritas takes over a disk—partition 3 stores Veritas housekeeping information and partition 4 holds the user's data—and henceforth data can only be retrieved with Veritas. The housekeeping information allows Veritas to identify the disk when the system is being booted.

Since the advent of soft partitioning in SVM 4.2.1, SVM and Veritas are equivalent in this regard.

Changes to Disk Device Names

Veritas's housekeeping information on each disk has one very important benefit: even if the disk's device name changes, the Veritas path to it remains the same.

Suppose a Veritas device `/dev/vx/rdsk/mydata/customer001` is located on an A5200 disk `/dev/rdsk/c12t32d0s2`. A number of possible events can cause the A5200 disk device name to change: events such as an OS upgrade to a new release of Solaris or a hardware change like failure and replacement of the A5200 controller. The old `c12` controller name may suddenly become `c15`. No action at all is necessary with Veritas, since the disk will be identified automatically as `/dev/vx/rdsk/mydata/customer001` when the system is booted. Even if you physically switch disks between controllers, at boot time Veritas will recognize the changes automatically without need for manual intervention.

Any of these changes are catastrophic for applications using SVM metapartitions unless you realize the changes have happened and modify the SVM device definitions.

Equally, applications using disk names directly rather than volume manager volumes will be affected by controller name changes, whether they use raw devices or UFS partitions on affected disks.

Automatic Error Recovery

Veritas will automatically reestablish the failed component of a mirrored volume by setting up and synchronizing a new mirror copy wherever it can find an appropriately sized chunk of free disk. Automatic recovery is achieved by the relocation daemon (`vxrelocd`), which is started at boot time by the `/etc/rc2.d/S95vxvm-recover` script. While this feature seems like a great idea, it can do violence to a careful disk layout.

I first discovered this behavior during a data warehouse benchmark when my query performance dropped inexplicably. I traced it to a disk bottleneck. One disk now hosted two volumes from the same mirrored stripe. The cause was `vxrelocd`—an unrecoverable read error had caused Veritas to take a subdisk offline and relocate it elsewhere. My mirror was preserved but my performance was compromised in the process.

I choose to prevent `vxrelocd` from starting by commenting it out in `/etc/rc2.d/S95vxvm-recover`. The downside is that I am now dependent on my own vigilance to detect disk failures that disable half of a mirror.

Veritas can have the same effect with hot spares, too. If a subdisk is taken offline because of disk failure, it is reestablished on a hot spare disk if one has been allocated. Other subdisks on the same disk are left intact. If the failed subdisk was positioned at the end of the disk, it is now positioned at the start of the hot spare disk. If I move the remaining subdisks off the failing disk to the hot spare so it can be replaced, my original disk layout is now scrambled. It is possible to reconstruct the original layout manually by using an intermediate disk, but once again I prefer to do the relocation myself from the beginning.

If availability is more important than performance, these automatic features will prove very welcome. But in either case, it is useful to be aware of them.

Storage Cocktails

Different types of disks can be mixed and matched to achieve the best possible configuration for a user environment.

Some suggestions are given in Table 17-2.

Table 17-2 *Possible disk solutions for various workload types*

	Random Read/Write	Sequential Read	Synchronous Write
Typical Workload	*OLTP*	*Decision Support Systems*	*Database Load (& Database Logs)*
SPARCStorage Array	Good	Good (Max. 15 disks per array)	Good (use write cache)
StorEdge D1000	Very Good	Very Good	Average
StorEdge A1000	Very Good	Very Good	Best (use write cache)
StorEdge A3x00	Best	Better	Best (use write cache)
StorEdge A5x00	Best	Best	Good (if using StorEdge Fast Write Cache[a])
MultiPacks	Good	Good	Best (if using StorEdge SRC/P Controller[b])
StorEdge T3	Best	Best[c]	Best[d] (use write cache)

a. Only supported on E3x00 to E6x00 systems. "Average" if not used.
b. Only supported on E250 and E450 systems. "Average" if not used.

c. Can be classed as "Best" for large I/Os (128 Kbytes or larger). Throughput is lower for smaller I/O sizes.

d. Optimal write performance is achieved when the cache is configured with a `writebehind` rather than `writethrough` policy.

For greatest simplicity, optimal performance, and availability when configuring StorEdge T3 arrays, I suggest using a 7+1 RAID 5 layout with one hot spare or an 8+1 RAID 5 layout. The cache operates most efficiently in `write-behind` mode; for T3 ES pairs, `auto` mode will default to `writebehind` provided the battery and both power supplies are functioning correctly.

It may be useful to choose A5x00 disks for OLTP data and A1000 disks for database logs, for example. In Database Engineering we have used A5x00 arrays for database logs with Sybase with no loss of performance (high throughput depends upon an adequately sized log buffer and striped log disks). Both Database Engineering and other groups within Sun have experienced significant benefit from using write caches with Oracle redo logs.

Table 17-3 presents some general guidelines for the use of various levels of RAID.

Table 17-3 *Using RAID with disk arrays*

	RAID 0 (Striping)	RAID 1 (Mirroring)	RAID 5
SPARCstorage Array	Yes	Yes	No
StorEdge D1000	Yes	Yes	No
StorEdge A1000	Yes	Yes	Yes
StorEdge A3x00	Yes	Yes	Yes
StorEdge A5x00	Yes	Yes	No
MultiPacks	Yes	Yes	Yes[a]
StorEdge T3	Yes	Yes	Yes

a. If used with the E250/E450 StorEdge SRC/P Controller. "No" otherwise.

Any storage solution can support mirroring or striping effectively (either within the array where that is supported or with software mirroring or striping on the server). RAID 5 can be implemented in software on any disk platform, including D1000 and A5x00 arrays and MultiPacks, but for best performance, use T3, A1000, or the older A3x00 arrays, or MultiPacks with the StorEdge SRC/P Intelligent SCSI Raid Controller, since they support RAID 5 in hardware.

Note that the StorEdge Fast Write Cache is only supported on A5x00 arrays on E3x00 to E6x00 systems, and the StorEdge SRC/P Intelligent SCSI Raid Controller is only supported on E250 and E450 systems with Multi-Packs.

Finally, Sun also makes available a range of SAN storage solutions from Hitachi Data Systems. The HDS systems are primarily targeted at environments requiring high-end storage solutions with high availability, large capacity, and high performance.

Disclaimer: The guidelines offered above represent the opinion of the author. Your mileage may vary!

Data Layout Recommendations

Effective data layout does not come for free; planning and discipline are required. The benefits far outweigh the cost, though. A carefully planned data layout strategy is easier to understand and maintain and can avert performance bottlenecks.

The Beauty of Simplicity

I remember on one occasion spending time with a user, tracking down a performance problem. The database in question used no more than 30 disks, yet we spent well over an hour trying to figure out which physical devices were associated with the small number of logical devices used by the database. I was astonished at the mazelike ingenuity with which logical volumes had been created, with a combination of Veritas, symlinks, and automounts. The performance uncertainties were further compounded with a single disk occasionally appearing more than once within a single stripe!

Unfortunately, simplicity doesn't just happen—it requires planning and discipline.

Recommendations

A few general data layout guidelines apply in most situations:

- Keep it simple! Remember that an incomprehensible disk layout is an indefensible disk layout.

- Maintain data layout diagrams. You won't always be able to avoid complexity, especially if you have many disks or extensive use of RAID, but at least you can manage it with good documentation.

- For optimal performance, configure as many spindles as you reasonably can. Don't overdo it, though; for most databases, the number of 18-Gbyte disks required to achieve the necessary capacity will probably be adequate.

- Always use raw devices or Direct I/O files for log files.

- Use raw devices for other database files if possible. If moving from UFS to raw devices, you may need to increase the size of your database buffer cache.

- Stripe tablespaces for both OLTP and DSS workloads.

- Use a stripe width of 64 Kbytes for OLTP workloads and 128 Kbytes for DSS workloads.

- Place stripes for data, index, and temporary tablespaces on the same disks.
- Keep log disks on separate disks if feasible.
- Use host-based write caches in combination with A5x00 where disk write latency is important (for example, database loads and database logs).
- Turn on file system logging for UFS database files to speed system recovery.

A Worked Example

To bring together many of the recommendations in this chapter, let's illustrate the principles by considering a server with four StorEdge T3s, containing 73-Gbyte disks, and two D1000 arrays—one with 36-Gbyte disks and one with 18-Gbyte disks. Each array is connected to the server by a dedicated host adapter. The T3s each have 9 disks, the 36-Gbyte D1000 array has 8 disks, and the 18-Gbyte D1000 array has 12 disks.

I would suggest placing the root file system, swap, and applications on one of the D1000 arrays. The D1000 arrays could also be used for miscellaneous file systems, including data transfer areas and database audit file storage (that is, online copies of old database logs). For improved levels of availability, the disks could be mirrored. Although the performance characteristics of the disks on the two D1000 arrays are different, they are not different enough to rule out either striping or mirroring across the arrays if necessary. The capacity difference (18 Gbytes compared to 36 Gbytes) would need to be taken into account when mirrors or stripes across both arrays are set up.

The T3s offer the most capacity but only support up to two LUNs each (for a maximum of eight LUNs on the four T3s). Clearly, the T3 storage cannot be configured in the same way as the D1000 storage. Probably the simplest layout for the T3s is to configure each T3 as a single RAID 5 LUN with seven data disks, one parity disk, and one hot spare disk. This configuration provides a good balance between high availability and effective use of disk capacity. If the T3s are configured as ES pairs, dynamic multipathing with Veritas Volume Manager offers a further level of high availability in the event of disk controller failure on the server.

Each LUN effectively becomes a stripe of eight data disks. To balance disk I/O, a volume manager could be used to create volumes striped across two T3 LUNs, giving an effective stripe of 16 data disks. Veritas Volume Manager, for example, could be used to create as many volumes as required, allowing the full capacity of the disks to be used. A two-level stripe has been created: one on the server using the volume manager, and the second within the disk array. A second stripe could be created on the other two T3 LUNs by using the other 16 data disks.

Live database files, including data, indexes, temporary tablespaces (and rollback segments for Oracle) could be distributed evenly between the two stripes. To facilitate backup, snapshots of volumes on the first stripe could be placed on the second stripe, and vice versa.

This layout adheres to the two rules of thumb outlined earlier for striping LUNs. No stripes have been constructed with a mixture of the T3 and D1000 disks, and the stripes inherent in each of the T3 LUNs have been taken into account.

What about the database logs? Since the D1000s do not have write caches, it is advisable to place the logs on the T3 stripes. Placing the log volumes on a single stripe affords the protection of RAID 5 within the array but does not protect the logs against the failure of an entire array. For additional redundancy, the logs could be mirrored across the two T3 stripes.

Part Four

Performance Monitoring and Tuning

- Troubleshooting Methods
- Major Contributors to Poor Performance
- System Performance Monitoring Tools
- Drill-Down Monitoring
- Monitoring and Tuning Oracle
- Monitoring and Tuning Sybase
- Monitoring and Tuning Informix XPS
- Monitoring and Tuning DB2 for Solaris
- Metrics: How To Measure and What to Report

18

TROUBLESHOOTING
METHODS

Imagine you are a performance consultant. You find yourself visiting a Sun customer with a major database application. On your way to the coffee machine a couple of anxious system administrators stop you in the hallway. "Our database server is performing badly. Can you look at it?" they plead.

What process would you go through to track down the problem? I routinely ask this question when interviewing candidates for our group (Performance and Availability Engineering at Sun). I receive some surprising answers.

Candidates fresh from college typically want to dive straight into the database or operating system source code and implement traces to monitor mutex contention for the critical sections of code. If that yields nothing, they will use hardware probes to check the efficiency of the first- and second-level CPU caches. Others are convinced the answer lies in tweaking the database configuration file (`init.ora` in the case of Oracle, for example). Still others want to dump the query plans for all the SQL in the applications.

It's possible that one of these approaches might bear fruit. Just as likely, though, everyone involved will end up exhausted, confused, and frustrated.

Have you ever seen some geek with impossibly thick glasses magically run to ground a problem that eluded everyone else's best efforts? After the geek somehow does it next time, too, the general consensus is that problem solving of this kind is a black art.

The boring truth is that there's little mystery about the process needed for solving performance problems. Sometimes the geek succeeds thanks to special technical knowledge that no one else possesses. But very often success comes to those who simply know how to attack a problem.

Problem-Solving Strategy Development

Occasionally in an interview someone outlines a credible strategy for finding the problem. The answer might go something like this:

"First, I would try to get some background to the problem. I'd ask what they mean by 'performing badly.' Are response times the issue? If so, how much improvement is needed: ten percent or one hundred percent?

"Then, I would ask when the problem first appeared. Did anything else happen at the same time; did they implement a new release of the application software or add fifty more users to the system?

"Where I went next would depend on the answers to these questions.

"If the only change was to the applications, I would refer the problem to the developers. If more users had been added, I would conclude that the system had run out of some critical resource. I would look at CPU, memory, disk, and network usage. Using the standard utilities available on the operating system, I would find which of these appeared to be the bottleneck. If a lot of paging was going on, for example, I would look for the memory hogs in the system. Once I found the right area to focus on, I would hope after more investigation to have some idea of what to do about it."

The answer points to three of the key elements of problem solving:

1. Understanding the nature of the problem.

2. Identifying all of the possible contributors to the problem.

3. Examining each in turn and drilling down to the one that appears anomalous to find the root cause.

Let's look at each of these elements more closely.

The Nature of the Problem

It's dangerously easy to make assumptions about the nature of a problem. I've seen it done many times and done it myself more often than I care to admit. The secret is to take a step back and make sure you can see the big picture. Don't get lost in the details.

A good place to start is to ask lots of questions. Questions help you understand:

- How the problem manifests itself.
- What characterizes normal behavior.
- When it first became a problem.
- Where it might be helpful to start looking.

Some people have a way of casually mentioning the most significant piece of information when you're despairing and almost ready to tear your hair out. Asking lots of questions can sometimes flush out crucial information at the beginning of the process.

In summary, don't attempt to solve a problem until you fully understand it.

Possible Contributors to the Problem

Not all problems are created equal. Some seem to be born with more vigorous genes. The next chapter looks at various potential problem areas and tries to identify those that have the greatest impact.

Drilling Down to Find the Root Cause

At some point it will become appropriate to monitor the system. You need to know which monitoring tools are available to you and what to look for in the bewildering array of data generated by the tools. The following chapters present monitoring tools and a step-by-step strategy for finding bottlenecks in the system, starting with the system and moving to the database.

19

MAJOR CONTRIBUTORS TO POOR PERFORMANCE

Sadly, good performance is a goal to be achieved rather than an inalienable constitutional right. And there are many potential pitfalls on the way to the goal.

Some of the most common problems in database server environments are:

- Inadequate hardware.

- Internal operating system architectural design problems.

- Poorly designed applications (including poorly written SQL).

- Problems with the user environment.

- Internal architectural inefficiencies in the DBMS being used.

- Poor data layout.

- Poor database design and implementation (including schema, choice of indexes, etc.).

- Operating system tuning.

- Database tuning.

In this chapter we briefly examine some of the major performance road-blocks. The emphasis is on identifying rather than resolving problems since many of the problems outlined above are beyond the scope of this book.

Performance Problem Identification

Don't decide your hardware is underconfigured until you've eliminated the other possibilities. Application issues can be major causes of performance problems and are an excellent starting point for an investigation.

Begin by understanding your limitations. Unless you are a kernel engineer working for Sun or Oracle, you probably can't change the internal architecture of the operating system or the database, so remove this ambition from your checklist. It makes sense to focus on the things you can fix and bypass the things you can't. But you might be able to fix problems with the user environment, with database layout, or with tuning.

A list of issues follows in order of importance. Decisions about relative importance are subjective, of course. These are my opinions and your mileage may vary!

Poorly Designed Applications

The impact on performance of a poorly designed application can be astonishing. Performance can be degraded significantly in the worst-case scenario.

I remember being called to a customer site where a remote terminal emulator was being used for a stress test on a new application. With a small number of users the system behaved normally, but as the load increased, response times climbed dramatically and throughput slowed to a standstill.

We ultimately discovered the cause of the problem after noticing a high number of fork(2) system calls. The application was logging each database transaction; the log included a timestamp and the terminal number (tty) of the user connection.

The developer who coded the transaction logging function knew only one way of identifying the tty name: the UNIX tty program. So, within his C program he used the system(3C) function to execute the tty program and redirect the output to a temporary file. He then opened the file, read in the tty string, and closed the file. Finally, he deleted the temporary file, once again using the system function, using the rm program since he was unaware of any better way of deleting a file from within the C programming language (such as unlink(2)).

Consequently, every database transaction required two system function calls, resulting in an expensive fork and exec(2) operation each time. The code ran to about 60 lines.

We replaced the 60 lines with two lines of code using the ttyname(3C) function, eliminating both system calls. Once the application was recompiled and deployed, the system behaved normally under load.

This example illustrates the potential of poorly written applications to bring your system to its knees. It also highlights the value of stress-testing applications before deployment. If you develop your own applications, I would strongly recommend using a remote terminal or browser emulator to test them during all phases of development to ensure that performance goals are met. (The book website includes the HandsOff Remote Terminal Emulator.)

Unfortunately, the reality is that while application functionality is tested by developers, application performance often remains untested, even for some major software packages. Consequently, performance problems are sometimes detected only when the application is deployed.

Poorly written SQL is another potential performance black hole. I have seen SQL consultants used to good effect as part of an application development review cycle. In an ideal world, database optimizers would find efficient ways of implementing even poorly coded SQL. That is the goal, but we're not there yet.

Poor Database Design and Implementation

An excellent logical design can prove inadequate under load. I have seen a widely used sequence number, read and incremented from the same heavily accessed row in the database, cause a major performance bottleneck. Heavy table inserts can also cause problems.

Some initial investment in profiling performance is usually worth the effort in the long run, as is an independent review by expert consultants.

Problems with the User Environment

User environment settings (typically established by the `.login`, `.cshrc`, or `.profile` files) may not seem an obvious place to look for performance problems. Yet a system can be crippled by poorly constructed environment variables.

I remember one occasion when a customer was unable to simultaneously log in 100 users to their server. The problem proved to be the `PATH` environment variable. The major application programs were on another server, accessed through the automounter. The `PATH` environment variable pointed first to several different automounted directories, then finally to `/bin`, `/usr/bin`, and other directories. The `.profile` contained some complex script code, including extensive use of `awk`, `sed`, `ls`, and other utilities.

Before any one of these UNIX utilities could be used, it first had to be located from the list of directories in `PATH`. So, to find `awk`, for example, the system first searched all of the automounted directories before finally locating `awk` in `/usr/bin`. Many users logging in at once caused the automounter to become a severe bottleneck.

Once the automounted directories were placed at the end of `PATH` instead of the beginning, user logins proceeded normally.

As with application performance issues, user environment problems can be most easily highlighted by a remote terminal emulator before they cause a problem in production systems.

Poor Data Layout

We have already considered the need for a carefully planned data layout strategy. The implications of poor choices here are not difficult to imagine, especially since they are so commonly experienced!

The Next Step

If you use packaged software, it may not be possible for you to tune either your applications or your database schema. And even if you do carry out your own development, it is neither realistic nor necessary to seek perfect performance in tuning your applications and database schema. The 80/20 rule applies here as elsewhere: 80 percent of your tuning effort could well be spent squeezing the last 20 percent of performance from your applications. Emphasize elimination of the major bottlenecks.

Once everything possible has been done to deal with the class of problems described above, we are now ready to proceed to the next stage: monitoring the operating system and database.

After monitoring, you should finally find yourself in a position to decide whether your hardware is adequate to achieve satisfactory performance.

But before we can develop a drill-down method for finding performance problems, we need to first look at the monitoring tools available to help with the task. The next chapter gives a snapshot of some of the useful system monitoring tools available for Solaris.

20

SYSTEM PERFORMANCE MONITORING TOOLS

Many monitoring tools are available today for the Solaris Operating Environment. Commercial tools such as BMC Best/1 offer capacity planning functionality and sophisticated monitoring capabilities. BMC Patrol and other such tools offer event mechanisms to notify the user if an exception occurs. All of the commercial tools automatically graph the key elements of system behavior, such as CPU utilization.

Another widely used tool is `virtual_adrian.se`, developed by Adrian Cockcroft, based on the SE toolkit; both are available on the book website. `virtual_adrian.se` monitors all the major elements of a system's performance and advises should any of them need attention. The SE toolkit and virtualAdrian are described in detail in *Sun Performance and Tuning*, Second Edition, Sun Press, by Adrian Cockcroft and Rich Pettit.

In this chapter we focus on tools that are freely available and do not require access to a GUI. One reason for keeping it simple is that sometimes systems are located on private subnets that do not lend themselves to graphical access. Another reason is that sometimes sophisticated presentation can actually mystify the process by removing the budding performance analyst one step from the raw data. Here, we focus on the relevant raw data with the aim of making it understandable.

Basic Solaris Tools

A number of tools for monitoring system behavior are supplied with Solaris. The most commonly used are the following:

277

- **iostat** — Disk utilization, service time, and related monitoring.

- **mpstat** — Per CPU monitoring. Also reports interrupt activity for each CPU.

- **netstat** — Network traffic monitoring.

- **nfsstat** — NFS monitoring.

- **ps** — Per process monitoring.

- **sar** — All aspects of system monitoring except networks.

  sar can optionally save data to a binary file. The data can be extracted later from the binary file, either for the entire monitoring period or according to a start and end time (with the -s and -e options). Data can also be selectively reported (for example, just CPU utilization or just disk statistics).

- **vmstat** — CPU, memory, swap, and run queue monitoring.

- **prstat** — Per process monitoring (only available as of Solaris 8).

Other tools that are widely used but do not ship with Solaris include the following:

- **vxstat** — Veritas Volume Manager volume throughput monitoring.

- **statit** — All major aspects of system monitoring.

  statit can be used to monitor the system for a specified period (for example, over a 30-second interval by running statit sleep 30), while a program is executing (statit *program_name*), or during an arbitrary period (use statit -x at the start of the period and statit -y at the end of the period to dump the statistics). Like sar, statit can save trace output at nominated intervals either to a text file or to a binary file for later display by statit.

  statit offers one additional benefit compared to sar: it reports network statistics for each network interface (although not packet size, unfortunately, only the number of packets).

- **top** — Per process monitoring (a curses-based tool).

  From Solaris 8, top is not required, since Solaris ships with the prstat utility, which provides similar functionality.

Of these tools, vxstat is only relevant to Veritas Volume Manager users and ships with Veritas Volume Manager; top (a third-party tool) and statit are both unsupported. The book website includes copies of statit and top.

Other more specialized tools such as lockstat and cpustat, which monitor kernel lock and low-level hardware behavior, are used within engineering by developers or specialized performance engineers. However, the tools listed above can identify the majority of the system performance problems found in real-world systems.

Monitoring Intervals

One common misconception is that use of these tools negatively impacts system performance. In fact, with the exception of ps and to a lesser extent top and prstat, it is quite safe to use any of them with intervals as small as 1 or 2 seconds. If you need convincing, try running vmstat 1 on an idle system. You will find that in spite of vmstat, the system still shows the CPU as 100% idle (apart from minor system daemon activity, which occurs every few seconds with or without vmstat running).

Considerable CPU is consumed by ps in particular, especially on a heavily loaded system; use it sparingly (every few minutes at the most on a busy system).

Monitoring with long intervals (five minutes or more) can be useful to get an overall perspective on performance. Beware, though—the results will be an average over the whole interval, so utilization peaks and troughs are smoothed out and can be completely missed.

To zoom in on a performance issue, don't use an interval longer than 10 seconds. A 5-second interval is a good choice for visual monitoring or for statistics collection over periods of up to 20 minutes (240 data points).

Note that some tools, such as vmstat, iostat, and vxstat, report the averages since boot time as the first data point. This first data point should normally be ignored. So, to get a single 5-second interval snapshot from vmstat, for example, use vmstat 5 2 and ignore the first line of information.

Other Monitoring Tools

An extremely useful set of tools, based on information held in /proc, can be found in /usr/proc/bin (as of Solaris 8, these tools are located in /bin, with symlinks in /usr/proc/bin pointing to the new location). They include the following:

- **pcred** — Prints the credentials (effective, real, and saved user IDs, or UIDs, and group IDs, or GIDs) of each process.
- **pfiles** — Reports fstat(2) and fcntl(2) information for all open files in each process.
- **pflags** — Prints the /proc tracing flags, pending and held signals, and other /proc status information for each lwp in each process.
- **pldd** — Lists the dynamic libraries linked into each process, including shared objects explicitly attached by dlopen(3X).
- **pmap** — Prints the address space map of each process.
- **psig** — Lists the signal actions of each process.
- **pstack** — Prints a hex+symbolic stack trace for each lwp in each process.
- **pstop/prun** — Stops or starts each process.

- **ptime** — Times a command, like the time(1) command but uses microstate accounting for reproducible precision.

- **ptree** — Prints the process trees containing the specified process IDs (PIDs) or users, with child processes indented from their respective parent processes. An argument of all digits is taken to be a process ID; otherwise, it is assumed to be a user login name. Default is all processes.

- **pwait** — Waits for all of the specified processes to terminate.

- **pwdx** — Prints the current working directory of each process.

Network traffic can be monitored with both netstat and statit, although both tools focus on the number of packets sent and received. An undocumented netstat option, -k, reports the number of packets received and sent by each network interface (ipackets and opackets), along with an almost overwhelming quantity of other kernel data. As of Solaris 2.6, netstat -k also reports the number of bytes received and sent (rbytes and obytes). The combination of packet count and byte statistics count allows the average packet size to be calculated for both incoming and outgoing packets. A new utility, kstat, introduced in Solaris 8, presents the same information in a more flexible manner, allowing statistics to be selectively extracted. An example of how kstat can be used is given on page 293.

A sophisticated tool referred to as memtool (developed by Richard McDougall) is also not officially supported but provides extremely useful information about memory usage for all processes on the system. memtool is available on the book website. A script based on this tool, procmem, is also included on the book website and is described on page 286.

Another useful tool is truss, which displays all system calls made by a running process. With the -c option, truss summarizes system call statistics for a monitored process. The statistics are reported when you interrupt truss with Control-C. Note, though, that truss can be intrusive on heavily loaded systems.

21

DRILL-DOWN
MONITORING

The time has come. Armed only with your wits, a little common sense, and some basic system knowledge, you're going to crack the performance problem bedevilling your database server. You roll up your sleeves and seat yourself firmly in front of a keyboard. A cluster of slightly awed colleagues watches wide-eyed over your shoulder.

OK, perhaps I'm getting a bit carried away here. Suffice it to say that the aim of this chapter is to develop a simple method for identifying performance problems on database servers.

I'm assuming you have already looked at the issues covered in earlier chapters. Your application's behavior is well understood and consultants in small doses have already done wonders with application performance. You've done what you can to fix any database schema design problems and the addition of a couple of crucial indexes has already calmed the users down a little.

You've checked out obscure things like environment variables and racked your brains for other issues that might need attention. But performance problems still persist. Perhaps you need to upgrade your hardware, but at this point you're not sure.

Where should you start? I'm going to suggest a five-step process that will walk you through the major components of the system: memory, disk I/O, network, and CPU, followed by database monitoring and tuning. If a problem becomes apparent in one of these areas, there may be further steps to narrow the problem. This kind of "drill down" approach is an effective way to identify and ultimately solve problems.

If you find a bottleneck (by which I mean a constriction of performance, just as the neck of a bottle limits the flow of liquid into or out of a bottle), does that mean you should look no further? I would suggest going through the whole process anyway to see what you can discover.

Bear in mind, though, that fixing a bottleneck in one place might expose another elsewhere. Suppose, for example, your system is paging severely due to a lack of memory, but no problems are apparent elsewhere. Adding memory might allow your throughput to improve to the point where one of the disks becomes overutilized, resulting in a disk bottleneck. Checking out the disks as well might give a hint of problems to come.

Once you've found and resolved a bottleneck, go through the entire process again.

Finally, is the order of the steps important? Of course there are many possible ways of tackling system monitoring, but I suggest you go through the steps in the order shown.

STEP 1. Monitoring Memory

To check for a memory bottleneck, use the vmstat utility, which shows, among other things, memory behavior for the system. A 5-second interval is a good choice for live monitoring.

The vmstat trace in Figure 21.1 shows a system with no evidence of memory shortfall.

Figure 21.1 *vmstat trace with no memory shortfall*

procs			memory			page						disk				faults			cpu		
r	b	w	swap	free	re	mf	pi	po	fr	de	sr	m1	m2	s6	sd	in	sy	cs	us	sy	id
0	8	0	3557104	1359368	0	621	0	0	0	0	0	0	0	0	0	417	11922	1190	12	2	86
0	7	0	3555728	1358080	0	729	0	0	0	0	0	0	0	0	0	449	12797	1985	20	2	78
5	9	0	3512184	1318120	0	3666	0	12	12	0	0	0	0	0	6	2198	32163	7404	70	10	20
3	15	0	3485016	1293944	0	939	0	24	24	0	0	0	0	0	1	892	30760	2842	50	4	46
0	18	0	3480520	1289912	0	813	0	0	0	0	0	0	0	0	1	616	27887	2895	31	4	65
0	17	0	3476216	1285992	0	547	0	3	3	0	0	0	0	0	0	516	31687	1716	21	2	77
1	16	0	3473000	1283232	0	542	0	6	6	0	0	0	0	0	0	663	43993	2112	30	3	67
2	16	0	3469568	1280368	0	712	0	8	8	0	0	0	0	0	1	666	39791	3176	34	3	62

Figure 21.2 shows a vmstat trace from the same system during a severe memory shortfall.

Figure 21.2 *vmstat trace with severe memory shortfall*

procs			memory		page					disk				faults			cpu		
r	b	w	swap	free	re	mf	pi	po	fr	de	sr	m1	m2	s6	sd	in	sy	cs	us	sy	id
0	31	0	2175384	47800	3	542	1	166	593	38656	141	0	0	0	1	689	26511	3549	19	4	78
0	27	0	2170608	47552	2	790	4	305	1116	45208	269	0	0	0	2	711	36787	6050	27	6	66
0	28	0	2168088	48704	4	788	1	190	432	47256	92	0	0	0	2	718	30558	3291	23	4	73
0	29	0	2164592	47664	1	699	8	158	574	47712	136	0	0	0	1	777	29870	3400	19	3	78
1	27	0	2162136	48184	2	734	9	140	403	42944	105	0	0	0	2	708	28258	3027	22	4	74
1	27	0	2158560	47688	0	498	4	166	606	38656	146	0	0	0	1	750	41527	3034	20	4	76
0	27	0	2155136	47408	1	489	6	240	796	38656	179	0	0	0	1	754	31926	3275	17	4	79
0	27	0	2151664	47824	1	581	6	187	622	47712	145	0	0	0	2	946	36169	3741	19	5	76

What to Look For

Look for po (pageouts—the kilobytes paged out per second) and sr (scan rate—the number of pages scanned by the clock algorithm). When both are consistently high at the same time (much more than 100 per second, say, on a system with up to 4 Gbytes of memory, more on a larger system), then it is possible the page daemon is being forced to steal free memory from running processes. Do you need to add more memory to the system? Maybe.

More memory may not help, though. That might sound crazy, but unfortunately the water is a little muddy here. Some explanation might help clarify the situation.

Pageouts can happen for a number of reasons, including the following:

- Dirty (modified) file system pages are being flushed to disk. Such flushing is normal behavior and does not represent a problem. If database files are placed on file system files, expect to see this kind of pageout.

- Application pages are being pushed out to the swap device to free up memory for other purposes. If the applications in question are active or about to become active, paging is bad!

- New memory has been allocated by an application and swap space is being assigned to it. This, too, is normal behavior and does not represent a problem.

- Memory pages have been freed by applications and are being flushed to disk. Isn't paging a waste of time if the memory is no longer required by the applications? You bet! Solaris 8 introduced a new madvise() flag called MADV_FREE to enable developers to tell the operating system not to bother to flush such pages to swap.

The *scan rate* is a measure of the activity of the page daemon. The page daemon wakes up and looks for memory pages to free when an application is unable to find enough memory on the free list (memory has fallen to the lotsfree system parameter). The greater the memory shortfall, the faster the page daemon will scan pages in main memory.

The major consumers of memory in a system are:

- Applications, including text (binary code), stack (which contains information related to the current phase of execution of the program and its functions), heap (which contains program working space), and shared memory.

- The file system page cache, which contains file system data (all file system disk blocks must first be read into memory before they can be used). This cache becomes important when database files are stored on file systems.

- The operating system kernel.

Normal Paging Behavior Prior to Solaris 8

Before Solaris 8, the `free` column reported by `vmstat` may not be a good indication of the available memory in the system. The reason is that once memory pages are used by the file system page cache, they are not returned to the free list. Instead, the file system data blocks are left in the cache in case they are needed again in the future.

When the page daemon detects a memory shortfall and scans for pages to free, it may well choose to free some of the pages in the file system page cache. If the pages have been modified, they are first flushed to disk. There is no simple way of finding out how much of main memory is being used by the file system page cache at any point, but you can bet it will be substantial if database files are located on UFS files rather than raw partitions. The `memtool` package (Richard McDougall's memory monitoring tool), available on the book website, can identify memory use by UFS files.

The problem is that the page daemon may free application memory pages as well as file system page cache pages since it doesn't know which is which. The result can be severe paging and major performance problems. Adding more memory won't help much, either. It will simply mean that more database pages can be cached in the memory. Fortunately, there is a solution.

Priority Paging

As of Solaris 7, a new feature called *priority paging* has been added. Priority paging lowers the priority of file system pages in memory so that the page daemon will choose to free them ahead of application pages. This behavior can make a huge difference to paging problems; priority paging should be enabled wherever databases coexist with active file systems, and especially where database files are placed on file systems.

You can activate priority paging by adding the following line to `/etc/system`:

```
set priority_paging = 1
```

Patches are available for Solaris 2.5.1 and Solaris 2.6 to add priority paging functionality. From Solaris 8, changes to the virtual memory system mean that priority paging is no longer required and should not be used.

UFS Files and Paging

If your database files are UFS files rather than raw devices, you may observe significant scanning even once you have enabled priority paging. In fact, the scan rate may increase since priority paging causes the page daemon to become active sooner. This behavior is a natural consequence of the need to bring all database pages into the UFS page cache before they can be accessed by the database. The ongoing need to find free memory gives rise to constant scanning activity on busy database servers using UFS files.

If your application carries out updates, inserts, and deletes, you should also expect to see pageout activity. All database writes must go through the UFS page cache before being written to disk. Although the page being written to disk would previously have been read into the UFS page cache, it might have since been reused if the scan rate is high. In that case the page must be reread from disk before the write to disk can proceed. This process in turn displaces another page, and the cycle continues.

How do you stop all this paging activity? To eliminate scanning (assuming you have enough memory for your applications), either use raw devices or mount your database partitions with the Direct I/O flag (forcedirectio).

A word of caution: eliminating paging activity with Direct I/O may not always result in instant performance improvements. The file system page cache acts as a second-level cache for database pages, and removing it from the picture will expose any inadequacies in the sizing of your database buffer cache. Make sure that your database buffer cache is adequately sized; otherwise, you may find yourself with plenty of free memory and a database buffer cache starved of buffers.

Enabling Direct I/O for database files, and especially for database logs, can offer significant performance benefits as of the Solaris 8 1/01 release; earlier versions of Direct I/O may not offer significant performance gains. Direct I/O is described in more detail in "Unix File System Enhancements" on page 21.

As a final caution, although Direct I/O can prove very useful for database files, do not enable it for nondatabase files without first examining carefully the performance implications of doing so.

Normal Paging Behavior as of Solaris 8

As we have seen, priority paging doesn't go all the way to solving the problem. Although the page daemon will choose file system pages in preference to application pages, the page daemon still has to search through the whole of memory to find them. And if large database buffer caches are being used, file system pages may only represent a small proportion of the total memory, so a lot of searching will be necessary.

As of Solaris 8, file system pages are separately accounted for, so they can be freed without a memory scan to find them. Consequently, the page daemon is not needed at all unless there is a major memory problem. As a result, the likelihood of paging problems is greatly diminished.

Drilling Down Further

If you want to find out where the memory is going, there are a number of options:

- For the final answer on memory consumption, use memtool. The proc-mem script described below will provide a detailed breakdown of process memory usage. Both memtool and procmem are available on the book website.

- Run dmesg and look for Avail mem. The difference between available memory and physical memory (use prtconf or /usr/plat-

`form/`arch -k`/sbin/prtdiag` to find out the physical memory)
indicates the amount of memory reserved for the kernel.

- Use `/usr/ucb/ps -aux` to find out which processes are the major memory hogs. This command lists the percentage of memory used by each process. Beware, though! The memory listed is virtual memory, not physical memory, and it may not be a good indication of how much physical memory is actually being consumed by the process at any given moment.

The `procmem` script requires you to install the unbundled `memtool` package since it uses the `pmem` program (similar to the standard Solaris `pmap` program, but with various bugs fixed on some Solaris releases). Some users are unwilling to install an unbundled package on a production system—an alternative version based on `pmap` is also available. The `procmem` script summarizes memory use for all processes and gives a breakdown into resident, shared, and private memory usage. Please note that both `procmem` and `memtool` are unsupported software.

Passing the `-h` parameter to `procmem` results in the following usage information:

```
usage: procmem [-v] [-h | -p pidlist | [ -u username ] [ searchstring ]]

Examples:
procmem -p 10784 10759
        - show memory usage for processes with pids 10784 10759
procmem -u root
        - show memory usage for all processes owned by the root user
procmem -u "daemon root"
     - show memory usage for all processes owned by the root & daemon users
procmem netscape
        - show memory usage for process(es) in 'ps -ef' with "netscape"
procmem -u fred netscape
        - show memory usage for "netscape" processes owned by fred
procmem
        - show memory usage for all processes (provided current user has
          superuser access privileges)

Definition of terms
   'Kbytes' is the total memory size of the process or file.
   'Resident' is that portion currently occupying physical memory.
   'Shared' is resident memory capable of being shared.
   'Private' is resident memory unique to this process or file.
   Resident = Shared + Private
Sizing
   For reporting purposes, the 'Shared' component has been counted once
   only while the 'Private' component has been summed for each process
   or file.  The /usr/lib shared libraries have been reported separately
   since they tend to be widely used across applications.  To be totally
   accurate, though, the shared component of these shared libraries
   should only be counted once across all applications, not once for
   every group of applications.  The same logic may apply to other
   shared libraries also used by multiple applications.
```

The `-v` flag offers additional detail. An example of `procmem` output follows for all processes on a server running an Oracle database.

Processes	Kbytes	Resident	Shared	Private
Process Summary (Count)				
-csh (3)	5376	2456	1064	1392
-ksh (8)	14624	2912	1456	1456
automountd (1)	4088	3656	1792	1864
cimomboot (1)	1576	1384	1256	128
cron (1)	1936	1744	1464	280
devfsadmd (1)	2776	2536	1592	944
devfseventd (1)	1272	1232	952	280
dmispd (1)	3160	2648	1744	904
dtlogin (1)	4920	2856	2192	664
dwhttpd (2)	20080	7440	4496	2944
esd (2)	24712	21768	3880	17888
grep (1)	968	936	832	104
in.ndpd (1)	1856	1488	1304	184
in.rdisc (1)	1616	1416	1272	144
in.rlogind (6)	10368	2464	1360	1104
inetd (1)	2648	2384	1384	1000
init (1)	1888	1608	1136	472
iostat (1)	1824	1784	904	880
ksh (5)	9040	2320	1456	864
lockd (1)	1896	1656	1264	392
lpsched (1)	3040	1768	1552	216
mibiisa (1)	2952	2752	1504	1248
mountd (1)	2952	2536	1528	1008
nfsd (1)	1888	1672	1264	408
nscd (1)	3200	2928	1528	1400
ora_ckpt_bench (1)	1405264	1372488	1371824	664
ora_dbw0_bench (1)	1406976	1374208	1371824	2384
ora_dbw1_bench (1)	1406968	1374200	1371824	2376
ora_dbw2_bench (1)	1406968	1374200	1371824	2376
ora_dbw3_bench (1)	1406968	1374200	1371824	2376
ora_lgwr_bench (1)	1405248	1372472	1371824	648
ora_pmon_bench (1)	1405696	1372920	1371824	1096
ora_reco_bench (1)	1405160	1372384	1371824	560
ora_smon_bench (1)	1405192	1372424	1371824	600
oraclebench (50)	70258944	1400768	1371824	28944
powerd (1)	1632	1576	976	600
rpcbind (1)	2584	2088	1296	792
sac (1)	1736	1488	1296	192
sendmail (1)	2936	2280	1816	464
sh (4)	4176	1320	912	408
snmpXdmid (1)	3744	3184	2024	1160
snmpdx (1)	2144	1920	1520	400
statd (1)	2592	2208	1464	744
syslogd (1)	4192	3008	1456	1552
tail (1)	968	936	792	144
tee (2)	1808	952	792	160
tpccload (50)	418800	38944	3344	35600
ttymon (2)	3464	1744	1336	408
utmpd (1)	1000	944	816	128
vmstat (1)	1312	1280	808	472
vold (1)	2696	2408	1768	640
vxconfigd (1)	14656	13944	1328	12616

File (Count)	Kbytes	Resident	Shared	Private
/usr/lib Shared Library Totals	291936	27928	2856	25072
Other Shared Library Totals	1473544	29304	7248	22056
Mapped File Totals	560	488	488	0
Binary File Totals	1378632	18864	13328	5536
Shared Memory Totals	80280128	1360688	1360688	0
Anonymous Memory Totals	89680	84008	0	84008
Grand Totals	83514480	1521280	1384608	136672

The bulk of the 1.5 Gbytes of resident memory used on this server is accounted for by 1.3 Gbytes of shared memory, which also constitutes the major component of the memory used for the Oracle processes.

The script can be used to report the physical and virtual memory consumption for a group of processes. For example, `procmem ora` will report memory consumption for all processes that have the string `ora` in a `ps -ef` report (Oracle processes typically meet this criterion). If another Oracle user running the same applications is added to the system, you would not expect an increase in the `Shared` component of memory for `/usr/lib` shared libraries, other shared libraries, binary files, or shared memory segments. The `Private` component would be expected to grow, though, for the shared libraries, the mapped files, and anonymous memory. The additional private memory required would probably be roughly equivalent to the private memory total for these applications divided by the current number of users.

Detail is available for all processes, as well as summaries for `/usr/lib` shared libraries (which tend to be used by many processes throughout a system and so should be counted only once for sizing purposes), other shared libraries (for example, Oracle shared libraries), mapped files (memory-mapped file system files), binary files (executable programs), shared memory segments, and anonymous memory (heap and stack).

The `procmem` script will accurately show all memory directly used by processes, but not memory belonging to UFS files that are resident in the file system page cache. Since pages from UFS database files are not directly mapped into the address spaces of database processes, they will not appear in the totals. The `memps -m` command from `memtool` provides this information (it requires the `memtool` kernel module—installed when the `memtool` package is first set up—to be loaded).

What You Can Do to Reduce Paging

If you are using file systems for your database files, the first step is to upgrade to Solaris 8 or else enable priority paging for earlier releases of Solaris. If necessary, you could also consider include the following steps to relieve memory pressures on your database server:

- Add more memory to the system.

- Use Direct I/O for database files.

- Reduce the size of the database buffer cache. This reduction may result in additional database I/O, but that is almost always preferable to paging.

- Remove applications from the server. If applications are running on the server, move them to a client system and run the applications in client/server mode. Memory should be freed up as a result.

- Reduce the number of users on the system.

STEP 2. Monitoring Disks

If you've made it to Step 2, then you know by now exactly what is going on with memory on your system. The next step is to find out whether you have any disk bottlenecks or disks that may soon become bottlenecks.

Use `iostat`, `statit`, or `sar` to check for a disk bottleneck. The `statit` utility is available on the book website.

Try `iostat -xn 5` (the -n option, which displays disk names in the *cnt-ndn* format, is only available from Solaris 2.6 on). If you have a lot of disks, you may be so overwhelmed by the output that you find it hard to make sense of all that data. You can use `grep` to remove idle disks from the display (after asking yourself why you have idle disks!):

```
iostat -xn 5 | grep -v "0.0  0.0    0.0    0.0  0.0  0.0    0.0   0   0"
```

Don't try to key this command in—you need exactly the right delimiters between all the 0s. I simply extract the `grep` string shown above from an `iostat` trace and save the whole command as `iostat2` for future use.

If you want to save a disk activity report for later reference, you will find the `sar` binary file format useful since each data point has an associated timestamp.

What to Look For

The `statit` extract in Figure 21.3 shows disk behavior for three disks. The first disk is fully utilized, the second is almost idle, and the third is appropriately utilized. The key information is `util%` (the percentage utilization of the disk) and `srv-ms` (service time in milliseconds). Note that service time (the time taken to complete the I/O at the disk) is mislabeled; it is actually response time: the time taken to complete the I/O from the time it leaves the disk device driver on the host, including queuing effects at the controller and the disk. `iostat` also reports the same values (`util%` is shown as `%b`, and `srv-ms` as `svc_t`).

Figure 21.3 *statit output for three disks*

```
Disk I/O Statistics (per second)
Disk    util%   xfer/s   rds/s   wrts/s  rdb/xfr  wrb/xfr wtqlen svqlen   srv-ms
c2t4d2  100.0   137.4    133.8    3.7     4081     2048    0.00   12.34    89.8
c2t4d3    0.3     1.0      0.0    1.0        0    14811    0.00    0.02    16.5
c2t4d4   35.5    46.7     42.7    4.1     2048     2048    0.00    0.48    10.3
```

For OLTP workloads, if utilization is consistently greater than about 60% or response time is consistently greater than about 35 msecs, the load on this disk is likely to negatively affect application performance.

For DSS workloads, utilization may exceed 60% and response times may exceed 35 msec—a single 1-Mbyte transfer from a 36-Mbyte disk could take 35 msecs. The `wtqlen` field in Figure 21.3 (wait in `iostat`) reports how many other I/O requests are queued and, therefore, how much of the response time is due to queuing time. The svqlen field (actv in iostat) shows the number of requests taken off the queue and actively being processed. With queue lengths consistently greater than 1.0 and response times consistently larger than 35 msecs, disk load is likely to negatively affect application performance.

For both workloads, the key issue is to check how busy the other disks are. You want to avoid the situation where some disks are busy and others are idle. In that respect, the disk utilization and service times shown in Figure 21.3 reveal a disk layout that is sadly lacking. Disk layout recommendations are discussed in Chapter 17.

An extract from an iostat trace (iostat -xn 5) is shown in Figure 21.4 for reference.

Figure 21.4 *iostat trace*

```
                              extended device statistics
   r/s   w/s    kr/s    kw/s  wait actv  svc_t  %w  %b device
  33.2   0.0    66.4     0.0   0.0  0.6   18.4   0   25 c2t4d0
   0.0   2.4     0.0    27.8   0.0  0.0    1.7   0    0 c2t4d1
  60.2   0.0   120.4     0.0   0.0  1.2   19.4   0   48 c2t4d2
  53.8   0.0   107.6     0.0   0.0  0.6   11.8   0   26 c2t4d3
   4.0   0.0   254.3     0.0   0.0  0.1   13.5   0    5 c2t4d4
   0.0   1.2     0.0    19.8   0.0  0.0    2.6   0    0 c3t0d0
   0.0   5.6     0.0    54.4   0.0  0.0    1.9   0    1 c3t0d1
```

The disk utilization shown in this trace is once again unbalanced, suggesting that improvements in the disk layout are needed.

Some utilities, such as sar, for example, report disk names as sd*n*, or ssd*n*, rather than c*n*t*n*d*n*. Having identified a hot disk, you may then find it difficult to locate the disk in question. Thanks to the /etc/path_to_inst file, it is possible to convert the name to a more recognizable form. The procedure is illustrated below.

Suppose a sar trace on host pae280 identifies a host disk with the name ssd4. First we need to find out more about ssd4.

```
pae280% grep " 4 " /etc/path_to_inst | grep ssd
"/pci@8,600000/SUNW,qlc@4/fp@0,0/ssd@w2100002037e3d688,0" 4 "ssd"
```

The complicated string returned from the /etc/path_to_inst file (the first string surrounded by double quotes) corresponds to the details for the disk in the /devices tree. Entries in the /dev/rdsk directory (and also in /dev/dsk) are actually symlinks to the /devices tree, so we can search for the entry above in the /dev/rdsk directory:

```
pae280% ls -l /dev/rdsk/*s2 | grep \
"/pci@8,600000/SUNW,qlc@4/fp@0,0/ssd@w2100002037e3d688,0"
lrwxrwxrwx   1 root   root   74 Jun 27 18:43 /dev/rdsk/c2t1d0s2 ->
../../devices/pci@8,600000/SUNW,qlc@4/fp@0,0/ssd@w2100002037e3d688,0:c,raw
```

This final step shows that the disk corresponding to ssd4 is /dev/rdsk/c2t1d0s2.

You can use the same procedure by substituting the appropriate details for 4 and `ssd` in the first step. The string returned can then be substituted for the string beginning `/pci` in the second step.

Drilling Down Further

Note that recent versions of `iostat` have the `-p` option, which shows per partition disk statistics. This option can be helpful in tracking down exactly which database device is responsible for a performance problem.

For systems using Veritas Volume Manager (Veritas), the partition is less useful because Veritas places all its volumes in partition 4. However, Veritas provides the `vxstat` program to monitor I/O activity per volume. This program is invaluable for drill-downs to find the volumes associated with heavy I/O, especially important when multiple volumes reside on the same disk.

The `vxstat` utility can be run as follows:

```
vxstat -g group -i interval -c iterations
```

BEWARE: Unlike `vmstat` and `iostat`, the statistics reported by `vxstat` represent totals for the whole interval period, not per second. Consequently, you need to divide the reported bytes read and written by the number of seconds in the interval (to get bytes read and written per second) and also by 1024 (to get kilobytes per second).

What You Can Do to Avoid Bottlenecks

To overcome a disk bottleneck, try one of the following:

- Stripe the data on the disk across a greater number of disks. Take into account, though, the recommendations in "Deciding How Broad to Make a Single Stripe" on page 249. Bear in mind, too, that the wider the stripe, the greater the number of disks that will be affected by the failure of a disk within the stripe.

- If there is more than one database volume on the disk, move one or more volumes to other disks.

- Increase the size of the database buffer cache to try to reduce the number of reads to the disk.

- Add more spindles and disk controllers.

An effective disk layout will avoid most disk bottlenecks. If you see uneven disk utilization, revisit the disk layout recommendations in Chapter 17.

STEP 3. Monitoring Networks

After checking memory and disks for bottlenecks, look next at any networks connected to the server. Although network bottlenecks are not likely to directly affect the performance of the database server, they can have a big impact on application response times.

When database applications are running in client/server mode, a slow network between the client and the server impacts interactions between the database and the applications. When the slow network sits between the applications and the user interface, the user perception could well be that the database server is slow.

What to Look For

A simple way of determining the impact of network latency on response times is to log and plot ping round-trip times from the client to the server. The following command pings a host called adelaide every 5 seconds and reports the round trip time in milliseconds.

```
alpaca% ping -s -I 5 adelaide
PING adelaide: 56 data bytes
64 bytes from adelaide (129.158.93.100): icmp_seq=0. time=147. ms
64 bytes from adelaide (129.158.93.100): icmp_seq=1. time=150. ms
64 bytes from adelaide (129.158.93.100): icmp_seq=2. time=150. ms
64 bytes from adelaide (129.158.93.100): icmp_seq=3. time=150. ms
^C
----adelaide PING Statistics----
4 packets transmitted, 4 packets received, 0% packet loss
round-trip (ms) min/avg/max = 147/149/150
```

Some application transactions involve multiple trips to the database server, each of which incurs the round-trip penalty. I have seen network latencies account for a significant portion of application response time in wide area networks.

One effective way of quantifying application response times on a wide area network is to enter a dummy transaction with a remote terminal or browser emulator and measure the response time. Dummy transactions can be entered from each remote location at regular intervals. The transaction response times in conjunction with round-trip times captured with ping can help determine whether the server or the network has the major impact on performance.

The netstat utility shows packet activity on a network; see Figure 21.5 for an example.

Figure 21.5 *Network traffic on hme0*

```
alameda% netstat -i -I hme0 5
    input   hme0       output                input (Total)    output
packets   errs   packets  errs colls      packets  errs  packets  errs   colls
36717966 261164 25214401   12 187668      36718099 261164 25214534  12    187668
       2      0        1    0      0             2      0        1   0         0
```

Watch for collisions (`colls`) greater than 10% of output packets (`output packets`). The use of switches makes collisions less an issue than in the past when many devices shared the same subnet.

Unfortunately, this `netstat` report shows only the number of packets sent and received and not the size of the packets. Without the size of packets it is difficult to assess the effective throughput of the network.

A number of tools are available to provide the number of bytes as well as the number of packets transmitted on a network. The `tcp_mon` script, which is part of the SE toolkit (available on the book website) reports network traffic in both packets and bytes. For the sake of simplicity, divide the theoretical bandwidth by 10 to get the effective throughput in Mbytes. So, a 10-Mbit Ethernet subnet will not be able to exceed approximately 1 Mbyte per second, and a 100-Mbit Ethernet subnet will not be able to exceed 10 Mbytes per second.

The undocumented `netstat` option, `-k`, reports the number of packets received and sent by each network interface (`ipackets` and `opackets`), and as of Solaris 2.6, `netstat -k` also reports the number of bytes received and sent (`rbytes` and `obytes`). The `kstat` utility, introduced in Solaris 8, allows network statistics to be selectively extracted. The following example displays the number of packets and bytes sent and received by all network interfaces on a host called `apollo`.

```
apollo% kstat -p -s "*packets"
hme:0:hme0:ipackets 362997
hme:0:hme0:opackets 480774
hme:1:hme1:ipackets 0
hme:1:hme1:opackets 0
ipdptp:0:ipdptp0:ipackets 124649
ipdptp:0:ipdptp0:opackets 180857
lo:0:lo0:ipackets 45548
lo:0:lo0:opackets 45548
apollo% kstat -p -s "*bytes"
hme:0:hme0:obytes 394165502
hme:0:hme0:rbytes 47823373
hme:1:hme1:obytes 0
hme:1:hme1:rbytes 0
```

The interfaces in the above example are two 100-Mbit Ethernet interfaces (`hme0` and `hme1`), a dial-up PPP connection (`ipdptp`), and the loopback interface (`lo`). The numbers are cumulative; that is, they represent the total since the last reboot. Calculating the average packet sizes (`rbytes/ipackets` and `obytes/opackets`) shows that the average packet received on the `hme0` interface was 131 bytes in size and the average packet sent was 819 bytes in size.

Although we are focusing on database servers and not NFS file servers, for completeness it is worth mentioning that `nfsstat` monitors NFS traffic. From a client, use `nfsstat -c`. Watch for timeouts greater than 5% of calls, or "not responding" messages when the server was running: they indicate either network problems or an overloaded NFS server.

As of Solaris 2.6, `iostat` also shows NFS mounts, so all disk statistics available under `iostat` are also available for NFS mounts.

For a comprehensive treatment of NFS monitoring, refer to Chapter 9 of *Sun Performance and Tuning* by Adrian Cockcroft and Richard Pettit, Second Edition, Sun Press, 1998.

What You Can Do to Minimize Network Bottlenecks

To overcome a network bottleneck, try one of the following:

- Install multiple network adapters and split the traffic across multiple subnets if network traffic becomes an issue. Expanding the network in this way is usually easier in the case of a local area network (LAN) than a wide area network (WAN). Current LAN technology is relatively inexpensive and performs acceptably in most environments. WAN technology is available to satisfy even heavy throughput requirements, although it is still relatively expensive.

- Use Solaris Bandwidth Manager to manage network traffic on servers running mixed workloads.

STEP 4. Monitoring CPUs

Having identified any memory, disk, and network bottlenecks, we are finally ready to look at CPU utilization.

One of the reasons for leaving CPU until last is that there is more to monitor with CPUs. If you start here, you risk getting bogged down in detail and losing sight of the big picture. But the main reason for monitoring CPU last is that it isn't necessarily bad if your CPUs are heavily utilized.

Why would server CPUs be less than heavily utilized? CPUs on a well-tuned server (one with no memory, disk, or network bottlenecks) will either be idle because there is no work to do or will be busy much of the time.

If there is work to do, you should expect the CPUs to be doing it. If there is work to do and the CPUs aren't busy, it is probably because there is a bottleneck somewhere else, perhaps in the I/O or memory subsystems. Non-CPU bottlenecks should be resolved if at all possible to allow work to proceed uninterrupted.

The aim, then, is to ensure that your workload is CPU-limited rather than limited by memory availability, disk performance, or network performance. Once you have achieved that, optimization remains important, especially application optimization, to ensure that the CPUs are not wasting cycles.

If CPU power were infinite, a server would never be CPU-bound. In the real world, however, significant idle CPU suggests the system has been over-sized.

That said, on a multiuser system there are nearly always periods when some users are idle. If CPUs are heavily utilized doing useful work all or most of the time, check user response times and batch job completion times. If response and completion times prove barely acceptable during periods of normal processing load, the server is unlikely to be able to handle peak periods gracefully. On a large multiuser SMP system, a reasonable average CPU utilization is 70%, increasing to 90% during peak periods.

Don't immediately assume that a CPU-limited system is behaving normally, though. To monitor the health of a system with respect to CPU, start by looking at system utilization.

What to Look For: System Utilization

First, use vmstat to check how busy the CPUs are. We're not looking for detail initially—the aim at this point is to get the view from 20,000 feet. The relevant statistics to look at are CPU user% (us) and system% (sy), and the size of the run queue (r).

Consider the vmstat trace in Figure 21.6.

Figure 21.6 *vmstat trace of a lightly loaded system*

```
procs      memory            page              disk          faults      cpu
 r b w   swap    free   re mf pi po fr de sr m1 m2 s6 sd  in   sy    cs   us sy id
 0 1 0 3294648 1215024  0 980  1  9  9  0  0  0  0  0  1 1057 13629 5621 35  4  61
 0 1 0 3294256 1214664  0 642  0  3  3  0  0  0  0  0  0  746 13709 4285 20  3  78
 0 2 0 3292192 1212320  0 473  0  0  0  0  0  0  0  0  0  825 11790 4292 17  3  81
```

The CPU is only lightly utilized: id (CPU idle%) is significantly greater than zero. Not surprisingly, the run queue (r under procs) is zero, meaning no runnable processes are waiting for CPU time.

By contrast, the vmstat trace in Figure 21.7 shows a fully utilized system:

Figure 21.7 *vmstat trace of a fully utilized system*

```
procs       memory              page              disk         faults       cpu
  r b w    swap      free   re  mf pi po fr de sr m1 m2 s6 sd  in   sy    cs us sy id
 49 4 0 2984600  916176   0  31  0  0  0  0  0  0  0  0  0  652 5459 2003 84 16  0
 31 5 0 2983504  914880   0  22  0  0  0  0  0  0  0  0  0  653 4957 1980 82 18  0
```

The run queue shows between 30 and 50 runnable processes and 4 or 5 blocked for I/O, and no idle CPU at all. The run queue does not include processes currently executing on the CPUs, only processes waiting for CPU time. A large number of processes blocked for I/O (the b column under procs) can suggest a disk bottleneck.

Is it a problem to have an average of 40 processes waiting on the run queue for a turn on the CPUs? That depends entirely on the number of CPUs in the system: on a 64-CPU system, that situation may not be an issue; on a single CPU server, it is likely to be a major problem.

The *us/sy* (user/system) ratio in Figure 21.7 is over 4.5/1, which typically indicates a very healthy balance between CPU time spent on user applications and on kernel activity (including I/O). If system% approaches or exceeds user%, a lot of time is being spent processing system calls and interrupts, possibly indicating that excessive time is being spent on disk or network I/O.

What to Look For: Kernel Statistics

The information in Figure 21.8 is extracted from a statit trace monitoring system activity over a 30-second period (run with statit sleep 30). Most of the disk information has been removed to reduce the size of the output.

Figure 21.8 *statit trace*

```
Hostid: 808d5e57 Hostname: "alameda" Version: 6.00 Command: sleep 30
                  Elapsed Time Statistics
      30.03 time (seconds)        100.00 % Start time: Wed Mar 10 16:04:50 2000
       0.00 idle time               0.00 %
      24.21 user time              80.62 %
       3.70 system time            12.32 %
       2.12 wait time               7.06 %


CPU Stats       idle%        user%       system%      wait%  Total%   Total (secs)
CPU  0           0.0         79.7         13.3         7.0    100.0      30.0
CPU  1           0.0         81.6         11.4         7.1    100.0      30.0
Totals           0.0        161.2         24.6        14.1    200.0      60.1


                   Average Load Statistics
        30 secs - monitoring interval       6.20 avg jobs waiting on I/O
      5.00 avg runnable processes           0.87 avg runque occupancy
      0.00 avg swapped jobs                 0.00 avg swap device occupancy
                 Average Swap Statistics in Pages
 111814.16 avg freemem                 103848.90 avg reserved swap
  96036.93 avg allocated swap          370944.53 avg unreserved swap
 378756.50 avg unallocated swap
                 Sysinfo Statistics (per second)
      0.00 phys block reads               4.96 phys block writes
(sync+async)
    160.54 logical block reads           29.10 logical block writes
    189.94 raw I/O reads                  0.00 raw I/O writes
   3264.90 context switches             958.11 traps
   1620.41 device interrupts           9813.75 system calls
   2202.96 read+readv syscalls        1501.63 write+writev syscalls
6066097.10 rdwr bytes read           254117.65 rdwr bytes written
      0.43 forks + vforks                0.53 execs
      0.00 msgrcv()+msgsnd() calls     128.07 semop() calls
```

```
   16.68 pathname lookups (namei)           1.20 ufs_iget() calls
    0.00 inodes taken w/ attach pgs         0.00 inodes taken w/ no attach pgs
    5.59 directory blocks read              0.00 inode table overflows
    0.00 file table overflows               0.00 proc table overflows
     100 % bread hits                     687.41 intrs as threads(below clock)
    3.73 intrs blkd/released (swtch)      143.62 times idle() ran (swtch)
    0.00 rw reader fails (swtch)            0.00 rw writer fails (swtch)
 1166.60 involuntary context switches     687.85 xcalls to other cpus
    0.67 thread_create()s                 221.65 cpu migrations by threads
  179.35 failed mutex enters                0.00 times module loaded
    0.00 times module unloaded              4.23 physical block writes (async)
                    Vminfo Statistics (per second)
    0.13 page reclaims (w/ pageout)         0.13 page reclaims from free list
    0.00 pageins                            0.00 pages paged in
    0.13 pageouts                           0.17 pages paged out
    0.00 swapins                            0.00 pages swapped in
    0.00 swapouts                           0.00 pages swapped out
   39.96 ZFOD pages                         0.17 pgs freed by daemon/auto
    0.00 pgs xmnd by pgout daemon           0.00 revs of page daemon hand
    0.00 minor pgflts: hat_fault          101.70 minor pgflts: as_fault
    0.00 major page faults                 12.89 copy-on-write faults
   21.84 protection faults                  0.00 faults due to s/w locking req
    0.43 kernel as as_flt()s                0.00 times pager scheduled
                Directory Name Cache Statistics (per second)
   87.28 cache hits  ( 96 %)                3.23 cache misses (  3 %)
    0.23 enters into cache                  0.00 enters when already cached
    0.00 long names tried to enter          0.00 long names tried to look up
    0.00 LRU list empty                     0.00 purges of cache
                    Segment Map Operations (per second)
   12.22 number of segmap_faults            0.00 number of segmap_faultas
 1334.90 number of segmap_getmaps           8.39 getmaps that reuse a map
 1324.48 getmaps that reclaim               1.80 getmaps reusing a slot
    0.00 releases that are async            0.00 releases that write
    2.63 releases that free                 3.03 releases that abort
    0.00 releases with dontneed set         0.00 releases with no other action
    2.63 # of pagecreates
                    Buffer Cache Statistics (per second)
  160.64 total buf requests               160.64 buf cache hits
    0.00 times buf was alloced              0.00 times had to sleep for buf
    0.13 times buf locked by someone        0.00 times dup buf found
                    Inode Cache Statistics (per second)
    1.20 hits                               0.00 misses
    0.00 mallocs                            0.00 frees
    0.00 puts_at_frontlist                  0.00 puts_at_backlist
    0.00 dnlc_looks                         0.00 dnlc_purges
                    Char I/O Statistics (per second)
  187.48 terminal input chars          20398.83 terminal output chars
Network Statistics (per second)
Net      Ipkts   Ierrs   Opkts   Oerrs   Colls   Dfrs  Rtryerr
hme0       404       0     248       0       1       0       0
lo0          0       0       0       0       0       0       0
```

		Disk I/O Statistics (per second)							
Disk	util%	xfer/s	rds/s	wrts/s	rdb/xfr	wrb/xfr	wtqlen	svqlen	srv-ms
md10	0.0	0.0	0.0	0.0	0	0	0.00	0.00	0.0
md20	0.0	0.0	0.0	0.0	0	0	0.00	0.00	0.0
c6t6d0	0.0	0.0	0.0	0.0	0	0	0.00	0.00	0.0
c2t0d0	97.1	125.6	124.6	1.1	3822	2048	0.00	5.10	40.6
c2t0d1	0.3	0.6	0.0	0.6	0	18312	0.00	0.01	13.2
c2t0d2	0.0	0.0	0.0	0.0	0	0	0.00	0.00	0.0
c2t0d3	46.8	67.8	63.2	4.6	2048	2048	0.00	0.66	9.8
c2t0d4	0.0	0.0	0.0	0.0	0	0	0.00	0.00	0.0
c2t1d0	8.6	83.5	2.2	81.3	56763	2048	0.00	0.76	9.1
c2t1d1	0.0	0.0	0.0	0.0	0	0	0.00	0.00	0.0

statit shows a lot of information, including CPU, memory paging, and network and disk statistics. Part of the attraction of statit is the comprehensiveness of the information it provides. Let's look at a few highlights.

- When looking at CPU utilization, don't be confused by I/O wait time. I/O wait time is highly misleading and should be regarded simply as idle. So add wait time and idle time together to determine the true idle time. Do the same for sar also (add wio and idl to determine idle time).

- Check context switches and involuntary context switches. A *context switch* occurs when a process or thread is moved onto or off a CPU. An *involuntary context switch* occurs when a running process or thread has consumed its allocated time quantum or when it is preempted by a thread with a higher priority. If the ratio of context/involuntary is significantly less than about 3/1, it can indicate that processes are being preempted before they have completed processing (usually processes will yield—that is, give up—the CPU when they request an I/O). A high level of involuntary context switching suggests there might be a benefit from using a modified TS dispatch table if your server is not a Starfire server (refer to "The TS Class" on page 220 for more information).

- Semaphore operations (semop() calls) and message queue calls (msgrcv()+msgsnd() calls) are the typical mechanisms used by databases for Interprocess Communication (IPC) and indicate the degree of synchronization traffic between database processes (usually primarily for internal locks and latches).

  Semaphore operations can increase exponentially when a database server becomes significantly overloaded. Such behavior is a symptom rather than a cause of poor performance, but it is a good indication that the CPU is unable to effectively complete the work it is doing and that more CPU resource is required.

- For the sake of reference, pageouts and pgs xmnd by pgout daemon are equivalent to po and sr, respectively, in a vmstat trace.

- A high level of faults due to s/w locking reqs can suggest that ISM is not being used when shared memory is attached (ISM is described in "Intimate Shared Memory" on page 24). Oracle and Sybase, for example, will try to attach shared memory as ISM, but if unsuccessful will attach shared memory without ISM. In each case an advisory message is placed in the database log file, but the onus is on you to notice it. A method of determining whether ISM is being used is discussed in "EXTRA STEP: Checking for ISM" on page 304.

Drilling Down Further

Monitoring Processes

Sometimes individual processes hog CPU resource, causing poor performance for other users. Use /usr/ucb/ps -aux, or prstat as of Solaris 8, to find out the processes consuming the most CPU (note that the ps process is itself a reasonably heavy consumer of CPU cycles, especially on systems with many processes). The sdtprocess utility (shipped as part of the CDE package within Solaris) offers a useful X11-based representation of the same data.

Figure 21.9 shows a trace where no particular process is hogging CPU.

Figure 21.9 *ps trace of multiple Oracle shadow processes*

```
alameda% /usr/ucb/ps -aux | head -10
USER         PID %CPU %MEM    SZ   RSS TT     S    START  TIME COMMAND
oracle     12545  0.4  2.57955276608 ?        R 17:37:52  0:09 oraclegl P:4096,4,
oracle     13200  0.3  2.57804075000 ?        S 17:40:11  0:04 oraclegl P:4096,4,
oracle     13250  0.3  2.57804074960 ?        R 17:40:21  0:04 oraclegl P:4096,4,
oracle     12236  0.3  2.57804074960 ?        S 17:36:47  0:10 oraclegl P:4096,4,
oracle     13102  0.3  2.57808075000 ?        R 17:39:51  0:04 oraclegl P:4096,4,
oracle     12598  0.3  2.57804074960 ?        S 17:38:02  0:09 oraclegl P:4096,4,
oracle     12323  0.3  2.57804074960 ?        R 17:37:04  0:11 oraclegl P:4096,4,
oracle     12263  0.2  2.57804074960 ?        R 17:36:51  0:11 oraclegl P:4096,4,
oracle     13615  0.2  2.57833675400 ?        R 17:41:30  0:02 oraclegl P:4096,4,
```

In this example, a lot of processes are running, but none are taking more than 0.4% of all available CPU.

In Figure 21.10 a couple of processes are consuming many times more CPU than other processes.

Figure 21.10 *ps trace of CPU hogging processes*

```
alameda% /usr/ucb/ps -aux | head -5
USER         PID %CPU %MEM    SZ   RSS TT     S    START  TIME COMMAND
root       13428 12.5  0.0   808   400 pts/2  O 17:41:00  5:38 /tmp/badboy2
root       13422 12.4  0.0   808   400 pts/2  O 17:40:58  5:40 /tmp/badboy1
oracle     14850  0.6  2.57804874952 ?        R 17:46:19  0:02 oraclegl P:4096,4,
oracle     14838  0.5  2.57808075040 ?        R 17:46:10  0:00 oraclegl P:4096,4,
```

The TIME column also shows that the CPU hogs have each consumed 5 minutes of CPU time. How much performance impact they will have depends on the number of online CPUs and other active processes. The %CPU column shows the percentage of all available CPUs, not the percentage of a single CPU. In this example, the two rogue processes are each consuming one full CPU out of eight (hence 12.5 %CPU). You can use pstack and truss to get an indication of what these CPU-hogging processes are doing.

Figure 21.11 illustrates a method of finding the process consuming the most CPU (with ps), then listing the system calls the process is running (with truss). I stopped truss after about 10 seconds with Control-C; at that point the system call stats were printed.

Figure 21.11 *truss system call trace of single process*

```
alameda./opt/bin /usr/ucb/ps -aux | head -2
USER         PID %CPU %MEM   SZ   RSS TT      S    START    TIME COMMAND
oracle     14870 1.2  2.57849675552 ?        S 17:48:24  0:06 oraclegl P:4096,4,
alameda./opt/bin truss -c -p 14870
^Csyscall      seconds   calls  errors
read             .06       239
lseek            .02       197
semsys           .00         5
context          .00         3
setitimer        .00         6
                ----       ---    ---
sys totals:      .08       450      0
usr time:       1.18
elapsed:       19.45
```

Read system calls dominated, with lseek close behind. The use of lseek indicates that the application is not using the pread(2) system call, which saves a system call by eliminating the need for lseek(2).

Monitoring Interrupts

The trace in Figure 21.12 is from mpstat on an 8-CPU server.

Figure 21.12 *mpstat trace for an 8-CPU server*

CPU	minf	mjf	xcal	intr	ithr	csw	icsw	migr	smtx	srw	syscl	usr	sys	wt	idl
6	84	0	87	3	1	221	1	10	8	0	403	6	3	91	0
7	24	0	98	4	1	256	2	14	9	0	261	8	2	90	0
10	76	0	81	4	0	149	3	8	138	0	735	44	3	53	0
11	99	0	44	237	228	251	2	14	8	0	722	6	3	91	0
14	28	0	253	120	118	261	2	11	139	0	1139	7	4	90	0
15	115	0	30	2	0	174	2	10	7	0	353	26	3	72	0
18	89	0	74	204	3	245	2	13	10	0	853	6	4	89	0
19	24	0	119	5	0	303	4	11	8	0	374	13	3	85	0

Note that interrupts (intr) are not evenly spread across all CPUs. CPUs 11, 14, and 18 are processing more interrupts than the other CPUs. These

CPUs show the highest system (sys) activity, but not the highest user (usr) activity.

Disk array and network drivers are bound to specific CPUs when Solaris boots. These CPUs handle interrupts related to these devices on behalf of all other CPUs. Notice, too, that Solaris has scheduled the running processes on the CPUs that are not busy servicing interrupts (CPUs 10, 1, and 19 show significantly greater user activity).

What You Can Do to Optimize CPU Usage

Following is a list of some causes of heavy CPU utilization, along with ways to track down the causes, and remedies to apply.

- **An unusually high level of system calls.** If the ratio of user% to system% is low, try to find out the causes by using truss -c to identify the main system calls for a few of the most CPU-intensive processes. If read I/Os are a major factor, increasing the size of the database buffer cache might reduce the number of read I/Os.

- **A low ratio of context switches to involuntary context switches.** On non-Starfire platforms, load the Starfire TimeShare Dispatch Table (see Chapter 15).

- **One or more inefficient applications.** Monitor processes with ps to identify the applications consuming the most CPU. Poorly written applications can have a major impact on CPU requirements and therefore offer one of the most fruitful places to begin looking when you are trying to free up CPU resources.

- **Poor database tuning.** The next chapters might help you identify inefficient database behavior. A high level of latch contention, for example, can cause CPU to be consumed for little benefit. If latch contention is the cause of heavy CPU utilization, adding more CPUs may not always help.

- **Insufficient CPU resources.** If your CPUs are consistently fully or heavily utilized and there are many more processes on the run queue than there are CPUs, you may simply need to add more CPUs. Fortunately, Solaris scales well enough that more adding CPUs is likely to help when CPU resources are scarce.

  An alternative might be to remove applications from the database server onto another server to use the database's client/server capabilities. Removing applications can make a big difference to CPU utilization on the database server.

STEP 5. Monitoring and Tuning a Database

A well-tuned database system has the following characteristics:

- The system is mostly CPU-bound.

- Disk I/O is well-balanced.

- The buffer cache is working effectively.

- The database is configured to run efficiently.

As we have already noted, the applications must also be coded efficiently if the database system is to run efficiently.

Having investigated memory, disks, networks and CPUs, you need to undertake the final step: monitor and tune the database, a process explored in detail in the following chapters for Oracle, Sybase, Informix, and DB2. Monitoring and tuning the buffer cache is a vital element of database tuning. A brief review of the main issues is presented in the next section, but before proceeding to the database tuning chapters, you would do well to review Chapter 7, which is dedicated to the buffer cache. Finally, although application efficiency is a crucial component in any well-tuned system, we will not be considering it since it is beyond the scope of this book. Refer to *Techniques for Optimizing Applications: High Performance Computing*, by Rajat Garg and Ilya Sharapov, Sun Microsystems Press, 2001 for a discussion on application optimization.

The Buffer Cache

One of the main metrics in monitoring database performance for OLTP workloads is the buffer cache hit rate. The buffer cache stores in memory as many database blocks read from disk as possible. The expectation is that the same database blocks will often be used by different transactions; the *buffer cache hit rate* shows how often a requested block was retrieved from the cache rather than from the disk. Since memory access is so much faster than disk access, a high cache hit rate is important for good performance with OLTP workloads.

For DSS workloads the buffer cache is less important. Some databases (for example, Oracle and Informix) avoid the buffer cache entirely when carrying out table or index scans. DB2 for Solaris does use the buffer cache, but there may be little opportunity for reuse of buffers since the volume of data brought into the cache is typically much greater than the cache size. So, cache buffers tend not to stay in the buffer for long. Similar behavior applies to batch jobs processing large volumes of data.

A Closer Look at the Cache Hit Rate

The cache hit rate can be misleading. For example, how much better is a 95% cache hit rate than a 90% cache hit rate? Does it represent a 5% improvement?

The answer is no! A 90% cache hit rate means 90% of all read I/Os are satisfied from the cache—only 10% of the reads result in a physical disk access. A 95% cache hit rate means only 5% of reads go to disk. So, improving the cache hit rate from 90% to 95% means physical disk reads are *halved*, not improved by only 5%! Depending on the number of physical reads, halving them may make a significant difference to the load on the disks.

Given this potential confusion, it is often more useful to think in terms of the *miss rate* (100 minus cache hit rate).

You can usually improve the cache hit rate by increasing the size of the database buffer cache, although a point is eventually reached when any improvement is not worth the extra memory. Cache sizing and effectiveness are discussed in more detail in Chapter 7.

An Appropriate Cache Hit Rate

A cache hit rate of 80% might be quite suitable in one situation while a much higher hit rate of 95% might be inadequate in another. How can you tell when you need to increase the size of the buffer cache to try to improve the cache hit rate?

You should consider three factors when determining an appropriate cache hit rate:

- **The amount of memory available.** Avoid paging at all costs. If increasing the size of the buffer cache causes application paging, then it is better to leave the cache as it is. If free memory is available, then increasing the cache is an option.

- **The load on the database disks.** Determine the disk utilization of the database disks by looking at either `iostat`, `sar`, or `statit` statistics for the relevant disks. Check, too, how many of the I/Os are due to reads. If the database disks are showing high utilization or high service times (as defined in "STEP 2. Monitoring Disks" on page 289) and a significant number of the I/Os are reads, then increasing the cache hit rate could take the pressure off the disks.

- **Application response times.** Retrieving disk blocks from the cache is faster than retrieving them from disk and also consumes less CPU. So improving cache hit rate might also reduce response times. Many factors contribute to response times, though, so any improvement may be less than you were hoping for.

Aftereffects of Database Monitoring and Tuning

Given that the database may be the major application on the system, investigating the behavior of the database should shed further light on the data already collected. Monitoring and tuning the database is an iterative process. Tuning the database may change the behavior of the system, in which case it will be important to briefly revisit the previous steps covered in the chapter.

EXTRA STEP: Checking for ISM

Unfortunately, before Solaris 8 it isn't easy to tell whether a shared memory segment is using ISM (described in "Intimate Shared Memory" on page 24). As of Solaris 8, the ipcs utility includes a -i parameter that shows how many shared memory segments have been attached as ISM (the ISMATTCH column), and pmap shows whether a particular process has attached a shared memory segment as ISM (ism will appear immediately before the shmid parameter). For Solaris 7 and earlier Solaris releases, the procedures shown in Figure 21.13 through Figure 21.17 can be used to answer the question.

Figure 21.13 is based on a server running an Oracle database.

Figure 21.13 *ps trace of Oracle shadow process*

```
     UID   PID  PPID  C    STIME TTY      TIME CMD
  oracle  4498  4479  0 15:58:20 ?        0:02 oraclegl P:4096,3,8,
```

The ps -aef command shows a number of Oracle processes, including pid 4498.

In Figure 21.14, the pstack command shows that pid 4498 is currently doing a read.

Figure 21.14 *pstack trace for process*

```
alameda# /usr/proc/bin/pstack 4498
4498:   oraclegl P:4096,3,8,
 ef7385e8 read       (3, 681150, 1000)
 ef7385e8 _libc_read (3, 681150, 1000, 0, ef7a227c, 5b4fc) + 8
 0005b4fc osnprc    (ffffffff, 6800d8, 681150, 681150, 3, 0) + 4a8
 000d91e4 opitsk    (67df80, 67dfcc, 67dfc8, 0, a, 6801d8) + 334
 001396c4 opiiino   (0, 67e000, 64, 67c7f8, 0, 67dd7c) + 53c
 000daf44 opiodr    (0, 1, 1, 0, 0, 67df84) + f64
 000cb43c opidrv    (67c7f8, 0, 0, 3c, 0, 67c7f8) + 56c
 000ca020 sou2o     (effff844, 3c, 4, effff834, 0, 0) + 10
 00058e70 main      (2, 0, effff8d0, 67f800, 0, 0) + 8c
 00058dcc _start    (0, 0, 0, 0, 0, 0) + 5c
```

In Figure 21.15, the pmap command shows that pid 4498 has attached to a shared memory segment shmid=0x5401, size 69144K bytes, base address 0xD0000000.

Figure 21.15 *pmap trace for process*

```
alameda# /usr/proc/bin/pmap 4498
4498:   oraclegl P:4096,3,8,
00010000   6504K read/exec         /FIN/ora713fin/oracle7.1.3/product/
   7.1.3/bin/oracle.ORIG.before_debug.121694
00678000     32K read/write/exec   /FIN/ora713fin/oracle7.1.3/product/
   7.1.3/bin/oracle.ORIG.before_debug.121694
00680000    408K read/write/exec       [ heap ]
D0000000  69144K read/write/exec/shared   [ shmid=0x5401 ]
EF5A0000     16K read/exec         /usr/platform/sun4u/lib/libc_psr.so.1
EF5B0000      8K read/write/exec       [ anon ]
EF5C0000     16K read/exec         /usr/lib/libmp.so.2
EF5D2000      8K read/write/exec   /usr/lib/libmp.so.2
EF5E0000     24K read/exec         /usr/lib/libaio.so.1
EF5F4000      8K read/write/exec   /usr/lib/libaio.so.1
EF5F6000      8K read/write/exec       [ anon ]
EF600000    448K read/exec         /usr/lib/libnsl.so.1
EF67E000     32K read/write/exec   /usr/lib/libnsl.so.1
EF686000     24K read/write/exec       [ anon ]
EF6B0000     88K read/exec         /usr/lib/libm.so.1
EF6D4000      8K read/write/exec   /usr/lib/libm.so.1
EF6E0000     32K read/exec         /usr/lib/libsocket.so.1
EF6F6000      8K read/write/exec   /usr/lib/libsocket.so.1
EF6F8000      8K read/write/exec       [ anon ]
EF700000    592K read/exec         /usr/lib/libc.so.1
EF7A2000     24K read/write/exec   /usr/lib/libc.so.1
EF7A8000      8K read/write/exec       [ anon ]
EF7B0000      8K read/exec/shared /usr/lib/libdl.so.1
EF7C0000    112K read/exec         /usr/lib/ld.so.1
EF7EA000     16K read/write/exec   /usr/lib/ld.so.1
EFFF8000     32K read/write/exec       [ stack ]
 total    77616K
```

Now, use the crash program to discover more about this process. In Figure 21.16, the data from the other processes on the system has been removed to reduce the size of the following trace.

Figure 21.16 *crash program proc output*

```
alameda# crash << EOF
proc
EOF
dumpfile = /dev/mem, namelist = /dev/ksyms, outfile = stdout
proc
> PROC TABLE SIZE = 16394
SLOT ST  PID  PPID  PGID   SID   UID  PRI     NAME        FLAGS
1705  s  4498  4479  4498  4498  2256  58    oracle.ORIG.befo  load
```

Next, use the SLOT information to find out whether this process is using ISM. In Figure 21.17, the output from crash has been reduced to save space.

Figure 21.17 *crash program as output*

```
alameda# echo "as -f 1705" | crash
dumpfile = /dev/mem, namelist = /dev/ksyms, outfile = stdout
>
```

PROC	PAGLCK	CLGAP	VBITS HAT		HRM	RSS	
SEGLST	LOCK		SEGS	SIZE	LREP	TAIL	NSEGS
1705	0		0	0x0	0x66104370	0x0	
0x63a592a0	0xefffff318		0x67de6ce0	79978496	0	0x65ccf5c0	26

BASE	SIZE	AS	NEXT	PREV	OPS	DATA
0x00010000	65a000	0x680d5f40	0x68b4f260	0x00000000	segvn_ops	0x63aca2f0
0x00678000	8000	0x680d5f40	0x6547d9a0	0x67de6ce0	segvn_ops	0x6440cbb0
0x00680000	66000	0x680d5f40	0x63a592a0	0x68b4f260	segvn_ops	0x64422fe0
0xd0000000	4400000	0x680d5f40	0x67263520	0x6547d9a0	segspt_shm	0x6721a060
0xef5a0000	4000	0x680d5f40	0x63905ac0	0x63a592a0	segvn_ops	0x67fcab38
0xef5b0000	2000	0x680d5f40	0x65ccee40	0x67263520	segvn_ops	0x64898b00

We saw before that the shared memory segment had a base address of 0xD0000000 (hex). The equivalent line on this trace shows a size of 4400000 (hex), which is equivalent to 71,303,168 bytes, or 69,632 Kbytes. This size agrees with that shown by pmap (rounded up to the nearest megabyte). The OPS value shows segspt_shm. This value definitely shows that the ISM driver is in use for this shared memory segment. If the value is segvn_ops, then ISM is not in use.

22

MONITORING AND TUNING ORACLE

In this chapter we consider tuning recommendations for Oracle in both OLTP and DSS environments after first considering methods of monitoring and configuring Oracle. We also explore Oracle9i enhancements that support dynamic reconfiguration, and we investigate issues related to crash recovery.

Managing Oracle Behavior

Oracle can be monitored and managed with Oracle Enterprise Manager (OEM), a powerful GUI-based tool that allows detailed monitoring of all aspects of database behavior and that supports database management. Oracle also provides access to the database information stored in its memory-resident performance tables (often referred to simply as system tables). This information can be retrieved either with SQL or supplied scripts. In this section we discuss these monitoring methods, explore ways of displaying and changing Oracle tunable parameters, and consider explain plans (query execution plans).

Running Administrative Commands

Starting and shutting down Oracle require special privileges, as do alter system statements. The method of connecting to Oracle to run administrative commands has changed more than once over the last few releases; the different methods for the major versions are shown below.

Before Oracle7.3, the `sqldba` command was used as shown in the following example based on Oracle7.1.3.

```
alameda% sqldba mode=line

SQL*DBA: Release 7.1.3.2.0 - Production on Mon Aug 6 12:10:17
2001
Copyright (c) Oracle Corporation 1979, 1994. All rights reserved.

Oracle7 Server Release 7.1.3.2.0 - Production Release
With the parallel query option
PL/SQL Release 2.1.3.2.0 - Production

SQLDBA> connect internal
Connected.
```

From Oracle7.3, the most commonly used command was `svrmgrl`, as shown in the following example based on Oracle 8.0.5.

```
1.oracle8 svrmgrl

Oracle Server Manager Release 3.0.5.0.0 - Production

(c) Copyright 1997, Oracle Corporation.  All Rights Reserved.

Oracle8 Enterprise Edition Release 8.0.5.0.0 - Production
PL/SQL Release 8.0.5.0.0 - Production

SVRMGR> connect internal
Connected.
```

From Oracle9i, `svrmgrl` is no longer supported. The approved connection method is based on the `sqlplus` command. This method also works with earlier versions of Oracle, such as Oracle8 and Oracle8i. The connection can be achieved in two steps, as shown in the example below, which is based on Oracle8.1.5.

```
oracle8.1.5% sqlplus /nolog

SQL*Plus: Release 8.1.5.0.0 - Production on Mon Aug 6
12:16:19 2001

(c) Copyright 1999 Oracle Corporation.  All rights reserved.

SQL> connect / as sysdba
Connected.
```

The same effect can be achieved with a single command, as shown in the following example based on Oracle9.0.1.

```
pae280% sqlplus "/ as sysdba"

SQL*Plus: Release 9.0.1.0.0 - Production on Mon Aug 6 12:19:15
2001

(c) Copyright 2001 Oracle Corporation.  All rights reserved.

Connected to an idle instance.
```

Throughout the rest of this chapter, I use "sysdba" as an abbreviation of the command sequences used to connect to Oracle to run administrative commands. You should substitute the appropriate command for your Oracle release (sqldba, svrmgrl, or sqlplus).

Viewing Current Oracle Tunable Parameters

You can display parameter settings for the current Oracle instance by running the show parameters command as sysdba. You can also display the settings for a single parameter or a group of parameters. For example, to display all settings for parameters containing the string block, run the following command as sysdba:

```
SQL> show parameter block

NAME                                     TYPE      VALUE
---------------------------------------- -------   ------------
db_block_buffers                         integer   8192
db_block_checking                        boolean   FALSE
db_block_checksum                        boolean   FALSE
db_block_lru_latches                     integer   1
db_block_max_dirty_target                integer   8192
db_block_size                            integer   2048
db_file_multiblock_read_count            integer   8
hash_multiblock_io_count                 integer   0
sort_multiblock_read_count               integer   2
```

Changing Tunable Parameters for Oracle

Most Oracle tunables reside in a file called init${ORACLE_SID}.ora (usually referred to as init.ora), where $ORACLE_SID is the environment variable used to set the instance ID of the current Oracle instance. The init.ora file is typically located in the $ORACLE_HOME/dbs directory.

This file allows the database administrator to set values for the tunable parameters that determine the behavior of the Oracle instance. System default values are used for any parameters that are not set. The parameter values in the init.ora file are only used when Oracle is started.

Some parameters can be changed dynamically with the set clause of the alter system commands; the number of such parameters has increased with recent versions of Oracle.

Some sites also use a `config.ora` file, referenced from `init.ora` with the `ifile` parameter, to store static parameters such as `db_name` and `db_block_size`.

Making Dynamic Parameter Changes Persistent

Oracle9i introduced a method of storing and maintaining configuration parameters based on a new *Server Parameter File* (`spfile`). As we have seen, tunable parameters can be changed dynamically with the `set` clause of the `alter system` statement. The `spfile` allows such changes to survive a database reboot. Without the `spfile`, all changes are lost when the database is shut down; unless the database administrator remembers to separately update the `init.ora` file, changes do not persistent across database reboots.

An `spfile` can be created from an `init.ora` file by the following statement run as `sysdba`:

```
SQL> create spfile='$ORACLE_HOME/dbs/spfileaccts.ora'
  2  from pfile='$ORACLE_HOME/dbs/initaccts.ora';

File created.
```

It is not actually necessary to supply the `spfile` name; if no name is specified, the name and location of the new `spfile` will default to `$ORACLE_HOME/dbs/spfile$ORACLE_SID.ora`. The `spfile` is a binary file that must not be manually edited; changes should be made with the `alter system` statement instead.

After an `spfile` is created, the database must be shut down and restarted before the file takes effect. If a startup command is issued without a `pfile` clause, the server parameter file will be used rather than the `init.ora` file. You can still boot Oracle with the `init.ora` file by supplying a `pfile` clause identifying the `init.ora` file. The new `SPFILE` configuration parameter can be used to specify the location of the `spfile`.

When parameters are modified with the `alter system` statement, a scope clause can be used to specify the scope of the change. Supported values are:

- **scope=spfile.** The change is made to the `spfile` only. Changes to both dynamic and static parameters take effect only when the database is next started.

- **scope=memory.** The change is applied to the running instance only and takes immediate effect for dynamic parameters. This option is not supported for static parameters.

- **scope=both.** The change is applied to both the `spfile` and the running instance and takes immediate effect for dynamic parameters. This option is not supported for static parameters.

The default scope is both if the database was started with an spfile, and memory if it was not.

A parameter can be returned to its system default value with the following statement:

```
alter system set parameter = '';
```

You can create an init.ora file from an spfile with the following command:

```
create pfile='$ORACLE_HOME/dbs/backup_initaccts.ora
       from spfile='$ORACLE_HOME/dbs/spfileaccts.ora'
```

The file names can be eliminated if default names are used for init.ora and spfile.

Finally, the current active parameters can be viewed with the show parameters statement or by querying the v$parameter view (or the v$parameter2 view). The v$spparameter view displays the current contents of the spfile, or NULL values if the spfile is not in use.

Viewing and Changing Hidden Parameters

As well as the init.ora parameters described above, Oracle includes a number of hidden init.ora parameters, each of which begins with an underscore (_). These hidden parameters can be set in the init.ora file just as for the normal parameters. There are occasions when modifying a hidden parameter can prove beneficial for performance reasons, and later in this chapter I identify some situations where modifying a hidden parameter might be helpful.

Let me issue an **Important Disclaimer**, though: the parameters are hidden by Oracle for a reason! Before changing them on a production system, discuss your plans with Oracle support. I will take no responsibility for database corruption or other problems resulting from your unsupported use of hidden parameters, and you should expect Oracle and Sun to take the same position.

That said, the following query will display hidden parameters for Oracle8 and later releases:

```
select a.ksppinm "name", a.ksppdesc "description",
       b.ksppstvl "current", b.ksppstdf "isdefault"
       from x$ksppi a, x$ksppcv b
       where a.indx = b.indx
       and substr(a.ksppinm,1,1) = '_'
       order by a.ksppinm;
```

The isdefault column shows whether the current value for this parameter is the default (true or false). Note that similar information can be obtained from Oracle7, although that release only provides the x$ksppi view, and not the x$ksppcv view.

On the book website I have included a script called _params that simplifies this process for Oracle8 and later releases. If run with no parameters, it displays all hidden parameters. If a string is passed to the script, it displays all hidden parameters matching the string.

Monitoring Error Messages

Oracle writes error, warning, and notification messages to the $ORACLE_HOME/rdbms/log/alert${ORACLE_SID}.log file. This file is often referred to simply as alert.log. The alert log is a good first place to visit when trying to understand and resolve problems with an Oracle instance.

Using Oracle Enterprise Manager

Oracle Enterprise Manager (OEM) provides access to database monitoring and administration capabilities with an intuitive graphical user interface. OEM displays the buffer cache hit rate and many other important Oracle metrics.

Since the Oracle8.1.6 release, the OEM console runs on Solaris as well as on Windows platforms. To invoke the OEM console, run the oemapp command from the command line (after first ensuring that your DISPLAY environment variable is set appropriately):

```
oracle% oemapp console &
```

It may first be necessary to run the Enterprise Manager Configuration Assistant program, emca, to create a repository.

Rather than considering OEM in any detail, in this chapter I focus on the lower-level data provided by scripts in the hope that such a focus will offer more insight into the underlying mechanisms used by Oracle.

Monitoring Oracle System Tables

Oracle maintains a number of internal views that record statistics about the database and offers scripts that present the same information in a more understandable fashion.

v$ Views

Oracle's internal views have names starting with v$. Although they appear to be tables, they are actually internal memory structures that are not persistent—that is, they only exist while the instance is active.

A few examples of v$ views are given in the following list:

- **v$system_event:** Shows a summary of all the events waited for in the instance since it started.

- **v$session_event:** Shows a summary of all the events the session has waited for since it started.

- **v$session_wait:** Shows the current waits for a session. This view is an important starting point for finding current bottlenecks.

- **v$sysstat:** Shows system statistics.

- **v$sesstat:** Shows system session statistics.

- **v$session:** Shows user-session-related information.

- **v$parameter:** Shows session parameters. To see the current parameter settings, try running the following command as sysdba:

    ```
    select name, value from v$parameter
    ```

    The **v$system_parameter** view shows systemwide parameters for the instance.

- **v$waitstat:** Shows buffer wait statistics (the number of times a user process had to wait for various buffers).

- **v$filestat:** Shows file access statistics.

We will encounter a number of other v$ views later in this chapter.

The utlbstat and utlestat Scripts

Although all the v$ views can be accessed with standard SQL statements, Oracle provides a simpler mechanism in the form of two scripts, utlbstat.sql and utlestat.sql. The first is run at the start of a measurement interval, and the second at the end of the measurement interval. The results are saved in a file called report.txt in the current directory. Many of the more important v$ views are represented in this report. Before running the scripts, make sure that Oracle is collecting timed statistics. If the timed_statistics parameter is set to false, you can change it dynamically as sysdba with the following command:

```
alter system set timed_statistics = true;
```

The parameter can be reset to false in the same way after the scripts have been run.

You can also permanently set the timed_statistics parameter to true in init.ora. The CPU overhead associated with timed statistics is small, and Oracle recommends setting the parameter permanently.

The way to run the utlbstat and utlestat scripts is shown below:

```
oracle$ sqlplus "/ as sysdba"
<< Various messages deleted >>
SQL> @$ORACLE_HOME/rdbms/admin/utlbstat
<< Pause for a suitable period of time... >>
<< Database activity during this period will be reported >>
SQL> @$ORACLE_HOME/rdbms/admin/utlestat
```

A sample `report.txt` for Oracle9i is presented later in this chapter, along with detailed comments and monitoring suggestions.

The Statspack Scripts

Oracle8.1.6 also introduced the `statspack` scripts. These scripts report information similar to that reported by the `utlbstat` and `utlestat` scripts, although more data is collected and some useful ratios are calculated for you. The `utlbstat/utlestat` scripts will eventually be phased out—this chapter focuses on their output rather than `statspack` output because they cover a broader range of releases.

For detailed information about installing and running the `statspack` scripts, refer to `$ORACLE_HOME/rdbms/admin/spdoc.txt` in the Oracle9i release and `$ORACLE_HOME/rdbms/admin/statspack.doc` in the Oracle8i release.

After installation (carried out with the `spcreate.sql` script for Oracle9i and with the `statscre.sql` script for Oracle8i), as `sysdba` you create snapshots in the following way:

```
SQL> connect perfstat/perfstat
SQL> execute statspack.snap;
```

To create a report, run the `spreport.sql` script (Oracle9i) or the `statsrep.sql` script (Oracle8i). The following example shows the appropriate syntax for Oracle9i.

```
SQL> @?/rdbms/admin/spreport
```

This script prompts for the IDs of two previously created snapshots and, after prompting for a report file name, creates a report based on activity occurring between the two snapshots.

Generating Explain Plans

Before retrieving data in response to a query, the database optimizer determines how best to access the data. In practice, especially for DSS queries, there is often more than one path the optimizer can choose (for example, either to retrieve the data with an index or directly from the base table). The sequence of steps the optimizer chooses is referred to as a query execution plan, or explain plan (the role of the database optimizer is discussed in detail in Chapter 8).

In an ideal world, the optimizer would always choose the optimal plan. The real world is rarely so straightforward, unfortunately. So because the query plan is so important, especially to DSS performance, it is often necessary to provide the optimizer with hints that can be embedded in SQL statements.

As previously stated, it is beyond the scope of this book to cover application and SQL tuning. Nonetheless, it is sometimes useful to know how to generate an execution plan for an SQL statement.

As of Oracle 7.3, generating an explain plan from sqlplus is as easy as running the set autotrace on command before running the query. Note that if the plan_table has not already been created, you will need to run the $ORACLE_HOME/rdbms/admin/utlxplan.sql script first:

```
SQL> @?/rdbms/admin/utlxplan

Table created.
```

As this example illustrates, the ? character can be used instead of $ORACLE_HOME within sqlplus.

An example of autotrace is shown below.

```
SQL> set autotrace on
SQL> select scale, power, company
  2  from tpcd
  3  where company like '%Sun%'
  4  order by scale, power;

     SCALE      POWER COMPANY
---------- ---------- ------------------------------------------
        30      702.8 Sun
       100    13738.7 Sun
       300     2009.5 Sun
       300     3270.6 Sun
       300     8113.2 Sun
      1000     8870.6 Sun
      1000    12931.9 Sun
      1000    70343.7 Sun
      1000   121824.7 Sun

9 rows selected.


Execution Plan
----------------------------------------------------------
   0      SELECT STATEMENT Optimizer=CHOOSE
   1    0   SORT (ORDER BY)
   2    1     TABLE ACCESS (FULL) OF 'TPCD'


Statistics
----------------------------------------------------------
        203  recursive calls
          4  db block gets
         58  consistent gets
         17  physical reads
         60  redo size
        894  bytes sent via SQL*Net to client
        715  bytes received via SQL*Net from client
          4  SQL*Net roundtrips to/from client
          5  sorts (memory)
          0  sorts (disk)
          9  rows processed
```

Explain plans can also be generated with the `utlxplan` script. This method, which also works with earlier versions of Oracle, is illustrated below. Once again, if the `plan_table` has not already been created, you will need to run the `utlxplan.sql` script, as shown.

```
SQL> @$ORACLE_HOME/rdbms/admin/utlxplan

Table created.

SQL> explain plan
  2  set Statement_ID = 'TEST'
  3  for
  4  select a.invoice_date
  5  from gl_je_lines a, gl_je_headers b
  6  where je_line_num = 1
  7  and a.je_header_id = b.je_header_id
  8  order by invoice_date desc;

Explained.

SQL> select
  2  LPAD(' ',2*Level)||
  3  Operation||' '||Options||' '||
  4  decode(Object_Owner,NULL,'',
  5  Object_Owner||'. '||Object_Name)||' '||
  6  decode(Optimizer,NULL,'',Optimizer)
  7  Q_Plan
  8  from PLAN_TABLE
  9  connect by prior ID = Parent_ID and Statement_ID ='TEST'
 10  start with ID = 0 and Statement_ID = 'TEST';

Q_PLAN
-------------------------------------------------------------
  SELECT STATEMENT    RULE
    SORT ORDER BY
      NESTED LOOPS
        TABLE ACCESS FULL GL. GL_JE_HEADERS ANALYZED
        TABLE ACCESS BY ROWID GL. GL_JE_LINES ANALYZED
          INDEX UNIQUE SCAN GL. GL_JE_LINES_U1 ANALYZED

6 rows selected.
```

When using this method of printing explain plans, it is simplest to execute the following SQL command between explain plans:

```
delete from PLAN_TABLE where Statement_ID = 'TEST';
```

Note that the first statement, which runs the `utlxplan` script, only needs to be run once (it creates the `PLAN_TABLE` table).

As of Oracle 7.2, the `select` statement above can be enhanced as follows:

```
select
LPAD(' ',2*Level)||
```

```
Operation||' '||Options||' '||
decode(Object_Owner,NULL,'',
Object_Owner||'. '||Object_Name)||' '||
decode(Optimizer,NULL,'',Optimizer)||' '||
decode(Cost,NULL,'',
       ' Cost='||Cost||
       ' Rows Expected='||Cardinality)
Q_Plan
from PLAN_TABLE
connect by prior ID = Parent_ID and Statement_ID = 'TEST'
start with ID = 0 and Statement_ID = 'TEST';
```

Oracle9i introduced a new view—v$sql_plan—that provides access to the execution plans for recently executed cursors. The information provided is similar to that produced by an explain plan statement. Unlike the explain plan statement, which shows a theoretical plan, the v$sql_plan view shows the actual plan that was used.

Calculating the Buffer Cache Hit Rate

As we saw in Chapter 7, the buffer cache hit rate plays an important role in database performance, especially for OLTP workloads. The Oracle buffer cache is sized according to the db_block_buffers parameter in init.ora (or the db_cache_size parameter in Oracle9i).

The statspack report shows the buffer cache hit rate (under Buffer Hit Ratio for Oracle8.1.6, and under Buffer Hit % for later releases). The report.txt file produced by the utlbstat and utlestat scripts does not calculate the hit rate, although all the necessary information is there.

The Buffer Cache Hit Rate Formula

The buffer cache hit rate can be calculated from the variables listed below (not all of them are used for all Oracle releases):

- **physical reads:** The number of read requests that required a block to be read from disk.

- **physical reads direct:** The number of read requests that read a block from disk, bypassing the buffer cache. Reads carried out during parallel table scans, for example, bypass the buffer cache.

- **physical reads direct (LOB):** The number of large-object (LOB) read requests that read a block from disk, bypassing the buffer cache.

- **db block gets:** Incremented when blocks are read for update and when segment header blocks are read.

- **consistent gets:** The number of times a consistent read was requested for a block.

  This statistic measures the number of block accesses involving System Change Number (SCN) checks. The SCN is a unique number assigned by Oracle to data file and block headers in ascending sequence to identify transaction modifications. It is checked to ensure that data is up-to-date. If the SCN for a row has changed since the transaction started, then the row must have been updated by another transaction; the before-image of the row will have been stored in a rollback segment.

The SCN is incremented as changes are made to data. Each row (and the block in which it is stored) holds a copy of the SCN that was current when the row was last changed. When the block is flushed to disk by the Database Writers, the SCN on disk will match the SCN for the same block in the buffer cache.

Oracle uses the SCN to ensure that data remains consistent and to assist in recovery after a crash. During roll-forward recovery, if the SCN for a block on disk is the same or later than the SCN in the redo log, there is no need to roll forward the transaction.

Figure 22.1 shows the formula for calculating the cache hit rate before the Oracle8i releases.

Figure 22.1 *Oracle Buffer Cache Hit Rate Formula before Oracle8i*

$$cachehitrate = \left(1 - \left(\frac{physicalreads}{(dbblockgets + consistentgets)}\right)\right) \times 100$$

Figure 22.2 shows the formula for calculating the cache hit rate for the Oracle8.1.5 and Oracle8.1.6 releases.

Figure 22.2 *Oracle Buffer Cache Hit Rate Formula for Oracle8.1.5/8.1.6*

$$cachehitrate = \left(1 - \left(\frac{physicalreads - physicalreadsdirect}{(dbblockgets + consistentgets - physicalreadsdirect)}\right)\right) \times 100$$

For Oracle8.1.7 and Oracle9i, use the formula shown in Figure 22.3 to calculate the buffer cache hit rate.

Figure 22.3 *Oracle Buffer Cache Hit Rate Formula for Oracle8.1.7/9i*

$$\left(1 - \left(\frac{physicalreads - physicalreadsdirect - physicalreadsdirectLOB}{(dbblockgets + consistentgets - physicalreadsdirect - physicalreadsdirectLOB)}\right)\right) \times 100$$

Cache Hit Rate Prediction

Oracle9i introduced a new view—v$db_cache_advice—to help with the challenging task of determining the optimal size for the buffer cache. Before this view can be used, the following statement must be executed:

```
alter system set db_cache_advice = on;
```

This statement will cause approximately 100 bytes to be allocated in the shared pool per buffer and will also result in a small CPU overhead. The shared pool memory can be preallocated by setting the `db_cache_advice` parameter to `ready` or `on` in `init.ora` before the database is started. The default value for `db_cache_advice` is `off`.

After a workload has been running for a time, the view can be queried. The collecting of statistics is terminated when the `db_cache_advice` parameter is set to `off` or to `ready`.

The `v$db_cache_advice` view reports the estimated number of physical reads that would have been required for 20 different buffer cache sizes, ranging from 10% of the current size to 200% of the current size. The information helps you to assess the likely impact on the I/O subsystem of either decreasing or increasing the size of the buffer cache.

Monitoring Oracle with utlbstat/utlestat

To illustrate the process of monitoring Oracle, we examine an Oracle9i `report.txt` file created with the `utlbstat.sql` and `utlestat.sql` scripts (described in "The utlbstat and utlestat Scripts" on page 313). The report is interspersed with comments about some of the highlights; my objective is to explore the main statistics that might require action rather than to attempt to explain every item.

Note that although we follow the order used by `report.txt`, the best way to begin understanding instance behavior is to examine wait events. The `statspack` scripts recognize this by reporting the top five wait events almost at the beginning of the report.

The Library Cache

The first section of the report deals with the library cache. The library cache stores SQL and PL/SQL statements for reuse by other applications (in the SQL AREA), and also caches other objects for Oracle's internal use.

```
SQL> column library  format a12 trunc;
SQL> column pinhitratio   heading 'PINHITRATI';
SQL> column gethitratio   heading 'GETHITRATI';
SQL> column invalidations heading 'INVALIDATI';
SQL> set numwidth 10;
SQL> Rem Select Library cache statistics.The pin hit rate should be high.
SQL> select namespace library,
  2            gets,
  3            round(decode(gethits,0,1,gethits)/decode(gets,0,1,gets),3)
  4              gethitratio,
  5            pins,
  6            round(decode(pinhits,0,1,pinhits)/decode(pins,0,1,pins),3)
  7              pinhitratio,
  8            reloads, invalidations
  9     from stats$lib;
```

LIBRARY	GETS	GETHITRATI	PINS	PINHITRATI	RELOADS	INVALIDATI
BODY	1172	1	1172	.999	1	0
CLUSTER	0	1	0	1	0	0
INDEX	818	.001	818	.001	0	0
JAVA DATA	0	1	0	1	0	0
JAVA RESOURC	0	1	0	1	0	0
JAVA SOURCE	0	1	0	1	0	0
OBJECT	0	1	0	1	0	0
PIPE	0	1	0	1	0	0
SQL AREA	517004	.986	2246870	.991	9115	4878
TABLE/PROCED	26899	.974	1739839	.999	1254	0
TRIGGER	0	1	0	1	0	0

11 rows selected.

Gets measure the number of times Oracle set up a reference to objects in the cache, and pins measure the number of times objects were referenced. The gethitratio and pinhitratio should be as close to 1 as possible (at least .95), and reloads should be no more than 2% of gets. These elements cannot be individually tuned, but increasing the size of the shared pool (the shared_pool_size parameter in init.ora) can help improve the hit ratios.

User Connections

The next section of the report deals with database connections.

```
SQL> column "Statistic"         format a27 trunc;
SQL> column "Per Transaction" heading "Per Transact";
SQL> column ((start_users+end_users)/2) heading "((START_USER"
SQL> set numwidth 12;
SQL> Rem The total is the total value of the statistic between the time
SQL> Rem bstat was run and the time estat was run.  Note that the estat
SQL> Rem script logs on to the instance so the per_logon statistics will
SQL> Rem always be based on at least one logon.
SQL> select 'Users connected at ',to_char(start_time, 'dd-mon-yy
hh24:mi:ss'),':',start_users from stats$dates;
```

```
'USERSCONNECTEDAT'      TO_CHAR(START_TIME     '      START_USERS
--------------------    --------------------   -     ------------
Users connected at      17-aug-01 10:01:30     :            41
```

```
SQL> select 'Users connected at ',to_char(end_time, 'dd-mon-yy
hh24:mi:ss'),':',end_users from stats$dates;
```

```
'USERSCONNECTEDAT'      TO_CHAR(END_TIME,'     '      END_USERS
--------------------    --------------------   -     -----------
Users connected at      17-aug-01 10:31:24     :            41
```

```
SQL> select 'avg # of connections: ',((start_users+end_users)/2) from
stats$dates;
```

```
'AVG#OFCONNECTIONS:'     ((START_USER
--------------------     ------------
avg # of connections:             41
```

The number of connections at the start and end of the monitoring period and the average number of connections all help track user connectivity. Note that connections do not necessarily equate to users, though, since some users may have more than one connection and administrative scripts (including the one used to create this report) also count as connections. Conversely, transaction monitors allow multiple users to share a single connection.

The duration of the monitoring period is also shown at the end of the report. In this case it was almost exactly 30 minutes.

Database Statistics

The statistics below include some of the most important measures to be monitored. If you examine the SQL command that generated these results, you will notice that only statistics with non-zero values are reported. Consequently, if you run `utlbstat/utlestat` again later, you might find that new rows appear in this section of the report and other rows may have disappeared.

```
SQL> select n1.name "Statistic",
  2        n1.change "Total",
  3        round(n1.change/trans.change,2) "Per Transaction",
  4        round(n1.change/((start_users + end_users)/2),2)  "Per Logon",
  5        round(n1.change/(to_number(to_char(end_time,   'J'))*60*60*24 -
  6        to_number(to_char(start_time, 'J'))*60*60*24 +
  7        to_number(to_char(end_time,   'SSSSS')) -
  8        to_number(to_char(start_time, 'SSSSS')))
  9    , 2) "Per Second"
 10  from
 11        stats$stats n1,
 12        stats$stats trans,
 13        stats$dates
 14  where
 15        trans.name='user commits'
 16   and  n1.change != 0
 17  order by n1.name;
```

Statistic	Total	Per Transact	Per Logon	Per Second
CR blocks created	11909	.04	290.46	6.64
Cached Commit SCN reference	158232	.49	3859.32	88.2
DBWR buffers scanned	590396	1.82	14399.9	329.09
DBWR checkpoint buffers wri	704570	2.18	17184.63	392.74
DBWR checkpoints	2	0	.05	0
DBWR free buffers found	402083	1.24	9806.9	224.13
DBWR lru scans	22320	.07	544.39	12.44
DBWR make free requests	22320	.07	544.39	12.44
DBWR summed scan depth	590396	1.82	14399.9	329.09
DBWR transaction table writ	68	0	1.66	.04
DBWR undo block writes	32991	.1	804.66	18.39

SQL*Net roundtrips to/from	421556	1.3	10281.85	234.98
background checkpoints comp	2	0	.05	0
background checkpoints star	2	0	.05	0
background timeouts	3947	.01	96.27	2.2
branch node splits	1210	0	29.51	.67
buffer is not pinned count	7280085	22.48	177563.05	4058.02
buffer is pinned count	1530511	4.73	37329.54	853.13
bytes received via SQL*Net	101119623	312.28	2466332.27	56365.45
bytes sent via SQL*Net to c	235602857	727.59	5746411.15	131328.24
calls to get snapshot scn:	501750	1.55	12237.8	279.68
calls to kcmgas	408813	1.26	9971.05	227.88
calls to kcmgcs	83029	.26	2025.1	46.28
cleanouts and rollbacks - c	8645	.03	210.85	4.82
cleanouts only - consistent	4922	.02	120.05	2.74
cluster key scan block gets	6431181	19.86	156858.07	3584.83
cluster key scans	6431132	19.86	156856.88	3584.8
commit cleanout failures: b	1	0	.02	0
commit cleanout failures: b	69	0	1.68	.04
commit cleanout failures: c	303	0	7.39	.17
commit cleanout failures: c	676	0	16.49	.38
commit cleanouts	4006646	12.37	97723.07	2233.36
commit cleanouts successful	4005597	12.37	97697.49	2232.77
consistent changes	11959	.04	291.68	6.67
consistent gets	10345798	31.95	252336.54	5766.89
consistent gets - examinati	2841078	8.77	69294.59	1583.66
cursor authentications	26	0	.63	.01
data blocks consistent read	11954	.04	291.56	6.66
db block changes	13297163	41.06	324321.05	7412.02
db block gets	9020588	27.86	220014.34	5028.2
deferred (CURRENT) block cl	2208212	6.82	53858.83	1230.89
dirty buffers inspected	42360	.13	1033.17	23.61
enqueue releases	423982	1.31	10341.02	236.34
enqueue requests	423997	1.31	10341.39	236.34
enqueue waits	11430	.04	278.78	6.37
execute count	2275386	7.03	55497.22	1268.33
free buffer inspected	42398	.13	1034.1	23.63
free buffer requested	763898	2.36	18631.66	425.81
hot buffers moved to head o	831102	2.57	20270.78	463.27
immediate (CR) block cleano	13567	.04	330.9	7.56
immediate (CURRENT) block c	530423	1.64	12937.15	295.66
leaf node splits	66072	.2	1611.51	36.83
logons cumulative	2	0	.05	0
messages received	320324	.99	7812.78	178.55
messages sent	320326	.99	7812.83	178.55
native hash arithmetic exec	4836175	14.94	117955.49	2695.75
no work - consistent read g	6989419	21.58	170473.63	3896
opened cursors cumulative	121	0	2.95	.07
parse count (failures)	1	0	.02	0
parse count (hard)	5	0	.12	0
parse count (total)	120	0	2.93	.07
physical reads	678283	2.09	16543.49	378.08
physical reads direct	94	0	2.29	.05
physical writes	935315	2.89	22812.56	521.36
physical writes direct	94	0	2.29	.05
physical writes non checkpo	603082	1.86	14709.32	336.17
prefetched blocks	1558	0	38	.87

```
recursive calls                2034976       6.28    49633.56    1134.32
redo blocks written            4683822      14.46   114239.56    2610.83
redo buffer allocation retr         72          0        1.76        .04
redo entries                   6864072       21.2   167416.39    3826.13
redo log space requests             72          0        1.76        .04
redo size                   2276348068    7029.82 55520684.59 1268867.37
redo synch writes               328737       1.02     8017.98     183.24
redo wastage                  46160068     142.55  1125855.32   25730.25
redo writes                     186021        .57      4537.1     103.69
rollback changes - undo rec      39610        .12       966.1      22.08
rollbacks only - consistent       3257        .01       79.44       1.82
rows fetched via callback       173830        .54     4239.76       96.9
serializable aborts              12052        .04      293.95       6.72
session logical reads         19366372      59.81   472350.54   10795.08
session pga memory            50759728     156.76  1238042.15   28294.16
session pga memory max        50653084     156.43  1235441.07   28234.72
session uga memory            38770192     119.73   945614.44   21611.03
session uga memory max        38828836     119.91   947044.78   21643.72
shared hash latch upgrades      450999       1.39    10999.98     251.39
shared hash latch upgrades           2          0         .05          0
sorts (disk)                       857          0       20.90        .48
sorts (memory)                   71791        .22        1751      40.02
sorts (rows)                   1924399       5.94    46936.56    1072.69
summed dirty queue length       263847        .81     6435.29     147.07
switch current to new buffe         11          0         .27        .01
table fetch by rowid            201420        .62     4912.68     112.27
table scan blocks gotten          3002        .01       73.22       1.67
table scan rows gotten             948          0       23.12        .53
table scans (short tables)          12          0         .29        .01
transaction rollbacks             4917        .02      119.93       2.74
user calls                      421017        1.3    10268.71     234.68
user commits                    323813          1     7897.88      180.5
user rollbacks                   13640        .04      332.68        7.6
write clones created in for        356          0        8.68         .2

100 rows selected.
```

Note that four sets of values are reported for each statistic:

- **Total.** This value shows the total number of events of this type during the monitoring interval.
- **Per Transaction.** This column is normalized according to the number of user commits (you will notice a value of 1 for that row). Note that the rate of user commits can provide an alternate measure of application workload in the absence of higher-level information about business transactions (such as the number of invoices processed during a specified period of time).
- **Per Logon.** Normalizing the statistic according to the number of logons (user connections) can help in predicting the impact of changing the number of users and user connections. Bear in mind, though, that logged-on connections may not all be active.

- **Per Second.** This value helps put the totals in perspective. For example, the I/O capability of a disk is usually expressed in I/Os per second, so knowing that 935,315 physical writes were completed is not as useful as knowing that on average 521 physical writes were completed per second. Early versions of Oracle did not include this useful column.

The Buffer Cache Hit Rate

Using the Oracle9i cache hit rate equation presented earlier in this chapter and the information reported above, we can calculate the cache hit rate for the monitoring interval:

$$Buffer\ Cache\ Hit\ Rate$$
$$= (1 - ((678283 - 94 - 0) \div (9020588 + 10345798 - 94 - 0)))$$
$$\times 100$$
$$= 96.5\%$$

Given a cache hit rate of 96.5%, the miss rate is 3.5%—a miss rate that could probably be reduced.

Is the hit rate acceptable? Given the rate of physical reads (approximately 380 per second) and the rate of physical writes (approximately 520 per second), the average disk I/O rate is 900 I/Os per second. That load could probably be handled by fifteen 7200 rpm disks or twelve 10000 rpm disks, although it would be wise to configure up to 50% more disks to allow for peaks of I/O activity.

If 20 to 25 disks are in use for the database and the I/O is balanced evenly across all the disks, it may not be necessary to try to improve the cache hit rate. On the other hand, if fewer disks are in use and they are heavily utilized, reducing the miss rate might significantly improve performance, provided adequate memory is available for the purpose (never increase the size of the buffer cache so much that applications begin to page). Remember, too, that increasing the cache size will make little change to the rate of physical writes.

The issues related to monitoring the buffer cache hit rate and sizing the buffer cache are explored in more detail in Chapter 7, beginning with "Monitoring the Buffer Cache" on page 76.

Other Statistics to Monitor

We conclude this section of the `report.txt` file by considering a few highlights from the long list of statistics reported by `utlbstat` and `utlestat`.

- **dirty buffers inspected.** This statistic measures the number of times a shadow process found a dirty buffer on the least recently used (LRU) list. Normally the Database Writers find such dirty buffers and move them to a linked list of dirty buffer headers. If the Database Writers are working effectively, this statistic should be zero (and therefore not appear in the report) or have a low value. Adding more Database Writers (the `db_writer_processes` parameter in `init.ora`) should help resolve a problem of this type. In this case, dirty buffers have been found 24 times a second, or on average for one in eight transactions, suggesting that the number of Database Writers could be usefully increased.

- **redo log space requests.** This statistic measures the number of times shadow processes stalled waiting for log file space. A common myth is that the statistic reports the number of times a process stalls during commits because there was not enough room in the log buffer. Stalls can occur during checkpoints.

- **sorts (disk)** and **sorts (memory).** The first of these statistics measures the number of sorts that spill to the temporary tablespace because they could not fit in the memory allocated by the sort_area_size parameter in init.ora. The second statistic shows the number of sorts that were able to complete in memory without resorting to the temporary tablespace. The report above shows 857 sorts to disk over a 30-minute period compared to 71,791 sorts in memory. So just over 1% of all sorts spilled to disk, at a rate of less than one per minute. There is little reason to increase sort_area_size in this case.

- **table scans (short tables)** and **table scans (long tables).** The first of these statistics shows the number of table scans carried out on short tables (less than or equal to 5 blocks in length) or on tables that have been flagged as cached.

    Tables can be specified as cached when the table is created, or later with the alter table command from sqlplus (for example, alter table customer cache;). Normally, blocks read during a full table scan are marked as least recently used, and the space they consume is quickly reclaimed. By contrast, blocks read from cached tables during a table scan are treated as most recently used blocks. Caching small, heavily accessed tables can improve performance in some cases.

    The second statistic shows the number of table scans on larger tables (none appeared in the report). Large table scans should be avoided in OLTP environments since they impact overall system performance and lower the buffer cache hit rate. Creating appropriate indexes or modifying the application can overcome the problem.

Systemwide Wait Events

You can dynamically view the events reported in the next section of the report.txt file by querying the v$system_event and v$session_event views as sysdba. The report below breaks down the wait events into two categories: nonbackground processes and background processes, where background processes are Oracle system processes like PMON, SMON, and LGWR. The wait events are sorted in descending order of total time spent waiting (in units of hundredths of seconds).

```
SQL> column "Event Name" format a32 trunc;
SQL> set numwidth 13;
SQL> Rem System wide wait events for non-background processes (PMON,
SQL> Rem SMON, etc).  Times are in hundredths of seconds.  Each one of
SQL> Rem these is a context switch which costs CPU time.  By looking at
SQL> Rem the Total Time you can often determine what is the bottleneck
SQL> Rem that processes are waiting for.  This shows the total time spent
SQL> Rem waiting for a specific event and the average time per wait on
SQL> Rem that event.
SQL> select  n1.event "Event Name",
     2              n1.event_count "Count",
     3              n1.time_waited "Total Time",
     4              round(n1.time_waited/n1.event_count, 2) "Avg Time"
     5       from stats$event n1
     6       where n1.event_count > 0
     7       order by n1.time_waited desc;
```

Event Name	Count	Total Time	Avg Time
db file sequential read	679244	2231864	3.29
SQL*Net message from client	423411	2164652	5.11
log file sync	329826	516878	1.57
enqueue	11472	71489	6.23
latch free	1736	2194	1.26
db file parallel read	40	481	12.03
log file switch completion	53	393	7.42
SQL*Net message to client	423405	327	0
control file sequential read	83	119	1.43
buffer busy waits	379	113	.3
SQL*Net break/reset to client	2284	61	.03

```
11 rows selected.

SQL> Rem System wide wait events for background processes (PMON,SMON,etc)
SQL> select  n1.event "Event Name",
     2              n1.event_count "Count",
     3              n1.time_waited "Total Time",
     4              round(n1.time_waited/n1.event_count, 2) "Avg Time"
     5       from stats$bck_event n1
     6       where n1.event_count > 0
     7       order by n1.time_waited desc;
```

Event Name	Count	Total Time	Avg Time
rdbms ipc message	331631	779378	2.35
db file parallel write	229188	603152	2.63
pmon timer	597	175435	293.86
smon timer	5	150002	30000.4
log file parallel write	186846	80079	.43
db file scattered read	377	2168	5.75
control file parallel write	613	1021	1.67
latch free	155	248	1.6
LGWR wait for redo copy	747	142	.19
control file sequential read	96	101	1.05
async disk IO	100	63	.63
db file sequential read	7	10	1.43
log file single write	4	4	1
direct path read	94	2	.02
log file sequential read	2	1	.5
direct path write	94	0	0

```
16 rows selected.
```

The `SQL*Net message from client` wait event simply means that the shadow process is waiting for the client to do something. Consequently, substantial wait times for this event do not usually indicate a problem (unless the waits are due to network delays). The converse event, `SQL*Net message to client`, shows the delay when shadow processes send messages to clients; large delays could indicate network problems.

Wait events that should be monitored include those in the following list:

- **free buffer waits.** A lot of time spent waiting for free buffers suggests that the Database Writers are not flushing dirty buffers fast enough to keep up with demand. This event does not appear in the report above, but if it should appear as a major wait event, try increasing the `db_writer_processes` parameter in `init.ora`.

- **buffer busy waits.** Buffer busy waits occur when shadow processes were unable to access a buffer because it was in use by another process. The report above shows a tiny number of waits of this type.

  If buffer busy waits are one of the top wait events in terms of percentage of time waited, check the `v$waitstat` view to find out what type of blocks are affected (this information is also presented later in `report.txt`, in "Buffer Busy Wait Statistics" on page 331).

  You can also check the `v$session_wait` view to find out the file ID (the `P1` column) and the block ID (the `P2` column) of the affected block. The file ID can be used to query the `dba_extents` view (you will need to add a `where file_id = n` clause, where n is the file ID from the `v$session_wait` view) to get the details of the segment that the block ID falls within.

  Each data block supports a limited number of concurrent accesses for update or delete operations; a table with a large number of rows per block and high concurrency can experience frequent `buffer busy wait` events as a result. The `INITRANS` parameter determines the number of concurrent accesses (the default is 1 for tables and 2 for indexes). If the segment identified in `v$session_wait` belongs to a table or index, you could increase the `INITRANS` storage parameter. The `INITRANS` parameter can only be set during table or index creation, so it may be necessary to drop and recreate the table or index.

  For tables subject to high insert concurrency, increase the `FREELISTS` storage parameter to improve performance if the `buffer busy wait` events are related to inserts. The `FREELISTS` parameter also must be specified at create time.

- **enqueues.** Although this wait event appears in the report above, the number of events and wait time do not suggest a problem. If enqueue waits represent a high proportion of the time spent waiting, you can try to identify the enqueue waited for. Oracle9i provides a view—`v$enqueue_stat`—for this purpose; see `statspack` for more information before Oracle9i. Enqueue waits are a symptom of some other problem.

Latch Wait Events

Latch wait information can be obtained from the `v$latch` view. When a latch is not available, in some cases the requesting process may spin (that is, consume CPU) for a time before trying again, depending on the nature of the latch request. If the latch is still unavailable, the process will go to sleep and try again when it wakes up. The next section of `report.txt` deals with latches of this type. The same information can also be obtained from the `name`, `gets`, `misses`, and `sleeps` columns in the `v$latch` view.

The subsequent section deals with no-wait latches. Processes unable to acquire latches requested in this way do not sleep, but time out and retry immediately. The `immediate_gets` and `immediate_misses` columns in `v$latch` also provide this information.

When monitoring latches, check the hit ratio, which indicates the degree of contention on the latch. Check also the number of gets, which indicates how hot (that is, how much in demand) a latch is, and the number of sleeps, which indicates the number of times the process had to sleep while waiting for the latch.

The worst-case scenario with latches is that a process will be preempted by the operating system while holding a high-contention latch. Database performance for some Solaris systems (particularly midrange systems) improves if the CPU allocation available to processes is increased. This issue and its resolution are discussed in "The TS Class" on page 220.

Latches with Waits

The first section of the latch report deals with latches with waits.

```
SQL> column latch_name format a18 trunc;
SQL> set numwidth 11;
SQL> Rem Latch statistics. Latch contention will show up as a large value
for
SQL> Rem the 'latch free' event in the wait events above.
SQL> Rem Sleeps should be low.The hit_ratio should be high.
SQL> select name latch_name, gets, misses,
  2    round((gets-misses)/decode(gets,0,1,gets),3)
  3      hit_ratio,
  4    sleeps,
  5    round(sleeps/decode(misses,0,1,misses),3) "SLEEPS/MISS"
  6  from stats$latches
  7    where gets != 0
  8    order by name;
```

LATCH_NAME	GETS	MISSES	HIT-RATIO	SLEEPS	SLEEPS/MISS
FIB s.o chain latc	8	0	1	0	0
FOB s.o list latch	75	0	1	0	0
active checkpoint	135993	82	.999	4	.049
cache buffers chai	67102082	5408	1	131	.024
cache buffers lru	1211707	386	1	8	.021
channel handle poo	4	0	1	0	0
channel operations	582	0	1	0	0
checkpoint queue l	5377441	1310	1	92	.07
child cursor hash	12	0	1	0	0

dml lock allocatio	110	0	1	0	0
enqueue hash chain	859206	1146	.999	117	.102
enqueues	1047133	820	.999	23	.028
event group latch	2	0	1	0	0
hash table column	4	0	1	0	0
ktm global data	5	0	1	0	0
latch wait list	958	0	1	0	0
library cache	4660957	12857	.997	465	.036
list of block allo	892019	301	1	44	.146
loader state objec	4	0	1	0	0
messages	1158227	551	1	42	.076
multiblock read ob	834	0	1	0	0
ncodef allocation	29	0	1	0	0
post/wait queue la	655696	1722	.997	152	.088
process allocation	2	0	1	0	0
process group crea	4	0	1	0	0
redo allocation	7233318	20538	.997	374	.018
redo copy	136	80	.412	93	1.163
redo writing	1166363	1394	.999	140	.1
row cache objects	121417	7	1	0	0
sequence cache	3	0	1	0	0
session allocation	334950	295	.999	7	.024
session idle bit	1009326	512	.999	26	.051
session switching	29	0	1	0	0
shared pool	224	0	1	0	0
sort extent pool	34	0	1	0	0
transaction alloca	1263687	2378	.998	77	.032
transaction branch	29	0	1	0	0
undo global data	1376947	2983	.998	77	.026
user lock	4	0	1	0	0

39 rows selected.

No-Wait Latches

The remainder of this section of the report deals with no-wait latches. It is followed by suggestions on latch monitoring.

```
SQL> set numwidth 16
SQL> Rem Statistics on no_wait gets of latches. A no_wait get does not
SQL> Rem wait for the latch to become free, it immediately times out.
SQL> select name latch_name,
  2        immed_gets nowait_gets,
  3        immed_miss nowait_misses,
  4        round((immed_gets/(immed_gets+immed_miss)), 3)
  5          nowait_hit_ratio
  6      from stats$latches
  7      where immed_gets + immed_miss != 0
  8      order by name;

LATCH_NAME             NOWAIT_GETS    NOWAIT_MISSES NOWAIT_HIT_RATIO
------------------ ---------------- ---------------- ----------------
cache buffers chai          806427               38                1
cache buffers lru           763359             1090             .999
process allocation               2                0                1
redo copy                  6861266            55595             .992
```

The hit_ratio should be close to 1. The following list indicates the main latches to monitor:

- **cache buffers chains.** When searching for a block in the cache, a shadow process uses a hashing algorithm to find the appropriate hash bucket and then follows a hash chain to scan for the block. Fewer hash buckets means longer hash chains, more searching, and higher contention on the `cache buffers chains` latch. Inefficient SQL statements, such as heavily accessed statements using indexes that are not highly selective, can cause high contention for this latch.

  Identify the scale of any potential problem with the following SQL (for Oracle8 and later releases) as `sysdba`:

  ```
  select count(*) from x$bh;
  select dbarfil "File", dbablk "Block", count(*)
      from x$bh group by dbafil, dbablk
      having count(*) > 1;
  ```

- **cache buffers lru chains.** This latch protects the LRU chain. High contention could indicate that the Database Writers are not operating efficiently, for example, due to a slow or overloaded I/O subsystem.

- **library cache.** A number of factors contribute to high library cache latch contention. Sometimes you can alleviate the contention simply by increasing the size of the shared pool (the `shared_pool_size` parameter in `init.ora`). Other changes that might be necessary to relieve library cache contention include those in the following list:

  - Keep large SQL statements into the shared pool (with the `dbms_shared_pool.keep` procedure).

  - Use bind variables to reduce SQL statement parsing. For example, the following two statements are parsed and stored independently in the shared pool, even though they are almost identical:

    ```
    select cust_name from customer
        where cust_id = 12345;
    select cust_name from customer
        where cust_id = 23456;
    ```

    The preferred approach is to use a bind variable (for example, `:cust_id`) and to assign the value for `cust_id` to the bind variable. The two statements can then be consolidated into a single statement:

    ```
    select cust_name from customer
        where cust_id = :cust_id;
    ```

    Use of bind variables reduces latch contention and also reduces the pressure on free space in the shared pool.

  - Fully qualify object names. For example, use:

    ```
    select * from accts.customer;
    ```

    rather than:

    ```
    select * from customer;
    ```

- Flush the shared pool if fragmentation occurs (run the `alter system flush shared_pool` command as `sysdba`). Fragmentation problems are typically accompanied by the `ORA-4031` error message: `More shared memory is needed than was allocated in the shared pool.` Note that flushing the shared pool provides short-term relief at the cost of a short-term performance hit but does not solve the problem. The previous suggestions should provide longer-term solutions.

- **redo copy.** If the hit ratio is low for the `redo copy` latch, it may be possible to reduce the contention by increasing the number of `redo copy` latches with the hidden `_log_simultaneous_copies` parameter in `init.ora`. Normally this parameter is based on the number of CPUs on the system. Do not change this parameter in Oracle9i. For more information on hidden parameters, including caveats, refer to "Viewing and Changing Hidden Parameters" on page 311.

Buffer Busy Wait Statistics

The following statistics are useful if buffer busy wait events suggest high contention on buffers. The issues are discussed earlier in this chapter in "Systemwide Wait Events" on page 325.

```
SQL> Rem Buffer busy wait statistics.  If the value for 'buffer busy wait' in
SQL> Rem the wait event statistics is high, then this table will identify
SQL> Rem which class of blocks is having high contention.  If there are high
SQL> Rem 'undo header' waits, then add more rollback segments.  If there are
SQL> Rem high 'segment header' waits, then adding freelists might help. Check
SQL> Rem v$session_wait to get the addresses of the actual blocks having
SQL> Rem contention.
SQL> select * from stats$waitstat
  2    where count != 0
  3    order by count desc;
```

CLASS	COUNT	TIME
data block	288	0
undo header	49	0
undo block	38	0
free list	4	0

Rollback Segments

The `v$rollstat` view presents detailed information on rollback segment behavior. The purpose of rollback segments is described in "Segments" on page 112.

```
SQL> set lines 159;
SQL> set numwidth 19;
SQL> Rem Waits_for_trans_tbl high implies you should add rollback segments.
SQL> select * from stats$roll;
```

UNDO_SEG	TRN_TBL_GETS	TRN_TBL_WAITS	UNDO_BYT_WR	SEG_SIZE_BYT	XACTS	SHRINKS	WRAPS
0	6	0	0	458752	0	0	0
1	36385	0	24940942	2762752	0	0	293
2	35993	0	24685736	2353152	1	0	289
3	35937	0	24726410	6858752	1	0	290

```
<< rows deleted >>
```

As transactions proceed, rollback segments gradually grow in size. Oracle reclaims this space periodically by automatically eliminating extents to return a rollback segment to the optimal size (set by the OPTIMAL parameter in the STORAGE clause of the rollback segment). A substantial number of shrinks can indicate that the optimal rollback segment size is too small. Be aware, though, that setting the OPTIMAL parameter too large wastes space.

If waits are more than 5% of gets, increase the number of rollback segments.

Note that I have abbreviated some of the column headings above for formatting purposes.

Modified init.ora Parameters

The following section of the report.txt file displays current init.ora parameters that have been modified from the defaults.

```
SQL> set lines 79;
SQL>
SQL> column name  format a39 trunc;
SQL> column value format a39 trunc;
SQL> Rem The init.ora parameters currently in effect:
SQL> select name, value from v$parameter where isdefault = 'FALSE'
  2     order by name;
```

NAME	VALUE
db_block_buffers	605600
db_block_size	2048
db_file_multiblock_read_count	4
db_files	350
db_name	accts
db_writer_processes	5
dml_locks	2500
log_buffer	8097792
log_checkpoint_interval	999999999
shared_pool_size	33554432
sort_area_size	1000000
transactions	1000

```
<< rows deleted >>
```

Dictionary Cache Statistics

The dictionary cache stores data dictionary information for all objects in the database. Consequently, it tends to be heavily accessed. Details of dictionary cache statistics can also be queried with the v$rowcache view.

```
SQL> column name format a15 trunc;
SQL> column scan_reqs heading 'SCAN_REQ';
SQL> column scan_miss heading 'SCAN_MIS';
SQL> column cur_usage heading 'CUR_USAG';
SQL> set numwidth 8;
SQL> Rem get_miss and scan_miss should be very low compared to requests.
SQL> Rem cur_usage is the number of entries in the cache being used.
SQL> select * from stats$dc
  2    where get_reqs != 0 or scan_reqs != 0 or mod_reqs != 0;
```

NAME	GET_REQS	GET_MISS	SCAN_REQ	SCAN_MIS	MOD_REQS	COUNT	CUR_USAG
dc_tablespaces	39923	0	0	0	0	14	13
dc_free_extents	28	6	6	0	18	42	4
dc_segments	29	0	0	0	6	141	123
dc_rollback_seg	600	0	0	0	0	66	61
dc_used_extents	6	6	0	0	6	88	55
dc_tablespace_q	23	0	0	0	23	23	8
dc_users	56	0	0	0	0	14	6
dc_user_grants	52	0	0	0	0	14	4
dc_objects	18	0	0	0	0	313	301
dc_usernames	3	0	0	0	0	21	4
dc_object_ids	10	0	0	0	0	230	218
dc_profiles	1	0	0	0	0	3	1

```
12 rows selected.
```

Once the database has been running for a while, look for a high proportion of misses compared to gets. If misses are significant, increase the size of the shared pool (the shared_pool_size parameter in init.ora).

Tablespace and Database File I/O Activity

The following section of report.txt shows I/O activity by tablespace and by database file, including the number of physical reads and writes and the time taken to complete each type of I/O (in hundredths of seconds). If times are shown as 0, set the timed_statistics parameter in init.ora to TRUE.

Mapping database files to physical disks can be complicated if a volume manager is used to stripe the database files. Nonetheless, information about the I/O activity for each file can be useful in data layout planning (discussed in detail in Chapter 17). For more information about monitoring disk utilization, refer to "STEP 2. Monitoring Disks" on page 289.

```
SQL> set lines 157;
SQL> column table_space format a80 trunc;
SQL> set numwidth 10;
SQL> Rem Sum IO operations over tablespaces.
SQL> select
   2    table_space||'       '
   3    table_space,
   4    sum(phys_reads) reads,  sum(phys_blks_rd) blks_read,
   5    sum(phys_rd_time) read_time,  sum(phys_writes) writes,
   6    sum(phys_blks_wr) blks_wrt,  sum(phys_wrt_tim) write_time,
   7    sum(megabytes_size) megabytes
   8    from stats$files
   9    group by table_space
  10    order by table_space;
```

TABLE_SPACE	READS	BLKS_READ	READ_TIME	WRITES	BLKS_WRT	WRITE_TIME	MEGABYTES
SYSTEM	410	1528	2321	28333	28333	0	262
TABLESPACE1	415	415	1610	1331	1331	0	52
TABLESPACE10	22847	22847	62941	49582	49582	0	189
TABLESPACE12	15288	15287	51655	2	2	0	157
TABLESPACE15	2	2	0	5102	5102	0	31
TABLESPACE16	2	2	0	2	2	0	210
TABLESPACE5	291653	291643	916007	225756	225755	0	2310
TABLESPACE6	77249	77249	201654	116744	116746	0	2520
TABLESPACE7	252514	252506	961914	491426	491428	0	3528

`<< rows deleted >>`

```
SQL> set lines 196;
SQL> column table_space format a48 trunc;
SQL> column file_nameformat a48 trunc;
SQL> set numwidth 10;
SQL> Rem I/O should be spread evenly across drives. A big difference
between
SQL> Rem phys_reads and phys_blks_rd implies table scans are going on.
SQL> select table_space, file_name,
   2    phys_reads reads, phys_blks_rd blks_read, phys_rd_time read_time,
   3    phys_writes writes, phys_blks_wr blks_wrt, phys_wrt_tim write_time,
   4    megabytes_size megabytes,
   5    round(decode(phys_blks_rd,0,0,phys_rd_time/phys_blks_rd),2) avg_rt,
   6    round(decode(phys_reads,0,0,phys_blks_rd/phys_reads),2) "blocks/rd"
   7    from stats$files order by table_space, file_name;
```

TABLE_SPACE	FILE_NAME	READS	BLKS_READ	READ_TIME	WRITES
BLKS_WRT	WRITE_TIME	MEGABYTES	AVG_RT	blocks/rd	
SYSTEM	/home2/dbfiles/sys001	410	1528	2321	28333
28333	0	262	1.52	3.73	
TABLESPACE1	/home3/dbfiles/wdi001	415	415	1610	1331
1331	0	52	3.88	1	
TABLESPACE10	/home2/dbfiles/iord2001	22847	22847	62941	49582
49582	0	189	2.75	1	
TABLESPACE12	/home2/dbfiles/icust001	15288	15287	51655	2
2	0	157	3.38	1	
TABLESPACE15	/home2/dbfiles/roll001	2	2	0	5102
5102	0	31	0	1	

`<< rows deleted >>`

Date, Time, and Version Details

The final section of `report.txt` shows the start and end time of the report and the Oracle version.

```
SQL> set lines 79;
SQL>
SQL> column start_time format a25;
SQL> column end_time   format a25;
SQL> Rem The times that bstat and estat were run.
SQL> select to_char(start_time, 'dd-mon-yy hh24:mi:ss') start_time,
  2    to_char(end_time,'dd-mon-yy hh24:mi:ss') end_time
  3    from stats$dates;

START_TIME                END_TIME
------------------------  ------------------------
17-aug-01 10:01:30        17-aug-01 10:31:24

SQL> column banner format a75 trunc;
SQL> Rem Versions
SQL> select * from v$version;

BANNER
---------------------------------------------------------------------------
Oracle9i Enterprise Edition Release 9.0.1.0.0 - Production
PL/SQL Release 9.0.1.0.0 - Production
CORE       9.0.1.0.0 - Production
TNS for Solaris: Version 9.0.1.0.0 - Production
NLSRTL Version 9.0.1.0.0 - Production

SQL> spool off;
```

Monitoring the Shared Pool

The Oracle shared memory area is called the System Global Area (SGA). After the buffer cache, the shared pool is typically the largest component of the SGA.

The shared pool includes memory for the library cache, which caches information about database objects such as stored procedures and views, the cursor cache, which caches SQL statements and, if the Shared Server (previously known as the MultiThreaded Server, or MTS) is in use, a cache for session-specific information such as the context area and the sort area.

If the shared pool is too small, performance can suffer. It can be increased with the `shared_pool_size` parameter in `init.ora`. To monitor the shared pool, run the following statements as `sysdba`:

```
select value from v$parameter where name = 'shared_pool_size';
select name, bytes from v$sgastat where name = 'free memory';
```

If free memory is more than 40% of the shared pool, you may be able to decrease the size of the shared pool. It is less easy to determine whether the shared pool is too small; a system with only 10% free memory in the shared pool might be running efficiently. Look for RELOADS in the library cache statistics to see how often objects have been aged out of the shared pool (see

"The Library Cache" on page 319 for details). Frequent reloads can indicate that the shared pool is too small.

Tuning Oracle

Once the system has been appropriately configured (see Chapters 13 through 17, and especially the data layout recommendations in Chapter 17), it is appropriate to find out if Oracle is properly configured. Oracle tuning is carried out with init.ora parameters, of which there are many; we focus on the most important parameters.

Tuning init.ora

When Oracle is installed, the init.ora file assumes a "small model" with just 400 Kbytes set aside for database buffers. For many end-user sites, several init.ora parameters will need to be changed in order for Oracle to work effectively.

A number of general tunable parameters unrelated to performance need to be assigned values large enough to support the required number of users and transactions:

- **processes:** The number of concurrent processes supported.
- **sessions:** The number of concurrent sessions supported.
- **dml_locks:** The number of locks that can be set. Needs to be set high enough to avoid "DML Lock" error. Try eight times the number of transactions.
- **db_files:** The number of database files that can be open while the database is running.
- **transactions:** The number of concurrent transactions supported.

Setting Tunable Parameters for OLTP Workloads

The most important init.ora tunable parameters for OLTP workloads are the following:

- **db_block_size:** Database block size in bytes. This parameter must be set when the database is created. You cannot change the block size once it is set without exporting and reimporting the data. All database blocks use this size. Use 2 Kbytes (set db_block_size to 2048), 4 Kbytes (4096), or 8 Kbytes (8192) for OLTP workloads.

  As of Oracle9i, different block sizes can be used for different tablespaces. The blocksize clause of the create tablespace statement can be used to achieve this effect.

- **db_block_buffers:** The amount of memory in database blocks set aside for the database buffer cache. The block size is defined by the db_block_size parameter. For OLTP workloads, this parameter is probably the most important tunable for performance. If you change it, monitor the buffer cache hit rate before and after to see how much improvement you have gained. Refer to "Calculating the Buffer Cache Hit Rate" on page 317 for details.

- **buffer_pool_keep** and **buffer_pool_recycle:** Parameters that reset the recycle and keep pools, described in "System Global Area (SGA)" on page 108. These pools can be especially useful for improving the performance of OLTP workloads. Set the buffer_pool_keep and buffer_pool_recycle parameters in init.ora to the number of blocks that should be reserved for the keep and recycle pools, respectively. The number of blocks in the main (default) buffer pool will consist of those assigned to db_block_buffers minus those assigned to buffer_pool_keep and buffer_pool_recycle.

  To assign a table to the keep pool, for example, add the storage (buffer_pool keep) clause to either a create table or an alter table statement. The following statement illustrates the required syntax:

  ```
  alter table customer storage (buffer_pool keep);
  ```

- **db_cache_size:** Replacement for db_block_buffers in Oracle9i, although the older parameter is still supported for backward compatibility. The recommended approach is now to use db_cache_size, which uses a unit of bytes rather than blocks, making it easier to understand. If you use db_block_buffers, you won't be able to dynamically resize the buffer cache (described in "Reconfiguring Oracle9i Dynamically" on page 344).

  As previously stated, Oracle9i also supports different block sizes for different tablespaces. Consequently, separate caches must be configured for these tablespaces. The following new parameters are used to configure caches for tablespaces with 2-, 4-, 8-, 16-, and 32-Kbyte cache sizes, respectively:

  ```
  db_2k_cache_size
  db_4k_cache_size
  db_8k_cache_size
  db_16k_cache_size
  db_32k_cache_size
  ```

  Any new caches will be configured in addition to the cache that is sized according to the db_cache_size parameter. One parameter must be avoided, though: the cache size parameter corresponding to the current block size. For example, if the standard db_block_size is set to 4096, the db_4k_cache_size parameter cannot be used. The appropriate parameter for tablespaces using the standard block size is db_cache_size.

- **shared_pool_size:** The size in bytes of the shared pool in the SGA. The shared pool stores the library cache, the shared SQL area, and session-specific data (only when the Shared Server is being used). This parameter is also important for performance. Depending on the environment and the amount of memory available, set it to a minimum of 20 Mbytes. Larger sites will require much more memory for the shared pool.

- **sort_area_size:** The maximum size in bytes of user memory available for sorting. Sorting is required during index creation and as a result of the sort by and order by clauses of the select statement. Increase this parameter if sorts (disk) in v$sysstat (or report.txt) is more than 5% of sorts (memory) and disk sorts are occurring frequently. Note that the statspack report calculates the In-memory sort %. The sort_area_size parameter determines the memory allocation per user, so a large setting can quickly consume memory. Use 64 Kbytes, or more if plenty of memory is available.

- **log_buffer:** The size in bytes of the redo log buffer in the SGA. Log data is cached here before being written to the redo logs. Try 1 Mbyte.

- **db_writer_processes (db_writers** in Oracle7): The number of DBWR processes available to flush dirty pages from the buffer cache. For small systems you can use the default of 1, although for large OLTP systems more than one will probably be necessary. Increase the number of DBWR processes if free buffer waits appears as one of the most frequent wait events or the dirty buffers inspected statistic is much greater than zero in the report.txt file. Note that you should increase db_writer_processes rather than the dbwr_io_slaves parameter.

  In Oracle7, multiple db_writers could be used only if async_write was set to FALSE.

- **rollback_segments:** The rollback segments available for transactions. Rollback segments need to be big enough to complete large transactions, and you need enough of them to support multiple concurrent transactions without undue contention. Increase the number of rollback segments if undo header waits in v$waitstat is high and increasing.

- **disk_async_io:** A boolean parameter designating whether or not asynchronous I/O should be used. Use the default of TRUE. In Oracle7, set async_read and async_write to TRUE. In combination with raw partitions, asynchronous I/O allows the use of Kernel Asynchronous I/O (KAIO). Note, however, the recommendations and limitations on the use of asynchronous I/O explained in "Using Oracle with File Systems" on page 340.

Setting Tunable Parameters for DSS Workloads

Following are the most important tunable parameters for DSS workloads:

- **db_block_size:** Database block size in bytes. Set when the database is created. All database blocks use this size. Use 16 or 32 Kbytes for DSS workloads.

- **db_block_buffers:** The amount of memory in database blocks (as defined by db_block_size) set aside for the database buffer cache. For DSS workloads, large buffer caches are less useful and this parameter is usually set much lower than for OLTP workloads. As described above in "Setting Tunable Parameters for OLTP Workloads" on page 336, a new parameter, db_cache_size, is provided as of Oracle9i.

- **shared_pool_size:** The size in bytes of the shared pool in the SGA. The shared pool stores the library cache and the shared SQL area. This parameter is also important for performance. Depending on the amount of memory available, set shared_pool_size to a minimum of 20 Mbytes.

- **sort_area_size:** The maximum size in bytes of user memory available for sorting. Increase if sorts (disk) in v$sysstat is more than 10% of sorts (memory). This amount of memory can be allocated per user, so large values can cause Oracle to quickly consume memory. Set to 1 Mbyte or more if you have the memory available.

- **sort_direct_writes:** A boolean parameter designating whether or not writes to temporary segments should bypass the buffer cache (as of Oracle 7.2). Set to TRUE for DSS workloads to improve performance. This parameter was made obsolete in Oracle8i; direct writes now occur automatically.

- **log_buffer:** The size in bytes of the redo log buffer in the SGA. Buffers log data before writing to the redo logs. This parameter can be important for performance, especially during database updates. Try 1 Mbyte.

- **db_file_multiblock_read_count:** The number of database blocks read at once when a tablescan is performed. Set it to 64 to get 1 Mbyte reads with a db_block_size of 16 Kbytes.

- **rollback_segments:** The rollback segments available for transactions. Rollback segments need to be big enough to complete large transactions, and you need enough of them to support multiple concurrent transactions without undue contention. Increase if undo header waits in v$waitstat is high and increasing.

- **hash_area_size:** The maximum size in bytes that will be used for hash joins (the default is twice sort_area_size). This parameter is per user and is private memory, so multiple users can easily consume more than 4 Gbytes, even with 32-bit databases on 32-bit Solaris. A large hash area can make a big difference to hash join performance for large tables. If you have a lot of memory, make it larger than 2 Mbytes.

- **parallel_max_servers:** The maximum size of the query server pool. This parameter determines the degree of parallelism during table scans. Use an upper limit of four times the number of CPUs. Set parallel_min_servers to the same value.

- **optimizer_percent_parallel:** A weighting factor used by the optimizer to determine how much weight to give to query parallelism. For fastest, greedy use of resources, set to 100 (favors table scans). Lower settings favor index scans.

- **query_rewrite_enabled:** A boolean parameter designating whether or not the optimizer should rewrite queries to take advantage of previously created materialized views. Set to TRUE to enable materialized views (Oracle 8i onwards). The query rewrite option can also be set by an alter system or alter session SQL command.

Applying Other Tuning Tips

This section presents a number of miscellaneous tuning tips related to file systems, load and index performance, and relinking of the oracle binary to allow shared memory segments larger than 2 Gbytes in size.

Using Oracle with File Systems

The issues associated with using database files on file systems are discussed elsewhere in this book:

- "Unix File System Enhancements" on page 21 outlines the enhancements made in Solaris to improve UFS database performance.

- "Raw Devices vs. UFS" on page 242 discusses the performance implications of UFS.

- "UFS Files and Paging" on page 284 explores UFS files in the context of system monitoring.

The bottom line is that if you decide to place your data files on UFS, use Direct I/O as of the 1/01 release of Solaris 8, especially for redo log files.

Asynchronous I/O with File Systems

Although all recent versions of Oracle support asynchronous I/O on Solaris raw devices, not all support asynchronous I/O on Unix file systems. Asynchronous I/O and its benefits are described in "Kernel Asynchronous I/O" on page 21.

The use of asynchronous I/O by Oracle is controlled by the disk_async_io parameter in init.ora (in Oracle7, the async_read and async_write parameters are used instead). The default of TRUE should be used for raw devices.

Versions of Oracle before Oracle8.1.5 also support asynchronous I/O for database files residing on file systems. The Oracle8.1.5 and 8.1.6 releases, however, automatically disable asynchronous I/O for database files on file systems, whatever the setting of disk_async_io.

For releases as of Oracle8.1.7 (including Oracle9i), asynchronous I/O is once again supported on file systems, and a hidden parameter, _filesystemio_options, has been introduced to control its behavior. This parameter accepts the following values:

- **async.** This is the default setting, and means that asynchronous I/O is enabled for database files on Unix file systems.
- **directIO.** Enable Direct I/O, but not asynchronous I/O, for database files on Unix file systems.
- **setall.** Enable both Direct I/O and asynchronous I/O for database files on Unix file systems. You can also achieve this effect with the default setting of async and by mounting file systems with the forcedirectio option.
- **none.** Do not enable either asynchronous I/O or Direct I/O for database files on Unix file systems.

Recommended Settings with File Systems

For database files on Unix file systems, use asynchronous I/O whenever it is supported, since asynchronous I/O allows the database writers to work more effectively by issuing multiple writes simultaneously. In addition, use Direct I/O as of the 1/01 release of Solaris 8.

For database files on raw devices, always use asynchronous I/O, the default setting.

To remain consistent with my earlier caution about the use of hidden parameters (see "Viewing and Changing Hidden Parameters" on page 311), I suggest you leave the default for _filesystemio_options as async and enable Direct I/O (as of Solaris 8 1/01) by mounting file systems with the forcedirectio option. This combination will result in the same effect as the setall option.

Optimizing Oracle Load Performance

DSS workloads in particular tend to require periodic loads, often of large volumes of data.

To reduce load times, use the sequence outlined in the following steps.

Load the Database Tables

You save significant time by avoiding access to the online redo log and archive logs during data loading. You can run Oracle in NOARCHIVELOG mode. Alternatively, you can disable redo generation with the alter table state-

ment before loading the data and use the same statement to reenable generation of redo data after the load has completed. Remember to back up the
database files after the load completes. An example is given below.

```
SQL> alter table customer nologging;
Table altered.
SQL>
< -- Load data into table -- >
SQL> alter table customer logging;
Table altered.
```

Presorting the data according to index columns and loading with the
SORTED INDEX option can also save time if indexes already exist.

Use direct path loading to bypass SQL processing and buffer cache access
(the direct=true parameter). Note that direct path loading imposes some
restrictions, such as requiring exclusive access to the table during load; check
any restrictions for your version of Oracle before attempting to use the direct
path load feature.

Use load parallelism if possible to shorten the load time. The load commands for a two-way parallel load are shown in the following example:

```
sqlldr userid=id/pwd control=c1.ctl direct=true parallel=true
sqlldr userid=id/pwd control=c2.ctl direct=true parallel=true
```

Note that each load session requires its own control file.

Analyze the Database Tables

This step is important to allow the optimizer to recognize data skew. Analyze
all columns that are likely to be queried (but not comment or description columns unless you know they will be queried). Analyze commands are shown in
the following examples:

```
analyze table item compute statistics;
analyze table stock estimate statistics sample 15000 rows;
```

The second example illustrates a command that might be appropriate for
very large tables in which the distribution of data in a subset of the table can
be expected to represent the overall data distribution.

Note that the DBMS_STATS package can also be used to gather statistics.

Create the Indexes

Index creation is fastest if done after the tables have been loaded rather than
during load. Index creation is also 10% to 15% faster after the tables have
been analyzed. Drop indexes before the load to ensure that index creation
does not take place during the load.

Use the parallel option when creating indexes if multiple CPUs are available. For example:

```
create index custname_idx on customer (cust_name)
     parallel (degree 8);
```

Analyze the Indexes

The final step is to analyze the indexes for the benefit of the optimizer. Examples of the `analyze index` command are shown below.

```
analyze index w_idx compute statistics;
analyze index d_idx compute statistics;
analyze index custname_idx estimate statistics sample 2 percent;
```

Note that the `DBMS_STATS` package can also be used to gather index statistics, and that the `compute statistics` keywords can be applied to the `create index` statement, eliminating the need for a separate analyze step.

Planning for Indexes

The primary key of a table normally has an associated index. Apart from that, deciding when to create an index is not always easy. Here are some general guidelines:

- If between one-half of 1% and 2% or more of the data in a table will be retrieved as a result of a query predicate, a table scan will be faster than retrieving the data from the base table with an index. So in this case you may be better off without an index, since an optimizer will often choose to use an index if one is present.
- If you know which columns are usually accessed in a table, consider a concatenated index to bypass the base table.
- If a query is stable and frequently run, consider the materialized view feature in Oracle8i.

Using an SGA Larger Than 2 Gbytes

Some applications need all the shared memory they can get, especially in high-throughput environments where extra memory in the buffer cache can benefit performance significantly. With 32-bit versions of Oracle, though, you will need to change the base address of the Oracle shared memory segment (sgabeg) and relink the `oracle` binary before you can use an SGA larger than 2 Gbytes. The method varies slightly with different versions of Oracle; the procedure for Oracle8 and later releases is documented in this section.

The standard `oracle` binary ships with sgabeg = 0x80000000, which allows a little less than 2 Gbytes of SGA shared memory. To allow for an SGA of around 3.75 Gbytes in size, lower sgabeg to 0x08000000.

The procedure outlined below will rebuild the `oracle` binary with sgabeg set to 0x08000000:

```
oracle$ nm -P $ORACLE_HOME/bin/oracle | grep sgabeg
sgabeg      n 80000000      0
oracle$ cd $ORACLE_HOME/rdbms/lib
oracle$ genksms -s 0x08000000 > ksms.s
```

```
oracle$ make -f ins_rdbms.mk ksms.o
oracle$ make -f ins_rdbms.mk ioracle
<< various messages deleted >>
oracle$ nm -P $ORACLE_HOME/bin/oracle | grep sgabeg
sgabeg      n  8000000         0
oracle$
```

The `make -f ins_rdbms.mk ksms.o` line is only needed for some older Oracle8 releases, but it does no harm on later releases, including Oracle9i.

To allow for the maximum possible shared memory segment size, ensure that the `shmmax` parameter in `/etc/system` is set high enough. Use the following line, which sets `shmmax` to the largest possible setting for 32-bit databases:

```
set shmsys:shminfo_shmmax = 0xffffffff
```

For 64-bit versions of Oracle, set `shmmax` as shown in the following line:

```
set shmsys:shminfo_shmmax = 0xffffffffff
```

When increasing the size of the SGA, remember to leave enough room for your applications so that the system does not page. Any performance benefits from a large buffer cache will be more than outweighed by the negative performance impact of paging. Refer to "STEP 1. Monitoring Memory" on page 282 for information about how to recognize memory paging.

Reconfiguring Oracle9i Dynamically

Dynamic Reconfiguration (DR) support in Solaris and on Sun hardware is described under "Dynamic Reconfiguration" on page 26, along with a discussion on its implications for databases.

Oracle9i Dynamic System Global Area

Oracle's Dynamic System Global Area (SGA) capability, released with Oracle9i, for the first time offers the capability of altering the size of the SGA while the database is live. In particular, Oracle9i supports changes to the sizes of the buffer cache and shared pool, the two major components of the SGA. When intimate shared memory (ISM) is used for the SGA, the amount of memory allocated to the buffer cache and the shared pool can be traded off against each other, although the total amount of memory allocated to the SGA cannot change. For example, the buffer cache can first be reduced in size, and then the shared pool increased by the same amount (and vice versa). When Dynamic ISM (DISM) is used for the SGA, the total size of the SGA can be changed dynamically.

After connecting to Oracle as `sysdba`, you can change the buffer cache and shared pool with the following statements:

```
alter system set db_cache_size = new_size_in_bytes;
alter system set shared_pool_size = new_size_in_bytes;
```

The `db_cache_size` tunable parameter is the recommended way of setting the size of the buffer cache. The old `db_block_buffers` parameter is still supported for backward compatibility, but it cannot be used if dynamic SGA capabilities are required.

Oracle9i also introduces a new optional `init.ora` parameter: `sga_max_size`. If `sga_max_size` is not set, Oracle will calculate it automatically in accordance with the user-supplied settings for `shared_pool_size`, either `db_cache_size` or `db_block_buffers`, and other SGA memory requirements. More significantly, on Solaris, if `sga_max_size` is *not* set, then ISM rather than DISM will be used for shared memory attaches. ISM will also be used if `sga_max_size` is set less than or equal to the total of `db_cache_size` and `shared_pool_size`.

How Oracle Chooses Between ISM and DISM

When the `sga_max_size` parameter is set larger than the total of `db_cache_size`, `shared_pool_size`, and the other smaller SGA components used by Oracle, Oracle9i automatically uses DISM. In this case, the amount of memory initially locked will be equal to `db_cache_size` plus `shared_pool_size` plus the other SGA components. When the buffer cache or shared pool is resized later, Oracle will either lock additional memory or unlock and release existing memory, depending on whether the change results in an increase or decrease in size.

Oracle also makes available a sample Reconfiguration Coordination Manager (RCM) script to allow the buffer cache and shared pool to be automatically resized if a DR event takes place. A sample script is included on the book website. Database administrators should modify the script according to local requirements. For example, if a DR operation that will remove 2 Gbytes of memory is attempted, the script should decide which instances should be adjusted and by how much.

Oracle9i program global area (PGA) memory can also be resized. This memory is local to each Oracle process rather than allocated as shared memory, so neither ISM nor DISM is used for PGA memory.

The Benefits of Using Dynamic SGA

When memory must be removed from a running system, a DR operation can be attempted. The DR event may fail, though, for example, if locked memory cannot be relocated onto other system boards. Consequently, there are times when the only alternative to dynamic SGA resizing is to disconnect all users from the database, shut it down, modify the SGA size, restart the database, and reconnect the users. Application availability is clearly compromised without the flexibility to resize SGA segments. For this reason, Oracle9i represents a significant leap forward in database availability.

Two scenarios can be considered to illustrate the impact of DR events on the database administrator. The first scenario covers the case where no RCM script has been configured to allow automatic reconfiguration of the SGA. If memory is to be removed, the buffer cache or shared pool must first be resized with the appropriate `alter system` commands. Once the resizing is done, the system board can be removed. If memory has been increased by addition of a system board, the buffer cache and the shared pool can be increased at any time with a suitable `alter system` command.

The second scenario covers the case where an RCM script has been configured to automatically issue the `alter system` commands in response to memory changes in the system. In this case, the DR event can take place without operator intervention.

In summary, Oracle9i effectively leverages the DR and RCM features in Solaris 8 (starting from the 4/01 release) to provide a significant boost to application availability.

Recovering Oracle

When you configure Oracle, it is wise to take into account recovery time as well as performance. In this section we focus on crash recovery, rather than database restore and roll-forward recovery after media failure.

Crash recovery should not happen often, but when it does you'll probably be grateful for any steps you took with a view to reducing the recovery time. In this section we explore Oracle tunables that relate to checkpoints and recovery and consider the trade-off between performance and recovery time. Checkpoints are described briefly in "Pagecleaners" on page 55, and crash recovery is described in "Database Recovery Process" on page 55.

Checkpoints and recovery time are an issue in environments where insert, update, and delete database operations feature prominently, so the discussion that follows has less relevance to read-only and read-mostly environments. OLTP workloads are typically good candidates for consideration of the implications of crash recovery.

The Influence of Checkpoints on Recovery Time

Recovery time is influenced significantly by checkpoint frequency. Oracle checkpoints are triggered when one of the following events takes place:

- An online redo log fills, causing a log file switch to occur.
- The checkpoint interval expires.
- A database administrator manually requests a checkpoint (`alter system checkpoint`) or redo log switch (`alter system switch logfile`).

Recovery is fastest when a system crash occurs immediately after a checkpoint, since all modified pages will have been flushed to disk. The longer the interval between a checkpoint and a crash, the more work will be required to recover the database.

Oracle does not wait until a checkpoint to flush its dirty buffers, so the recovery time is not directly proportional to the interval between a checkpoint and a crash. The graph in Figure 22.4 shows read and write I/O activity for an Oracle8.1.5 data disk with checkpoints near the start and end of the monitoring period.

Figure 22.4 *Data disk activity during and between checkpoints*

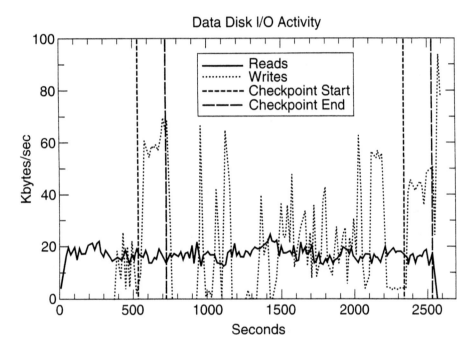

The graph shows that writes to disk continue sporadically between checkpoints. This write activity is needed to maintain a supply of clean buffers for applications as well as to reduce recovery time.

The Influence of Checkpoints on Performance

Checkpoint frequency affects system performance as well as recovery time. Table 22-1 shows results from a series of tests that measured performance and recovery time as the checkpoint interval was varied. By "checkpoint interval," I mean the period of time between the start of successive checkpoints. Checkpoints were initiated manually with the `alter system checkpoint` command as `sysdba`.

Table 22-1 *Checkpoint interval, performance, and crash recovery time*

Checkpoint Interval (secs)	Checkpoint Interval Relative to Baseline	Transaction Throughput Relative to Baseline	Recovery Time (secs)	Recovery Time Relative to Baseline
150	1	1.00	252	1.0
300	2	1.06	242	1.0
600	4	1.19	646	2.6
900	6	1.27	963	3.8

Some of the conclusions that can be drawn from these results are listed below.

- Transaction throughput for the workload improves as the checkpoint interval increases. Throughput increases by 27% if checkpoints are only run every 900 seconds instead of every 150 seconds. Further increases in the checkpoint time beyond 900 seconds resulted only in minor throughput improvements.

  The reason for the performance improvement is that dirty buffers are flushed less frequently, freeing CPU cycles to do application work. As expected, monitoring shows that the average number of I/Os per transaction drops with longer checkpoint intervals, as does the average number of CPU cycles consumed per transaction.

- Recovery time does not increase as much as you might expect when checkpoints are run less frequently. For example, quadrupling the checkpoint time does not quadruple the recovery time. Nonetheless, compared to 150-second checkpoints, the recovery time more than doubles with 600-second checkpoints and more than triples with 900-second checkpoints.

CPU utilization during recovery for the four tests ranged between 42% and 45% on a four-CPU server, comprising 7% to 8% user activity and 35% to 38% system activity. The high system utilization reflects the heavy I/O activity during recovery.

The v$instance_recovery view

Oracle8i introduced a new v$ view, the v$instance_recovery view. This view offers an estimate of how long it would take to complete crash recovery if the database crashed at the moment of the query.

The following example from an Oracle8.1.7 instance shows the estimated number of I/Os that would be required to recover the instance following a crash.

The recovery_estimated_ios statistic is actually a measure of the number of dirty buffers in the buffer cache.

```
SQL> select recovery_estimated_ios from v$instance_recovery;

RECOVERY_ESTIMATED_IOS
----------------------
                814540
```

The number of I/Os required for recovery goes only partway toward answering the question. Most database administrators will be more interested to know how long it will take to recover. Database Engineering carried out tests to answer this question by deliberately crashing a database immediately after querying the v$instance_recovery view. Table 22-2 shows the results of the tests.

Table 22-2 *Recovery estimated I/Os and recovery time*

Recovery Estimated I/Os	Actual Recovery Time (secs)	Estimated I/Os per Recovery Time
1,500,160	1,802	833
868,745	1,011	859
814,540	981	830
284,210	340	836
187,520	249	753

The tests showed that for this instance, the recovery_estimated_ios statistic from the v$instance_recovery view could be divided by approximately 800 to estimate the recovery time in seconds. The results will differ in other environments because of differences in the hardware configuration, the Oracle version, and other local differences.

Oracle8i also introduced an init.ora parameter related to the v$instance_recovery view. The fast_start_io_target parameter, available only in Oracle8i Enterprise Edition, allows a database administrator to set a high-water mark for the number of I/Os that will be required to carry out instance recovery. Once this mark is reached, the Database Writers will begin flushing dirty buffers without waiting for a checkpoint. If the default value of 0 is used, the parameter will be ignored. The db_block_max_dirty_target fulfills a similar function in Oracle Standard Edition.

In one Database Engineering test, fast_start_io_target was set to 200 Kbytes. The result was a 27% hit in throughput, but recovery finished 20 times faster compared to recovery after no recent checkpoints and without this parameter set.

In Oracle9i, another more useful metric was added to the v$instance_recovery view: estimated_mttr, the estimated mean time to recover (MTTR) in seconds. An example from an environment running Oracle9.0.1 is shown below:

```
SQL> select estimated_mttr from v$instance_recovery;

ESTIMATED_MTTR
--------------
          1714
```

Oracle9i also introduced a new `init.ora` parameter to complement the new `v$instance_recovery` column: `fast_start_mttr_target`, the maximum desired recovery time, in seconds. This new parameter allows the database administrator to set the approximate maximum recovery time that is acceptable for this instance.

Once this high-water mark is reached, the Database Writers will begin flushing dirty buffers. The default value of 0 means that the parameter is ignored. If the `fast_start_mttr_target` parameter is set, then refer to the `target_mttr` column instead of `estimated_mttr` in the `v$instance_recovery` view (that is, use `select target_mttr from v$instance_recovery`). Note that the `db_block_max_dirty_target` `init.ora` parameter in Oracle8i has been converted to an underscore (hidden) parameter in Oracle9i (`_db_block_max_dirty_target`). For more information on hidden parameters, including caveats, refer to "Viewing and Changing Hidden Parameters" on page 311.

Other Parameters Influencing Recovery

Apart from the parameters already discussed, the main `init.ora` parameters that influence recovery are outlined in the following list:

- **`log_checkpoint_interval`:** The number of blocks in the redo log file that will be written before a checkpoint is triggered. This parameter has no effect if it is set larger than the size of a redo log file, since every log switch automatically triggers a checkpoint. If redo log files are sized appropriately, this parameter can simply be set to a very high number and ignored. Note that redo log files should all be set to the same size to ensure consistency in checkpoint frequency.

- **`log_checkpoint_timeout`:** The maximum number of seconds that should expire before a checkpoint is triggered. If the default value of 0 is used, this parameter will be ignored. In read-mostly environments this parameter can be used to ensure that checkpoints do happen regularly, even if the write activity is not sufficient to trigger frequent redo log switches.

Carefully sizing redo log files offers a good way of managing the checkpoint interval. Set the `log_checkpoints_to_alert` parameter to `true` to allow Oracle to report redo log switches in the `alert.log` file. You can monitor redo activity by running the following command as `sysdba`:

```
SQL> select name, value from v$sysstat
  2  where name = 'redo blocks written';

NAME                                                          VALUE
------------------------------------------------------------- ----------
redo blocks written                                           1489089
```

The value reported is cumulative, so you will need to run the command multiple times and calculate the difference.

23

MONITORING AND TUNING SYBASE

In this chapter we consider tuning recommendations for Sybase, focusing on OLTP environments but including information on Sybase's parallel processing features. We begin by exploring the alternatives for monitoring Sybase and modifying its configuration parameters.

Sybase ASE Monitoring

Sybase provides two tools for monitoring Adaptive Server Enterprise (ASE) performance. The first is Sybase Central, a graphical management tool introduced with ASE 11.5, and the second is a stored procedure called sp_sysmon, bundled with the Sybase distribution.

Sybase Central includes a client plug-in performance monitor tool, providing a graphical presentation of data. It is a powerful tool for identifying causes of bottlenecks in ASE, but its usefulness is restricted in that it runs only on Windows clients (although it can monitor ASE running on non-Windows servers). The data is updated at regular intervals, and monitoring does not have a significant impact on the performance of the ASE being monitored. An overview of the capabilities of the tool is presented below. For more complete information on the tool, refer to the *Managing and Monitoring Sybase Adaptive Server Enterprise* manual from Sybase.

Sybase Central for ASE consists of the following four components:

- **ASE Monitor Server** — Runs on the same system as the ASE and captures performance data by accessing the ASE shared memory.

351

- **Historical Server** — Obtains ASE performance data and saves the files for later analysis.

- **Monitor Plug-in** — Obtains ASE performance data from Monitor Server for viewing in Sybase Central.

- **Monitor Client Library API** — Enables users to write their own monitoring applications.

Sybase Central Monitor Output

Sybase Central monitors performance of the ASE as a whole without focusing on individual databases or database objects. It helps monitor the following performance areas:

- **Data and procedure cache effectiveness.** Sybase Central shows physical and logical reads and writes for both data and procedure caches. The data cache window also shows cache hit rates for each of the individual named caches along with the spinlock contention on these caches. This information is useful for proper configuration of named caches and for determining which objects should be bound to which named cache.

- **Database device activity.** The Sybase Central Device I/O window shows the rate of device I/Os for each ASE device and the hit rate for each device. The hit rate in this case measures the number of times I/O was successfully requested without waiting for a lock on the device or for an internal resource, compared with the total I/Os requested. The device hit rate is a measure of contention on devices by the server engines.

- **Network traffic.** The Network I/O window shows the network traffic for ASE in number of packets and number of bytes sent and received. It also shows the average size of packets sent and received. This information is useful in determination of the right values for network parameters such as the default and maximum packet size. A high number of small packets might also indicate a need to disable tcp batching.

- **Lock activity.** The Object Lock Status windows of Sybase Central provide information on lock activity for each object in the database, object page number, and status of each lock. This information can be used to check for lock contention on database objects.

- **Object I/O activity.** The object page I/O window in Sybase Central provides information on the logical and physical reads and writes carried out on each database object. This information can help identify "hot" (that is, heavily accessed) objects that could be assigned to specific named caches to improve performance.

- **User processes.** Data on a single process, a group of processes, or all processes executing in ASE can be displayed. The information provided includes CPU usage, page I/O, and process state for each process and can be used to identify specific processes or applications contributing to bottlenecks and lock contention.

The Performance Summary window shows a snapshot of the above information. The Performance Trends window allows the collected data to be graphed to show trends in resource usage and locking. All data gathered can be logged for further analysis.

Sybase sp_sysmon Stored Procedure Output

The sp_sysmon stored procedure provides more detailed information than Sybase Central but in a nongraphical format.

The sp_sysmon stored procedure is run from an isql session and takes a time interval as a parameter. It collects ASE usage statistics during this interval and at the end outputs the data to the isql session. Output can also be limited to a nominated section of the report by use of sp_sysmon with an additional parameter.

A sample sp_sysmon session, initiated by a user with sa privileges, is shown in Figure 23.1 (the results have been truncated).

Figure 23.1   *A sample sp_sysmon session*

```
sybase% isql -Usa_user -Pprasanta
1> sp_sysmon 10
2> go
DBCC execution completed. If DBCC printed error messages, contact a
user with System Administrator (SA) role.

=====================================================================
Sybase Adaptive Server Enterprise System Performance Report

=====================================================================
Run Date                    Oct 10, 2000
Statistics Cleared at          21:10:59
Statistics Sampled at          21.20:59


<< results deleted >>
```

The results for a particular event typically appear under four headings: per sec (the number that occurred per second), per xact (the number that occurred per transaction), count (the total number observed during the measurement interval), and % of total (the percentage of total meaning varies according to the event being measured). When investigating an unusually high percentage for an event, remember to check the count as well. A high percentage might not matter if the number of occurrences for the event is low.

The sp_sysmon stored procedure provides performance data in the following categories of ASE activity:

Application queue management	Monitor access to executing SQL
Asynchronous prefetch usage	Network I/O management
Data cache management	Parallel query management
Disk I/O management	Procedure cache management
Index management	Recovery management
Kernel utilization	Task management
Lock management	Transaction management
Memory management	Transaction profile
Metadata cache management	Worker process management

Configuring Sybase ASE

Sybase stores its configuration parameters in the sysconfigures and syscurconfigs tables in the master database. When ASE is started, configuration parameters are copied from sysconfigures to syscurconfigs. The two sets of configuration parameters might differ as a result of changes made while the database is running.

Sybase provides the sp_configure stored procedure to display and modify the configuration parameters. When called with no arguments, sp_configure displays each parameter and its settings. Before System 11, the settings shown were the allowable minimum, allowable maximum, sysconfigures table setting (config_value), and syscurconfigs table setting (run_value). As of System 11, the settings are conveniently displayed in logical groups such as Cache Manager, Disk I/O, and General Information. The values shown have also slightly changed to Default, Memory Used, Config Value, and Run Value.

Settings for an individual parameter can also be displayed with sp_configure by giving it a single argument. Figure 23.2 illustrates the use of sp_configure to display configuration parameter settings.

Figure 23.2 *Displaying individual configuration parameter settings*

```
1> sp_configure "recovery"
2> go
Configuration option is not unique.

Parameter Name                  Default Memory Used Config Value Run Value
----------------------------    ------- ----------- ------------ ----------
print recovery information      0            0           0            0
recovery interval in minutes    5            0           5            5

(return status = 1)
1> sp_configure "recovery interval"
2> go
Parameter Name                  Default Memory Used Config Value Run Value
----------------------------    ------- ----------- ------------ ----------
recovery interval in minutes    5            0           5            5

(return status = 0)
```

As the example demonstrates, it is not necessary to supply the full name of the configuration parameter to display its settings.

Settings can also be changed with `sp_configure`. Figure 23.3 shows how the recovery interval parameter can be changed and shows as well the results of making the change.

Figure 23.3 *Changing a configuration parameter*

```
1> sp_configure "recovery interval", 10
2> go
00:2001/07/04 10:12:56.32 server  Configuration file 'MySYBASE.cfg' has been
written and the previous version has been renamed to './MySYBASE.010'.
00:2001/07/04 10:12:56.36 server  The configuration option 'recovery interval
in minutes' has been changed by 'sa' from '5' to '10'.
Parameter Name                  Default    Memory Used Config Value Run Value
----------------------------    ---------- ----------- ------------ ---------
recovery interval in minutes    5              0           10           10
Configuration option changed. The SQL Server need not be rebooted since the
option is dynamic.

(return status = 0)
```

Before Sybase 11, the change shown in Figure 23.3 would have required a subsequent `reconfigure` command, telling Sybase to check the validity of the change and put it into effect.

The comment immediately before the `return status` highlights the fact that some configuration parameters are dynamic and can be changed without the need to reboot Sybase. By contrast, changes to static options require a Sybase reboot before taking effect. ASE 12.5 converted many of the frequently changed static configuration parameters to dynamic configuration parameters and introduced a number of new dynamic parameters to replace obsolete static parameters. Approximately 75% of configuration parameters in ASE 12.5 are dynamic, compared to about 50% in ASE 12.0.

The initial comment also points to a configuration file, in this case called MySYBASE.cfg, which has been updated to reflect the change. The configuration file, introduced with System 11, is typically stored in the $SYBASE directory and is a normal text file that can be modified with your choice of text editor. Parameters in the configuration file are grouped into logical subdivisions such as Cache Manager, Named Cache, Disk I/O, and Network Communication.

Sybase can be booted with a configuration file by the following command:

```
sybase% $SYBASE/$SYBASE_ASE/bin/dataserver -cMySYBASE.cfg
```

A configuration file offers a number of advantages, including the ability to change values more easily, to keep different configuration settings for different purposes (for example, database load versus normal running), and to back up the configuration settings in a text-readable form.

If ASE is unable to boot as a result of invalid settings in the configuration file, error messages are displayed in the errorlog. The configuration file should be changed and ASE booted again.

Figure 23.4 shows an extract from a working configuration file. Note the syntax required for named caches, including those with multiple I/O Buffer Pools of different sizes.

Figure 23.4 *An extract from an ASE 11.9.3 configuration file*

```
###########################################################################
#
#Configuration File for the Sybase SQL Server
#
#Please read the System Administration Guide (SAG)
#before changing any of the values in this file.
#
###########################################################################

[Configuration Options]

[General Information]

[Backup/Recovery]
recovery interval in minutes = 2000
print recovery information = DEFAULT
tape retention in days = DEFAULT

[Cache Manager]
number of oam trips = DEFAULT
number of index trips = DEFAULT
procedure cache percent = 1
memory alignment boundary = DEFAULT
global async prefetch limit = DEFAULT
global cache partition number = 16

[Named Cache:c_customer]
cache size = 8M
cache status = mixed cache
cache replacement policy = DEFAULT
local cache partition number = 2
```

```
[2K I/O Buffer Pool]
pool size = 8M
wash size = 512 K
local async prefetch limit = 0

[Named Cache:c_log]
cache size = 20M
cache status = HK ignore cache
cache replacement policy = DEFAULT
local cache partition number = 1

[2K I/O Buffer Pool]
pool size = 1M
wash size = 64 K
local async prefetch limit = 0

[8K I/O Buffer Pool]
pool size = 19M
wash size = 160 K
local async prefetch limit = 0

[Named Cache:default data cache]
cache size = 2128K
cache status = default data cache
cache status = HK ignore cache
cache replacement policy = DEFAULT
local cache partition number = 2

[2K I/O Buffer Pool]
pool size = 2128K
wash size = DEFAULT
local async prefetch limit = 0

[Disk I/O]
allow sql server async i/o = DEFAULT
disk i/o structures = 8192
page utilization percent = DEFAULT
number of devices = 100

[Network Communication]
default network packet size = DEFAULT
max network packet size = 4096

[O/S Resources]
max async i/os per engine = 1012
max async i/os per server = 1012

[Physical Memory]
total memory = 11482112
additional network memory = 14745600

[Processors]
max online engines = 24
min online engines = DEFAULT

[SQL Server Administration]
event buffers per engine = 3
cpu accounting flush interval = DEFAULT
housekeeper free write percent = 0
```

```
[User Environment]
number of user connections = 650
user log cache size = 4096

[Lock Manager]
number of locks = 60000
deadlock checking period = DEFAULT
max engine freelocks = DEFAULT
lock spinlock ratio = 10
address lock spinlock ratio = 10
table lock spinlock ratio = 1
```

Note that from ASE 12.5, a new `max memory` parameter has been introduced. The implications of this change are discussed in "Memory Management" on page 124.

Calculating the Buffer Cache Hit Rate

The simplest way of calculating the buffer cache hit rate is with `sp_sysmon`. This stored procedure displays the cache hit rate for all caches and for each individual named cache. Monitoring the cache hit rate is discussed in more detail in "Data Cache Monitoring" on page 363.

Monitoring Error Messages

Sybase ASE reports error messages in the `errorlog` file, which normally is found in the `$SYBASE` directory. You can specify an alternative error file by passing the `-e` parameter to Sybase at boot time, as shown in the following command:

```
sybase% $SYBASE/$SYBASE_ASE/bin/dataserver -cMySYBASE.cfg -e/home/err.log
```

Generating Query Plans

It is useful to be able to identify the queries that consume the most CPU time and cause the most I/O, since it might be possible to rewrite the query in a less expensive manner.

Use `set showplan on` from within an `isql` session to view the query execution plan generated by the optimizer. When you submit a query, Sybase shows the query plan and executes the query. Use `set statistics io on` to report the number of logical and physical reads and the number of writes, and use `set statistics time on` to report the CPU time and elapsed time required to execute the query.

To generate a plan without executing the query, you can use `set noexec on`. Note that all session settings and trace flags need to be in place before you execute `set noexec on`, since ASE will not actually execute any subsequent commands apart from `set noexec off`. Figure 23.5 shows the results of submitting a query from `isql` with `showplan`, `statistics io`, and `statistics time` all set on.

Figure 23.5 *A sample Sybase query plan*

```
1> select min(cust_id) from customer
2> go

QUERY PLAN FOR STATEMENT 1 (at line 1).


  STEP 1
     The type of query is SELECT.
     Evaluate Ungrouped MINIMUM AGGREGATE.

     FROM TABLE
        customer
     Nested iteration.
     Index : custindex
     Ascending scan.
     Positioning at index start.
     Scanning only up to the first qualifying row.
     Index contains all needed columns. Base table will not be read.
     Using I/O Size 2 Kbytes.
     With LRU Buffer Replacement Strategy.

  STEP 2
     The type of query is SELECT.

Parse and Compile Time 0.
SQL Server cpu time: 0 ms.


 -----------
         1
Table: customer  scan count 1, logical reads: 1, physical reads: 0
Total writes for this command: 0

Execution Time 0.
SQL Server cpu time: 0 ms.  SQL Server elapsed time: 3 ms.

(1 row affected)
```

The showplan, statistics, and noexec settings are all turned off by default when you begin an isql session; other sessions are not affected by these settings being turned on since they are session specific.

You can force the optimizer to adhere to the join order you specify in a query, rather than the join order it determines is optimal. You achieve this behavior by running the command set forceplan on before executing the query. Be careful with this option, though, since it might not yield improvements in execution time, and remember to turn it off once the query has completed.

You can also force the optimizer to use a nominated index by including the index ID in brackets after the table name. This method works for all versions of Sybase. Figure 23.6 illustrates the procedure.

Figure 23.6 *Forcing Sybase to use a specified index*

```
1> select 'table'=o.name, 'index'=i.name, indid
2> from sysindexes i, sysobjects o
3> where i.id = o.id and o.type = 'U'
4> order by 1, 3
5> go
 table                            index                            indid
 ---------------------------      ----------------------------     ------
 customer                         customer                              0
 customer                         custindex                             2

(2 rows affected)
1> select * from customer (2)
2> where cust_id between 1 and 50000
3> go
```

In this example, we instructed the optimizer to use the index custindex by specifying the index ID of the customer index, that is, 2, after the table. A table scan would be forced in this case by 0. As of Sybase 11, you can directly supply the index name by replacing (2) with (index custindex) or (index customer) to force the optimizer to use the index or a table scan on the base table, respectively. Once again, use this option cautiously. Before permanently forcing index selection, first check the likely impact of each alternative by running the query with the showplan and statistics options set.

The reasons behind the choices made by the Sybase optimizer might not always be clear. Fortunately, you can gain more insight into how the choices were made by turning on trace flags with the Database Consistency Checker (dbcc). For example, you can turn on the trace options with a command like dbcc traceon (3604, 302), which turns on trace flags 3604 and 302. One or more trace flags can be turned on with a single command.

The most interesting trace flags are listed below:

- **-1** — Applies trace flags to all user sessions.

- **302** — Reveals index selection information for each table.

- **310** — Reveals join order selection information.

- **3604** — Sends trace output to the client session.

- **3605** — Sends trace output to the Sybase errorlog.

Tuning Sybase ASE

The discussion in this section focuses on Sybase System 11 and subsequent releases (System 11.5, 11.9.2, 12, and 12.5). Although the same basic principles apply to System 10 and earlier releases, not all features are available.

Tuning Memory

ASE 12.5 supports dynamic changes to the shared memory segment size. We consider this functionality and conclude with general memory tuning recommendations.

Dynamic Memory Tuning

Before ASE 12.5, the amount of shared memory could not be changed dynamically—a database restart was required after the parameters were changed. The `total memory` parameter, grouped under `Physical Memory` in the configuration file, determined the size of shared memory. Memory was allocated to named data caches according to the parameter settings, and the remaining memory was allocated to the default data cache and the procedure cache.

The ASE 12.5 release introduces the `max memory` parameter, which determines the absolute upper limit of shared memory allocation. The actual size of the initial shared memory segment allocated by ASE is now determined by the sum of the sizes of the following pools and caches: the kernel stack pool, the server static pools, the server dynamic pools, the data cache, and the procedure cache. The size of the default data cache is now an absolute value. The procedure cache (described in "Procedure Cache" on page 126) is also specified as an absolute value (in 2-Kbyte pages), rather than as a percentage of available memory. Accordingly, the `procedure cache percent` parameter has been replaced by the new `procedure cache size` parameter. The procedure cache size can now be changed dynamically. Data cache creation is still static, but buffer pools within a data cache can be resized dynamically.

A new read-only configuration parameter, `total physical memory`, shows the physical size of shared memory allocated to ASE at any point in time, and a second new read-only parameter, `total logical memory`, shows the amount of memory required for the current configuration (which may be different from the physical memory actually allocated).

The default behavior of ASE 12.5 is to allocate shared memory on demand, up to `max memory`. This behavior can be changed, though, with the `allocate max shared memory` parameter. If the value of this parameter is set to 0, shared memory will be allocated dynamically; a value of 1 means that a shared memory segment, sized according to `max memory`, will be established at boot time and not changed. Note that `allocate max shared memory` can be changed dynamically; changing from 0 to 1 will cause `max memory` to be allocated, whereas changing from 1 to 0 will have no effect.

ASE 12.5 also permits dynamic allocation of memory resources. A new configuration parameter, `dynamic allocation on demand`, has been introduced to control the behavior of this feature. The default value of 1 means that specified memory resources will only be partially allocated at boot time. As demand for the resources increases, more memory will be allocated. A value of 0 will cause the full allocation to be configured immediately.

When ASE dynamically adds an additional shared memory segment, it will attempt to allocate intimate shared memory (ISM), just as it does when making the initial shared memory allocation. ISM is explained in "Intimate Shared Memory" on page 24.

Note that the shared memory allocation cannot be shrunk without an ASE reboot.

Memory Tuning Guidelines

As a general rule, the more memory available to cache database pages, the better. Never allow ASE to page because it lacks memory, though. It is preferable to do extra physical I/Os by allocating less memory to ASE than to have insufficient memory for the operating system and hence cause ASE to page fault. When physical I/O is initiated by an ASE engine thread, it is done asynchronously. Hence, other ASE threads can continue to do useful work while the I/O completes. However, if the ASE application is paged out because of memory starvation, the entire process is blocked and no useful work can be done until the required pages are brought into memory. Use Solaris utilities to ensure that the system is not paging after each increase in memory. The available tools are described in Chapter 20, and the process of monitoring memory is described in "STEP 1. Monitoring Memory" on page 282.

Note that enabling parallelism adds to the memory requirements of a system. Worker processes use additional memory that would otherwise go to the data cache, and the area required for the procedure cache needs to be larger to support parallel query plans.

Data Caches and Buffer Pools

The Logical Memory Manager in System 11 enables you to create named caches and to bind database objects (for example, tables and indexes) to these caches. As a result, specific tables and indexes can be associated with dedicated caches instead of being serviced by the same general cache. For more information, refer to "Named Caches" on page 124.

The named caches can be configured with buffer pools of various sizes (2-, 4-, 8-, and 16-Kbyte buffers for 2-Kbyte page sizes) to enable different physical I/O block sizes. Refer to "Large I/O and Multiple Buffer Pools" on page 125 for more information about buffer pools in named caches.

Named caches can be used to reduce spin lock contention in an SMP environment, to reduce contention between applications, to provide a high data cache hit rate for hot objects, and to pin objects in memory.

Buffer pools larger than 2 Kbytes enable large block I/O, which has the effect of both reducing the total number of I/O operations required and prefetching data pages. Use `sp_cacheconfig` or edit the ASE configuration file to create named caches (Figure 23.4 on page 356 shows an example of a configuration file with named caches, including buffer pools of different sizes). Use `sp_bindcache` to bind an object to a specific data cache. Use `sp_poolconfig` to create buffer pools of nondefault size.

Start with the default data cache configuration and monitor the system closely before attempting to tune the data cache configuration.

The most effective method of tuning the data cache is to monitor I/O for each database object. Once you have identified the hot objects, bind them to their own named caches to reduce the amount of physical I/O. In an SMP environment, named caches can also be used to reduce spinlock contention, and the default and named caches can be further broken into partitions for the same purpose (the number of partitions must be a power of 2). Refer to the global cache partition number and local cache partition number lines in Figure 23.4 for examples of the use of partitions within caches.

If you want to cache index pages for longer than usual (in the absence of a dedicated cache for indexes), you can use the number of index trips configuration parameter to set the number of trips an index page makes through the MRU-LRU chain of the cache before being discarded. Refer to "Page Cleaning" on page 124 for more information about the MRU-LRU chain.

In environments where significant space allocation is being carried out, it is useful to keep the Object Allocation Map (OAM) pages in cache longer. The number of oam trips configuration parameter is provided for this purpose: set it higher than the default of 0. OAM pages are described in "Logical Data Storage" on page 126.

Data Cache Monitoring

Figure 23.7 shows context switches caused by a range of events, including lock contention and misses in a data cache.

Figure 23.7 *Cache search misses (sp_sysmon)*

```
Task Context Switches Due To:
  Voluntary Yields                 174.0        13.0      104533      1.3%
  Cache Search Misses              149.3        11.1       89682      1.1%
  Logical Lock Contention            1.1         0.1         673      0.0%
  Address Lock Contention           78.1         5.8       46917      0.6%
  Log Semaphore Contention           3.7         0.3        2240      0.0%
  Group Commit Sleeps               18.4         1.4       11071      0.1%
  Last Log Page Writes              21.4         1.6       12880      0.2%
  I/O Device Contention              4.2         0.3        2509      0.0%
  Network Packet Received         1802.2       134.4     1082643     13.7%
  Network Packet Sent             1800.3       134.2     1081508     13.7%
  SYSINDEXES Lookup                155.4        11.6       93341      1.2%
  Other Causes                    8907.5       664.2     5351099     67.9%
```

A high percentage of Cache Search Misses suggests that more cache memory is needed or that caches are poorly configured. This event measures the percentage of task switches that occurred because a required page could not be found in the data cache. ASE switches to another task while the page is being read into the cache.

Figure 23.8 shows a sample of the Data Cache Management results from sp_sysmon.

Figure 23.8　*Data cache management (sp_sysmon)*

```
Data Cache Management
---------------------
Cache Statistics Summary (All Caches)
-------------------------------------
Cache Search Summary
Total Cache Hits          27293.5      2035.3     16396405        99.5%
Total Cache Misses          149.3        11.1        89682         0.5%
----------------------    ---------   --------    ---------
Total Cache Searches      27442.8      2046.4     16486087
Cache Turnover
Buffers Grabbed              39.6         3.0        23768          n/a
Buffers Grabbed Dirty         0.0         0.0            0         0.0%
Cache Strategy Summary
Cached (LRU) Buffers      25153.4      1875.7     15110753       100.0%
Discarded (MRU) Buffers       0.0         0.0            0         0.0%
Large I/O Usage
Large I/Os Performed         51.8         3.9        31143        87.5%
Large I/Os Denied             7.4         0.6         4437        12.5%
---------------------     --------    --------    ---------
Total Large I/O Requests     59.2         4.4        35580
Large I/O Effectiveness
Pages by Lrg I/O Cached        3.0         0.2         1808          n/a
Pages by Lrg I/O Used          0.0         0.0            0         0.0%
Dirty Read Behavior
Page Requests                  0.0         0.0            0          n/a
-----------------------------------------------------------------------
default data cache
                          per sec     per xact      count % of total
----------------------    ---------   --------    ---------  ----------
Spinlock Contention          n/a          n/a         n/a        69.9 %
Utilization                  n/a          n/a         n/a       100.0%
Cache Searches
Cache Hits                27293.5      2035.3     16396405        99.5%
Found in Wash                71.9         5.4        43211         0.3%
Cache Misses                149.3        11.1        89682         0.5%
----------------------    ---------   --------    ---------
Total Cache Searches      27442.8      2046.4     16486087
```

The statistics shown are for all caches and for the default data cache. The `Total Cache Searches` count for all caches and for the default data cache are the same, indicating there are no named caches in this case. If named caches are in use, additional statistics will be shown for each one.

The final column in the `Total Cache Hits` line shows the cache hit rate percentage, indicating the overall effectiveness of the caching strategy. In this case the cache hit rate is very high (99.5%). Refer to Chapter 7 for a discussion about determining appropriate cache hit rates.

A non-zero count for the `Buffers Grabbed Dirty` event indicates problems with the buffer wash parameter (`wash size` in the configuration file). This event occurs when a buffer taken from the LRU end of the cache proves to be dirty (that is, modified), forcing the thread to stall while the buffer is flushed to disk. The offending cache should be identified and the wash marker for this cache increased to ensure that pages are being cleaned quickly enough. See "Page Cleaning" on page 124 for an explanation of the wash marker.

If the percentage of Large I/Os Denied is high, identify the cache concerned and consider increasing the size of the large I/O buffer pool to allow more of the large I/O requests to succeed, especially if the Pages by Lrg I/O Used percentage is high (indicating that most pages brought into the cache by large I/O operations were later accessed by applications).

Spinlock contention is caused on SMP systems when multiple Sybase engines attempt to access a data cache at the same time. You can reduce a high Spinlock Contention percentage by creating new named caches and binding objects to them. Such a reduction should improve performance. Splitting a cache into partitions can also help reduce spinlock contention.

If the Found in Wash percentage is high, the wash marker might be set too high. Note, though, that if a fetch-and-discard strategy (see "Fetch-and-Discard Strategy" on page 125) is being used for the cache, a page will be placed directly in the wash area after it is first accessed.

Tuning I/O

Managing I/O effectively is critical to database performance. In this section we examine performance and monitoring issues related to asynchronous prefetch, log performance, and I/O balance across disk devices.

Asynchronous Prefetch

Asynchronous prefetch (APF), introduced with ASE 11.5, attempts to bring pages into cache before a query requests them. Prefetching can improve the performance of sequential scans, dbcc checks, recovery, and other activities requiring large amounts of data to be read in. It is less applicable for most OLTP queries, where sequential scans usually indicate a problem (such as a missing index).

ASE makes intelligent choices about which pages to fetch and when to automatically disable APF to avoid unnecessary I/O. It is important to avoid excessive prefetching; otherwise, pages containing prefetched data might need to be reclaimed before the data has been referenced.

APF tries to make use of large I/Os, so it is helpful if you allocate enough 16K I/O buffers, especially in multiuser environments or databases with partitioned tables.

In tables with heavy insert, update, and delete activity, page chains can become kinked or can split across different extents or different allocation units, reducing the efficiency of APF. Specify a low value for fillfactor (defined by either sp_configure or the create index command) to allow space for growth in indexes. Bear in mind, though, that setting fillfactor too low increases the number of pages to be read during an index scan and increases the amount of buffer cache memory required to cache index pages.

The max_rows_per_page value can be lowered for tables to allow space for growth within rows (max_rows_per_page can be defined by either sp_chgattribute, the create index, create table, or alter table commands). Recreating the indexes or reloading tables will eliminate page chain kinking.

Figure 23.9 shows sp_sysmon output for asynchronous prefetch activity.

Figure 23.9 *Asynchronous prefetch activity (sp_sysmon)*

```
Asynchronous Prefectch Activity
    APFs Issued                        3.3        0.0        1999      28.1 %
    APFs Denied Due to
        APF I/O Overloads              0.0        0.0           6       0.1 %
        APF Limit Overloads            0.0        0.0           0       0.0 %
        APF Reused Overloads           1.1        0.0         661       9.3 %
    APF Buffers Found in Cache
        With Spinlock Held             0.0        0.0           0       0.0 %
        W/o Spinlock Held              7.4        0.0        4440      62.5 %
    -------------------------      --------   --------   --------
    Total APFs Requested              11.8        0.0        7106

Other Asynchronous Prefetch Statistics
    APFs Used                          2.8        0.0        1698       n/a
    APF Waits for I/O                  1.1        0.0         668       n/a
    APF Discards                       0.0        0.0           0       n/a

Dirty Read Behavior
    Page Requests                      0.0        0.0           0       n/a
```

A high value for APFs I/O Overloads suggests problems with disk I/O structures (you can manage this behavior by increasing the disk i/o structures configuration parameter) or problems with disk semaphore contention. If the Device Semaphore Waited event in sp_sysmon shows a high percentage, investigate the physical placement on disk of heavily utilized Sybase objects and consider implementing a more balanced disk layout.

APF Limit Overloads means that APF requests exceeded the pool limits set globally by the global async prefetch limit configuration parameter. This limit can also be managed for each buffer pool with sp_poolconfig.

APF Used and APF Discards provide insight into cache usage. If APF Discards is high but APF Used is very low, the system might be prefetching data that isn't useful. If both are high, then increasing the buffer pool size might keep pages in cache long enough to be used.

Log Performance

System 11 features a user log cache (ULC) that batches log writes in a log buffer. This cache reduces the contention on the log semaphore. The ULC sizing should take into account the average transaction size. The ULC size is set with the user log cache size configuration parameter.

The I/O block size to the syslog object can also be tuned to get better throughput. Experience has shown that a 4-Kbyte I/O block size provides optimal performance in most cases. Use sp_logiosize to change the I/O block size for `syslog`. Note that you will need a buffer pool of a size corresponding to the log I/O size for best performance.

Figure 23.10 shows `sp_sysmon` output relevant to log device performance.

Figure 23.10 *Transaction management (sp_sysmon)*

```
Transaction Management
----------------------
PLC Flushes to Xact Log        per sec      per xact      count    % of total
-----------------------        ----------   ----------    ------   ----------
by Full PLC                       31.1          2.3        18673      50.3%
by End Transaction                12.8          1.0         7714      20.8%
by Change of Database              0.1          0.0           57       0.2%
by System Log Record               6.2          0.5         3725      10.0%
by Other                          11.6          0.9         6940      18.7%
                               ----------   ----------    ------
Total PLC Flushes                 61.8          4.6        37109
PLC Log Records                 1215.9         90.7       730441        n/a
Max PLC Size                       n/a          n/a         2044        n/a
PLC Spinlock Requests
Granted                         2490.7        185.7      1496293      100.0%
Waited                             0.0          0.0           12        0.0%
                               ----------   ----------    ------
Total PLC Spinlock Req          2490.8        185.7      1496305
Log Semaphore Requests
Granted                           76.4          5.7        45914       95.3%
Waited                             3.7          0.3         2240        4.7%
                               ----------   ----------    ------
Total Log Semaphore Req           80.2          6.0        48154
Transaction Log Writes            50.9          3.8        30606        n/a
Transaction Log Alloc             58.9          4.4        35354        n/a
Avg # Writes per Log Page          n/a          n/a      0.00000        n/a
```

Note that PLC and ULC refer to the same thing (that is, the user log cache). ULC flushes `by Full PLC` (caused when the ULC for a process becomes full) should be low, and `by End Transaction` (caused by a transaction `commit` or `rollback`) should be high. If ULC flushes `by full PLC` are high (greater than 20%), increase the size of the ULC by changing the `user log cache size` configuration parameter.

If ULC size is too small, the result will be excessive flushes of the ULC to the last log page, with possible contention on the log semaphore (reported by `sp_sysmon` under `Task Context Switches Due To: Log Semaphore Contention`). Figure 23.10 also shows `Log Semaphore Requests`—a large value for `Waited` compared to `Granted` can also indicate problems.

I/O Balance Across Devices

The more you can spread I/O across multiple devices, the less likely you are to experience I/O contention. Below are some basic principles for avoiding contention and improving I/O response times:

- **Use as many physical and logical devices as practicable.** Increasing the number of physical devices increases the I/O bandwidth available to the system. I/O bandwidth becomes more important as disk capacities increase in size. It is important to consider the number of spindles as well as just the disk capacity.

Stripe tables across multiple disks with either a volume manager or by using sp_placeobject within Sybase. Increasing the number of logical Sybase devices ensures minimal contention for ASE I/O queues.

- **Consider using a separate disk for the transaction log.** In an update-intensive environment, consider placing the log device on a separate disk. Use the sp_logdevice stored procedure to direct all logging to that device.

- **Partition applications into multiple databases to increase log throughput.** Since there is one log device per database, partitioning the data into multiple databases will increase the number of log devices and hence the throughput to the logs.

These recommendations apply to both small and large databases, regardless of whether tables are partitioned or intraquery parallelism is enabled. Partitioning and parallelism do, however, place an additional burden on database designers and make the disk and device layout particularly important for performance.

Figure 23.11 shows loading by disk device, as reported by sp_sysmon.

Figure 23.11 *Disk device load balancing (sp_sysmon)*

```
/dev/sybase/log2
LOG2                         per sec     per xact      count   % of total
------------------------     ----------  ----------   --------  ----------
Reads                           0.0         0.0             7       0.3%
Writes                          3.4         0.3          2038      99.7%
------------------------     ----------  ----------   --------  ----------
Total I/Os                      3.4         0.3          2045       1.6%
Device Semaphore Granted        3.4         0.3          2045     100.0%
Device Semaphore Waited         0.0         0.0             0       0.0%
------------------------------------------------------------------------
/dev/sybase/datadev2
DBDATADEVICE1                per sec     per xact      count   % of total
------------------------     ----------  ----------   --------  ----------
Reads                           1.2         0.1           706      31.6%
Writes                          2.5         0.2          1525      68.4%
------------------------     ----------  ----------   --------  ----------
Total I/Os                      3.7         0.3          2231       1.8%
Device Semaphore Granted        3.7         0.3          2231     100.0%
Device Semaphore Waited         0.0         0.0             0       0.0%
------------------------------------------------------------------------
/dev/sybase/datadev3
DBDATADEVICE10               per sec     per xact      count   % of total
------------------------     ----------  ----------   --------  ----------
Reads                           1.1         0.1           637      31.5%
Writes                          2.3         0.2          1386      68.5%
------------------------     ----------  ----------   --------  ----------
Total I/Os                      3.4         0.3          2023       1.6%
Device Semaphore Granted        3.4         0.3          2023     100.0%
Device Semaphore Waited         0.0         0.0             0       0.0%
```

The data reported by sp_sysmon includes both the total I/O to each device and the mix between read and write I/Os. Chapter 17 offers suggestions about data layout across disks and placement of heavily accessed disk files.

A high percentage of total I/Os concentrated on a single disk device or a small number of devices could point to a performance bottleneck if the devices have not been striped effectively.

Remember that striping means there is not a one-to-one relationship between Sybase devices and disks. Check `iostat` for disk-level information; refer to "STEP 2. Monitoring Disks" on page 289.

Tuning the CPU

In this section we examine the way Sybase engines use the CPU and consider ways of increasing the effectiveness of CPU utilization by ASE.

Engine CPU Utilization

In an SMP environment, CPU usage is controlled by the number of data-server engines. The number of engines is set by the `max on-line engines` configuration parameter. Use `sp_sysmon` to identify CPU utilization. If utilization is high, configure additional engines. If the current number of engines is not heavily utilized, consider reducing the number of engines. It is better to have a few heavily utilized engines than many idle engines. The reason is that a Sybase engine will consume CPU cycles even when it is not completely busy; the CPU time is spent looking for transactions to process. Never configure more engines than the physical number of CPUs.

To help identify the amount of time Sybase actually spends processing transactions, `sp_sysmon` shows the utilization of the Sybase kernel. Figure 23.12 illustrates the engine utilization information reported by `sp_sysmon`.

Figure 23.12 *Sybase engine utilization (sp_sysmon)*

```
Engine Busy Utilization:
Engine 0                        55.7%
Engine 1                        55.9%
Engine 2                        56.8%
Engine 3                        58.6%
Engine 4                        58.1%
-----------        ---------------- ----------------
Summary:
  Total: 1367.4%        Average: 57.0%
```

This example shows 57% engine usage by ASE, indicating that ASE is looking for work 43% of the time. The `sp_sysmon` stored procedure also shows the `CPU Yields by Engine`. If engine utilization is low and CPU yields are also low, the engines may have been starved of CPU time by the operating system rather than being idle. Consistently high CPU yields and low engine utilization suggest that the number of engines could be reduced.

The Scheduler

ASE's clock rate is the number of microseconds in a "tick" and is controlled by the configuration parameter sql server clock tick length. Changing the clock tick length might help CPU-intensive environments where a few tasks monopolize the CPU, but you should not make such a change without first consulting Sybase technical support. If necessary, it is wiser to reduce the time slice configuration parameter to limit CPU allocation to batch jobs and to allow disk and network I/O checks to be performed more often. An ASE thread yields the CPU when its time slice expires and the next thread in the queue is started. Note that setting the time slice too low increases the thread-switching overhead since thread switching will occur more frequently.

The configuration parameter io process polling count controls the frequency at which network and disk I/O checks are made. The value of this parameter can be increased to improve I/O throughput or decreased to improve application response time.

When ASE has completed all tasks at hand, it continues to loop and look for runnable tasks for a certain period before relinquishing the CPU. The number of times it loops is controlled by the runnable process search count configuration parameter. When a task becomes runnable there is usually some latency before the task is scheduled to run on a CPU. Increasing this variable on an SMP system can reduce that latency. In some CPU-bound environments, reducing the value of this variable might help free up some CPU cycles. On uniprocessor systems it should be set to 1.

Usefulness of Binding Engines to CPUs

Consider binding Sybase engines to processors. Binding is generally useful in environments where ASE engines consume most of the available CPU time and are rarely descheduled. Binding engines to CPUs minimizes the operating system overhead caused when engines are migrated between processors and can help provide each engine process with a warm cache when it is rescheduled. If possible, use the mpstat utility to choose a CPU with a low number of interrupts so that the engine will not need to be descheduled often.

As of Solaris 2.6, you can create a processor set and bind ASE engines to that set. In a larger system or in systems with a number of ASE instances, using a processor set might be better than binding individual engines to individual CPUs. With processor sets, only the processes bound to the set can run within the set; this restriction eliminates interference from other processes. Each instance can have its own processor set, effectively isolating it from other workloads on the system.

Adding CPUs will help performance in multiuser situations where additional ASE engines can be configured to run user tasks in parallel or in DSS situations where parallel query execution is possible. Adding more CPUs does not help single-threaded applications.

Tuning Parallel Features

ASE 11.5 introduced the capability of sharing queries across multiple ASE threads. The following section considers tuning of ASE parallel features.

Parallel Queries

As of ASE 11.5, Sybase supports intraquery parallelism, allowing a single query to be split into multiple ASE tasks. Query parallelism can greatly improve performance for large queries, particularly in DSS environments. Although query run times can be reduced dramatically, more resource is consumed in running queries in parallel compared to normal processing with a single thread. For this reason it is important to balance the performance needs of DSS workloads with those of OLTP workloads. Dedicating system resources for the sake of a few large queries can impact the performance of OTLP queries.

The configuration parameters that control query parallelism are listed below:

- **number of worker processes** — Determines the total size of the pool of available threads for all parallel query activity.

- **max parallel degree** — Determines the maximum number of worker processes available for partition scans and the total number of worker processes available for join queries involving parallel access to multiple tables.

- **max scan parallel degree** — Determines the maximum number of worker processes available for hash table scans and nonclustered index scans.

Here are some rules of thumb relating to parallel queries:

- Parallel queries consume more system resources than do serial queries.

- If CPU utilization is high and OLTP performance is critical, do not increase the degree of parallelism.

- If CPU utilization is low and I/O is not saturated, slowly increase the degree of parallelism.

- The degree of parallelism should be greater than or equal to the largest number of partitions for a single table.

- It is not necessary to partition tables in order to use Intra-Query Parallelism. Multiple worker processes can divide and scan a single table, although partitioning is often more efficient and allows greater degrees of parallelism.

  Partitioning a table can take time. When testing degrees of parallelism, you need not repartition tables for each test. Once you decide on a reasonable level of parallelism, it might be beneficial to repartition and retest.

- If large queries deadlock when executing serially, changing to parallel execution can increase the number of deadlocks. In addition, when deadlocks occur, the OLTP queries are most likely to be rolled back since the DSS queries have more accumulated CPU time.

- Each worker process in an ad hoc query stores a copy of the plan in the procedure cache. Be sure the procedure cache is large enough to support this duplication.

To fully understand how the system is performing for parallel queries, you must analyze worker process management and parallel query management together. Figure 23.13 shows worker process management information reported by sp_sysmon.

Figure 23.13 *Worker process management (sp_sysmon)*

```
Worker Process Management
-----------------------------

                                  per sec    per xact      count    % of total
    -----------------------       --------   ---------    --------  -----------
Worker Process Requests
    Requests Granted                72.1        0.2        43277     100.0 %
    Requests Denied                  0.0        0.0            0       0.0 $
    -----------------------       --------   ---------    --------
    Total Requests                  72.1        0.2            0

    Requests Terminated              0.0        0.0            0       0.0 %

Worker Process Usage
    Total Used                     216.4        0.5       129831       n/a
    Max Ever Used During Sample      2.3        0.0         1392       n/a

Memory Requests for Worker Processes
    Succeeded                     2157.0        5.4      1294221     100.0 %
    Failed                           0.0        0.0            0       0.0 %
    -----------------------       --------   ---------    --------
    Total Requests                2157.0        5.4      1294221

Avg Mem Ever Used by a WP (in bytes) n/a        n/a         26.3       n/a
```

If the percentage of Requests Denied is large and your engines are not fully utilized, increase the number of worker processes to allow more queries and sorts to be parallelized. If Memory Requests for Worker Processes shows a high percentage of Failed requests, you may have to increase the memory per worker process configuration parameter. Requests Terminated shows the number of times a user terminated a parallel query (for example, with Control-C).

Figure 23.14 illustrates parallel query management data displayed by sp_sysmon.

Figure 23.14 *Parallel query management (sp_sysmon)*

```
Parallel Query Management
-------------------------

   Parallel Query Usage        per sec    per xact      count    % of total
   -------------------------   --------   ----------   --------  ----------
   Total Parallel Queries         72.1         0.2       43278       n/a
   WP Adjustments Made
     Due to WP Limit               0.0         0.0           0       0.0 %
     Due to No WPS                 0.0         0.0           0       0.0 $

   Merge Lock Requests         per sec    per xact      count    % of total
   -------------------------   --------   ----------   --------  ----------
   Network Buffer Merge
   Locks
       Granted with no wait      216.4         0.5      129823     100.0 %
       Granted after wait          0.0         0.0           0       0.0 %

   Result Buffer Merge Locks
       Granted with no wait        0.0         0.0           0       0.0 %
       Granted after wait          0.0         0.0           0       0.0 %

   Work Table Merge Locks
       Granted with no wait        0.0         0.0           0       0.0 %
       Granted after wait          0.0         0.0           0       0.0 %
   -------------------------   --------   ----------   --------
   Total # of Requests           216.4         0.5      129823
```

The Total Parallel Queries statistic reports the number of queries eligible for parallel processing.

WP Adjustments Made occurs when the optimizer suggests a degree of parallelism but either the number of available worker processes was too small or no worker processes were available at all. If the WP Adjustments values are non-zero, increase the number of worker processes parameter.

Parallel Sort Performance

Most processes that require a sort can benefit from parallel sorting. Many of the same issues occur in parallel sorting as in parallel query processing. Parallel sorting requires more system resources than does serial sorting. Worker processes for sorting are divided into producer processes that depend on the number of partitions in a table or index, consumer processes that depend on the number of database devices in tempdb, and a coordinating process that handles the final merge. The number of worker processes required depends on the number of partitions on a table or the number of devices configured for a table.

Here are some rules of thumb relating to parallel sort performance:

- Sorts for clustered indexes on partitioned tables *must* be performed in parallel. If there are not enough worker processes, the create will fail.

- Apart from clustered index creation, the optimizer assigns a single consumer process if it sees only one device in tempdb. If you are using a large RAID device that can handle parallel sort I/O or if tempdb is located on /tmp (that is, using tempfs), the with consumers clause allows you to specify the number of consumer processes to use when creating indexes. It does not allow control of consumer processes for internal sorts in parallel queries.

Sort Buffer Waits in Figure 23.14 reports contention for parallel sort buffers. Increase the number of sort buffers configuration parameter if the waits are high.

Tuning Other Aspects

A number of other tuning tips are explored in the final section of this chapter, including tips on network and lock monitoring, BCP and index create performance, and recovery interval tuning.

Network Monitoring

Figure 23.15 shows task context switches caused by sending and receiving network packets, as reported by sp_sysmon.

Figure 23.15 *Task context switches due to network traffic (sp_sysmon)*

```
Task Context Switches Due To:
Voluntary Yields              174.0         13.0     104533    1.3%
Cache Search Misses           149.3         11.1      89682    1.1%
Logical Lock Contention         1.1          0.1        673    0.0%
Address Lock Contention        78.1          5.8      46917    0.6%
Log Semaphore Contention        3.7          0.3       2240    0.0%
Group Commit Sleeps            18.4          1.4      11071    0.1%
Last Log Page Writes           21.4          1.6      12880    0.2%
I/O Device Contention           4.2          0.3       2509    0.0%
Network Packet Received      1802.2        134.4    1082643   13.7%
Network Packet Sent          1800.3        134.2    1081508   13.7%
SYSINDEXES Lookup             155.4         11.6      93341    1.2%
Other Causes                 8907.5        664.2    5351099   67.9%

Total Bytes Sent            per sec      per xact     count % of total
-------------------------   ---------    ----------   -------- ----------
Engine 0                        5.7          0.4       3450    0.0%
Engine 1                     9661.3        720.5    5803975    7.1%
Engine 2                     9118.2        680.0    5477698    6.7%
Engine 3                    10149.4        756.9    6097198    7.5%
Engine 4                     7338.9        547.3    4408804    5.4%
Engine 5                    10276.5        766.3    6173525    7.6%
-------------------------   ---------    ----------   -------- ----------
Total Bytes Sent           135527.0      10106.4   81416885
Avg Bytes Sent per Packet       n/a          n/a         75    n/a
```

Data packets sent between Sybase clients and servers use a network-independent protocol called Tabular Data Streams (TDS). The default size of a TDS packet is 512 bytes, adequate for most purposes with OLTP workloads. A larger size might be appropriate for some workloads.

When part of a multiple-packet TDS message is received by ASE, the thread is context-switched while waiting for the remaining packets to arrive. TDS packets are sent one at a time, and the thread sleeps while waiting for each packet to be sent. If large numbers of context switches occur because of sent or received network packets, increasing the TDS packet size might help. The `default network packet size` configuration parameter can be changed if necessary to increase the TDS packet size, and the `max network packet size` and `additional network memory` can also be modified if necessary.

Lock Monitoring

Before System 11, when an application took out more than 200 page locks on a table, the lock was automatically escalated to a table lock. On large tables, this behavior could result in a negative performance impact, so Sybase made the escalation point configurable in System 11. Lock promotion is reported by `sp_sysmon` only if it occurs; if the number of lock promotions is high, you can consider increasing the `page lock promotion HWM` (high-water mark), to increase the number of locks that trigger an escalation. An escalation will only occur if the `page lock promotion LWM` (low-water mark) has been reached for a table and one of `page lock promotion HWM` or `page lock promotion PCT` (percentage) has also been reached. The percentage ensures that small tables can benefit from lock escalation without having to reach a high-water mark appropriate for larger tables.

Figure 23.16 shows an extract from the Lock Management information provided by `sp_sysmon`.

Figure 23.16 *Lock management (sp_sysmon)*

```
Lock Management
---------------
Lock Summary                 per sec       per xact      count % of total
-------------------------  ------------  ------------  --------- ---------
Total Lock Requests          25528.5        1903.7     15336086     n/a
Avg Lock Contention             79.2           5.9        47590     0.3%
Deadlock Percentage              0.6           0.0          378     0.0%

Lock Detail                  per sec       per xact      count % of total
-------------------------  ------------  ------------  --------- ---------
Exclusive Table                  0.0           0.0            0     n/a
-------------------------  ------------  ------------  --------- ---------
Total EX-Table Requests          0.0           0.0            0     0.0%
Shared Table
Granted                          0.0           0.0           30   100.0%
Waited                           0.0           0.0            0     0.0%
-------------------------  ------------  ------------  --------- ---------
Total SH-Table Requests          0.0           0.0           30     0.0%
```

`Avg Lock Contention` shows the amount of lock contention as a percentage of the total locks requested. `Deadlock Percentage` shows the number of deadlocks as a percentage of the total locks requested.

If either of these is high, use `sp_sysmon` to get additional lock information and determine where the problem contention is occurring. Take note, too, of the number of `Shared Table` lock requests that `Waited` compared to the number that were `Granted`.

Putting hot tables into named caches, partitioning tables, or creating clustered indexes can all help reduce lock contention.

The Recovery Interval

The recovery interval of ASE determines the amount of time taken by ASE to recover from a crash. It is controlled by the `recovery interval in minutes` configuration parameter, which determines the frequency at which the checkpoint process runs. The checkpoint process scans the data cache for dirty pages and writes them out to disk. If checkpoints are done often (based on a low value of recovery interval), ASE should recover from a crash in a shorter time, but more physical I/O is carried out during normal running because of pages being written to disk more often. Hence, recovery interval tuning is a trade-off between higher availability and lower I/O overheads at run time.

System 11 added a new task, the *housekeeper task*, to assist the checkpoint process by scanning each buffer pool page chain during free CPU cycles and writing dirty pages to disk. This proactive flushing reduces the I/O overhead from checkpointing. For more information on the housekeeper task, refer to "Page Cleaning" on page 124.

In high transaction environments, checkpoints can often be completed more quickly if you increase the number of writes per batch. By default, the checkpoint process only writes 10 I/Os per batch to avoid flooding the I/O subsystem. If you have adequate I/O bandwidth, you can increase this value up to a maximum of 50, as illustrated in the following `dbcc` command:

```
dbcc tune (maxwritedes, 25)
```

Data Load Performance

Sybase provides a high-speed data load utility called the Bulk Copy Program (bcp). Fast bulk copy, which becomes possible when a table has no indexes or triggers, greatly reduces load time. ASE carries out reduced logging when carrying out a fast bulk copy (only page allocation is logged).

ASE 11.5 introduced parallel data load capabilities with `bcp`, allowing you to load multiple partitions at one time. You can start multiple `bcp` sessions, each reading from a different source file into a different partition.

To improve `bcp` performance, use the `number of pre-allocated extents` configuration parameter to preallocate extents (between 2 and 31), thereby reducing thread sleeps and logging of extent allocations. Increasing the `number of oam trips` configuration parameter will keep the OAM pages in cache longer and will also help `bcp` performance. Keeping memory size low and the buffer wash setting high will force a stream of I/O to disk during `bcp`.

ASE 11.5 allows tables to be partitioned into multiple page chains. Partitioning reduces the contention on the last page of a heap table during heavy inserts and improves some parallel queries. If possible, partition a table into multiple chains so that there are between one and four partitions per disk device. Large I/O (16 Kbytes) greatly improves `bcp` performance.

When creating a database, increase the `number of large i/o buffers` configuration parameter (introduced in System 11.9.2) beyond the default of 6 (the maximum value supported is 32). The value establishes the number of disk devices on which parallel I/O can be carried out simultaneously. This parameter became dynamic in System 12 (meaning that it takes effect without an ASE reboot after being changed).

Index Creation Time

You can improve index creation time by tuning the following parameters:

- **`number of extent io buffers`.** Increase this configuration parameter to improve the availability of extent buffers for reading and writing intermediate and final results.

- **`number of sort buffers`** and **`sort page count`.** Adjust these configuration parameters to improve sort performance.

  The `number of sort buffers` parameter sets the number of pages used to hold pages from the base table. Set the value to `number of extent io buffers` multiplied by 8. The `sort page count` parameter specifies the maximum memory `sort` can use; set the value to the `number of sort buffers` multiplied by 2.

24

MONITORING AND TUNING INFORMIX XPS

In this chapter we explore tuning options and recommendations for Informix XPS and examine XPS configuration parameters and monitoring options. The focus is on DSS environments.

Informix XPS Monitoring

We begin by considering the main utilities provided by Informix to monitor XPS. We also examine ways of configuring XPS, generating query execution plans, and monitoring buffer pool behavior.

Examining Informix Utilities

XPS includes a number of utilities for accessing, managing, and monitoring database instances. Of these, the `onstat` utility is probably the most important for monitoring. It monitors many aspects of coserver activity and reports various XPS statistics, some of which are reviewed later in the chapter. Running `onstat` with the `--` argument lists the available options.

Several other important utilities are outlined in the following list:

- **dbaccess:** Provides an SQL command interface to XPS. If called without arguments, the `dbaccess` program runs in full-screen mode with menu-based operation. It also takes two optional arguments: the database name and the name of a file containing SQL commands to be executed.

To run dbaccess in interactive mode with the accts database, use the following syntax (supplying the - character instead of a file name):

```
dbaccess accts -
```

To execute SQL commands stored in a file called cust_update.sql, use the following syntax (assuming the commands should be run against the accts database):

```
dbaccess accts cust_update
```

SQL commands can also be piped to dbaccess, in which case the optional file name parameter is not required.

- **oninit:** Initializes shared memory and brings the database server online according to the settings of the INFORMIXSERVER environment variable (which identifies the server name) and the ONCONFIG environment variable (which identifies the name of the onconfig configuration file, described in the next section). This command is used in conjunction with the xctl utility (described below) to start all coservers at once.

  The -i option causes oninit to destroy all existing data and reinitialize the root dbspaces.

- **onlog:** Displays the contents of a logical-log file. onlog can be useful when you are debugging an application by looking at transaction details.

- **onmode:** Changes the database server and coserver operating modes, forces checkpoints, and allows some parameters to be dynamically changed.

- **onutil:** Defines and modifies XPS objects such as cogroups, dbslices, dbspaces, logical logs, and logical logslices. It also includes check commands for monitoring database server status.

  For example, the following command will display detailed space allocation information for the sysmaster database:

```
onutil check allocation info in database sysmaster display
```

- **xctl:** Runs database server utilities such as oninit, onlog, onmode, and onstat on one or more coservers. Also executes operating system commands on one or more nodes in a cluster environment.

  For example, the following command initializes shared memory and brings all coservers online:

```
xctl -C oninit -y
```

The following command shuts down all coservers:

```
xctl onmode -ky
```

The following command reports the status of all coservers:

```
xctl onstat -
```

Changing Informix XPS Tunable Parameters

Most XPS tunable parameters are found in a configuration file located in `$INFORMIXDIR/etc/$ONCONFIG`. The configuration file includes global and coserver-specific sections.

Parameters in the global section apply to all coservers. When global parameters, such as the `ROOTPATH` parameter, have different names on each coserver, a substitution string representing the coserver number, `%c`, can be included as part of the name. The coserver number will be substituted for each coserver when the name is expanded.

The coserver-specific section of the configuration file consists of groups of parameters delimited by the `coserver` *coserver_number* and `END` keywords. XPS will establish a coserver for each of these parameter groups.

Connectivity details are located in the `$INFORMIXDIR/etc/sqlhosts` file. Lines from a sample `sqlhosts` file with two coservers on a host called `alameda` are shown below:

```
alameda         onipcshm      alameda       alameda.1
alameda.1       onipcshm      alameda       alameda.1
alameda.2       onipcshm      alameda       alameda.2
```

The first column shows the `dbservername`, and the second shows the `nettype`—in this case, communication is based on shared memory and Interprocess Communication (IPC) rather than on network protocols (the standard method on a single SMP system). The third column shows the `hostname`, and the final column shows the `servicename`.

Monitoring Error Messages

XPS messages are written to the file whose path is defined in the `MSGPATH` parameter in the `onconfig` file. The following line illustrates the use of this parameter:

```
MSGPATH    /usr/informix/online.log # System message log file path
```

The file contains error, warning, and notification messages for all coservers. An extract from an `online.log` file is shown below.

```
[002] Sat Sep  1 18:51:56 2001

[002] 18:51:56  Dynamically allocated new shared memory segment (size 8388608)

[002] 23:36:54  Checkpoint Completed:  duration was 0 seconds.

[001] Sat Sep  1 23:39:12 2001

[001] 23:39:12  Checkpoint Completed:  duration was 0 seconds.
[002] 23:42:00  Checkpoint Completed:  duration was 0 seconds.
```

Each line begins with the reporting coserver number and a timestamp.

Generating Query Plans

Query execution plans (QEPs) can help you understand query behavior. Once you have created an index, for example, there is no guarantee that the optimizer will use it. A QEP sheds light on the strategy the optimizer uses in satisfying a particular query. Optimizers are discussed in Chapter 8.

If an SQL statement is preceded by the `set explain on` command, the QEP will be dumped to a file called `sqexplain.out` in the current directory. The contents of one such `sqexplain.out` file are shown below.

```
QUERY:
------
select a.staff_id as id, staff_name as name, project_name as project,
    project_lead as lead, project_manager as mgr
  from staff a, current_projects b, project c
  where b.project_id = c.project_id and a.staff_id = b.staff_id
    and c.project_stage = 'Current'
  order by a.staff_id

Estimated Cost: 3
Estimated # of Rows Returned: 81
Temporary Files Required For: Order By

1) informix.b: SEQUENTIAL SCAN
2) informix.c: SEQUENTIAL SCAN

    Filters: informix.c.project_stage = 'Current'

DYNAMIC HASH JOIN (Build Outer Broadcast)
    Dynamic Hash Filters: informix.b.project_id = informix.c.project_id

3) informix.a: SEQUENTIAL SCAN

DYNAMIC HASH JOIN (Build Inner Broadcast)
    Dynamic Hash Filters: informix.b.staff_id = informix.a.staff_id

# of Secondary Threads = 6

XMP Query Plan
    oper      segid   brid    width   misc info
    ----------------------------------------------
    scan      4       0       1       b
    scan      5       0       1       c
    hjoin     3       0       1
    scan      6       0       1       a
    hjoin     2       0       1
    sort      1       0       1

XMP Query Statistics
  Cosvr_ID: 1
  Plan_ID: 187
    type   segid brid information
    ----   ----- ---- -----------
    scan    4     0    inst cosvr time   rows_prod  rows_scan
                       ---- ----- ----   ---------  ---------
                        0    1     0       144        144
                       --------------------------------------
                        1                  144        144

    scan    5     0    inst cosvr time   rows_prod  rows_scan
                       ---- ----- ----   ---------  ---------
                        0    1     0       37         65
                       --------------------------------------
                        1                  37         65
```

hjoin 3 0	inst	cosvr	time	rows_prod	rows_bld	rows_probe	mem	ovfl	tmp
	0	1	0	77	144	37	64	0	0
	1			77	144	37	(1592)		

scan 6 0	inst	cosvr	time	rows_prod	rows_scan
	0	1	0	45	45
	1			45	45

hjoin 2 0	inst	cosvr	time	rows_prod	rows_bld	rows_probe	mem	ovfl	tmp
	0	1	0	77	45	77	8	0	0
	1			77	45	77	(1592)		

sort 1 0	inst	cosvr	time	rows
	0	1	0	77
	1			77

The optimizer evaluates the Estimated Cost for a number of possible plans and selects the plan with the lowest cost. The unit used in the estimated cost is roughly equivalent to a typical disk access. The Estimated # of Rows Returned is based on the statistics collected on the tables (refer to "Collecting Statistics" on page 396 for more information).

The plan above uses sequential scans to read the three tables and hash joins as the join strategy. Finally, a sort satisfies the order by clause. Six threads are used. The width column shows the number of threads allocated to each operation.

During a hash join, a hash structure is built for the first table, and each row of the second table is used to probe this structure. Individual details are given for each operation, including the coserver number, the number of rows involved in the operation, and the Kbytes of memory required to build the hash table (mem). A non-zero result in the ovfl column means that the hash join has overflowed to temporary space—an adjustment to the PDQPRIORITY parameter (described in "Memory Resources" on page 389) can help ensure that the query is granted enough memory. If -1 appears in the ovfl or mem columns, the operator did not build a hash table.

If a parallel scan is executed, any fragment elimination is reported. The following line shows a plan involving fragment elimination, leaving only six fragments left to scan:

```
1) informix.b: SEQUENTIAL SCAN (Parallel, fragments: 196,
197, 198, 199, 200, 201)
```

The following line illustrates a report for a parallel scan plan with no fragment elimination.

```
1) informix.b: SEQUENTIAL SCAN (Parallel, fragments: ALL)
```

Monitoring Buffer Pool Behavior

Buffer pool usage can be monitored with `onstat -p`. An example is given below.

```
alameda.xps% xctl onstat -p
 --- Output of "onstat -p " id=1 node=alameda Sun Sep  2 23:23:16 2001

Informix Extended Parallel Server Version 8.31.FC1    -- On-Line -- Up 2
days 07:41:49 -- 40960 Kbytes

Profile
dskreads pagreads bufreads %cached dskwrits pagwrits bufwrits %cached
573      573      71587    99.20   5448     8767     19281    71.74

isamtot  open     start    read    write    rewrite  delete commit  rollbk
101501   18387    18524    16082   5011     385      1239   697     0

ovlock   ovuserthread ovbuff    usercpu syscpu   numckpts flushes
0        0            0         18.48   12.10    13       1331

bufwaits lokwaits lockreqs deadlks  dltouts  ckpwaits compress seqscans
2        0        59791    0        0        3        225      477

ixda-RA  idx-RA   da-RA    RA-pgsused lchwaits
0        0        11       11         1033

 --- Output of "onstat -p " id=2 node=alameda Sun Sep  2 23:23:17 2001

Informix Extended Parallel Server Version 8.31.FC1    -- On-Line -- Up 2
days 07:41:50 -- 22528 Kbytes

Profile
dskreads pagreads bufreads %cached dskwrits pagwrits bufwrits %cached
23       23       340      93.24   3442     5301     160      0.00

isamtot  open     start    read    write    rewrite  delete commit  rollbk
175      26       40       43      2        0        0      6       0

ovlock   ovuserthread ovbuff    usercpu syscpu   numckpts flushes
0        0            0         12.87   7.91     4        1313

bufwaits lokwaits lockreqs deadlks  dltouts  ckpwaits compress seqscans
0        0        11       0        0        0        1        0

ixda-RA  idx-RA   da-RA    RA-pgsused lchwaits
0        0        0        0          60
```

In this case, the `xctl` utility was used to retrieve buffer pool information for all coservers (two in this case).

The read cache hit rate, `%cached`, appears immediately after the `bufreads` column on the first line of statistics. The `dskreads` and `dskwrits` columns show the number of physical disk I/Os due to reads and writes, respectively. Chapter 7 discusses the issues associated with buffer cache tuning.

The report shows various other useful statistics, including the number of checkpoints (numckpts), the number of times a thread had to wait for a free buffer (bufwaits), and read-ahead activity. If the sum of ixda-RA, idx-RA, and da-RA is not approximately equal to RA-pgsused, reduce the values for the read-ahead parameters (discussed in "I/O Read-ahead" on page 393).

Monitoring Scan Type

We saw in "Memory Management" on page 139 that XPS does not cache data pages in the buffer pool during light scans. To determine whether a query is using the buffer pool or DS memory, use the onstat utility with the -g scn arguments. An example is shown below:

```
alameda.xps% onstat -g scn

Informix Extended Parallel Server Version 8.31.FC1    -- On-Line -
- Up 05:20:27 -- 30720 Kbytes

RSAM sequential scan info

SesID Thread Partnum Rowid Rows Scan'd Scan Type Lock Mode   Notes
33    124    10119   14d   76            Buffpool  SLock+Test

RSAM index scan info

SesID Thread Partnum  Scan Type Lock Mode  Notes
```

In this example, a scan is in process with a scan type of Buffpool, signifying that the data is being read into the buffer pool. Other possible scan types are shown in the following list:

- **Light.** The scan is a light scan (it uses DS memory and bypasses the buffer pool).

- **Keyonly.** The scan is an index scan.

- **Rids.** The scan is an index scan returning row identifiers.

- **Skip scan.** The scan is an index scan sending row identifiers to a light scan.

Monitoring Queries

The onstat utility includes a number of options for monitoring live queries. We examine a few onstat options that provide useful information about the activity and status of running queries. For readability, comments follow the relevant section of each report rather than appearing at the end.

Queries Accessing Multiple Coservers

The first example is a report produced by `onstat` with the `-g rgm` arguments. It shows information about queries that access data across multiple coservers.

```
alameda.xps% onstat -g rgm

Informix Extended Parallel Server Version 8.31.FC1    -- On-Line
-- Up 04:00:08 -- 40960 Kbytes

Resource Grant Manager (RGM)
==============================

DS_ADM_POLICY:                    FAIR
DS_MAX_QUERIES:                   4
MAX_PDQPRIORITY:                  100
DS_TOTAL_MEMORY:                  512 KB
DS_TOTAL_TMPSPACE:                NO QUOTA

Coserver Capabilities
-------------------------------------------------------------
                       Number cosvrs   Active/Enabled
Total cosrvs           2               2
Compute Capable cosvrs 2               2
TempData Capable cosvrs 2              2
-------------------------------------------------------------

DS Total Memory Across Coservers:   1024 KB
```

The first section of the report shows the parameters determining the behavior of the Resource Grant Manager (RGM), including `DS_MAX_QUERIES` (the maximum number of memory-consuming queries that can be active concurrently on the database server) and `DS_TOTAL_MEMORY` (the maximum amount of memory that can be used for memory-consuming queries).

```
Queries:    Waiting    Active
            0          12

Memory:     Total      Free
(KB)        1024       0
```

The second section of the report shows the number of active queries. In this case, 12 queries are active and none are waiting for resources. The total memory available to be granted—1024 Kbytes in this case—is also shown, along with the amount of free memory (that is, memory not currently granted)—none in this case.

```
RGM Wait Queue:    (len = 0)
---------------
No waiting queries.

RGM Active Queue: (len = 12)
----------------
Lvl  Session  Plan  PdqPrio     Memory (KB)  #Cosvrs  Local Cosvr
50   1.90     190   0.00-0.00   128          1        1
50   1.96     191   0.00-0.00   128          1        1
```

```
50   1.92    192   0.00-0.00  128          1          1
50   1.88    193   0.00-0.00  256          2
50   1.98    194   0.00-0.00  *128         1          1
50   1.94    195   0.00-0.00  *256         2
50   1.104   196   0.00-0.00  *128         1          1
50   1.105   197   0.00-0.00  *128         1          1
50   1.110   198   0.00-0.00  *128         1          1
50   1.102   199   0.00-0.00  *128         1          1
50   1.100   200   0.00-0.00  *256         2
50   1.107   201   0.00-0.00  *256         2
```

The final section of the report shows the RGM Wait Queue and RGM Active Queue. The active queue shows the PDQPRIORITY range for the query (Pdq-Prio) and the memory currently granted to the query (Memory (KB)). An asterisk in the memory column indicates that the query was granted less memory than requested. The #Cosvrs column shows the number of coservers involved in executing the query, and, for local queries, the Local Cosvr column shows the coserver on which memory is allocated.

If queries had been waiting in this case, the statistics reported would have been similar to those shown in the following example:

```
Lvl   Session   Plan   PdqPrio    Local Cosvr   Candidate   Wait Time
50    1.16      210    0.00-0.00                 *           15
```

The PdqPrio shows the PDQPRIORITY range for the query. An asterisk in the Candidate column means the query is waiting for memory to become available, and the Wait Time shows the number of seconds the query has been waiting. Queries are usually kept waiting either because not enough memory is available or because the number of active queries has reached the limit set by DS_MAX_QUERIES in the onconfig file.

Query Segments and SQL Operators

The query segments and SQL operators currently executing on a coserver can be revealed by onstat -g xmp. A sample report is shown below.

```
alameda.xps% onstat -g xmp

Informix Extended Parallel Server Version 8.31.FC1    -- On-Line
-- Up 04:10:19 -- 40960 Kbytes

XMP Query Segments
segid  width  numbr  qryid  sessid  flags   seqno
0      1      1      296    1.220   0x11a   1
0      1      1      300    1.230   0x11a   1
2      1      1      300    1.230   0x118   5
1      1      1      296    1.220   0x118   7
0      1      1      301    1.223   0x11a   1
0      1      1      305    1.238   0x11a   1
3      1      1      305    1.238   0x118   3
1      2      1      301    1.223   0x118   6
6      1      1      305    1.238   0x118   4
0      1      1      298    1.234   0x11a   1
2      1      1      298    1.234   0x118   5
0      1      1      306    1.240   0x11a   1
3      1      1      306    1.240   0x119   2
```

The first section of the report shows the Query Segments for queries that are currently executing. The width column shows the number of parallel processes that can be involved in executing this operator (not only on this coserver). The seqno indicates the order in which the segments of the plan were executed.

```
XMP Query Operators
opaddr      qry  segid branch brtid opname  phase  rows in1        in2
0xc421ed8   300  2     0-0    1433  xchg    open   37   0xc422220  0x0
0xc422220   300  2     0-0    1433  hjoin   probe  75   0xc422620  0xc4227a0
0xc422620   300  2     0-0    1433  xchg    next   77   0x0        0x0
0xc4227a0   300  2     0-0    1433  xchg    done   45   0x0        0x0
0xc105bf0   296  1     0-0    1452  xchg    open   49   0xc1238f0  0x0
0xc1238f0   296  1     0-0    1452  sort    next   99   0xc123a18  0x0
0xc123a18   296  1     0-0    1452  xchg    done   144  0x0        0x0
0xc435180   305  3     0-0    1442  xchg    open   0    0xc4354c8  0x0
0xc4354c8   305  3     0-0    1442  hjoin   probe  0    0xc4358c8  0xc435a48
0xc4358c8   305  3     0-0    1442  xchg    done   144  0x0        0x0
0xc435a48   305  3     0-0    1442  xchg    open   0    0x0        0x0
0xc1cb788   301  1     0-0    1444  xchg    done   1    0xc1cb938  0x0
0xc1cb938   301  1     0-0    1444  flxins  close  35   0xc1cbb88  0x0
0xc1cbb88   301  1     0-0    1444  xchg    close  34   0x0        0x0
0xc348858   305  6     0-0    1450  xchg    done   45   0xc0ae438  0x0
0xc0ae438   305  6     0-0    1450  scan    close  45   0x0        0x0
0xb90e138   306  3     0-0    1451  xchg    done   52   0xb90e2e8  0x0
0xb90e2e8   306  3     0-0    1451  project close  52   0xb90e538  0x0
0xb90e538   306  3     0-0    1451  scan    close  52   0x0        0x0
```

The Query Operators section of the report shows memory addresses and IDs for the query, the segment within a plan, and the branch within a segment. The type of SQL operator is also shown (opname), as well as the processing phase (phase) and the number of rows processed in this phase (rows).

Query Plan Statistics

Running onstat -g xqs *qryid* will report query statistics for a specific query plan. Substitute a real query ID for *qryid* before running this command. Query IDs are shown in the qryid column of the report produced by the onstat -g xmp command and in the Plan column of the report produced by the onstat -g rgm command (both illustrated earlier in the chapter).

The following example shows the type of report produced by this command.

```
alameda.xps% onstat -g xqs 500

Informix Extended Parallel Server Version 8.31.FC1    -- On-Line -- Up
04:33:40 -- 49152 Kbytes

XMP Query Statistics

 Cosvr_ID: 1
 Plan_ID: 500
```

```
type  segid brid information
----  ----- ---- -----------
scan   3    0    inst cosvr time    rows_prod rows_scan
                 ---- ----- ----    --------- ---------
                 0    1     1       52        65
                 ---------------------------------------
                 1                  52        65

merge  2    1    inst cosvr time    it_count
                 ---- ----- ----    --------
                 0    1     2       65
                 1    2     2       0
                 ---------------------------
                 2                  65

group  2    0    inst cosvr time    rows_prod rows_cons  mem  ovfl  tmp
                 ---- ----- ----    --------- ---------   ---  ----  ---
                 0    1     3       34        34         16    0     0
                 1    2     3       31        31         16    0     0
                 -----------------------------------------------------
                 2                  65        65         (256)
```

The information shown in the report is similar to query plan output. Refer to "Generating Query Plans" on page 382 for more information.

Tuning Informix XPS

Achieving optimal tuning of XPS requires attention to parallel features, memory, I/O, and CPU, data load, and interserver communication.

Tuning Parallel Features

No single parameter establishes query parallelism in XPS. Instead, query parallelism is determined by a number of factors, including the number of available coservers, the number of VPs per coserver, data fragmentation, and query complexity. If data required by a query is fragmented across coservers, for example, then those coservers must all participate before the query can complete successfully.

Tuning Memory

Both the buffer pool and DS memory must be tuned for effective XPS performance. We examine the parameters available for memory tuning and consider ways of controlling the dynamic allocation of shared memory by XPS.

Memory Resources

The PDQPRIORITY parameter in XPS determines allocation of memory resources. If this parameter has a value of 100, a single query will be able to use all available memory resources. You can set this priority with the PDQ-

PRIORITY parameter in the onconfig file, and you can override it with the PDQPRIORITY environment variable. An application can override both of these settings with the SET PDQPRIORITY statement.

The total amount of memory available to a single query is also limited by the MAX_PDQPRIORITY parameter in onconfig. If PDQPRIORITY is set to 30 and MAX_PDQPRIORITY to 50, for example, the minimum required memory resources will be 15 (50% of 30), corresponding to 15% of DS_TOTAL_MEMORY.

The value of the MAX_PDQPRIORITY parameter can be changed dynamically with the -D option of the onmode utility.

XPS 8.3 also allows PDQPRIORITY ranges to be established. You can specify a high and low setting for a query. For example, you can run an SQL command before executing a query, as illustrated below.

```
set pdqpriority low 30 high 50
```

In this example, a minimum of 30% and a maximum of 50% of the memory available to memory-consuming queries will be used by a query. If more than the minimum of 30% of memory is available, such as 40%, the query will use the larger amount.

The PDQPRIORITY parameter enables the database administrator to limit the resources consumed by DSS queries, allowing OLTP workloads to gain a guaranteed share of resources, for example. If the parameters are set too low, though, queries will stall until the minimum amount of memory becomes available. The onstat -g rgm command highlights queries waiting for memory and queries running with less memory than requested. Refer to "Queries Accessing Multiple Coservers" on page 386 for more information.

Buffer Pool

Buffer pool memory is configured with the BUFFERS parameter in the onconfig file. The unit is buffers rather than bytes, where the size of each buffer is determined by the page size (2, 4, or 8 Kbytes).

In DSS environments, buffer pool memory is typically required primarily for indexes and inserts. A practical minimum value of 5,000 buffers (20 Mbytes with 4-Kbyte pages) should be adequate to cache internal XPS catalog tables.

With large data sets, it is unlikely that indexes can be fully cached, and memory is probably more usefully allocated to table scans and sorts. Nevertheless, if a lot of users are accessing indexes, increase BUFFERS with a view to caching index nonleaf nodes at least.

Buffer requirements for inserts vary according to the type of insert. Random inserts require pages to be read in from disk and possibly split to accommodate the insert. Inserts at the end of a table require fewer buffers. Inserts into indexed tables require buffers for index as well as table pages.

Buffer pool memory monitoring is discussed in "Monitoring Buffer Pool Behavior" on page 384.

Dirty Buffer Flushing

Modified buffers in the buffer pool are flushed to disk by pagecleaner threads, discussed in "Page Cleaning" on page 140. Pagecleaner behavior is managed with several parameters in the onconfig file:

- **CLEANERS:** The number of pagecleaner threads. The appropriate value depends on the number of disks and on how well pagecleaner threads are keeping up with their task. Monitor with onstat -R, illustrated below.

- **LRUS:** The number of LRU queues (or pairs of LRU queues, to be more accurate, since both an MLRU and an FLRU queue are established—see "Buffer Pool" on page 139 for more information). Set the parameter to four times the number of CPU VPs in the coserver.

- **LRU_MAX_DIRTY** and **LRU_MIN_DIRTY:** The point at which page cleaning begins and ends, respectively. For example, if these parameters are set to 60 and 40, pagecleaner threads will start when 60% of buffers are on the MLRU queue and will stop when the proportion drops to 40%.

Current queue lengths can be reported with the -R option of the onstat utility, as illustrated in the following example:

```
alameda.xps% onstat -R

Informix Extended Parallel Server Version 8.31.FC1    -- On-Line -- Up
   02:24:27 -- 22528 Kbytes

8 buffer LRU queue pairs                      priority levels
# f/m  pair total   % of    length    LOW   MED_LOW  MED_HIGH    HIGH
 0 f        126   100.0%       126    116      10         0         0
 1 m                0.0%         0      0       0         0         0
 2 f        126   100.0%       126    115      11         0         0
 3 m                0.0%         0      0       0         0         0
 4 f        126   100.0%       126    116      10         0         0
 5 m                0.0%         0      0       0         0         0
 6 f        126   100.0%       126    116      10         0         0
 7 m                0.0%         0      0       0         0         0
 8 f        124   100.0%       124    114       9         1         0
 9 m                0.0%         0      0       0         0         0
10 F        124   100.0%       124    114      10         0         0
11 m                0.0%         0      0       0         0         0
12 f        124   100.0%       124    115       9         0         0
13 m                0.0%         0      0       0         0         0
14 f        124   100.0%       124    115       9         0         0
15 m                0.0%         0      0       0         0         0
0 dirty, 1000 queued, 1000 total, 1024 hash buckets, 4096 buffer size
start clean at 60.00% (of pair total) dirty, or 75 buffs dirty, stop at
   50.00%
```

In this example, there are no dirty buffers at all: 100% of the buffers managed by each pair of FLRU/MLRU queues appear in the FLRU queue. Flushing will start when the percentage of buffers in the MLRU queue grows to 60% and will stop when the percentage drops to 50%.

Finally, checkpoints can be triggered at regular intervals with the CKPTINTVL parameter in onconfig, which specifies the checkpoint interval in seconds.

DS Memory

DS memory (described in "DS Memory" on page 140) is configured with the onconfig DS_TOTAL_MEMORY parameter. You can use the DS_MAX_QUERIES parameter to limit the number of active DSS queries using DS memory; the DS_MAX_QUERIES parameter determines the maximum number of memory-consuming queries that can be run concurrently (a memory-consuming query is one with its PDQPRIORITY set to a high value). Both parameters can be changed dynamically with the onmode utility: onmode -M to change DS_TOTAL_MEMORY, and onmode -Q to change DS_MAX_QUERIES.

Achieving an optimal balance between BUFFERS and DS_TOTAL_MEMORY is important to the efficient operation of XPS. Finding this balance may require some experimentation. In a totally DSS environment, try setting DS_TOTAL_MEMORY to 90% of SHMTOTAL (described in the next section). In a mostly DSS environment, try setting DS_TOTAL_MEMORY to between 50% and 80% of SHMTOTAL.

Non-zero values in the ovfl column of a query plan output report or the onstat -g xqs report signify that an overflow to temporary space resulted from a shortfall in DS memory.

Shared Memory Allocation

A number of other onconfig parameters have an important bearing on system configuration, especially since XPS dynamically allocates additional shared memory as required. The most important parameters are listed below.

- **SHMTOTAL.** This parameter limits the total amount of shared memory a single coserver can allocate. A value of 0 means unlimited, in which case the practical limit will be determined by the operating system.

- **SHMVIRTSIZE.** The size of the initial shared memory segment allocated by XPS is determined by this parameter. When this memory is exhausted, XPS will attempt to allocate more segments, with the size of each segment determined by the value of the SHMADD parameter.

  Note that XPS restrictions prevent more than 2 Gbytes being allocated initially. To allocate more than 2 Gbytes, set SHMVIRTSIZE to 2 Gbytes and add an extra shared memory segment with the xctl onmode -a 1380000 command, for example.

  Preallocating a single block of contiguous memory is better than allowing memory to be dynamically allocated in a fragmentary fashion.

- **RESIDENT.** This value determines whether XPS will use intimate shared memory (ISM). ISM can offer significant performance benefits. See "Intimate Shared Memory" on page 24 for more information. A value of 1 means XPS will attempt to allocate ISM; note that sufficient contiguous free memory must be available.

Tuning I/O

As we saw in "Fragmentation" on page 145, XPS supports fragmentation of table data. When a table is scanned, a single scan thread is assigned to each fragment. Careful data layout can result in efficient use of the I/O subsystem. For example, if fragments are placed on several disks, table data can be retrieved from each of them in parallel.

I/O Parallelism

If query predicates enable the optimizer to eliminate some fragments, it is possible that only a small number of chunks will be scanned in parallel, leading to idle CPU while I/O is being completed. Increasing the number of fragments, and hence the number of active threads, can improve this situation. Striping the fragments across multiple disks is another way of ensuring that the available disk bandwidth is used effectively.

Increasing the number of threads to improve I/O throughput can lead to problems, though, since additional threads bring with them increased CPU costs. Once the number of active threads significantly exceeds the number of CPUs, the CPU overheads associated with thread switching can degrade performance.

General recommendation: try to partition large tables with one fragment per disk to minimize disk contention between two scan threads active on the same disk. If table scans are expected to benefit from fragment elimination, it might be possible to place multiple fragments on a single disk and still avoid disk contention during scans of large tables.

Another important factor to consider is the expected number of active users. Multiple queries that result in simultaneous scans of various large tables can also place pressure on the I/O subsystem. Thin and wide stripes are the best overall strategy to achieve balanced disk I/O. Refer to "The Right and Wrong Way to Stripe" on page 246 for more information.

I/O Read-ahead

Two `onconfig` parameters determine read I/O behavior during sequential table scans, index build, and `update statistics` processing. The `RA_PAGES` parameter sets the size of individual read I/Os, both into the buffer pool and into DS memory. If you have adequate I/O bandwidth, a good choice is 64, resulting in 256-Kbyte reads with a 4-Kbyte page size. The `RA_THRESHOLD` parameter sets the point at which the next read I/O will take place. Set `RA_THRESHOLD` to half the value of `RA_PAGES`.

The equivalent parameters for index page read-ahead are `IDX_RA_PAGES` and `IDX_RA_THRESHOLD`.

Isolation Levels

For optimal XPS query performance, set the isolation level to Repeatable Read. Repeatable Read causes XPS to take out table locks, reducing overhead but also limiting concurrency. A more flexible alternative is to set Cursor Stability and introduce the ISOLATION_LOCKS parameter into the onconfig file. This parameter determines the maximum number of rows that can be locked at one time while Cursor Stability is in effect. The default value is 1 if it is not set. Ensure that the LOCKS parameter (the maximum number of locks) is set to a sufficiently large value to hold locks acquired as a result of the ISOLATION_LOCKS parameter.

The isolation level can be set globally with the set isolation level statement. For example:

```
set isolation level to repeatable read;
```

The isolation level can also be set for the subsequent transaction with the set transaction isolation level statement.

Tuning CPU

The number of CPUs per coserver is set with the NUMCPUVPS parameter in the onconfig file. For example:

```
NUMCPUVPS8# Number of user vps (CPUs)
```

This number is set in the global section of the onconfig file, so the number of CPUs in each coserver will always be the same. Two other parameters should also be set for SMP environments:

```
MULTIPROCESSOR1
SINGLE_CPU_VP0
```

Tuning Log Buffers

The LOGBUFF and PHYSBUFF parameters in the onconfig file determine the size in Kbytes of the logical-log and physical-log buffers, respectively. The size of these buffers influences how quickly they fill and therefore how frequently the buffers will be flushed to disk. The circumstances in which these buffers will be flushed to disk are discussed in "Page Cleaning" on page 140.

The logs can be monitored with the onstat -l command, as illustrated in the following report:

```
alameda.xps% onstat -l

Informix Extended Parallel Server Version 8.31.FC1    -- On-Line -- Up
10:17:57 -- 30720 Kbytes

Physical Logging
Buffer bufused  bufsize   numpages numwrits pages/io
  P-1  0        8         28       4        7.00
     phybegin            physize  phypos   phyused   %used
     1:65                375      231      0         0.00

Logical Logging
Buffer bufused  bufsize   numrecs  numpages numwrits recs/pages pages/io
  L-2  0        8         274      43       43       6.4        1.0
```

address	number	flags	uniqid	begin	size(p)	used(p)	%used
a1843d0	1	U------	1	1:440	512	512	100.00
a184400	2	U------	2	1:952	512	512	100.00
a184430	3	U---C-L	3	1:1464	512	487	95.12
a184460	4	F------	0	1:1976	512	0	0.00
a184490	5	F------	0	1:2488	512	0	0.00
a1844c0	6	F------	0	1:3000	512	0	0.00

The report shows buffer statistics and the amount of space used in each log file. If PHYSBUFF is sized appropriately, the pages/io for the physical log should be approximately 75% of the bufsize. The nature of access to the logical log makes it inappropriate to set a similar goal for LOGBUFF.

Optimizing Load Performance

XPS offers a number of methods for loading data. We consider some of the alternatives relevant to DSS environments and discuss options for statistics collection.

Loading Data

Informix has been able to speed up and simplify the parallel loading of data in XPS with the Pload/XPS utility. Pload maps external data to internal data by treating the external data file as a table with a special type of "external" (refer to "Tables and Indexes" on page 144 for more information on table types in XPS).

Pload uses an enhanced SQL interface to read data from the external file. The necessary conversion is carried out to create the row, and data that cannot be converted is written to a reject file.

After you have created the table, define the external file as shown in the following example:

```
create external table cust_ext sameas customer using (
    format "delimited",
    datafiles("disk:1:/data1/customer.tbl"));
```

The sameas keyword specifies that the contents of the delimited fields in /data1/customer.tbl exactly match the table columns in the customer table. The delimiter is the | character, as illustrated in the following example of data ready to be loaded:

```
23114|Smith and Sons Inc|12946.55|A|408-492-6875|86
921271|Bloggs and Co|499284.03|C|510-548-3874|6A
```

The load is performed with an SQL insert statement, as shown:

```
insert into customer select * from cust_ext;
```

To achieve the fastest load rates for data warehouse loads, start with an empty Operational table with no indexes. Alter the table to Raw and load the data with express mode. Alter the table back to Operational after the load. You must create indexes separately. The following example illustrates an express-mode load, with the data loaded from pipes rather than from a file:

```
create external table cust_ext sameas customer using (
    format "delimited",
    datafiles ("pipe:1:/tmp/customer.pipe.%r(0..2)",
        "pipe:2:/tmp/customer.pipe.%r(3..5)"),
    rejectfile "/tmp/cust%c",
    express);
```

In this example, `pipe:1` specifies a pipe in coserver 1, and `customer.pipe.%r(0..2)` will be expanded to `customer.pipe.0`, `customer.pipe.1`, and `customer.pipe.2`. So three pipes (0, 1, and 2) will feed coserver 1, and pipes 3, 4, and 5 will feed coserver 2. One reject file will be created for each coserver (the `%c` will be expanded to the coserver number).

If a pipe is used, a separate process is needed to feed the pipe with data. Pipes can be useful if data conversion is required; the conversion phase can proceed concurrently with the load.

Pipe-based loads use FIFO VPs. By default, two are configured per coserver, but more can be specified with the `NUMFIFOVPS` parameter in the `onconfig` file, up to a limit of the number of physical CPUs per coserver. For best performance, set `NUMFIFOVPS` equal to the number of pipes per coserver.

For inserts into tables that already have indexes, `deluxe` mode is an alternative to `express` mode, as shown in the following example based on four coservers:

```
create external table order_ext sameas order using (
    format "delimited",
    datafiles ("disk:1:/data1/order.aa",
        "disk:2:/data1/order.ab"),
        "disk:3:/data1/order.ac"),
        "disk:4:/data1/order.ad"),
    deluxe);
```

The insert modifies the indexes, checks constraints, and logs all changes. You can share the table while the updates are proceeding, too, by locking the table in share mode.

Collecting Statistics

The optimizer bases its query plans on the column statistics available to it. Statistics are collected with the `update statistics` SQL statement. Three levels of statistics collection are supported:

- **HIGH.** Exact distribution information is collected. For large tables, this option can be time consuming, with scans required for all specified columns.

- **MEDIUM.** Sampling techniques are used to establish data. A single scan of the data is required, but the overall operation is much faster than for HIGH.

Statistics are collected into bins, each of which contains a subset of the data. The proportion of the data summarized in each bin is determined by the `resolution` parameter.

A confidence interval can also be specified, representing the frequency with which the statistic should be expected to equal a value collected with HIGH.

- **LOW.** Minimal information is collected, and the statement typically takes only seconds to complete. Column distributions are ignored.

The following example illustrates the syntax used in statistics collection:

```
update statistics medium for table stock resolution 0.1 0.95;
```

In this example, column data will be summarized in bins, each of which contains 0.1% of the data. The final parameter (set to 0.95 in the example) specifies the confidence value.

Statistics collection inevitably involves trade-offs between the time taken to gather the statistics and the accuracy of the final results. A possible compromise is to specify HIGH for small tables and MEDIUM for large tables.

Creating Indexes

Don't overdo index creation. Although indexes can improve performance for some queries, they also introduce extra processing overhead and consume additional disk space. The time taken to build large indexes can be significant, and table updates—particularly bulk inserts and deletes—require maintenance of every affected index.

Tuning Inter-Coserver Communication

Communication among coservers is an important component of DSS performance with XPS. When all coservers are located on a single Solaris SMP system, inter-coserver communication takes place through shared memory (set the nettype in the sqlhosts file to onipcshm). When coservers are located on different nodes—in a cluster, for example—network protocols are required.

The following section considers the tuning that is required both for Solaris and for XPS on clusters (this tuning is not necessary on a single Solaris SMP system).

Configuring UPD on Solaris

All inter-coserver communication uses the eXtended Message Facility (XMF) layer in XPS. Each operating system supplies a datagram (DG) layer to carry out the low-level communication, presenting a well-defined API to XMF. The current Solaris implementation uses the User Datagram Protocol (UDP) to communicate between coservers on different systems. UDP is a simple datagram protocol layered directly above the Internet Protocol (IP). The DG layer accesses UDP with the Transport Layer Interface (TLI), where it supports the connectionless (T_CLTS) service type.

For optimal UDP configuration, execute the following commands from the Solaris command line:

```
ndd -set /dev/udp udp_recv_hiwat 65536
ndd -set /dev/udp udp_xmit_hiwat 65536
ndd -set /dev/udp udp_do_checksum 0
```

The first two commands result in an increase in system memory consumption. The default value for both `udp_recv_hiwat` and `udp_xmit_hiwat` is 8192 bytes. The values shown above are the maximum settings (in bytes); they can be decreased if necessary. The `ndd` program can also report the current variable settings, as illustrated in the following lines:

```
alameda% ndd /dev/udp udp_xmit_hiwat
65536
```

The simplest way of ensuring that these commands are run automatically is to place the commands in an executable script, called `S99infxsetup`, for example, and place it in the `/etc/rc2.d` directory.

Configuring Coserver Communications

The communication resources used by XPS are configurable. XMF uses buffers of three different sizes, configured with the following `onconfig` parameters:

- **SBUFFER.** The small buffer defaults to 880 bytes.
- **LBUFFER.** The large buffer defaults to 8 Kbytes.
- **HBUFFER.** The huge buffer defaults to 48 Kbytes.

These buffers cannot be reduced in size. Increasing these buffers beyond the defaults should be done cautiously since larger buffers can cause message fragmentation.

XMF also uses resources, called endpoints, to communicate between coservers on different systems. XMF uses *send endpoints* to send messages to other coservers. Send endpoints are specified for each CPU VP with the `onconfig` parameter SENDEPDS; the default value is 5. Each CPU VP controls its own endpoints, using them in a round-robin fashion. When a message is sent on a send endpoint, UDP buffers it immediately. XMF can send any type of message to a send endpoint. If too few send endpoints have been configured, XMF will buffer messages internally, increasing virtual memory consumption in the process.

Messages from other coservers are delivered to XMF on *receive endpoints*. The user has more options in specifying receive endpoints. Each CPU VP requires a configuration line in the `onconfig` file for small, large, and huge receive endpoints. The syntax is illustrated in the following examples:

```
SADDR     myhost:15000,8,0
LADDR     myhost:15010,25,0
HADDR     myhost:15050,1,0
```

Each endpoint parameter has a node name (`myhost` in the example), a port number (`15000` for small endpoints in the example), the number of endpoints (the example uses 8 for small endpoints), and the number of the CPU VP (0 in the example).

More than 90% of messages are received with large endpoints, so a useful rule of thumb is to set their number to at least twice that of small endpoints. Huge endpoints are rare, so one endpoint is usually sufficient. Experiment to find the optimal values for your environment, bearing in mind that endpoints use memory.

Monitoring XMF Traffic

Poorly configured endpoints can result in XMF retransmissions. Retransmissions degrade performance because they significantly increase the XMF code path. You can monitor XMF traffic for all coservers by executing the following command while a query is running:

```
xctl onstat -g xmf
```

A sample report created with this command is shown below.

```
alameda% onstat -g xmf

Informix Extended Parallel Server Version 8.31.FC1   -- On-Line -- Up
04:53:54 -- 49152 Kbytes

XMF Information
---------------
  Cosvr_id: 1    Domain_Cnt: 1

  Poll Information:

    Domain   Int   Cur   Ave   SvcCycle   NetPoll+     FastPoll+     InDG/Sig
    ------------------------------------------------------------------------
    0        50    65    65    265224     4883         4883          N / N

  End_point Information:

    Huge_rcvedps:    1
    Large_rcvedps:   1
    Small_rcvedps:   1
    Xmit_edps:       1
    Max_user_segsize: 48968
    Net_retry:       0
    Net_no_progress: 0

  Memory Usage:

          Buf_size   Total_bufs  Free_bufs  Allocs    Dallocs    H / SExpnds
          -----------------------------------------------------------------
    Sml:  1024       104         42         46148     46086      104 / 0
    Lrg:  8192       150         59         13911     13820      150 / 0
    Huge: 49152      10          6          226       222         10 / 0
    Dyn:  0          0           0          0         0            0 / 0

          XMF_Client XMF_Svc    XMF_Reltp  XMF_Net   XMF_DG
          -----------------------------------------------------
    Sml:  52         0          0          0         10
    Lrg:  81         0          0          0         10
    Huge: 0          0          0          0         4
    Dyn:  0          0          0          0         0
```

```
Coserver Information:

    ID  X_Msgs   X_Bytes     R_Msgs    R_Bytes    X_Rtrns  R_Dupls XOffs  XO_Cycls
    ---------------------------------------------------------------------------------
    L   13118   19077076    13118    19077076   0        0        0      0
    2   6688     4951217     6934     1556485   14        5        0      0
```

The following list outlines the meaning of some of the key columns in the report above:

- **X_Msgs:** The number of messages sent to this coserver.

- **X_Bytes:** The number of bytes in transmitted messages.

- **R_Msgs:** The number of messages received by this coserver.

- **R_Bytes:** The number of bytes in received messages.

- **X_Rtrns:** The number of retransmitted messages received by this coserver.

- **R_Dupls:** The number of duplicate messages received by this coserver.

If the Solaris UDP parameters have been set as recommended earlier, a significant proportion of retransmissions or duplicates most likely suggests the need for more endpoints.

One of the biggest challenges with coservers is data skew. Data skew causes some coservers to work harder than others, but it also results in more data being shipped between coservers. A better fragmentation strategy may help reduce data shipping, although it may not be possible to completely resolve the problem.

25

MONITORING AND TUNING DB2 FOR SOLARIS

In this chapter we consider tuning recommendations for DB2 Universal Database for Solaris in both DSS and OLTP environments, and we examine the pros and cons of splitting data across multiple logical database partitions (LDPs). First, though, we look at methods of monitoring DB2 and outline the way DB2 UDB tunable parameters can be modified.

Monitoring DB2

DB2 supplies a snapshot monitor to provide information about UDB behavior. The Snapshot Monitor can be invoked either by the Control Center, db2cc, a powerful graphical tool (Java-based as of DB2 UDB V6.1) that supports both monitoring and general database administration, or by commands to be executed by the DB2 command-line processor.

Underlying the monitoring tools is a series of switches that allow selective monitoring of the main DB2 subsystems. Information can be gathered about an instance, a database, tablespaces, tables, and database connections.

Switches can be turned on or off to monitor bufferpools (BUFFERPOOL), locks (LOCK), sort activity (SORT), SQL statements (STATEMENT), tables (TABLE), and unit of work (UOW) activity. Switches can be turned on for all or some of these elements. Monitoring does incur a small performance penalty, so it is wise to use it selectively.

The following example turns on the monitoring switches for bufferpools, locks, and sorting.

```
db2 "update monitor switches using BUFFERPOOL on LOCK on SORT on"
```

A snapshot on the current instance can be taken with the following command:

```
db2 "get snapshot for database manager"
```

A database snapshot on the CUSTOMER database would require the following command:

```
db2 "get snapshot for database on CUSTOMER"
```

A variant of the same command can be used to monitor tables and tablespaces associated with the CUSTOMER database: simply replace database with tables or tablespaces.

The db2mon script, available on the book website, takes two arguments (database name and monitoring interval), carries out database monitoring for the specified interval, and reports the results along with explanations and recommendations.

Changing DB2 Tunable Parameters

Monitoring isn't much use unless you can change database parameters. There are two types of DB2 tunable parameters: instance-level parameters and database-level parameters. Instance-level parameters apply to all databases belonging to the instance. Database-level parameters apply only to the affected database. Examples of instance-level (database manager) configuration parameters (referred to later in the chapter) are COMM_BANDWIDTH, SHEAPTHRES, and MAX_QUERYDEGREE. Examples of database-level configuration parameters are DFT_DEGREE, SORTHEAP, and LOCKLIST. In general, logger, bufferpool, and locking parameters are defined at the database level (and so can vary for different databases within the same instance).

DB2 tunable parameters are not updated by editing of a file. Instead, they are displayed and updated with special DB2 commands.

Displaying and Changing Instance-Level Parameters

Instance-level parameters can be displayed from a UNIX shell prompt with the following command:

```
db2 get database manager configuration
```

An abbreviated form can also be used:

```
db2 get dbm cfg
```

Instance-level updates are achieved with the following command:

```
db2 update database manager configuration using
    parametername value [parametername2 value2...]
```

As before, database manager configuration can be abbreviated to dbm cfg.

Displaying and Changing Database-Level Parameters

Database-level parameters can be displayed with the following command:

```
db2 get database configuration for databasename
```

Once again, an abbreviated form is available:

```
db2 get db cfg for databasename
```

Database-level updates are achieved with the following command:

```
db2 update database configuration for databasename using
parametername value [parametername2 value2...]
```

As before, `database configuration` can be abbreviated to `db cfg`.

Displaying and Changing DB2 Registry Variables

Although most DB2 UDB parameters are viewed and modified with the `db2 get` and `db2 update` commands, DB2 also uses a registry to store tunable parameters. The following command lists all supported registry variables:

```
db2set -lr
```

You can also change registry variables with the `db2set` command, as shown in the following example:

```
db2set registry_variable_name = newvalue
```

DB2 must be rebooted before changes to these parameters take effect.

Monitoring Error Messages

DB2 stores error, warning, and notification messages in the `db2diag.log` file, which can be found in the `$HOME/sqllib/db2dump` directory. If multiple logical database partitions are used, messages relating to all logical partitions are logged in the same `db2diag.log` file. If database partitions are located on different physical nodes, the same file can be used by all nodes, provided the file is accessible to each by an NFS mount.

Generating an Explain Plan

Finding and improving inefficient SQL statements can do wonders for performance. DB2 explain plans describe the query plan used to access data and indicate the cost associated with the query. One method of generating an explain plan is shown in the following sequence.

1. Go to the DB2 home directory and connect to the database. If you haven't already done so, create the system explain tables by running the SQL statements in EXPLAIN.DDL.

   ```
   db2 -tf sqllib/misc/EXPLAIN.DDL
   ```

2. Let DB2 know that you only want to generate an explain plan, not to execute the following SQL.

   ```
   db2 set current explain mode explain
   ```

3. Run the SQL. In this example, the SQL is held in a file called /tmp/query.sql.

   ```
   db2 -vtf /tmp/query.sql
   ```

4. Switch off explain mode.

```
db2 set current explain mode no
```

DB2 will have saved the details in its internal explain tables.

5. Retrieve the header information for this explain session by using the following SQL statement.

```
db2 "select explain_time, source_name, source_schema
    from explain_instance"
```

The timestamp, name, and schema information will be returned for your session and possibly for many previous sessions as well.

6. Identify the correct information and use it to retrieve the explain plan details. In this example, the database name is PROJECTS and the output will be written to a file called /tmp/query.log.

```
db2exfmt -d PROJECTS -w "2001-03-06-17.32.33.211516"
  -n SQLC28U5 -s NULLID '-#' 0 -o /tmp/query.log
```

The output file will include a tree-structured representation of the query execution plan as well as detailed costing information.

Monitoring the Cost of SQL Statements

Identifying expensive SQL statements can be difficult, especially if the SQL is embedded in applications. The DB2 UDB SQL event monitor provides one way of identifying SQL costs during the running of a program. The procedure below outlines a way of achieving that.

1. Create a directory for temporary storage (for example, /home/db2events) and establish an event monitor called COSTS in the PROJECTS database, using that directory. A lot of disk space could be required if a lot of SQL is to be monitored.

```
mkdir /home/db2events
db2 "create event monitor COSTS for statements
    write to '/home/db2events'"
```

2. Enable the event monitor.

```
db2 "set event monitor COSTS state = 1"
```

3. Run the application or execute the SQL. Each SQL statement will be costed and the details stored in the /home/db2events directory. When you are ready, disable the event monitor.

```
db2 "set event monitor COSTS state = 0"
```

4. Use the db2evmon tool to format the raw event data.

```
db2evmon -db PROJECTS -evm COSTS > /tmp/costs.txt
```

You will find the results in the /tmp/costs.txt file. The file is verbose and possibly very large if a lot of SQL statements were executed during the period the event monitor was active. Wading through a large event file is not a task for the faint-hearted, but at least you now have concrete information to work with.

Monitoring DB2 Processes

One unusual feature of DB2 for Solaris is that all DB2 system processes are shown as db2sysc when viewed in /bin/ps. Use /usr/ucb/ps -axw instead to reveal the names of each DB2 UDB process.

You can use an alias to simplify this process. In the C shell, try this:

```
ozalpaca% alias db2ps "/usr/ucb/ps -axw | grep -v grep |
grep db2"
```

Now you can look at the DB2 processes simply by executing db2ps.

```
ozalpaca% db2ps
 8287 ?          S   0:00  db2sysc 0
 8288 ?          S   0:00  db2gds 0
 8289 ?          S   0:00  db2ipccm 0
 8290 ?          S   0:00  db2resyn 0
 8291 ?          S   0:00  db2srvlst 0
 8299 ?          S   0:01  db2agent (PROJECTS) 0
 8345 ?          S   0:00  db2agent (idle) 0
 8437 ?          S   0:00  db2loggr 0
 8438 ?          S   0:00  db2dlock 0
 8439 ?          S   0:00  db2pfchr 0
 8440 ?          S   0:00  db2pfchr 0
 8441 ?          S   0:00  db2pfchr 0
 8442 ?          S   0:00  db2pclnr 0
 8286 pts/12     S   0:00  db2wdog 0
 8436 pts/12     S   0:00  /db2/db2ee/sqllib/bin/db2bp 8426 5
```

Managing Bufferpools

DB2 UDB allows you to create multiple bufferpools and to bind tablespaces to them. If you do not create multiple bufferpools, the default bufferpool (IBM-DEFAULTBP) will be used automatically.

Bufferpools can be created with the create bufferpool statement, and changed or removed with the alter bufferpool and drop bufferpool statements.

The following command creates an 80-Mbyte bufferpool, called customer, with a 4-Kbyte page size on all database partitions:

```
db2 "create bufferpool customer all nodes
        size 20000 pagesize 4096"
```

The new bufferpool will become active when the database is restarted.

A tablespace called customer1 can be bound to this new bufferpool with the following command:

```
db2 "alter tablespace customer1 bufferpool customer"
```

The details for all current bufferpools can be displayed as shown in the following example:

```
sanramon% db2 "select * from syscat.bufferpools"

BPNAME              BUFFERPOOLID NGNAME       NPAGES   PAGESIZE ESTORE
--------------      ------------ ------------ -------- -------- ------
IBMDEFAULTBP             1 -                   5000     4096 N
CUSTOMER                 2 -                   8000     4096 N
STOCK                    3 -                  20000     4096 N

  3 record(s) selected.
```

The bufferpool size is reported in the NPAGES column. If the size of a bufferpool is set to -1, the amount of memory allocated to the bufferpool will be determined by the BUFFPAGE configuration parameter. If BUFFPAGE is set to 1024, for example, 4 Mbytes of shared memory will be allocated to any bufferpools with NPAGES set to -1 and PAGESIZE set to 4096 (because 1024 × 4096 = 4 Mbytes).

Calculating the Cache Hit Rate

The cache hit rate for DB2 UDB can be calculated from the information produced either by a database snapshot, in which case activity is summarized for all bufferpools, or by a tablespace snapshot, in which case the bufferpool activity is shown for each tablespace. If no additional bufferpools have been created, the activity reported is only for the default bufferpool (IBM-DEFAULTBP).

The cache hit rate can be calculated as follows:

$$\left(1 - \frac{\text{(Bufferpool data physical reads + Bufferpool index physical reads)}}{\text{(Bufferpool data logical reads + Bufferpool index logical reads)}}\right) \times 100$$

The following extract from a database snapshot illustrates the kind of information provided by DB2:

```
Buffer pool data logical reads          = 5157626
Buffer pool data physical reads         = 1645052
Asynchronous pool data page reads       = 1597188
Buffer pool data writes                 = 0
Asynchronous pool data page writes      = 0
Buffer pool index logical reads         = 959999
Buffer pool index physical reads        = 55750
Asynchronous pool index page reads      = 32008
Buffer pool index writes                = 0
Asynchronous pool index page writes     = 0
```

Based on this example, the cache hit rate was

```
(1-(1645052+55750)/(5157626+959999)) ×100 = 72.2%
```

You can also separately calculate the data and index cache hit rates (68.1% and 94.2%, respectively) by including only the physical and logical reads for either data or index. As the hit rates suggests, index pages tend to be kept in the bufferpool for longer since they are more likely to be reused.

The `Asynchronous pool data page reads` and the `Asynchronous pool index page reads` show the number of pages read into the bufferpool by the prefetchers as a result of sequential read activity. The prefetchers tend to lower the cache hit rate since pages read by them are not resident in the bufferpool for long and so are rarely reused. If you deduct the prefetched pages from the totals, the cache hit rate improves significantly.

The `db2mon` script on the book website calculates the cache hit rate for you and reports other useful metrics.

Buffer cache sizing and tuning are discussed in detail in Chapter 7.

Tuning DB2 for Solaris for DSS Workloads

Many users have gained their first experience of DB2 for Solaris with Decision Support System (DSS) applications. For that reason we consider tuning for DSS workloads first. But a strength of DB2 for Solaris is its ability to effectively handle both OLTP and DSS workloads.

For background information on the architecture of DB2 for Solaris, refer to Chapter 12.

Choosing a Partitioning Method

Before we discuss tuning specifics, we need to examine the alternative methods of implementing a DB2 database. Thanks to the functionality of DB2 Extended Edition (EE) and Enterprise-Extended Edition (EEE), DB2 UDB offers more than one method of laying out a database. Even on a single SMP server, data can be stored as a single image or split across multiple database partitions. Consequently, choices must be made about how best to structure a database for DSS workloads. There are pros and cons associated with each approach. The optimal choice will depend on the size of the largest database tables and how the database will be accessed.

Smaller data warehouses (up to 200 Gbytes, for example) are more likely to lend themselves to a single database partition. With large volumes of data, multiple database partitions may prove more attractive. Some of the pros and cons associated with each option are discussed below.

Single Database Partition Advantages

Many smaller data warehouses will benefit from the advantages of using a single database partition. Single database partitions are attractive for the following reasons.

- They offer greatest ease of use in setup and ongoing administration. Data is stored as a single entity and so no data splitting across partitions is required. Configuring a single data image affects loading data, insert, update, and delete activity, and data administration generally.

- Query parallelism adjusts itself automatically as CPUs are added. Query parallelism is easy to manage (with the DFT_DEGREE database configuration parameter). Adding CPUs requires little change to the configuration before the CPUs can be used (only the DFT_DEGREE parameter need be changed, and not even that if it is set to -1). With multiple partitions, adding a CPU is likely to require more fundamental reorganization of the data.

  Note that the INTRA_PARALLEL parameter must be set to YES to allow parallelism within a database partition. Setting this parameter to SYSTEM is also equivalent to setting it to YES on an SMP server.

- Single partitions are more efficient than multiple database partitions. Since no interpartition communication is required, intrapartition parallelism tends to be more efficient.

- System administration is much simpler. A single partition without split data is easier to administer.

Single Database Partition Disadvantages

In spite of the attractive simplicity of single database partitions, they do have some disadvantages.

- Tables and tablespaces were restricted to 64 Gbytes with DB2 Universal Database V5.0, although this limit was increased to 256 Gbytes with V5.2 if 16-Kbyte page sizes are used, and further increased to 512 Gbytes with V6.1 and 32-Kbyte pages. Users with very large data warehouses may find this restriction a problem. The limit applies to each logical or physical database partition. With four logical (or physical) partitions, for example, the limit rises to 64 × 4 Gbytes, or 256 Gbytes (2 terabytes with 32-Kbyte pages).

- Each logical or physical database partition is subject to a limit of 4 Gbytes of shared memory. This limit may not be a major problem, though, since DB2 UDB is relatively modest in its shared memory requirements for data warehouse applications. Also, memory is relatively inexpensive at present.

  Nonetheless, unless EStore (the ability to use additional shared memory segments to go beyond 4 Gbytes) is used, intrapartition parallelism means a limit of around 3.7 Gbytes of shared memory (on Sun systems, less on some other UNIX systems). EStore became available for the first time in DB2 Universal Database V5.0. Be aware that its use does involve a performance penalty.

- Indexing and `runstats` take longer with intrapartition parallelism than with interpartition parallelism. Although the scan and sort phases of index creation are parallelized, the write phase is not. `runstats` is not parallelized at all. Consequently, index creation and `runstats` may run slower than with multiple database partitions.

  A workaround for this problem is to create indexes and collect statistics during the load operation. This approach offers some savings by eliminating double-handling of data and allows for a greater degree of parallelism than would otherwise be possible. An alternative strategy for `runstats` is to schedule `runstats` for multiple tables concurrently.

Multiple Database Partition Advantages

The use of multiple database partitions is pretty much a given for large DB2 UDB data warehouses or large systems (for example, an Enterprise 10000 or large Sun Fire systems). On a single SMP system, logical database partitions can be used to offer greater scalability than would otherwise be possible. Multiple domains are not required—multiple logical database partitions can coexist and achieve excellent scalability within a single domain.

Each logical partition operates as a shared-nothing entity: it has its own CPU resource, its own shared memory, and its own disk containers. It does not directly "see" the data stored in other partitions; if it requires rows held in another logical database partition (to carry out a join, for example), it must request them from the Fast Communication Manager (FCM). When a cluster or an MPP system is used, the data is not physically accessible because it is located on a physically separate node. With a single SMP system, of course, all memory pages and all disks are equally accessible—the shared-nothing architecture is imposed by the DB2 software implementation.

The advantages of multiple database partitions are summarized below.

- Because the 512-Gbyte table and tablespace size limit (as of V6.1) and the 4-Gbyte shared memory limit apply to each logical database partition, use of multiple logical partitions allows these limits to be stretched. In the Solaris Operating Environment, the 4-Gbyte shared memory limit associated with the 32-bit version of DB2 for Solaris is per process, not systemwide. Each process associated with a particular logical database partition attaches to the same shared memory segments. Thus, the 4-Gbyte shared memory limit amounts to a limit per logical database partition. The 64-bit version of DB2 for Solaris lifts this restriction.

- Index creation is better parallelized since all phases take place simultaneously across all affected logical database partitions.

- The `runstats` utility is significantly faster than with single database partitions since it scans only the data in one logical database partition. This data is assumed to be representative of the whole data set.

- Bulk inserts and updates are naturally and transparently parallelized across all nodes containing the relevant tablespaces (once they have been split). With a single database partition, bulk update data must be subdivided if more than one set of inserts or updates is to be run concurrently. Subdivision may also be necessary with multiple database partitions for optimal performance, though.

- The database system can scale beyond the biggest single SMP system, although with SMP systems with high CPU and memory capacities available from Sun, this need only be relevant for a subset of users.

Multiple Database Partition Disadvantages

The considerable benefits of multiple database partitions must be offset against the disadvantages. These advantages and disadvantages have nothing to do with the pros and cons of SMP versus MPP hardware architectures. Here, we are talking about a software architecture that can be implemented on either SMP, MPP, or cluster systems.

The Data Shipping Problem   Interpartition parallelism is, in effect, a shared-nothing software architecture that can be implemented on an SMP or a shared-nothing hardware platform. The most severe problem with a shared-nothing architecture for databases is that joins will almost always require data shipping across partitions or nodes. This problem increases in direct proportion to the number of partitions or nodes. It also increases with the number of tables involved in a join. On an SMP with logical partitions, the problem is somewhat improved compared to an MPP or cluster because internode communication takes place through shared memory rather than across a network, drastically reducing latency and improving throughput. However, data shipping is still necessary. With intrapartition parallelism (parallelism within a single database partition), data shipping is completely eliminated.

The optimizer will do its best to choose an execution plan that minimizes data shipping. How great a problem it will be depends on a number of factors:

- **The locality of rows in the join.**

    For a two-table join, the best-case scenario is when all rows to be joined for each table are resident in the same partition. This is referred to as a colocated join (also discussed in "Massively Parallel Processor (MPP) Systems" on page 32). In that case, no data shipping is required. While it may be possible to avoid data shipping for some queries, in practice data cannot be split so as to avoid data shipping for all queries.

    For example, consider three tables partitioned across four logical nodes: a customer table partitioned with the customer_id column, an order table partitioned with the order_id column, and an order_line table also partitioned with the order_id column. A join between the order and order_line tables based on the order_id column will be colocated. Since that column was used as the basis for data splitting, all the rows from both tables that need to be joined will already be located in the same partition.

A join between the `customer` and `order` tables, though, based on the `customer_id` column from both tables, will require data shipping. The `customer` table rows were split according to the `customer_id` column, but the `order` table was split according to the `order_id` column.

Once data shipping becomes necessary, the additional overhead will be directly related to the other factors listed below.

- **The number of nodes involved.**

  In the preceding example involving four nodes, the `customer` table and `order` table join will require approximately three-fourths of one of the tables to be shipped to other nodes. Let's explore the join in more detail to find out why.

  Suppose the optimizer chooses to scan the `order` table locally. Once the `order` table rows in logical node 0 have been scanned, the `customer_ids` in those rows can identify the rows required from the `customer` table to complete the join. Assuming the customer table rows are evenly distributed between the nodes, on average one-fourth of the required rows will already be in node 0, one-fourth will be located in node 1, and so on. So three-fourths of the required rows will have to be shipped, one-fourth from each of the other three nodes. The same process will be repeated in nodes 1, 2, and 3.

  With eight nodes, seven-eighths of the required `customer` table rows will need to be shipped. With 16 nodes, fifteen-sixteenths will need to be shipped. So the problem increases with the number of nodes.

- **The number of tables involved.**

  The more tables that are involved in a non-colocated join, the more data that will need to be shipped.

- **The number of rows to be shipped after predicates have been applied and any aggregation has been carried out locally.**

  Predicates will be applied in the node where the rows are located, to eliminate as many as possible before shipping. For example, suppose a query includes the following predicate:

  ```
  where customer_balance > credit_limit
  ```

  Any rows that do not match this criterion will not be joined anyway, and so do not need to be shipped.

In some cases, data shipping can be eliminated with replicated tables. DB2 allows tables to be replicated on each database partition, and since a replicated table is present in its entirety, all table joins involving that table will be colocated. Small dimension tables in a DSS environment are good candidates for replication. Recent versions of DB2 allow replicated tables to be updated from any database partition.

Other Disadvantages   Other disadvantages of multiple database partitions are listed below.

- Data reorganization can be more complex than with a single partition,
  especially if resplitting is required.

- Adding additional CPUs necessitates adding additional partitions and
  requires redistributing nodegroups.

- It is impossible to restrict the number of partitions (and hence the CPU
  resource, for example) involved in a query with Enterprise-Extended
  Edition, since all partitions with affected tablespaces will automatically
  be involved in the query. By contrast, the DFT_DEGREE configuration
  parameter can be used to limit the CPU resource committed to a query
  in the intrapartition case (Enterprise Edition).

Partitioning and the Optimizer

The DB2 UDB query optimizer knows how many database partitions will be
involved in a particular query and chooses a plan accordingly. DB2 Enterprise Edition, which supports multiple CPUs in a single partition, determines a serial explain plan and then parallelizes it afterwards depending on
the setting of DFT_DEGREE (and MAX_QUERYDEGREE at the instance level). It
inserts a single table queue (the final synchronization point for all subagents
participating in the query) into the new plan as late as possible because no
further parallelism takes place beyond it. DB2 has efficient mechanisms for
making sure that the work is shared evenly among subagents and therefore
the available CPUs, but the optimizer may not be able to parallelize some
phases of a query as effectively as others.

By contrast, an explain plan for DB2 EEE, running with single-CPU partitions, often looks more complicated. The optimizer takes into account all participating database partitions, and it is common to see more than one table
queue. Since the parallelism in DB2 UDB EEE had its roots in DB2 Parallel
Edition (the original MPP version of DB2), the optimizer is mature and well
proven in its handling of partitioned data. Query parallelism is an integral
part of the explain plan rather than applied post hoc to a serial plan. As for
DB2 EE, not all phases of a plan may execute with equal efficiency.

Finally, DB2 UDB EEE V5.2 combined the two approaches by supporting
multiple partitions, each with multiple CPUs. In this case, an EEE explain
plan is chosen on the basis of the database partitions, with intrapartition parallelism applied to the final plan by the optimizer in a post-processing phase.

Summary

Choice is usually regarded as a good thing. Nonetheless, the alternatives
available to the DB2 user implementing a data warehouse may seem complex and confusing. The good news is that while an MPP hardware solution
effectively dictates the use of DB2 UDB Enterprise-Extended Edition functionality, a large Sun SMP server is an excellent foundation for all the avail-

able choices. That means if you decide to change direction, you won't need to change your hardware platform.

Choosing a Page Size

DB2 UDB versions prior to V5.2 supported only a single page size (4 Kbytes), but as of Version 5.2, 8-Kbyte and 16-Kbyte page sizes are also available. As of DB2 UDB Version 6.1, 32-Kbyte page sizes are supported as well.

The key issue for DSS workloads is retrieving data efficiently during queries. Large I/O sizes are necessary to ensure adequate read performance. In the case of DB2 UDB, the read size is determined by the database page size multiplied by the extent size for the tablespace in question. Consequently, large reads can be achieved by an appropriate combination of the extent size and the page size, making the choice of page size less important for performance.

The significance of the page size, however, is in the maximum table and tablespace size per logical database partition. With 4-Kbyte pages, tables and tablespaces have a maximum size of 64 Gbytes. With 8-Kbyte pages, the maximum increases to 128 Gbytes, and with 32-Kbyte pages to 512 Gbytes. The larger sizes allow greater flexibility in choosing the number of logical database partitions.

Tuning I/O

Tablespace layout and the role of prefetchers are the key issues in achieving well-tuned I/O with DSS workloads. In this section we examine these factors as well as the influence of pagecleaners and log file layout.

Laying Out Tablespaces

DB2 data is stored in tablespaces, made up of multiple containers (which can be raw devices or UFS files). Each table lives in one and only one tablespace, although its indexes can live in a different tablespace. One of the benefits of DB2 is that data is automatically striped across all available containers in a tablespace. The width of the stripe is determined by the extent size of the tablespace. An extent size of 32 will result in a stripe width of 128 Kbytes if 4-Kbyte DB2 data pages are used.

In general, it is good to have as many disks available as possible to minimize head contention and maximize the amount of data that can be accessed simultaneously.

Should you locate your data and index tablespaces on separate disks, or should you stripe them both across all available disks? As discussed in Chapter 17, it is wise to stripe tablespaces as widely as possible (taking into account the potential recovery time after a disk failure, though). One reason is that few users have an oversupply of disks, even if they have adequate disk space available. This results because high-capacity disks are cheaper per gigabyte than low-capacity disks. A second reason is that when a query does a table scan, you want all available disks working on the problem. The same is true for an index scan. DB2 executes queries in discrete phases: large-scale access to a table or index (such as a scan) will be completed before the next scan is started.

Configuring Prefetchers

One of the major challenges in dealing with vast amounts of data is getting it into the system quickly and efficiently when it is needed. When DB2 detects sequential access (the SEQDETECT parameter must be set to TRUE), processes called *prefetchers* are invoked to preload the next set of pages into the buffer-pool. The result is that the pages are available when the agents (or sub-agents) need them. Provided enough prefetchers have been configured, one prefetcher will be assigned per container, up to the maximum prefetch size defined for the tablespace. Each prefetcher will read in one extent. So, the size of prefetched I/O can be controlled by adjustments to the extent size of the tablespaces.

Configuring Pagecleaners

Decision Support applications tend to be read-mostly. Consequently, tuning the pagecleaners (described in "Tuning DB2 for Solaris for OLTP Workloads" on page 418) is less an issue than it is for OLTP applications. Idle pagecleaners are no big problem; they are only invoked as required and will not degrade performance while not in use.

Configuring Log Files

Log file usage for DSS applications takes place when updates are run. Consequently, the log files may receive little usage during peak query activity. Updates tend to be batch based and often involve multiple inserts or updates before a commit. Hence, logger performance is less important than for OLTP applications where the online transactions stall until the log records have been written. UFS-based log files may be an option for DSS workloads, given that they are simpler to configure than raw log files.

Configure enough primary log files (LOGPRIMARY) to ensure that you never run out of log space. You can monitor your log file usage with the Next active log file and First active log file values reported when you run db2 get database configuration for *dbname*. The difference between these two values will reveal the current number of active log files. Set LOGSECOND to a minimum of 2 (it is not significant for performance).

Log retain mode (described in "Log Files" on page 155) is enabled by the LOGRETAIN parameter set to ON; circular logging is used if this parameter is set to OFF. The size of log files is determined by the LOGFILSIZ parameter (the unit is 4-Kbyte pages). Log files can be created up to 256 Mbytes in size, so the maximum amount of log space available is determined by LOGFILSIZ * LOGPRIMARY.

As of DB2 UDB Version 7.2, dual logging is supported—log records can be written concurrently to two log devices, eliminating the need for mirroring at the hardware or operating system level. A new registry variable, DB2_NEWLOGPATH2, specifies the path of the second log device.

I/O Tuning Recommendations

Our experience suggests the following practices:

- Stripe your data and index tablespaces across all available disks. Keep your log files on separate disks, though, and consider placing your temporary tablespaces on separate disks as well.
- An extent size of 32 is usually a good choice for both DSS and OLTP applications.
- Set the prefetch size for a tablespace to the number of containers in the tablespace multiplied by the extent size for the tablespace. Use the following command to find the prefetch size for tablespaces:

  ```
  db2 "list tablespaces show detail"
  ```

  Container details can be shown with the following command:

  ```
  db2 "list tablespace containers for TABLESPACE_ID
    show detail"
  ```

- Use multiple containers for the temporary tablespace to improve the performance of sorts that overflow to disk. The DB2 list tablespace containers command in the preceding bullet can identify the temporary tablespace; the number of containers is one of the properties shown.
- Configure as many prefetchers as there are containers in your widest tablespace. This rule of thumb applies even if your widest tablespace has a large number of containers (200, for example).
- Configure one pagecleaner for every two CPUs.

Tuning Bufferpools

Parallel queries running under DB2 UDB do not seem as sensitive to the size of the bufferpools as for OLTP applications. A single bufferpool of a few hundred megabytes is usually more than adequate for most queries. Since the amount of data being processed is typically too great to cache in memory and since individual pages are rarely able to be reused, the buffer cache is mainly needed to ensure that enough free pages are available for the prefetchers.

Some experiments have suggested a small performance benefit from using a separate bufferpool for the temporary tablespace(s). A separate bufferpool can reduce disk I/O to the temporary tablespace. In this case, a good starting point is to configure a "temp" bufferpool half the size of the main bufferpool. You might be able to fully cache small indexes, too; a separate index bufferpool with the relevant tablespaces attached to it is worth considering.

The DB2 optimizer sums the total number of pages in all bufferpools when deciding on a query plan and divides it by the number of concurrent applications configured with the database configuration parameter AVG_APPLS. If you have configured a lot of memory and the explain plans do not seem optimal, try increasing AVG_APPLS. Sometimes the best plans are those based on a conservative setting of memory. But you will still have the benefit of the additional pages in the bufferpools when it comes to executing the query.

Tuning Parameters That Influence the Optimizer

The DB2 UDB optimizer uses sophisticated algorithms and takes many factors into account when choosing an explain plan. These include the cost of CPU cycles, the cost of disk access and throughput, the average number of active users, the available resources such as memory, the degree of parallelism, the number of database partitions, the specifics of the query, and the profile of the relevant columns in the tables it references.

The following tunable parameters influence the optimizer.

- **DFT_QUERYOPT:** The query optimization class (0 to 10, with higher being more highly optimized). Higher values mean that more time will be spent trying to find the best plan. A good starting point for DSS queries is 7.

- **BUFFPAGE:** The total amount of memory allocated to any bufferpool with size set to -1 (as described in "Managing Bufferpools" on page 405). The unit of BUFFPAGE is a page; the size of the page is specified for each bufferpool. So a bufferpool with a page size of 32 Kbytes will be allocated BUFFPAGE × 32 Kbytes of shared memory.

- **AVG_APPLS:** The average number of active applications connected to the database. This parameter is used by the optimizer to estimate how much bufferpool space will be available at run time for the application. Set the value to the average number of heavy query applications you expect to be executing concurrently.

- **CPUSPEED:** The speed of the CPU and, hence, the cost of CPU operations. This value is set automatically and should not be changed by the user. A setting of -1 will force DB2 to reevaluate the setting each time DB2 is started.

- **SORTHEAP:** The amount of memory (in 4-Kbyte pages) available for piped sorts. If sufficient memory is available, sorts will complete in memory; otherwise, the sorts will overflow to the temporary tablespace. When setting this parameter, remember that DB2 may need to perform multiple sorts at the same time. Check Piped sorts requested and Piped sorts accepted in the output from the db2 "get snapshot for database manager" command. If the number of piped (in-memory) sorts requested is significantly less than those accepted, consider increasing the size of SORTHEAP.

- **MAX_QUERYDEGREE:** An instance-level parameter that determines the maximum degree of parallelism for any query run against all databases in the instance, and **DFT_DEGREE**, a database-level parameter specifying the degree of parallelism available to execute a query. Either or both of these parameters can be set to ANY, in which case a setting based on the number of CPUs in the system is used. ANY is a good choice unless there is a reason to restrict the number of CPUs involved in queries. Typically, a setting of between 1 and 1.5 degrees of parallelism per CPU has proved optimal in our testing at Sun. Note that these parameters will not take effect unless the **INTRA_PARALLEL** parameter is set to YES (the default on systems with multiple CPUs).

- **LOCKLIST:** The amount of memory to set aside for the lock list, and **MAXLOCKS**, the maximum percentage of lock list before escalating. For more information about locking, see "Controlling Lock Activity" on page 424.

- **COMM_BANDWIDTH:** The bandwidth available for communication between logical database partitions. A good choice for an SMP system is 200 (Mbytes/sec).

Tuning Other Important Parameters

The following tunable parameters are also worth considering:

- **SHEAPTHRES:** Sort heap threshold, in 4-Kbyte pages. This parameter determines the maximum amount of memory that can be used for in-memory sorts.

  Sort heap threshold is not a hard limit, but if it is exceeded, the faster "pipe" sorts will not be performed. The threshold impacts the total amount of memory that can be allocated for all concurrent sort heaps. In general, the more sort heap threshold memory the better. Try setting it to five times the **SORTHEAP** parameter.

  When **INTRA_PARALLEL** is set to YES, meaning that parallel operations are allowed within a database partition, the sort heap threshold memory is allocated as part of the database shared memory. As a result, the threshold does become a hard limit in this environment.

- **CHNGPGS_THRESH:** The changed pages threshold. Try setting it to 30. This parameter is discussed in more detail below in the context of OLTP workload tuning, where it is more important.

- **DB2_FCM_NUM_BUFFERS:** The number of internal communication buffers used for internode communication, in 4 Kbyte pages. Try setting it to 1024 if you are using multiple logical database partitions. FCM is an abbreviation for *Fast Communication Manager*. Each logical database partition has an FCM daemon that coordinates interpartition data requests.

- **DB2_FCM_NUM_RQB:** The number of FCM request blocks. Try a value of 1024.

Tuning DB2 for Solaris for OLTP Workloads

OLTP workloads vary considerably, making it difficult to establish a set of tuning rules with general applicability. But there are guidelines that should apply to most situations.

Successful tuning requires careful planning in the initial stages. Laying out the data is very important. Never forget, too, that applications have more potential to cause poor performance than does DB2 tuning. Once the applications have been tuned and the explain plans for your SQL seem reasonable, DB2 tuning can give you a small but welcome performance boost.

Choosing a Page Size

As of DB2 UDB V6.1 a choice of page sizes is available (4, 8, 16, or 32 Kbytes). For OLTP applications, a small page size is usually a good choice. Since most database rows are relatively small, many rows will fit into the same page. Since I/O access is random and there is usually little benefit from data locality (access to rows physically located together), a large page size means a lot of data is being accessed for no additional benefit. Larger pages also mean fewer pages in the bufferpool and therefore lower cache hit rates if there is poor data locality.

Tuning I/O

Tablespace layout, the bufferpool, pagecleaners, and log file layout are the key factors in achieving well-tuned I/O with OLTP workloads. In this section we examine these and other issues.

Laying Out Tablespaces

DB2's ability to stripe data automatically across all available containers in a tablespace is a big help for performance when it comes to DB2 tablespace layout for DSS applications. The same is true for OLTP workloads, although the reason is different. Whereas for DSS queries the striped data allowed simultaneous access to large amounts of data by the prefetchers, for OLTP applications striped data means that many users simultaneously accessing small amounts of data will have their I/O spread across multiple disks, thereby evenly spreading the load.

In this case the importance of the tablespace extent size is not that it is the number of pages read at one time by the prefetchers, since they are used infrequently if at all. Rather, the extent size is important because it is also the stripe width of data within the tablespace. Too wide a stripe will mean that I/O to the disk will be less well balanced. Too small a stripe can be inefficient. An extent size of 32 (128 Kbytes with 4-Kbyte pages) is a good choice.

As with DSS applications, it is important to have as many disks available as possible to minimize head contention and maximize the amount of data that can be accessed simultaneously. And once again it is wise to stripe data and index tablespaces as widely as possible rather than to separate data and index tablespaces onto separate sets of disks. Temporary tablespaces can also be placed on the same disks—they are not required as often for OLTP queries (and possibly not at all if adequate sort memory has been allocated). Even if sorts overflow to disk, they are likely to involve a lot less data.

Configuring Prefetchers

The random nature of I/O with OLTP applications means that prefetchers are less likely to be needed. That does not mean that none should be configured, though. Prefetchers are also used for other purposes, such as roll-forward recovery, so there should always be some configured. The prefetchers are only activated as required, so they do not cause a performance drain when not in use.

Configuring Pagecleaners

Tuning the pagecleaners is an important issue for OLTP applications since pagecleaners impact both recovery time and performance. The trick is to avoid cleaning pages more frequently than necessary. If, for example, a page is dirtied again immediately after it has been flushed to disk by a pagecleaner, a write could have been saved by slightly delaying the flush operation.

The following parameters influence pagecleaner behavior.

- **NUM_IOCLEANERS:** The number of pagecleaners. Start with one for every two CPUs.

- **CHNGPGS_THRESH:** The changed pages threshold. This parameter represents a percentage of dirty pages in each bufferpool. When this threshold is reached, the pagecleaners will be activated for the bufferpool. For small bufferpools (a few thousand pages in size) that sustain a lot of write activity, this parameter should not be set too high (that is, no more than 30); otherwise, the pagecleaners will not keep up and agents will be forced to clean pages themselves. For larger bufferpools (tens or hundreds of thousands of pages in size), the parameter can be set much higher (up to 90). Unfortunately, the parameter is set per database, not per bufferpool, so a compromise setting may be necessary if you have a mixture of large and small bufferpools.

You can discover the number of times the pagecleaners were triggered as a result of the threshold being reached by running db2 "get snapshot for database on DBNAME" and looking for Dirty page threshold cleaner triggers.

- **SOFTMAX:** The percentage of the log file reclaimed before a soft checkpoint. This parameter determines the point at which pagecleaner behavior changes from flushing the least recently used (LRU) pages to flushing the oldest pages. The larger this setting, the better the performance (since pages are cached for longer before being flushed), and the longer the recovery time. For real-world applications, 20 to 30 is probably more appropriate than the typical benchmark setting of 90.

  The usage of this parameter has changed between DB2 Version 2 and DB2 UDB. In Version 2, it represented the percentage of the total primary log space available (that is, the sum of all log files defined in LOGPRIMARY). Suppose, for example, there are 10 primary log files and a soft checkpoint is wanted every time 2 log files are filled. For DB2 Version 2, the SOFTMAX setting would be 20. As of DB2 UDB, the same result would be achieved by setting SOFTMAX to 200, since SOFTMAX is now relative to a single log file, not the sum of all primary log files.

  The number of times the pagecleaners were triggered as a result of SOFTMAX being exceeded is reported as LSN Gap cleaner triggers in a database snapshot.

Although flushing of dirty pages is normally carried out by the pagecleaners, if an agent cannot find an available page in the bufferpool, it can flush a page itself rather than stall waiting for the pagecleaners. Page flushing by agents is not as efficient as flushing by the pagecleaners, so it should be avoided. Compare Buffer pool data writes (the total number of data pages flushed) with Asynchronous pool data page writes (the number of data pages flushed by the pagecleaners) and the index page equivalents, Buffer pool index writes and Asynchronous pool index page writes. If less than 95% of pages are being written asynchronously (that is, by the pagecleaners), then increase NUM_IOCLEANERS (the number of page cleaners). In general, the more writes done by the pagecleaners the better, although if pages are cleaned too vigorously, you may be unnecessarily flushing pages that will soon be dirtied again.

When an agent steals a dirty page because the pagecleaners are not keeping up with demand, the pagecleaners will be triggered. The number of times this event occurred is reported as Dirty Page Steal Cleaner Triggers in a database snapshot.

Avoiding Table Scans

You should not normally expect to see table scans with OLTP workloads unless substantial batch jobs are running concurrently with user applications. To check for table scan activity, run the following commands (after first making sure that the bufferpool and table monitor switches are turned on):

```
db2 "get snapshot for database on DBNAME" > /tmp/db.snap
db2 "get snapshot for tables on DBNAME" > /tmp/tbl.snap
```

Look in the /tmp/db.snap file for Commit statements attempted and Rollback statements attempted and add them together to derive the total number of transactions. Next, sum the Rows read for the user tables from /tmp/tbl.snap. Divide the total number of rows by the total transactions. If the result—the average number of rows read per transaction—is in the hundreds or thousands range, review the Rows read for each table to find out which table is most influencing the result. An appropriately constructed index could significantly reduce the number of rows read and improve performance as a result.

Monitoring Sorts

Sorts are used to complete SQL statements with order by, group by, or distinct clauses. An area of memory (SORTHEAP, in 4-Kbyte pages) is set aside for this purpose. The number of sorts can be monitored with the db2 "get snapshot for database on DBNAME" command. Look for Total sorts, the total number of sorts carried out. Look also for Sort overflows, the number of sorts that began as the faster pipe sorts but ran out of memory and overflowed to the temporary tablespace. If many of the sorts overflow, try increasing the SORTHEAP.

Configuring Log Files

Logger performance for OLTP applications is critical since online transactions must wait until the log records have been written before completing. Raw log files, while more complex to configure, offer significantly better performance than UFS-based log files. Place log files on separate disks, and make each log file as large as possible (65,535 pages of 4 Kbytes each, or 256 Mbytes).

Configure enough primary log files (LOGPRIMARY) to ensure that you never run out of log space. You can monitor your log file usage with the Next active log file and First active log file values reported when you run db2 get database configuration for *dbname*. The difference between these two values is the current number of active log files. Set LOGSECOND to a minimum of 2 (it is not significant for performance).

Transactions are written to the log buffer before being written to the log file. The size of this buffer is determined by the LOGBUFSZ parameter (the unit is 4-Kbyte pages).

The MINCOMMIT parameter can be significant to logger performance. The logger will wait until MINCOMMIT transactions are ready to be written to the log file (or until 1 second passes) before writing a log record. This grouping of commits reduces log I/O and improves logger efficiency, although at the cost of slight delays in completing transactions. Settings of 3 or 4 have proved effective in high transaction-throughput environments.

I/O Tuning Recommendations

Our experience suggests the following practices:

- Stripe your data, index, and temporary tablespaces across all available disks. Keep your log files on separate disks.
- An extent size of 32 is usually a good choice for OLTP applications.
- Configure one pagecleaner for every two CPUs.
- Set SOFTMAX to 20 to 30 for real-world applications.
- Set the changed page threshold to 30 if small bufferpools are in use and up to 90 if only very large bufferpools (or a single bufferpool) are in use.
- Configure a small number of prefetchers.

Tuning Bufferpools

Bufferpools are usually extremely important to OLTP performance, and generally the bigger the better. The more pages that can be cached, the less I/O that is required. This efficiency in turn means internal latches are held for shorter periods and contention is reduced. Faster transactions at lower CPU consumption are the end result. All this depends upon reuse of data, or data skew. Fortunately, most OLTP applications feature considerable data reuse (for example, companies may do 80% of their business with only 20% of their customers).

The simplest approach is to configure one large bufferpool. With Solaris 2.6, the largest DB2 UDB bufferpool is around 3.45 Gbytes in size, plenty for most OLTP databases. With Solaris 7 and later releases, up to 3.7 Gbytes can be configured, and 64-bit versions of DB2 UDB allow significantly larger bufferpools. Studies have suggested it is optimal to configure between 5% and 15% of the database size as memory for the bufferpools (see "Sizing the Buffer Cache" on page 81 for more detail).

There can be benefits to using multiple bufferpools, and as of DB2 UDB, each tablespace can be assigned its own bufferpool, as described in "Managing Bufferpools" on page 405). Where data is not reused, there is little point in assigning a lot of memory for caching purposes. Such tables could be assigned to a small bufferpool. Note that some memory is still required to ensure that agents are able to find clean buffers; usually, a few thousand pages are adequate for the purpose.

Where data is reused, the more buffers the better. Small tables or indexes may be able to be cached completely, thereby limiting table I/O to the flushing of dirty pages. For large tables, it may not be practical to fully cache the table data, although full caching of indexes can prove easier to achieve and more useful. Some experimentation will be necessary to achieve the best results. The DB2 Snapshot Monitor can report cache details by bufferpool, enabling you to monitor the efficiency of each bufferpool.

The size of a bufferpool is determined by its specified size or by the BUFF-SIZE parameter for all bufferpools with size set to -1. Refer to the BUFFSIZE discussion in "Tuning Parameters That Influence the Optimizer" on page 416 for more information.

General Tuning Tips

Some tuning issues are relevant to workloads generally. Some of the most important of these are discussed below.

Balancing Tablespace Activity

In Chapter 21 we discussed ways of monitoring disk activity with Solaris tools. It can be useful, though, to monitor the I/O activity for each DB2 tablespace to assist in data layout. DB2 provides a command to monitor tablespace activity:

```
db2 "get snapshot for tablespaces on dbname"
```

The output from this command shows the number of physical reads and writes as well as the bufferpool activity for each tablespace.

If the database configuration "index sort flag" parameter (INDEXSORT) is set to YES, then index creation will require sort activity. This is advisable for performance reasons. The sort will be carried out in the temporary tablespace. For best performance, ensure that the temporary tablespace uses multiple containers to allow disk reads and writes to be striped. Use the following command to find out the number of containers for the temporary tablespace:

```
db2 "list tablespaces show detail"
```

The entry for the temporary tablespace will look something like this:

```
Tablespace ID                     = 1
 Name                             = TEMPSPACE1
 Type                             = System managed space
 Contents                         = System Temporary data
 State                            = 0x0000
    Detailed explanation:
       Normal
 Total pages                      = 1
 Useable pages                    = 1
 Used pages                       = 1
 Free pages                       = Not applicable
 High water mark (pages)          = Not applicable
 Page size (bytes)                = 4096
 Extent size (pages)              = 32
 Prefetch size (pages)            = 32
 Number of containers             = 1
```

In this case, the number of containers could usefully be increased, and the prefetch size set to the number of containers multiplied by the extent size.

Controlling Lock Activity

Lock activity is controlled by a number of database configuration parameters. The deadlock detector checks deadlocks at an interval (measured in milliseconds) determined by the DLCHKTIME parameter. A long deadlock checking interval means checks are carried out less frequently, and therefore less system time is consumed in the process. But it also results in longer delays for deadlocked applications before the deadlocks are resolved. To see how many deadlocks were detected, execute db2 "get snapshot for database on *dbname*" and look for Deadlocks detected.

The lock timeout interval (measured in seconds) can also be set with the LOCKTIMEOUT database configuration parameter. A LOCKTIMEOUT setting of -1 means lock timeout detection is turned off—not usually a good idea, especially for OLTP applications. The database snapshot returns the number of timeouts: look for Lock timeouts.

The interval for deadlock checking should be less than the lock timeout interval. Deadlocks can then be eliminated before locks that might otherwise be successfully set are rolled back.

DB2 uses an area of memory to store the list of locks. The size of this memory area is determined by the LOCKLIST database configuration parameter (measured in 4-Kbyte pages). If the lock list is too small, DB2 is forced to escalate locks to table locks. You can monitor the amount of lock list memory by looking at Lock list memory in use (Bytes), returned by a database snapshot. If more than half the lock list is in use (remember that LOCKLIST is expressed in 4-Kbyte pages, though, not bytes), increase the size of LOCKLIST.

To avoid an application consuming an excessive proportion of the lock list, DB2 provides a database configuration parameter called MAXLOCKS. This parameter defines a percentage of the lock list that must be filled by a connected process before DB2 performs lock escalation. Monitor the number of lock escalations by using a database snapshot (look for Lock escalations).

A database snapshot will also reveal other useful information, including Locks held currently and Agents currently waiting on locks. To calculate the average time (in milliseconds) spent waiting per lock, divide Time database waited on locks (ms) by Lock waits.

Configuring Agent Processes

Each user connection results in an agent process being forked to handle database access. The total number of agents that can connect to all databases for an instance can be controlled by the MAXAGENTS database configuration parameters. A second parameter, MAXCAGENTS, limits the total number of agents that can concurrently execute a database transaction. The default setting for MAXCAGENTS is -1, which sets the total number the same as MAXAGENTS. If the number of concurrent agents is set too low, users may be unable to execute their queries. In this case, an agent will be forced to wait for a token before it can continue. When one becomes available, the agent can complete its work. The database manager snapshot reveals the status of user connections: look for High Water Mark for Agents Registered (the peak number of concurrently active agents) and High Water Mark for Agents Waiting for a Token (the peak number of agents stalled because MAXCAGENTS was set too low). If agents have been forced to wait for a token, increase MAXCAGENTS.

After all user connections are terminated, a pool of idle agents will be retained to speed up new connections. This number is determined by the NUM_POOLAGENTS database manager configuration parameter. Note that before DB2 UDB Version 6.1, only local clients could use idle agents; from Version 6.1, both local and remote clients can share idle agents. You can also speed up first-time connections when the database is started by establishing an initial number of pool agents (set by the NUM_INITAGENTS parameter).

Limiting Open Files

DB2 allows you to set a database configuration limit, MAXFILOP, on the number of open files (tablespace containers). Each agent needs to open all tablespace containers associated with the tables accessed by the agent. If the open files limit is not set high enough, other containers will have to be closed to allow your agent to proceed. If the containers closed were active, others will then need to be closed before the agents can resume. The result can be a loss of performance.

The database snapshot will show Database files closed, the number of containers that needed to be closed due to a shortage of available file descriptors. The ideal result is zero—if it is greater than zero, increase MAXFILOP.

26

METRICS: HOW TO MEASURE AND WHAT TO REPORT

If you decide to monitor or benchmark your applications, one of the crucial decisions you must make is which metrics to calculate and report. Some benchmarks are designed solely to test application functionality, in which case the metric may be related to success or failure of the test. If the benchmark is testing performance, useful metrics are more likely to be related to transaction throughput, response time, and resource utilization.

Similar decisions must be taken when the objective is to monitor and profile live application behavior. Unfortunately, many users do not monitor their business transactions. Nevertheless, before server systems can be sized in a meaningful way, it is essential to understand application transaction throughput and response time characteristics.

Common Performance Metrics

Some useful metrics can be derived from data made available by the operating system. For a complete picture, some data will also need to be collected from applications. Both types of metrics are discussed below.

System Metrics

The most commonly reported system metrics are CPU utilization, disk input/output operations (I/Os) per second (IOPS), disk throughput, and network IOPS.

CPU utilization is the sum of user and system CPU percentage. For servers with multiple CPUs, the CPU utilization is the average of the percentages for each of the individual CPUs. Some tools, such as `sar`, report `%wio`, that is, the percentage of time spent waiting for I/O. Waiting for I/O should be treated as idle; user and system percentages are sufficient for an accurate picture of CPU utilization.

Disk I/Os are the total number of read and write operations per second. I/Os are usually reported per disk (or per LUN on a RAID array), so the total number of IOPS is calculated as the sum of those reported on each disk.

Disk throughput, usually reported in Mbytes/sec or Kbytes/sec, indicates the volume of disk I/O being processed. Along with disk IOPS, disk throughput gives an understanding of the size of disk transfers.

This data can be captured with standard Solaris tools such as `sar`, `vmstat`, and `iostat`.

Database system metrics such as the database cache hit rate and lock statistics should be calculated and stored for an understanding of workload behavior and for possible later reference.

Application Metrics

Application performance can be usefully monitored with some or all of the following measures:

- **Transaction throughput.** This is a measure of the rate at which transactions are processed and is typically expressed in terms of transactions per minute (tpm) or transactions per second (tps). Longer running transactions may be more usefully reported in transactions per hour (tph).

  The term *transaction* generally refers to the processing of a unit of work, but it can have a number of different meanings. *Business transactions* refer to events that achieve some business purpose such as recording a sales order, carrying out a stock inquiry, or printing an invoice. *Database transactions* typically refer to the database operations that occur between an SQL `begin transaction` statement and a `commit` or `rollback` statement. A single business transaction can carry out a number of database transactions. Lower-level transactions might involve interactions with the disk or system interconnect.

  Each of these transaction types can be usefully measured. When reporting transaction throughput, though, the business transaction rate is the most common choice since it is significant and well understood.

  Table 26-1 shows the transaction rate for a sample workload with four types of transactions each minute, in total and on average per minute.

Table 26-1 *Throughput for sample workload*

Time	Customer Orders	Inquiries	Purchase Orders	Payments
11:52:52	12	5	4	2
11:53:52	4	1	0	1
11:54:52	3	1	0	0
11:55:52	3	0	0	0
11:56:52	15	6	6	3
Total	**37**	**13**	**10**	**6**
Per Minute	**7.4**	**2.6**	**2.0**	**1.2**

- **Response time.** Time spent waiting for the system to complete an action is referred to as the *response time*. Response times are usually associated with Online Transaction Processing (OLTP) applications. For any given business transaction there may be more than one point at which response times could be measured. For example, when a customer sales order is entered, there may be a delay between the user entering the customer number and the system returning the customer's name and address, and further delays between the user entering each item code and the system responding with the item description. The total of these delays in completing one transaction provides the transaction response time as a whole.

  For batch jobs and for long-running queries, such as those typical of data warehouse systems, the response time is the completion time for the task.

The time taken to process an interactive transaction involves more than just the response time: keystroke delay and think time must also be included. *Keystroke delay* takes into account the speed at which users type; no one types infinitely fast. *Think time* represents natural delays while a user pauses to think, sip coffee, or refer to documentation. Both types of delay must be simulated in a benchmark, and both must be clearly understood before accurate system sizing is possible. Keystroke delays and user think time are not usually relevant for batch jobs and long-running queries.

Application Instrumentation

Discussing transaction throughput and response time is academic if they are not being collected. Some third-party applications do capture transaction statistics and make them available to end users. If you are using applications developed internally, you might be able to arrange for the application code to be modified to report basic throughput and response time information.

To simplify the reporting process, a working group associated with the Computer Measurement Group has established a set of libraries, called

Application Response Measurement (ARM), that is freely available on all major platforms and operating environments.

The ARM API enables applications to provide information to measure business transactions from an end-user perspective and the contributing components of response time in distributed applications. The information can be used to support service level agreements and to analyze response time across distributed systems.

To download the no-cost Software Developers Kit (SDK) or for more information, refer to http://www.cmg.org/arm.

In the absence of any way of measuring business transaction throughput, a crude alternative is to use the number of database commits and rollbacks; all the major databases provide monitoring tools that report this information. A breakdown like the one shown in Table 26-1 will not be possible, but commits and rollbacks at least provide a concrete indication of application activity.

System and Application Metrics Combined

The availability of both system and application metrics allows calculation of CPU cost per transaction and I/O operations per transaction. These metrics offer a means of making high-level assessments of the benefits or otherwise of changes made to applications or the operating system, assist in preparing server sizing estimates, and generally contribute to the understanding of application behavior. CPU and I/O cost per transaction are discussed in detail below, with worked examples.

- **Input/output operations per transaction.** Determining the transaction throughput, or the number of transactions processed during a given time interval, is the first step toward a sizing model for an application. The next step is to calculate the system resources needed to complete a transaction. Unfortunately, it is not easy to do that with any precision. Although it is not difficult to determine the CPU consumption and number of disk and network input/output (I/O) operations across the entire system, there may be no easy way of breaking down resource utilization into consumption for each type of transaction.

    Disk input/output operations (I/Os) can be calculated with the `iostat` or `sar` tools. If the number of transactions completed during the same period is known, the average number of I/Os per transaction can be calculated.

    For example, consider the disk throughput associated with the transaction throughput shown in Table 26-1. Figure 26.1 shows the disk I/O over the same period, collected with `sar -d 60 5`.

Figure 26.1 *Disk I/O for sample workload*

```
SunOS alameda 5.8 Generic_108528-01 sun4u     10/09/00

11:51:52   device     %busy   avque   r+w/s  blks/s  avwait  avserv

11:52:52   md10         0     0.0       0       0     0.0     0.0
           ssd8         2     0.0      10     153     0.0     2.5
           ssd15        2     0.0       7     118     0.0     3.1
           ssd173      13     0.1      10     165     0.0    13.1
           ssd180      10     0.1       9     146     0.0    10.5

11:53:52   md10         0     0.0       0       0     0.0     0.0
           ssd8        15     0.2      12     235     0.0    14.2
           ssd15        8     0.1      11     168     0.0     7.9
           ssd173      13     0.1      12     190     0.0    11.4
           ssd180      15     0.2      14     241     0.0    12.4

11:54:52   md10         0     0.0       0       0     0.0     0.0
           ssd8        10     0.1      10     158     0.0    10.8
           ssd15       14     0.2      13     203     0.0    12.4
           ssd173      11     0.1      10     160     0.0    12.0
           ssd180      11     0.1      11     182     0.0    10.9

11:55:52   md10         0     0.0       0       0     0.0     0.0
           ssd8        10     0.1       9     148     0.0    10.9
           ssd15        9     0.1      11     167     0.0     9.5
           ssd173       7     0.1       6     123     0.0    12.0
           ssd180      11     0.1      10     161     0.0    11.4

11:56:52   md10         0     0.0       0       0     0.0     0.0
           ssd8         3     0.0       7     108     0.0     4.1
           ssd15        3     0.0       8     125     0.0     4.0
           ssd173      11     0.1       9     143     0.0    12.4
           ssd180      10     0.1      10     159     0.0    11.1


Average    md10         0     0.0       0       0     0.0     0.0
           ssd8         8     0.1      10     160     0.0     9.1
           ssd15        7     0.1      10     156     0.0     8.1
           ssd173      11     0.1      10     156     0.0    12.2
           ssd180      11     0.1      11     178     0.0    11.3
```

The total number of disk I/Os over the five-minute period can be determined by summing the I/Os in the r+w/s column, which shows the
number of read I/Os plus the number of write I/Os, and multiplying by
60 since the results are per second, not per minute. The result is
$119 \times 60 = 11940$ I/Os in total over the five-minute period.

Since the total number of transactions is 66 (from Figure 26.1), we can
determine that, on average, 180 I/Os are required per transaction.

- **I/O throughput per transaction.** The disk throughput can be calculated by summing the contents of the `blks/s` column of Figure 26.1, which shows the number of 512-byte blocks transfered per second, and multiplying once again by 60. The result is 99,932,160 bytes, or 95.3 Mbytes. So the average transaction requires 95.3 ÷ 66 = 1.4 Mbytes of disk throughput.

- **CPU cost per transaction.** Like I/Os per transaction, the average CPU cost per transaction can be calculated if CPU utilization and transaction throughput are both known for a given period.

  Figure 26.2 shows the CPU utilization for the transaction load shown in Table 26-1, collected with `sar 60 5`.

Figure 26.2   *CPU utilization for sample workload*

```
    SunOS alameda 5.8 Generic_108528-01 sun4u      10/09/00

    11:51:52    %usr    %sys    %wio    %idle
    11:52:52     27      21      47       5
    11:53:52      2       7      69      22
    11:54:52      1       8      69      22
    11:55:52      0       8      71      21
    11:56:52     37      27      36       1

    Average      13      14      58      14
```

On average over the five minutes, the CPU utilization was 13% user and 14% system, for a total of 27% utilization (`%wio` and `%idle` can be ignored since both represent idle CPU). If four 900 MHz CPUs were used, then 3600 million cycles were available. Only 27% of them, or 972 million cycles, were actually used. So, the 66 transactions consumed an average of 14.7 million cycles each.

The preceding methods are useful ways of calculating the I/O and CPU cost per transaction, although a one-hour duration would probably prove more useful than the five minutes used in this example. The benefit of averaging over a long period is to lessen the likelihood that unusual behavior at any particular moment will skew the result.

An alternative method of determining the I/O and CPU cost per transaction is to use a snapshot and base the calculation on the results at that moment in time. The snapshot could be used to profile the peak load, for example. The transaction throughput at 11:56:52 could be used along with the CPU and I/O stats for the same interval, rather than the totals over five minutes.

Choosing Statistics

Data is typically presented in one or more of the following representations. Choose among the statistical types for the measurement most relevant to your purpose:

- **Mean.** The most commonly used means are the arithmetic mean and the geometric mean.

  The *arithmetic mean*, better known as the *average*, is calculated as the sum of the values divided by the number of values. The arithmetic mean of a sample $\{x_1,x_2,...,x_n\}$ of n observations, can be expressed as follows:

  $$\bar{x} = \frac{1}{n} \sum_{i=1}^{n} x_i$$

  An arithmetic mean is appropriate for handling multiple values of the same kind, such as repeated measurements of the response time for a stock inquiry.

  The *geometric mean* is calculated as the nth root of the product of the values. For a sample $\{x_1,x_2,...,x_n\}$ of n observations, the equation can be expressed as:

  $$\dot{x} = \left(\prod_{i=1}^{n} x_i \right)^{\frac{1}{n}}$$

  A geometric mean is often used to prepare a single result that represents values of different types. It would not be appropriate, for example, to calculate an average response time by using an arithmetic mean for a 2.3-second stock inquiry, a 5.1-second journal entry, and a 72.5-second backorder query, because response times for different transaction types are not comparable.

  To illustrate the point, consider the measurements in Table 26-2.

Table 26-2 *Response times for two tests*

	Test 1	Test 2	Change
Stock Inquiry	2.3	2.0	*−13%*
Journal Entry	5.1	4.1	*−20%*
Backorder Query	72.5	72.5	*0%*
Average	*26.6*	*26.2*	*−2%*
Geometric Mean	*9.47*	*8.41*	*−11%*

The results for Test 2 show a noticeable improvement in the Stock Inquiry and Journal Entry response times and no change in the Backorder Query response time compared to Test 1. The average is not meaningful, since the response times within each test are unrelated. The average is almost unchanged because the long Backorder Query response times dominate at the expense of the other values. By contrast, the geometric mean better reflects the improvement in two of the three response times.

The *harmonic mean* is used to summarize performance for data values expressed as rates. It can be defined as follows:

$$h = \frac{n}{\sum\limits_{i=1}^{n} \left(\frac{1}{x_i} \right)}$$

A common example is based on speeds. If you drive one mile at 60 miles per hour (m.p.h.) and a second mile at 20 m.p.h., how fast were you driving on average? The obvious answer—40 m.p.h.—is incorrect. At 60 m.p.h., the first mile would have been completed in one minute; the second mile, at 20 m.p.h., would have been completed in three minutes. So the two miles took a total of four minutes, or on average, two minutes per mile. So the average speed is actually 30 m.p.h.

The harmonic mean will correctly calculate this result:

$$h = \frac{2}{\left(\frac{1}{60} + \frac{1}{20} \right)} = 30$$

To pick a more relevant example, harmonic means can be used to summarize transaction rates. Suppose 1,000 transactions must be processed by two different batch applications in turn. If the first application completes transactions at a rate of 500 transactions per minute (tpm), and the second at the rate of 100 tpm, what is the average transaction processing rate?

The first application will take 2 minutes to complete and the second will take 10 minutes. Since the two applications take a total of 12 minutes, the average transaction rate can be calculated as follows:

Rate = $(500 \times 2/12) + (100 \times 10/12)$ = 166.67 tpm

The harmonic mean equation can more easily determine the average transaction rate:

h = $2 \div (1/500 + 1/100)$ = 166.67 tpm

- **Minimum and maximum.** The largest and smallest values give an indication of the range of values.

- **Standard deviation and the coefficient of variation.** The *standard deviation* is a measure of the degree to which values differ from each other. If values are all similar, the standard deviation will be low; if values vary wildly, the standard deviation will be high. The standard deviation of a sample $\{x_1, x_2, ..., x_n\}$ of n observations can be expressed as:

$$s = \sqrt{\frac{1}{n-1} \sum_{i=1}^{n} \langle x_i - \bar{x} \rangle^2}$$

Unfortunately, it is difficult to compare standard deviations across different groups of values. For example, the standard deviation for the range of numbers "10, 11, 12, 13" is 1.29, whereas the standard deviation for "100, 110, 120, 130" is 12.91. The means are 11.5 and 115, respectively. Although the degree of variation within each group of numbers is exactly the same, the standard deviation is influenced by the size of the raw values.

The *coefficient of variation* offers a metric that compares the degree of variation without influence from the size of the values. The coefficient of variation can be calculated by dividing the standard deviation by the mean, thereby normalizing the result. For both of the ranges of numbers shown above, the coefficient of variation is 0.11.

- **Percentiles.** The *nth* percentile measures the value that is greater than or equal to *n*% of all values in the sample. For example, a 90th percentile of 127 means that 90% of values are less than or equal to 127. The 90th percentile can be determined by sorting the sample values in ascending order, then selecting the value 90% of the way through the list.

Percentiles offer an insight into how values are distributed. For example, if the 90th percentile score of a mathematics test is 12 out of a possible 20, it means that only 10% of students achieved better than 12; most students taking the test performed poorly. For another test, a 10th percentile score of 13 out of 20 would indicate a better result, since 90% of students achieved a score better than 13.

- **Graphs.** Although the mean, the coefficient of variation, and the percentiles can provide useful data on the scale, the range, and the degree of variation of the values, none of these metrics offer any indication of trends. For example, suppose the following three sets of data are values captured at one-minute intervals. All three groups of values have the same mean, standard deviation, coefficient of variation, and percentiles:

        Group 1: "9, 8, 7, 6, 5, 4, 3, 2"
        Group 2: "2, 9, 3, 8, 4, 7, 5, 6"
        Group 3: "3, 2, 4, 7, 8, 9, 6, 5"

Figure 26.3 shows these three sets of values plotted against time.

Figure 26.3   *Using graphs to highlight trends in data sequences*

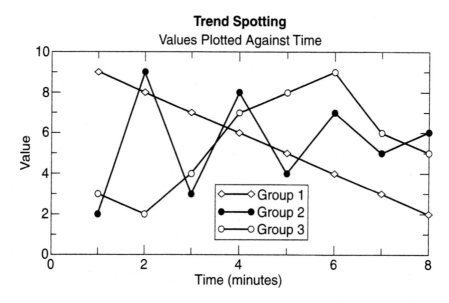

A simple list of numbers may fail to highlight trends that become obvious when the numbers are presented as a graph. The Group 1 trend in Figure 26.3 is obvious from both the list of numbers and the graph, but the Group 2 results are most clearly highlighted in the graph.

Other metrics can also be used, but in most situations those discussed above will prove adequate.

Scalability Demystified

Scalability refers to the server's behavior either as more work is added or as more resource is added, either separately or together. As system resource is increased, if the amount of workload that can be processed increases at the same rate, then the scalability is said to be *linear*. For example, if twice as many transactions can be completed by a doubling of the number of CPUs, then processing of transactions has scaled linearly.

Some workloads scale better than others; for example, data warehouse queries often scale almost linearly since there is little contention between processes. Some OLTP workloads may show poorer scalability characteristics.

Another way of achieving excellent scalability is to host multiple workloads on the same system. Provided the workloads do not interfere with each other, additional work can be processed efficiently as hardware resource is added.

Sun has invested considerable effort into improving the scalability of the Solaris Operating Environment and in working with software partners to improve the scalability of their products in the Solaris Operating Environment. This has led to many world-record benchmark results over a number of years on Sun's high-end platforms, such as the Enterprise 10000 (Starfire) server.

Whether the aim is to support a bigger workload or to process an existing workload faster, it seems logical that the goal could be achieved with more CPUs or faster CPUs. For example, the following propositions seem plausible:

- If a server with four fully utilized CPUs is capable of processing 2,000 transactions per minute, then a server with eight CPUs will be able to process 4,000 transactions per minute (linear scalability).

- If a fully utilized server can support 50 users processing 100 transactions per minute, then the same server supporting 100 active users should still be able to process 100 transactions per minute, even though response times would have doubled (also linear scalability).

It might also seem plausible that:

- A response time of two seconds on a four-CPU system will be reduced to one second on an eight-CPU system running the same workload. This logic might work up to a point, but eventually it will be like saying that if 50,000 workers can build a pyramid in two years, then 18 million workers could build it in two days.

- The completion time for a batch job can be halved by being run on a two-CPU server. If the batch job is single-threaded, only one CPU will be active. One balloonist might be able to circle the world in 80 days, but that doesn't mean that 80 balloonists, all launching from the same starting point, can do it in 1 day.

Reality has a nasty habit of intruding on the ideal world at times, unfortunately. As the pyramid workers would discover, some things just don't scale beyond a certain point. And once you've reached that point, throwing more resources at the problem can sometimes actually make things worse.

It is important to understand the scalability of your server and your application if you plan to increase the workload. If scalability is not linear, there are always reasons, and understanding the reasons can help lead to improvements. Scalability can suffer in these situations:

- A hardware resource becomes a bottleneck, preventing further increases in throughput or reductions in response time. For example, if a disk becomes fully utilized, it can prevent further increases in throughput.

- Competition for software resources (locks, mutexes, or latches) increases to the point where CPU time is wasted waiting for a lock to become available. Lock contention can be a relevant issue with database applications. More users will mean more contention, thereby compounding the problem.

- The number of user processes increases to the point where the overheads of interprocess communication and time spent in scheduling the processes interfere with carrying out useful work.

The best way to learn about the scalability of a workload is to gradually increase the load until the CPUs become saturated or some other bottleneck is encountered. Throughput may continue to increase linearly, it may continue to increase but at a diminishing rate, or it may reach a point beyond which it begins to fall.

Figure 26.4 illustrates three nonlinear workload scalability models.

Figure 26.4   *Nonlinear workload scalability models*

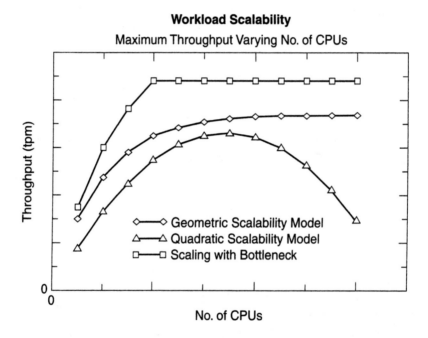

In each case shown in Figure 26.4, the number of users (and therefore the workload) has been increased at the same rate as the number of CPUs. The following three scenarios are shown:

- **The Geometric Scalability Model.** Throughput scales well initially but the rate of increase diminishes gradually until a peak value is approached. Contention for shared resources (such as locks) can lead to this kind of tail-off in throughput. Some OLTP workloads behave in this manner.

- **The Quadratic Scalability Model.** Throughput increases to a maximum and thereafter degrades. This model can reflect contention among processes that increase exponentially as the number of processes increases, resulting in a drop in the amount of real work carried out. The Quadratic Scalability model is useful for identifying the optimal number of CPUs for a workload.

- **A scaling model with a bottleneck.** Scalability is constrained at a particular point and never exceeded. This behavior might be observed when a disk becomes fully utilized, for example.

You can often improve scalability by identifying and eliminating the bottleneck or by finding ways of reducing interprocess contention.

Lies, Damn Lies, and Statistics

Statistics can lend an aura of scientific credibility to any sizing or benchmarking exercise. But don't be fooled by your own statistics. The line between credibility and the appearance of credibility can be exceedingly fine.

I'm not immune from being fooled, either—I have more than once wished I had paid more attention during Statistics 101! For that reason, before drawing conclusions from statistics, I try especially hard to understand the following factors:

- **The raw data used to calculate the metrics, how the metrics have been calculated, and what they mean.** Do low average response times signify satisfied users, for example? Maybe not, if response times are averaged across both quiet periods with low response times and busy periods where response times climb to unacceptable levels.

- **Whether *all* the relevant facts have been presented.** Application changes that lead to spectacular improvements in throughput, for example, may look less impressive if CPU requirements have climbed exponentially in the process. In particular, *when monitoring throughput or response times, always report CPU costs per transaction as well.*

- **The validity of any causal connections presented.** Suppose it could be shown that the fluctuation in the tonnage of oranges imported into the United Kingdom from Australia over a five-year period closely matched the changes in the infant mortality rate in Canada during the same period. Few people would try to argue a causal link (that is, a cause and effect relationship) between the two statistics.

  But suppose it could be shown that as application load increased, both disk response times and transaction response times increased. It might seem logical to conclude that the transaction response times are a result of the disks becoming overloaded, in which case adding more disks should improve transaction performance. If the disk response times had increased because the backplane bus was saturated, though, adding more disks would not help at all. The root cause in this case would be a third factor, and no causal connection would actually exist between disk load and transaction response times.

  I remember some years ago a PC dealer asserting confidently that an Ethernet segment could be saturated by a single 486 PC. He was embarrassed when a colleague demonstrated that his monitoring tool was actually measuring the capacity of the PC's network driver, not the capacity of the Ethernet.

Politicians and lobbyists are past masters at manipulating statistics for their own purposes, to the point where many people treat their statistical pronouncements with scepticism at best. But honest mistakes with statistics can be just as damaging as cynical manipulation of the facts, so it is always wise to ask questions before blindly accepting conclusions based on statistics.

When the Same Thing Isn't

Things are not always as they appear. Remember the "spot the differences" pictures we pored over in our childhood? It's hard enough finding the discrepancies when you know they're there; it becomes infinitely harder if you believe two pictures are the same.

Comparison of Methods

There are times when it appears that the right metrics are in use and the right data has been captured, but still there is a problem. This happened a few years ago in our group when a number of us compared notes on our scalability measurements. We had been finding the maximum OLTP throughput with various numbers of CPUs on the same hardware platform and the same Solaris release but using different RDBMS products. In each case we first established the maximum throughput with all CPUs turned on, then we turned off some CPUs and located the new maximum throughput, turned off more CPUs, and repeated the exercise down to a single CPU. The end result was a scalability curve from one CPU to the maximum number of CPUs for the hardware platform.

The comparisons were not at all what we expected. After investigation we discovered that although we appeared to be doing exactly the same thing, in fact each team had used a different method, leading to very different scalability results. The methods actually used by various teams are listed below:

- Team 1: As the number of CPUs was reduced, the amount of memory used for the database cache was left unchanged. Larger caches mean less physical disk I/O, reduced CPU costs per transaction, and higher throughput. For smaller numbers of CPUs, the cache size was large relative to the throughput, leading to higher throughput at the low end and apparently poor scalability as the number of CPUs increased.

- Team 2: As the number of CPUs was reduced, the database cache size was reduced in the same proportion. Consequently, throughput was lower for small numbers of CPUs, but scalability was better.

- Team 3: To eliminate any variation in the effect of the database cache, the cache size was modified experimentally at each measurement level to ensure that the number of physical disk I/Os per transaction was exactly the same for all measurements. Once again the result was relatively low throughput at low numbers of CPUs, but good scalability.

On reflection, my opinion is that Team 3 used the best method, although each approach certainly had its merits. The point, though, is that our results could not be directly compared. The lesson for all of us was to assume nothing and ask lots of questions.

Interval Discrepancies

Another trap for the unwary is making assumptions about the sampling interval used in collecting data. The longer the sampling intervals, the more certain that any peaks and troughs in throughput and utilization will be smoothed out. CPU utilization at 30-minute intervals, for example, will probably look very different from utilization at 30-second intervals. The finer-grained measurements may show brief but sustained utilization peaks not visible at the longer interval.

In selecting an interval, you must strike a balance between too much detail and too little detail. The right choice depends on the environment. As a rough rule of thumb, five seconds is a reasonable lower limit for a collection interval. At the other end of the scale, be very careful before basing conclusions on data collected at intervals longer than five minutes.

Data Collection and Presentation Discrepancies

A final pitfall is collecting data at one interval and then presenting it at another. I have seen CPU utilization data collected at 5-second intervals fed into a statistical package that plotted a 24-hour utilization graph. The results showed CPU utilization consistently higher than I had observed on the system. Upon further inquiry, it emerged that the graph did not have sufficient resolution to show each data point, so multiple data points had been combined for each plotted point.

How do you combine multiple CPU utilization data points? Take the average? The person preparing the graph had decided to plot the maximum! So if 10 data points averaged a utilization of 60% but one value peaked at 80%, that was the value plotted as representative of the entire interval. The result was an inflated view of system utilization.

It is better to synchronize collection and presentation intervals if at all possible. If that proves impossible, understand clearly the implications of the choices that must be made in presenting the data.

A Complete Picture

One of the key challenges in presenting data is to ensure that sufficient detail is shown to allow meaningful interpretation of the results. Consider, for example, the throughput for three tests graphed in Figure 26.5.

Figure 26.5   *Three test results: A partial picture*

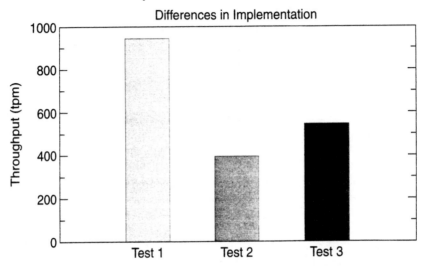

Repeated Tests on the Same Platform

Differences in Implementation

The graph shows the results of running the same test three times on the same platform, but with differences in the way the test was implemented. It would seem reasonable to conclude that whatever changed in the implementation resulted in significantly greater efficiency for Test 1, allowing throughput double that of the other tests. Not enough information is presented, however, to draw any firm conclusions about the reasons for such a big difference. For example, was the CPU consumption the same across all tests, or was the CPU cost per transaction for Test 1 half that of the other tests, allowing twice as many transactions to be processed?

The graph in Figure 26.6 helps answer the question.

Figure 26.6   *Three test results: The complete picture*

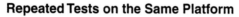

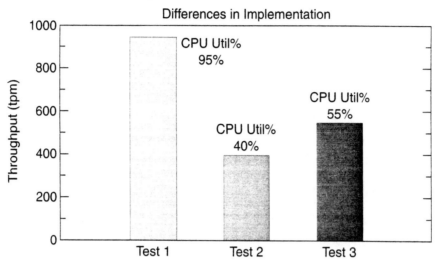

The graph is no different, but now additional information has been added: the CPU utilization for each test. It is immediately obvious that the CPU utilization is directly related to the throughput, so the CPU cost per transaction should be the same in each case. We still don't know why the different implementations gave rise to such different results, but it is likely that bottlenecks of some kind have prevented Test 2 and Test 3 from fully utilizing the CPUs and therefore achieving a higher throughput.

Make sure you supply all the information necessary and sufficient to understand and interpret the results you have invested so much effort to collect.

A Clear Picture

One final issue on data presentation: sometimes all the necessary information is presented, but in such a way that the implications are hard to understand. For example, consider the data in Table 26-3.

Table 26-3   *Confusing test results*

	Test 1	Test 2	Test 3
Throughput (tpm)	123,200	143,530	134,535
CPU Utilization %	68%	77%	70%

The data is both accurate and complete, but it is hard to precisely compare each test, since both the throughput and CPU utilization vary in each case. Normalizing the results in some way would greatly contribute to the readability of the results. For example, suppose eight 900 MHz CPUs have been used for the tests. In that case 7,200,000 thousand (or 7,200 million) CPU cycles are available. If the CPU cost per transaction, in thousands (K) of cycles, is shown, subtle differences between the runs become clear. Table 26-4 gives the complete picture, with the CPU cost per transaction included.

Table 26-4 *Test results clarified*

	Test 1	Test 2	Test 3
Throughput (tpm)	123,200	143,530	134,535
CPU Utilization %	68%	77%	70%
CPU Consumed (Kcycles)	4,896,000	5,544,000	5,040,000
CPU Cost Per Transaction (Kcycles/transaction)	39.74	38.63	37.46
Difference in CPU Cost/tx Relative to Test 1	0%	−2.8%	−5.7%

The CPU cost per transaction shows that, although Test 2 delivered the highest throughput, Test 3 was the most efficient in terms of CPU cost per transaction. The final row in the table quantifies the difference by presenting the percentage difference in the CPU cost per transaction relative to Test 1.

Conclusion and Recommendations

The value of carrying out performance measurements is greatly compromised unless the method, the choice of metrics, and the presentation of the data are all carefully planned in advance.

In particular, the method of measurement should only be selected after communication with other interested parties, the metrics to be used should be both comprehensive and comprehensible, and the data presentation should include enough detail to allow accurate and meaningful conclusions to be drawn.

When carrying out a series of tests, consider the following recommendations:

- Automate the capture and calculation of key statistics and metrics by using scripts. Automation will help prevent key data from being forgotten.

- Present enough information to allow meaningful conclusions and to discourage inaccurate inferences. Check that the presentation of information is simple and accessible enough that junior staff can make sense of it.

- Archive enough data to allow later interpretation or reinterpretation. Sometimes is it useful to be able to go back to previous test results and reevaluate them in the light of new information. That option is only possible if all necessary information has been saved.

Part Five

Other Topics

- Benchmarking
- Java, Middleware, and Databases

27

BENCHMARKING

The term *benchmark* refers to the practice of running a test on a known configuration, using a known workload, and monitoring the result. Sometimes the objective is to determine the maximum throughput the configuration is capable of or to determine the response times of specific operations. At other times the objective is simply to find out whether the hardware/software combination is able to execute the workload through to completion without failing. Benchmark performance is sometimes less interesting than system functionality and robustness.

A benchmark workload is usually one of the following types:

- **An emulation**, which aims to replicate a real environment. The goal is to copy a real workload and make it perform in the same way as a live version of the workload. The emulation is usually achieved with a software tool that mimics the behavior of end users. The data used in the emulation is likely to be a snapshot of live data.

- **A simulation**, which approximates a real workload. Simulated workloads are modeled on real workloads and share similar characteristics and behavior, although they are usually smaller and simpler. Simulations typically rely upon a small number of representative transactions rather than attempting to model every possible transaction. Data could be synthetically generated or could be based on a snapshot (possibly a subset) of live data.

A performance benchmark is most useful if it is based on real applications, real data, and real end-user behavior. Benchmarks are usually of limited value unless they can be clearly positioned relative to the target environment.

447

On one occasion a customer called to ask if I had an Oracle benchmark he could use to compare different hardware platforms. I asked what kind of benchmark and he replied "Oh, any benchmark will do." When I asked him how the proposed benchmark related to his own environment, it quickly became clear he had only a vague idea that a database benchmark was the appropriate way to do a hardware comparison. Even if I could have provided a benchmark, its value would have been questionable. Unfortunately, useful benchmarks rarely come gift-wrapped.

Later in the chapter we explore the issues involved in developing your own benchmark, but first we look at the major industry-standard database benchmarks—TPC-C, TPC-H, and the more recent TPC-W—and their relevance to real-world environments.

Industry-Standard Database Benchmarks

The best-known industry-standard database benchmarks are those developed by the Transaction Processing Performance Council, a nonprofit corporation established to define transaction processing and database benchmarks and to provide objective, verifiable performance data to the industry.

Founded in 1988 by eight companies, the TPC has grown to about 30 members, including Sun. During the last 10 years the TPC has defined and released six database benchmarks, of which four, TPC-C, an OLTP benchmark, TPC-H and TPC-R, DSS benchmarks, and TPC-W, a web-based benchmark, are still current. TPC-H and TPC-R are successors to TPC-D; they replaced it in April 1999. TPC-W, released in 2000, tests middleware such as web servers as well as the database.

TPC benchmarks are by no means the only industry-standard database benchmarks in common use. Other de facto standard benchmark suites include those created and promoted by SAP, Baan, Peoplesoft, Oracle, and others. Generally, such benchmarks are intended to test the application environment as a whole, not just databases.

Usefulness of Database Benchmarks

Database benchmarks serve a number of valuable purposes:

- **Stress testing RDBMS products and the servers and operating systems on which they are implemented.** Stress testing is sometimes used to ensure that hardware and software components work together. Testing of this type is called *integration testing*. The test environment can also be invaluable in comparing both the functionality and performance of new releases of software or hardware with that of previous releases. This activity is known as *regression testing*. Benchmarks can also help identify and resolve system bottlenecks that negatively impact performance.

- **Testing applications that use databases.** Wise customers benchmark their own applications with their own data before putting new applications into production. Database benchmarks, whether synthetic or based on real applications and data, are usually carried out with some form of remote terminal, PC, or browser emulator.

- **Comparing the relative performance of different databases, hardware platforms, and operating systems.** Competitive performance benchmarking has significant marketing potential. Consequently, companies often go to extreme lengths to position themselves favorably against their competition.

The excesses resulting from aggressive database benchmarking without agreed-on standards led to the formation of the TPC (Transaction Processing Performance Council). By creating and maintaining benchmarks and using a process involving broad industry participation and support, the TPC has succeeded in restraining many of the worst marketing abuses of database benchmarks. The TPC still has its flaws, but TPC benchmarks have become the de facto standard for database benchmarks.

Whether benchmarks are run by users or database companies, it is easy to draw false conclusions from the results, though. The only way to avoid wrong conclusions is to understand thoroughly the nature of the benchmark and the results it produces.

It is also important to have a good reason to embark on an often costly and painful benchmark process of your own. Benchmarks are only useful if they shed light on a real-world environment or problem.

Introduction to TPC-C

The TPC-C workload simulates a simple OLTP environment: multiple online terminal sessions in a warehouse-based distribution operation. It contains a mixture of read-only and update-intensive transactions based on a nonuniform data distribution while enforcing transaction (ACID) properties. Table 27-1 shows the five TPC-C transactions executed against nine tables.

Table 27-1 *TPC-C V3 transactions*

Transactions	Weight	Profile	Percentage Mix	90th Percentile Response
New-Order	Midweight	Read/write	< 45%	5 secs
Payment	Lightweight	Read/write	Min. 43%	5 secs
Order-Status	Midweight	Read-only	Min. 4%	5 secs
Stock-Level	Heavyweight	Read-only	Min. 4%	20 secs
Delivery	Heavyweight	Read/write	Min. 4%	80 secs

Of the nine tables, all except one (the Item table) scale with the number of warehouses. Table 27-2 shows the TPC-C tables and scaling rules.

Table 27-2 *TPC-C V3 tables*

Table Name	Cardinality
Warehouse	1 row per warehouse
District	10 rows per warehouse
Item	100k rows
Stock	100k rows per warehouse
Customer	30k rows per warehouse
Order	30k+ rows per warehouse
New-order	9k+ rows per warehouse
Order-line	300k+ rows per warehouse
History	30k+ rows per warehouse

The user population also scales with the number of warehouses—10 user sessions must be established per warehouse. Thus, the workload as well as the database size can be increased by scaling up the number of warehouses, allowing a broad range of servers to be tested. The TPC-C metrics include Throughput (new-order transactions per minute, or tpmC), Price/Performance (price per TPC-C throughput, or $/tpmC), and Availability Date, the date on which the tested system will be available for public purchase.

Benefits of TPC-C

TPC-C and slightly simplified variants are widely used within Sun Engineering and throughout the industry for performance and regression testing, as well as for published benchmarks. TPC-C is attractive for the following reasons:

- Although relatively simple, it is a challenging workload.
- It puts a load on all major system components, including the system bus, I/O subsystem, and network.
- It scales well, so very small and very large systems can be tested.
- It is stable, popular, and widely accepted.

Limitations of TPC-C

TPC-C is not representative of most user environments, so it is difficult to use published TPC-C results for sizing and configuring real-world OLTP systems. Some of the reasons include the following:

- The TPC transactions are limited in number and predictable in behavior, allowing implementers to exploit TPC transaction peculiarities. Real-world transactions are much more diverse.

- Since TPC transactions are much lighter in weight than most real-world OLTP transactions, the workload compensates by generating an unrealistically large number of transactions. The implications affect all database subsystems, and especially the logger and the pagecleaners (Database Writers).

- Much important system information is not disclosed (for example, CPU utilization, disk utilization and service times, and database metrics such as buffer cache hit rate).

- TP monitors are used to drastically reduce the number of user connections on the database server. TPC-C user multiplexing through a TP monitor can reduce database server connections by almost 100 times. TP monitors are not used for user multiplexing by most UNIX sites.

- TPC-C applications do not use forms software. Instead, they use simple block-mode screens, vastly reducing network traffic and database read accesses in contrast to forms software. For example, the New-Order transaction includes an average of 10 order lines as well as customer details. All of this data is keyed without validation and then sent to the server as a single block for processing. Most applications would dynamically validate the customer ID and each stock ID as they are keyed.

- TPC-C implementations typically use stored procedures for all transactions, reducing network traffic and database overhead. Few customers are able to implement all their SQL through stored procedures.

- Throughput is uniform; most real-world OLTP workloads are bursty.

- No user sessions are started or ended during the measurement interval. Most user environments incur the ongoing startup and shutdown costs associated with users logging in and out.

- There is no substantial batch component to the workload. Many real-world applications involve heavy-duty batch jobs or reports that can run for hours.

- Some of the biggest TPC-C results have been run on clustered systems. Many real-world workloads cannot be partitioned as easily as can TPC-C and therefore will not scale as well on clusters. Starting in 2000, some vendors went beyond clustering; some of the largest results used systems loosely networked together, in what has been termed "federated" database environments. Arbitrarily large results are now possible provided a vendor is willing to configure enough hardware, so the usefulness of the TPC-C benchmark is undermined.

- TPC-C implementations are highly optimized because the workload is so well known, much more so than user workloads.

- The database buffer cache benefits from data skew with TPC-C; if a user's data is uniform or skewed differently, that user may not attain the same benefits. The ratio of cache size to database size may also differ between TPC-C and user environments.

- Many recent TPC-C results use multiple caches that are carefully configured to achieve optimal results. Users may not be able to do as well with their own workloads.

Other things to be aware of:

- Reported throughput is based only on the new-order transaction, which is less than 45% of the full throughput. So, the total throughput is roughly double the quoted transactions per minute.

- TPC-C recoverability and availability requirements are unrealistically generous. Real-world workloads would be more likely to require RAID 5 or mirroring for data disk high availability and more frequent checkpoints.

- TPC-C databases and results have become so big they have moved beyond the realm of all but a handful of real users. Some published results have exceeded 500,000 transactions per hour, corresponding to roughly two transactions for every U.S. resident in an eight-hour day! This is not typical of warehouse-based distribution operations, to say the least.

Introduction to TPC-D, TPC-R, and TPC-H

The decision-support benchmark—TPC-D—originally released by the TPC has been superseded by two new benchmarks: TPC-H and TPC-R. Since the new benchmarks have their roots in TPC-D, all three are worth discussing.

TPC-D

The TPC-D V1 workload simulated a decision-support environment, specifically, a warehouse-based distribution operation. It comprised 17 complex queries and small-scale business data updates (inserts and deletes).

A TPC-D benchmark consisted of a timed database load, a power run, and a throughput run. The power run was a sequence comprising the first update function (data insertion), the 17 queries, and the second update function (data deletion). The throughput run comprised a vendor-selectable number of concurrent streams applied serially; each stream consisted of the 17 queries executed in a different predefined sequence plus an extra stream with one pair of update functions for each query stream.

TPC-D V1 allowed the benchmark sponsor to dispense with the throughput run and to calculate the TPC-D throughput metric from the power run. TPC-D V2, however, mandated a small number of streams, increasing with database scale.

TPC-D queries included minor ad hoc elements, encompassed various access patterns, and examined a large percentage of available data. Most queries necessitated sorted result sets (order by, group by), many involved aggregation and range predicates, and several included correlated subqueries. All but two of the queries required joins involving two to seven tables.

Performance, at least in theory, depended on the degree of data selectivity, query plan strategy, query parallelism available, and the appropriate use of indexes. All TPC-D data tables, except the Region and Nation tables, scaled according to a scale factor of 1, 10, 30, 100, 300, 1000, 3000, or 10000. Table 27-3 shows the TPC-D tables and scaling rules.

Table 27-3 *TPC-D tables*

Table Name	Cardinality
Region	5 rows
Nation	25 rows
Supplier	10k * scale factor rows
Customer	150k * scale factor rows
Part	200k * scale factor rows
Partsupp	800k * scale factor rows
Order	1500k * scale factor rows
Lineitem	6000k * scale factor rows

Scale factors correspond to the size of the raw data in gigabytes; so, a scale factor of 100 means a 100-Gbyte database. The database size does not include the space required for indexes, temporary tablespaces, and availability options such as mirroring or RAID 5.

TPC-D V1 included metrics for the following: Power, which was the inverse of the geometric mean of the 17 queries, and two update functions scaled according to the scale factor (QppD@xxGB); Throughput, a function of the number of streams, the elapsed time for the throughput and update streams, and the scale factor (QtdD@xxGB); and Price/Performance, based on the configuration cost and the geometric mean of the power and throughput metrics ($/QphD@xxGB).

The Power metric, being a geometric mean, was sensitive to a change in any query or update function. The Throughput metric was more like an arithmetic mean. Most published results show a strong correlation between these two metrics.

TPC-D V2 combined the power and throughput metrics into a single metric, Composite Query-Per-Hour Performance (QphD@xxGB), which was the geometric mean of the two.

TPC-D V2 came into operation in February 1999. It also dropped 1 query and added 6 more, for a total of 22 queries. No V2 test results were ever published.

Benefits of TPC-D

TPC-D was initially popular for database performance engineering work as well as for benchmarks, although its popularity declined as it became less and less relevant and useful. The original reasons for its popularity were these:

- Like TPC-C, it placed a heavy load on all major system components.

- It was much easier to implement than TPC-C.

- Hardware and database vendors used it to learn a lot about solving real-world DSS problems.

- TPC-D forbade the use of optimizer hints. As a result, database optimizers have been forced to become smarter, rather than relying on a clever database administrator to decide on the right query plan.

- While TPC-D did not scale perfectly, it scaled well enough to remain interesting over a wide range of different database sizes.

Limitations of TPC-D

TPC-D always had its limitations:

- It did not address all aspects of DSS. For example, the TPC-D data model did not include star schema.

- Although TPC-D included minor ad hoc elements, the queries were basically static.

The same limitations apply also to TPC-H and TPC-R.

The fact that TPC-D was not an ad hoc benchmark (in other words, the queries were known in advance) led to the gradual erosion of the credibility and value of TPC-D. The 17 queries became so well known and understood that elaborate strategies were devised by database vendors to defeat them. These strategies, discussed in more detail in "Reducing the Workload" on page 98, included:

- Join indexes, which construct index keys by using columns from more than one table, thereby eliminating the joins altogether at run time.

- Range partitioning, which vastly reduces the volume of data to scan for queries with range predicates.

- Concatenated indexes, which include column data that is not part of the index key, to avoid any access to the base table.
- Materialized views, which are internal database objects known to the database optimizer that permanently hold the result set from specific queries or views. The result is that a query can be satisfied by a simple table lookup rather than by execution of the query.

Each of these technologies is potentially useful to a user who knows queries in advance and executes them repeatedly. However, with the exception of range partitioning, they are mostly useless for ad hoc queries. In effect, TPC-D became an OLAP benchmark.

The impact of these results is shown in Figure 27.1, which shows Sun's 1000GB Starfire Oracle results from April 1998 to March 1999.

Figure 27.1 *Sun's TPCD V1 results from April 1998 to March 1999*

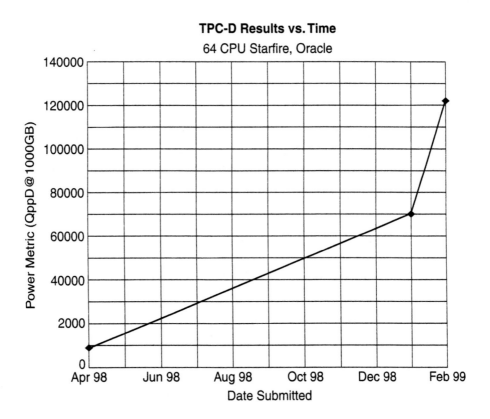

Over an 11-month period the Starfire power metric increased by no less than 1,373%! The first result used 336 MHz CPUs with Oracle8 8.0.4, and the last two results used 400 MHz CPUs with Oracle8i 8.1.5. All three results used Solaris 2.6.

The astonishing exponential improvement shown in the figure was not due to hardware improvements. Instead, it can be almost totally accounted for by the materialized-views technology introduced by Oracle, along with an intimate understanding of the TPC-D queries. IBM DB2 and NCR Teradata, using similar technology, achieved equally spectacular improvements.

The TPC realized that the credibility of TPC-D and of the organization itself was significantly compromised as a result. In response, the TPC decided in April 1999 to bifurcate TPC-D into two new benchmarks: TPC-R and TPC-H.

TPC-R

TPC-R continues the trend of TPC-D. All the tricks, including join indexes, concatenated indexes, and materialized views, are allowed.

TPC-R can be regarded as representing a DSS "Reporting" environment where queries are well known and frequently executed and where shortcuts are, therefore, welcome. It allows database vendors to continue the development and demonstration of exotic software technologies like those that emerged in the later years of TPC-D. These technologies may well find some use in end-user environments although they will probably never become mainstream in real-world appeal. Not surprisingly, most vendors have since ignored TPC-R.

TPC-H

TPC-H returns to the original spirit and intent of TPC-D. Join indexes, concatenated indexes, and materialized views are banned, leaving a much more ad hoc environment where queries have to be executed by more primitive and expensive operations such as table scans, index scans, and hash joins.

TPC-H is closer to many real-world ad hoc query environments. Because the queries are known in advance, though, it is not truly ad hoc. Consequently, database companies are most motivated to achieve good performance for 22 queries.

TPC-H, since it prohibits the creation of special database objects based on prior knowledge of the queries, is so far avoiding the special technologies that rendered TPC-D irrelevant. It is to be hoped it will not become debased in the same way as TPC-D.

Can published TPC results be used for system sizing? This issue is discussed in "Using Published TPC Results for Sizing" on page 184.

Introduction to TPC-W

In 2000, the TPC introduced a new benchmark, TPC-W. TPC-W sets out to simulate the performance and price performance of systems in transactional web environments such as electronic commerce, business-to-business, and intranet. It includes database access to data for generation of dynamic web pages, a secure user interface, and external secure transactions for payment authorization. Three types of web sites are represented: shopping, browsing, and business-to-business. The shopping site supports searching, browsing, and buying functions, the browsing site includes browsing and searching transactions, and the business-to-business site primarily carries out secure purchasing functions.

A bookstore storefront, similar in concept to www.amazon.com, was chosen as the model for TPC-W. The customer, using a web browser, starts at the store home page and carries out product searches, selecting some items for more detailed information. Items are added to a shopping cart for purchase, with personal and payment information supplied through a secure connection.

Three transaction mixes are used:

- Primarily browsing

- Typical shopping

- Primarily ordering or business to business

In total, 14 transactions, referred to as web interactions, are defined. The primary metrics are the shopping mix Web Interactions Per Second (WIPS) and a price performance metric defined as Dollars/WIPS ($/WIPS). Web interactions are subject to response time requirements (the Web Interaction Response Time, or WIRT). Web Interactions Per Second completed during the Browsing Interval (WIPSb) and Web Interactions Per Second completed during the Ordering Interval (WIPSo) are secondary metrics.

The mix of web interactions is shown in Table 27-4.

Table 27-4 *TPC-W web interactions*

Web Interaction	Browsing Mix (WIPSb)	Shopping Mix (WIPS)	Ordering Mix (WIPSo)
Browse	*95%*	*80%*	*50%*
Home	29.00%	16.00%	9.12%
New Products	11.00%	5.00%	0.46%
Best Sellers	11.00%	5.00%	0.46%
Product Detail	21.00%	17.00%	12.35%
Search Request	12.00%	20.00%	14.53%
Search Results	11.00%	17.00%	13.08%
Order	*5%*	*20%*	*50%*
Shopping Cart	2.00%	11.60%	13.53%
Cust. Registration	0.82%	3.00%	12.86%
Buy Request	0.75%	2.60%	12.73%
Buy Confirm	0.69%	1.20%	10.18%

Table 27-4 *TPC-W web interactions (Continued)*

Web Interaction	Browsing Mix (WIPSb)	Shopping Mix (WIPS)	Ordering Mix (WIPSo)
Order Inquiry	0.30%	0.75%	0.25%
Order Display	0.25%	0.66%	0.22%
Admin Request	0.10%	0.10%	0.12%
Admin Confirm	0.09%	0.09%	0.11%

Most web interactions must have a 90th percentile WIRT of either 3 or 5 seconds, except for the Admin Confirm web interaction (20 seconds) and the Search Results web interaction (10 seconds).

The TPC-W tables and scaling rules are shown in Table 27-5.

Table 27-5 *TPC-W tables*

Table Name	Cardinality (in rows)	Typical Table Size
Customer	2880 * no. EBs	2,188,888 Kbytes
Country	92	5.44 Kbytes
Address	2 * Customer	887,040 Kbytes
Orders	9 * Customer	570,240 Kbytes
Order_line	3 * Orders	1,026,432 Kbytes
Author	25 * Item	1,575 Kbytes
Cc_xacts	1 * Orders	207,360 Kbytes
Item	1, 10, 100 Kbytes, 1, 10 Mbytes	8,600 Kbytes

Unlike scaling in TPC-C, scaling in TPC-W takes place in two dimensions. The number of items controls the size of the inventory, and the number of emulated browsers (EBs) controls the size of the customer population. The number of items can vary between 1,000 and 10,000,000. The number of emulated browsers must be increased as the throughput increases, to ensure that the number of WIPS falls between one-seventh and one-fourteenth of the number of emulated browsers.

TPC-W improves on TPC-C and TPC-H/TPC-R by requiring system utilization to be reported in addition to throughput. In particular, the following must be reported:

- CPU utilization, including a graph covering the measurement interval.

- Page/swap activity.

- Database I/O activity (logical and physical reads and writes).

- Total system I/O rate, including network I/O, reported as single averages across the measurement interval.

- Average I/O rates and service times for each disk device.

- Web server statistics, including connections per second, HTTP requests per second, HTTP errors per second, bytes per second, and successful returns per second.

As for TPC-C and TPC-D, the benefits and limitations of TPC-W will become clearer over time as benchmark results are published and vendors discover its peculiarities.

TPC Results in a Competitive Environment

The information presented above should help you better understand any marketing claims made by other vendors about their own TPC results.

When using TPC results, vendors are responsible to ensure that they do not violate the TPC's fair use policy. That means:

- Never quoting estimated TPC results except under a Non-Disclosure Agreement.

- Quoting *all* primary metrics when putting a TPC result into writing (including proposals, presentations, external web pages). For example, TPC-C results should never be published showing only tpmC; $/tpmC and availability dates must also be disclosed.

- Comparisons of the TPC results of different vendors cannot be used unless all the results are current and have not been withdrawn or superseded by a better result on similar hardware. Go to http://www.tpc.org/ for a full list of current results.

In December 1998, one vendor formally quoted TPC-C and TPC-D estimates at a Gartner Group conference. These estimates were later used by Gartner and Merrill Lynch in reports. Sun and other vendors were represented at the conference, and a challenge was brought to the TPC. The vendor was found to be in major violation, fined, and later required to send retractions to analysts and competitors.

Sun and other vendors spend millions of dollars producing and publishing TPC benchmarks. Any irresponsible person with access to PowerPoint can produce an impressive estimate for free. Such unreasonable practices do no service to anyone in the industry.

It is also worth noting that TPC prices are not subject to audit, and vendors have at times resorted to "creative" pricing practices. Although TPC prices are supposed to represent typical street pricing, discounts exceeding 50% have been used for published results. This abuse had not been dealt with by the TPC at the time of this writing.

Running Your Own Benchmark

Industry-standard benchmarks rarely provide an adequate approximation to real-world environments because of differences in applications, data, and implementation. As a result, users often choose to develop and run their own benchmarks, in spite of the investment cost.

Reasons for Running a Benchmark

Among the many reasons for running your own benchmark are the following:

- To compare competing hardware platforms.
- To compare competing software products.
- To tune applications and environments and to identify and deal with bottlenecks independently of a production environment.
- To plan for change by determining in advance system utilization for new applications or environments.

If you decide to run your own benchmark, make sure you clearly document in advance why you are doing it. That statement might sound so obvious it's insulting, but, as I said in the introduction to this chapter, sound reasoning doesn't always happen.

Sometimes people start out with clear objectives and simply get distracted. For example, consider a competitive benchmark where the users have indicated they need a system capable of completing their batch workload within two hours. Vendor A completes the workload in 90 minutes and Vendor B in 75 minutes. After more tweaking, Vendor A manages to finish in 72 minutes. Not to be outdone, Vendor B calls in some gurus and reduces the time to 68.5 minutes.

In such competitive environments I have seen users eagerly follow each new attempt at reducing the completion time, having completely lost sight of the fact that either system will comfortably meet their business requirements. The goal posts have moved without any clearly stated rationale.

Factors That Make a Benchmark Meaningful

A benchmark will be meaningful if it is:

- **Relevant.** The benchmark should be appropriate for the environment under consideration. Ideally, that means the user's own applications, data, and workload profiles form the basis of the benchmark.
- **Scalable.** In other words, the load on the system can be increased in a meaningful way. Often, the number of users and the data volumes are increased to see how the system responds.

- **Understandable.** Both the benchmark and the derived results should be clearly understandable; otherwise, it will be difficult to draw meaningful conclusions. Sometimes it is useful to simplify the workload to avoid unnecessary complexity. For example, a few representative transactions can be chosen rather than the full range of live transactions.

- **Repeatable.** If the same benchmark when run twice does not yield roughly the same result, there is a problem with the benchmark. Possible solutions include restoring the database or removing data entered during the benchmark run, thereby returning the system to its original state.

- **Portable.** If the benchmark is to be run on multiple hardware or software platforms, it must be designed to be portable. Portability ensures that any differences in the benchmark on different platforms are not significant to the end result.

Parameters to be Measured

The decision about what is to be measured depends on the nature of the benchmark. Transaction response time or query or workload completion time might be the key issue. Alternatively, the objective might be to see how much work a system can process before predefined response or completion times are exceeded. This subject is discussed in more detail in Chapter 26, "Metrics: How to Measure and What to Report."

Useful metrics include the following:

- **Transaction throughput**. The throughput may be transactions per minute (for example, for OLTP workloads), queries completed per hour, or batch jobs completed in a nominated period of time.

  This metric may not be as simple as it sounds, though. If one class of transactions completes in around one second and another class in ten minutes, it isn't terribly meaningful to simply add together the total number of transactions completed during the benchmark run or to average the throughputs of each transaction type.

  TPC-C addresses this problem by locking down the transaction mix (the required percentage of each type of transaction) and reporting the transaction throughput for only one type of transaction (the new-order transaction).

  Another way of deriving a single metric from unlike values (for example, the average throughput per minute for each of several different transactions) is to use a geometric mean (the nth root of the product of n values). Be careful with geometric means, though. They have some strange characteristics, and if you don't understand them, you will find you don't understand your primary metric!

- **CPU quanta per transaction.** Using throughput as the primary metric can bring traps for the unwary. When comparing results on different systems, make sure think time or system bottlenecks do not constrain the throughput. Put another way, account for system utilization as well as the throughput.

  For example, suppose you run a test on a system with 8 CPUs and achieve 10,000 transactions per minute. You then run the same test on the same system with 16 CPUs and achieve only 11,000 transactions per minute. The obvious conclusion—that the system does not scale—may be quite incorrect. Suppose the CPU utilization for the 8-CPU test was measured at 100%, whereas the CPU utilization for the 16-CPU test was only 55%.

  One way of comparing the two results is to calculate CPU utilization per transaction. Suppose the CPU clock speed is 900 MHz. Let's arbitrarily define the CPU quanta available per CPU as 900 (corresponding to 900 million CPU cycles per second). For the 8-CPU system, 7,200 quanta are available, and for the 16-CPU system, 14,400 quanta are available. The 8-CPU test showed 100% CPU utilization, so the quanta consumed was $7200 \times 100 \div 100 = 7200$, and the quanta consumed per 1000 transactions was $7200 \div 10 = 720$. The 16-CPU test showed 55% CPU utilization, so the quanta consumed was $14400 \times 55 \div 100 = 7920$, and the quanta consumed per 1000 transactions was $3520 \div 11 = 720$. So, the quanta consumed per 1000 transactions was actually the same in both cases.

  Why did the throughput increase only marginally on the more powerful system? Perhaps because insufficient load had been placed on the system under test, leaving 45% of CPU idle. Alternatively, some kind of bottleneck, such as a fully utilized disk, may have prevented the system from processing more than 11,000 transactions per minute.

  Using CPU clock speed to compare systems with different architectures is inadvisable. You can't assume, for example, that a 900 MHz Pentium has the same processing power as a 900 MHz UltraSPARC CPU.

- **Response time or completion time.** The response time for OLTP transactions and completion time for batch jobs and DSS queries are primary metrics in any performance-related benchmark. It is also valuable to keep the minimum, maximum, standard deviation, and some key percentiles (for example, 10th percentile and 90th percentile) as well as the average. The 90th percentile is the value greater than or equal to 90% of all values. To calculate it, sort the list of values in ascending order and take the value nine-tenths of the way through the list.

- **System utilization.** Keep track of at least the CPU utilization, disk utilization, network utilization, and memory paging. As discussed earlier in "CPU quanta per transaction," these metrics are necessary for a proper understanding of the behavior of a system.

- **Database statistics.** Calculate and keep the cache hit rate, lock statistics, and other database-specific metrics, both to understand workload behavior and for later reference.

- **Price.** If the purchase of a system is the primary outcome of the benchmark process, be sure to keep track of the total price of the system required to support the workload. Before comparing system prices, make sure you understand whether quoted prices are list, street, or "negotiated" prices.

- **Price/performance.** When comparing different systems, it is often useful to calculate price/performance as well as absolute price. Price/performance is the total price divided by the throughput (for example, transactions per minute or queries completed per hour). A system that is 50% more expensive may be capable of twice the throughput, for example. The price/performance metric should reflect that fact.

Pick two or three of the above as your key metrics. The final choice should be influenced by the purpose of the benchmark.

Benchmark Requirements

To run a benchmark, you need all of the following:

- **Hardware.** In addition to the database server and adequate disk, you may need additional disks to hold online backups of the data so the database can periodically be restored to its original state to ensure repeatability of benchmark runs. You may also need separate application servers and networking hardware.

- **Software.** Web browsers and other specialized software can be included as well as a database.

- **Applications.** Packaged software, applications developed in-house, and some benchmark special applications and scripts are all important. The key question is: Are the applications real-world?

- **Data.** You must decide how to load the data: drop the tables and reload from flat files, or insert into existing tables.

  If production data is being used, you will need to transfer it and possibly massage it for use in the applications.

  If the data is to be synthetically generated, you must find a suitable generation method. The data should be meaningful, as should the data relationships (for example, foreign keys, referential integrity). The data distribution should also reflect the final production data: some column values may have a normal distribution; others, negative exponential distribution; and others, uniform distribution.

- **Workload profiles**. Each work shift is likely to have a different profile of logged-in users, concurrent users, transaction types, and background batch load. The think time associated with transactions may also change. In some cases, the most important shift for benchmarking is the end of period processing (end of week, month, quarter, or year, for example). You might also have to emulate the load caused by users logging in and starting applications and by users logging out.

- **Some means of generating a workload.** The alternatives are lots of people, trained monkeys, scripts, or some kind of remote terminal or remote browser emulator. Remote terminal emulators will not only emulate users, they will typically allow you to apply think time and analyze the response times and produce detailed reports with a range of useful statistics.

  The HandsOff Remote Terminal emulator available on the book website can be used to emulate text-based applications (anything that can be run from a telnet session). Various commercial RTEs are also readily available, typically offering support for the full range of applications, including GUI-based and browser-based applications.

- **Plenty of time!** Don't underestimate the time required to develop a benchmark properly. There are definite benefits from thorough development, such as finding major application bottlenecks before putting the applications into production.

The best-case scenario is to use the applications, data, and workload profile of the target environment as the benchmark workload.

Running the Benchmark

The timing of a benchmark exercise is often crucial. Make sure you allow enough time for the following elements:

- **Once-only tasks.** These might include developing and testing the Remote Terminal Emulator scripts. Development and testing might take weeks rather than days, depending on the complexity of the benchmark environment.

- **Setting up the hardware and software.** Allow at least a day.

- **Loading the database.** Depending on database size and your ability to parallelize the load process, the database load could take many hours.

- **System tuning.** Allow a couple of days to ensure that your environment is properly tuned and working.

- **Each benchmark run.** The steady state duration of a typical benchmark is between 30 minutes and 60 minutes, plus ramp-up and ramp-down time. There are often other scripts to be run at the beginning and end of each run, increasing the total run time to between 90 minutes and 120 minutes. If you are using some kind of run queueing mechanism, you can launch benchmarks unattended overnight and on weekends.

- **Contingency.** Sometimes unexpected tasks can prove surprisingly greedy with time!

If you are running competitive benchmarks on a number of different platforms, make sure you allow adequate setup time on each. Be prepared to set aside a total of weeks or even months before embarking on such an exercise.

Competitive Benchmarks

When planning a competitive benchmark, remember:

- The benchmark will probably prove very expensive to the vendors bidding for the business, especially if they are lending hardware or support resources. Trying out your new application on borrowed hardware is an inexpensive way of finding out how much hardware resource will be required. Be reasonable and realistic in your expectations, and find ways of making it worthwhile for all participants.
- Be clear in advance about the benchmark rules and the evaluation criteria. Don't move the goal posts during the benchmark without a compelling reason. Ensure a level playing field.
- Allow flexibility where possible if it doesn't unfairly offer advantage or disadvantage to one vendor.
- Freely communicate with vendors the details of their own performance. It probably isn't wise to broadcast other vendors' results, though, unless all vendors have agreed to it.
- In a competitive environment, vendors often appreciate some rough indication of how their performance stands relative to competitors so they know how much extra tuning effort they might need to invest.
- If you expect the vendor to run an acceptance test with the same workload after purchase, make that clear in advance.
- Allow time to watch over the shoulders of vendors—you might learn a lot.

I have seen users commence major benchmark exercises before their own software is fully functional. I have also seen users decide not to purchase anything at the end of a major competitive benchmark, even though at least one vendor was able to demonstrate a viable solution. It should go without saying that such behavior is unreasonable, especially when vendors are investing significant hardware and time.

I have also seen decision-making undermined by confusion about the meaning of the statistics produced by sophisticated, commercial remote-terminal-emulator packages. When users and vendors alike have made super-human efforts to deliver a high-quality result, it makes sense to invest whatever is necessary to properly understand that result.

Finally, if each vendor has used its own performance and tuning gurus, ensure that you understand what they have done to improve performance. If key tuning parameters are not set to the same values across all platforms, a valid comparison between the platforms may not be possible. Beware also of tuning tricks that cannot be applied to real-world environments.

What Often Goes Wrong with Benchmarks?

In my experience, common pitfalls are poor estimates for the following performance factors:

- **Concurrent versus logged-in users.** The concurrent user load is often overestimated, resulting in oversizing. Use transaction throughput as a reality check for user load.

- **User think time**. Think time is often underestimated, leading to oversizing.

- **CPU required to run the workload.** CPU horsepower is often underestimated in advance, leading to big surprises for all concerned when the benchmark is run, especially by vendors unable to readily supply a larger server.

- **The degree of application tuning required**. Tuning is often underestimated, with negative impacts on the benchmark schedule.

Conclusion

TPC benchmarks have considerable value to database and system vendors for stress testing and regression testing. They are well established, stable, scalable, and widely accepted throughout the industry.

At the same time, they are highly optimized and differ significantly from most end-user application environments and, as such, rarely offer a good basis for system sizing. For the same reasons, they are not the best choice for comparing the performance of competing hardware or database platforms.

For sizing and for performance comparisons, the best measure is a user's own workload. If that workload is based on an established application suite, such as SAP, Oracle Applications, or Peoplesoft, then published benchmarks for those platforms are better choices than TPC-C, for example. If no published results are available, it is more useful to base comparisons on a range of different results than just on TPC-C.

When software is being developed in-house, benchmarks form an important part of a testing strategy for both the functionality and performance of applications. They sometimes also have a place in a competitive environment if not abused.

When you do conduct a benchmark, remember that the end result will only be as good as the investment made.

28

JAVA INTERFACES, MIDDLEWARE, AND DATABASES

The Java programming language has become an integral part of the Information Technology landscape, so it is not surprising that Java has a role to play with databases. This chapter explores the Java interfaces supported by the major database vendors and considers the burgeoning market for middleware based on Java standards.

Java in the Database

All four major databases—Oracle, DB2 for Solaris, Sybase, and Informix—allow developers to store Java code in the database engine, as stored procedures and sometimes as user-defined functions (UDFs). *Stored procedures* are compiled functions containing both SQL and business logic. The code is treated as an extension to the database engine; when the stored procedure is called, the logic code is executed and the SQL statements are run against the database.

Both a JDBC driver (described later in this chapter) and a Java virtual machine (JVM) are typically supplied with the database. The JVM is loaded into the address space of the database engine to execute the Java stored procedure code. The JDBC driver provides an application programmer interface (API) to support client access to the database from Java classes.

The ease of development and portability of the Java language and the efficiency of stored procedures together enable the deployment of scalable Java-based code for both client and database server applications.

Oracle Java stored procedures are compiled into the Oracle database and can be called by any database client. Java stored procedures function in the same way as PL/SQL stored procedures and can interact seamlessly with existing PL/SQL and SQL code.

DB2 for Solaris supports the creation and use of stored procedures in Java as for other languages, and also supports Java-based UDFs. DB2's Stored Procedure Builder (SPB) offers a wizardlike interface that aims to simplify the development of Java stored procedures by assisting in the creation of SQL queries, and to estimate the cost of invoking a stored procedure.

Sybase's Java in Adaptive Server supports Java UDFs and the use of Java classes as SQL datatypes. Java classes are installed in the Adaptive Server database and can be invoked from an SQL session and from client systems. The Java API can be used in classes, in stored procedures, and in SQL statements.

Informix delivers Java capabilities in the database server by providing J/Foundation, an embedding architecture for existing JVMs. Unlike the architectures from other vendors, J/Foundation supports standard JVMs rather than including a proprietary JVM with the database. The implementation still allows the Java code to be executed in the address space of the database server rather than in a separate process. Informix also supports user-defined routines (UDRs) and DataBlade modules written in the Java programming language.

Java Interfaces to Databases

Database access from Java applications and applets can be achieved with either JDBC or the more recent SQLJ. Each is outlined in the following section.

JDBC

The best-known method of accessing databases from a Java program is with the JDBC API. JDBC provides a vendor-neutral way of accessing relational databases. JDBC permits a Java applet or application to do the following things:

- Connect to a database.
- Send SQL statements to the database.
- Receive the results after they have been processed.

The features provided by JDBC classes include simultaneous connections to several databases, cursor support (scrollable result set), large-object support, batch updates, calls to stored procedures, and database dictionary access. JDBC supports both static and dynamic SQL.

The JDBC API contains two major interfaces, one for application developers and the other for developers writing JDBC drivers. Java applications and applets can connect to databases with JDBC in a number of different ways, as Figure 28.1 illustrates.

Figure 28.1 *Java database connectivity alternatives*

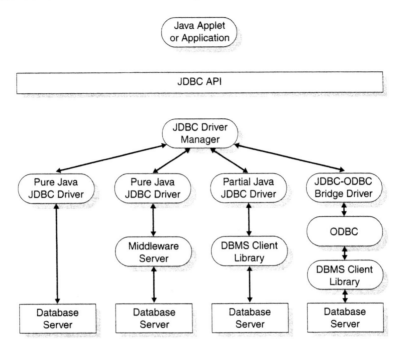

The first two drivers use pure Java technology. The first driver converts JDBC calls directly into the network protocol used by the database and permits direct connection from the client to the database server. The second driver converts JDBC calls into the network protocol used by a middleware server. The middleware server then manages the interaction with the database server.

The third driver requires proprietary client code on the client system. It converts the JDBC calls into client API calls for Oracle, DB2, Sybase, Informix, or other database products. The client library then manages the database server interaction. The fourth driver requires both proprietary client code and an ODBC driver on the client system. The JDBC-to-ODBC bridge driver provided by Sun converts the JDBC calls to ODBC calls, and the ODBC driver manages the database interaction.

SQLJ

SQLJ is a standard developed by the major database vendors, including Oracle, IBM, Sybase, and Informix. It is similar in concept to embedded C, except that SQLJ provides embedded SQL functionality for the Java programming language. SQLJ, like other embedded SQL languages, is preprocessed at compile time since it is not pure Java code. The SQL code is parsed at compile time, its syntax is checked for errors, and database schema references are validated.

SQLJ does not replace the JDBC API, although the two products have considerable overlap. Oracle's SQLJ implementation, for example, uses JDBC for its database connectivity.

JDBC supports both static and dynamic SQL, whereas SQLJ supports only static SQL (static SQL statements are known at development time; dynamic SQL statements are constructed at run time). On the other hand, SQLJ code is more concise than JDBC code.

Unlike JDBC, SQLJ code supports Java host variables, so a result set is not needed when only a single row is returned. Further, because SQLJ code is parsed at compile time, SQL syntax errors are detected before the program is run. By contrast, the Java compiler used to compile JDBC code knows nothing of SQL syntax, so errors are only detected at run time.

Since SQLJ does not support dynamic SQL, it allows direct interoperability with JDBC to overcome this limitation.

J2EE Middleware

Developers have increasingly been adopting the strategy of using Java for application portability and XML for message portability. The task of developing enterprise applications with Java and XML has been greatly simplified with the advent of standards-based middleware from a number of major software vendors supporting the Java 2 Platform, Enterprise Edition (J2EE). The remainder of this chapter examines J2EE and the major architectures it comprises and discusses the way it provides access to databases.

J2EE Middleware Suppliers

The Java 2 Platform, Enterprise Edition (J2EE) defines a standard for developing multitiered enterprise applications. J2EE simplifies enterprise application development and deployment by basing them on standardized, modular components, by providing a complete set of services to those components, and by handling many details of application behavior automatically, without requiring complex programming.

Since the release of J2EE technology in December 1999, 25 companies have become licensees, representing a significant majority of the application server market. Many of them have passed the J2EE technology Compatibility Test Suite (CTS) and are currently shipping certified J2EE technology-based applications.

With a dominant proportion of the application server market currently using the J2EE platform, the J2EE platform has become the de facto standard for middleware development. J2EE leverages extensible markup language (XML) and offers enhanced features, including the Enterprise JavaBeans (EJB) specification, the JavaServer Pages (JSP) framework, the

Java Servlet API, J2EE blueprints, the J2EE Connector architecture, and the Java API for XML Parsing (JAXP).

Major implementations of middleware servers supporting J2EE include WebLogic from BEA, Oracle9iAS Containers for J2EE (OC4J) from Oracle, Websphere from IBM, and IAS from iPlanet.

The J2EE Framework

Modern distributed enterprise applications must be capable of scaling to thousands of users while maintaining the security and integrity of the data that they provide access to. The Java 2 Platform, Enterprise Edition (J2EE) is a framework that has been developed to meet these needs. J2EE is beginning to deliver a scalable, transactional, and multiuser secure architecture for the development of distributed enterprise applications.

J2EE takes advantage of many features of the Java 2 Platform, Standard Edition (J2SE), such as application portability, JDBC API for database access, CORBA technology for interaction with existing enterprise resources, and a security model that protects data even in Internet applications. Building on this base, J2EE adds full support for Enterprise JavaBeans (EJB) components, Java Servlets API, JavaServer Pages (JSP) and XML technology. The J2EE standard includes complete specifications and compliance tests to ensure portability of applications across the wide range of existing enterprise systems capable of supporting J2EE.

JavaServer Pages

JavaServer Pages (JSP) technology enables web designers to rapidly develop platform-independent web pages that are easy to maintain. JavaServer Pages extend the familiar and powerful HTML and XML languages with special scriptlets written in the Java programming language. A normal HTML page is downloaded into the user's browser, but embedded in the page are special XML-like tags that invoke Java code on the web server to generate the designated content. In this way JavaServer Pages separate the user interface from content generation, allowing designers to modify the layout of a web page without altering the underlying dynamic content.

JSP technology supports reusable components, so developers can rapidly build web-based applications. Application logic can reside in JavaBeans components, for example.

JSP technology is an extension of the Servlet technology, described in the next section. JavaServer Pages compile into servlets.

The Java Servlet API

The Java Servlet API is a standard extension to the Java platform that gives developers a simple mechanism for expanding the capability of a web server.

Servlets are Java modules; they are like applets, except that they run on the web server and have no user interface.

Servlets extend web server functionality while fitting seamlessly into the web server's environment. They are platform independent and require minimal maintenance and support. Since servlets have access to the full range of Java APIs, servlets can provide web servers with access to databases through JDBC.

XML

XML is an acronym for eXtensible Markup Language. XML and HTML share SGML as a common ancestor, and they look similar in many respects. But XML broadens considerably the usefulness of tags—developers can embed information about the nature of the data in with the data. Where an HTML table contains only data, XML might also let you know what the columns and rows represent. XML allows for more sophisticated style sheets than does HTML.

J2EE takes advantage of XML and also provides classes that automatically parse XML (the Java API for XML Parsing: JAXP).

Enterprise JavaBeans

Although possibly less well known than JSP and Servlets, an important cornerstone of the J2EE framework is Enterprise JavaBeans (EJB). EJB is an architecture for developing Java-based components. Put more simply, it is the specification for Java middleware that defines how things like user connection pooling and database access are provided.

Components of Enterprise JavaBeans are transaction-aware Java objects that run in an EJB container. They typically provide an object-oriented view of relational database tables and legacy applications. Since EJB is Java based, the write-once run-anywhere paradigm still applies, with one exception: the "beans" must be deployed into a server that implements the EJB specification. Middleware servers implementing EJB relieve the application developer from coding connection logic and database access as well as from dealing with threads, security, memory management, and component life-cycle issues.

EJB should not be confused with JavaBeans, which is a special kind of Java class that implements the JavaBeans API. In particular, the JavaBeans API exposes its methods so that a builder tool can make them available to other beans. Beans can be used for anything from business logic to GUI components. EJBs also expose themselves to builder tools; a number of commercially available tools take advantage of this characteristic. All beans are classes, although not all classes are beans.

In summary, EJB is the component model for server-side Java, and JavaBeans is the component model for client-side GUI components.

Session Beans

Session beans are nonpersistent components that represent a client session with an EJB application. Session beans are analogous to business objects; they represent activity (business process) that takes place to fulfill a business task (for example, purchasing goods, sending payments, and changing an order). They implement the business logic, business rules, and workflow required to accomplish a defined task.

Session beans derive their name from the fact that they live only as long as the client session. When the client session is finished, the EJB container destroys the session bean. Session beans are not shared; there is a one-to-one relationship between clients and session beans. There are two types of session beans: stateless session beans and stateful session beans.

- *Stateless session beans* represent business processes that can be performed by a single method request—calculating the cost of ordered goods, validating credit cards, and making payments, for example.

- Some business processes last across multiple method requests and transactions. Further, they require that the state of the process be available to all methods of the process. *Stateful session beans* represent such processes. They maintain state on behalf of a single client. If the state of a session bean is changed during a method request, the same state will be available to that same client upon the subsequent request.

Entity Beans

Entity beans are persistent. They provide an object-oriented view of data in the underlying data store. Traditionally, applications deal with data by storing it in tables in a relational database, reading and writing the data as required. Entity beans are object-oriented representations of the data in the underlying relational (or other) database. They enable the developer to treat data in tables as objects. A row can be read from a table directly into an entity bean and manipulated by a call to the entity bean's methods. When changes are made to in-memory entity beans, the EJB container takes care of updating the underlying database. Thus, entity beans combine the persistence of a database with the convenience of object-oriented programming.

Because entity beans are just in-memory views of data in a persistent data store, they survive failures, such as an EJB server crash or machine crash. After a machine or EJB server crash, the entity beans can be reconstructed by a rereading of the data from the underlying database. The life of an entity bean depends on how long the data represented by the bean remains in the database.

As with session beans, there are two subtypes of entity beans: *bean-managed persistence* (BMP) entity beans and *container-managed persistence* (CMP) entity beans. As already stated, entity beans are persistent—their state is saved to an underlying data store. A BMP entity bean requires the bean developer to write all persistence code, including code for the locating, loading, and saving of data. CMP beans transfer the responsibility of persistence from the bean developer to the EJB container, thus freeing the developer to concentrate on business logic.

Key differences between entity beans and session beans include the following:

- Session beans represent business process and work flow, whereas entity beans represent the underlying business data.
- Session beans are nonpersistent, short-lived objects, whereas entity beans are long-lived, persistent objects.
- Each client uses its own session bean, whereas multiple clients share an entity bean.
- Session beans usually use entity beans to represent the data required to perform a business process. Session beans often act as a façade to a subsystem of an EJB application. This strategy decreases coupling between subsystems, thus making the subsystem easier to use.

Message Beans

Message beans are a new type of bean that became available in the EJB 2.0 specification. Message beans facilitate peer-to-peer messaging and can create asynchronous messages.

Importance of J2EE to End Users

EJB provides a framework for server-side, component-oriented middleware, enabling users to purchase off-the-shelf components from vendors, combine them with their own or other vendors' components, and run them all in an application server. This approach should reduce the overall development cost of building enterprise applications.

The Enterprise JavaBeans architecture was designed to achieve the following goals:

- Provide a standard architecture for the development of distributed business applications.
- Enable developers to build distributed applications by combining prebuilt components.
- Make distributed application development easier by taking care of complexities such as multithreading, transaction control, and connection pooling.
- Take advantage of the write-once run-anywhere philosophy of the Java programming language.
- Simplify the issues associated with the development, deployment, and run time of an enterprise application.
- Provide a framework that enables tools from multiple vendors to deploy components that can interact at run time.

- Offer compatibility with existing server platforms and enable vendors to extend their existing products to accommodate EJB.

- Maintain compatibility with other Java APIs.

- Enable non-Java-based applications to interact with EJB.

J2EE inherits the portability of Java; some J2EE implementations are written entirely in the Java programming language. The platform neutrality of J2EE allows software vendors to provide middleware solutions based on industry standards rather than on proprietary programming interfaces.

J2EE Availability

Customers want availability at the end-user application. Availability means long Mean Time Between Failure (MTBF), short recovery times, and little or no operator intervention during recovery. The goal can be achieved in various ways, including the use of reliable components and redundant components with automatic failover. Availability often focuses on hardware and operating systems, but the behavior of middleware components is equally vital.

The relevant software components in this context are web servers, middleware servers, and databases. The availability issues associated with databases are relatively well understood; we are interested here primarily in middleware servers and in web servers to the extent that they are associated with middleware servers.

End users deploying middleware services want to minimize recovery incidents by making use of a resilient architecture that limits the likelihood of downtime. J2EE implementations typically address this concern by supporting some form of software clustering with failover. Developers are thus free to focus on ensuring that their applications detect and respond appropriately to failures elsewhere in the system and that their applications recover to a consistent state after they themselves have failed. The Java programming language provides a robust exception-handling framework, and J2EE middleware extends this exception handling to cover connectivity and database access. The J2EE model significantly frees the developer from much of the burden normally involved in identifying and handling errors.

In addition to the software clustering typically provided by J2EE, availability can be further enhanced by hardware clustering. Sun Cluster 3.0 is the latest release of Sun's high availability or clustering product (for details see http://www.sun.com/clusters). It is designed to extend the Solaris Operating Environment by enabling core Solaris services such as file systems, devices, and networks to be clustered yet presented to the user as a single service. Other services, such as LDAP, database, and mail services, can be layered on top of the core Solaris services in a clustered environment with the Sun Cluster framework.

Other Related Technologies

Here, we briefly introduce a number of other technologies that are relevant to Java-based middleware.

Java Messaging Services (JMS) is an XML Message Broker. JMS allows users to store their data formats in an XML schema repository and an XSL stylesheet repository. When two applications communicate, they don't need to know what data format the other needs because the message broker does the translation, thanks to the information in the repository. Both applications can be loosely coupled, that is, grow, change, and version independently, without breaking the message capability.

Remote Method Invocation (RMI) is the original way of getting distributed Java applications to talk to each other. RMI can also run over the top of the Internet Inter-Orb Protocol (IIOP), although this alternative is more difficult to implement. Since it is difficult to get IIOP working through firewalls, running XML over HTTP has become a popular alternative for web-based application connectivity.

In Conclusion

Figure 28.2 illustrates the application development model enabled by J2EE, and brings together many of the elements discussed in this chapter.

Figure 28.2 *Application development model based on J2EE middleware*

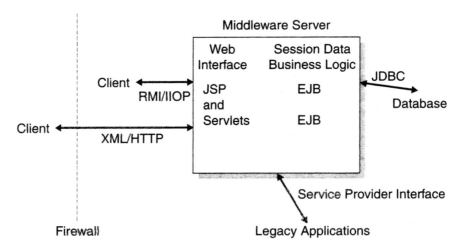

Client interfaces are based on JavaServer Pages and Servlets, with EJB providing the connection pooling, database access, and access to legacy applications. Connections inside the firewall use RMI over IIOP, and connections outside the firewall are based on XML/HTTP. Database access is achieved with JDBC. Most middleware based on J2EE includes a bundled web server.

J2EE middleware and the Web deliver a new and substantially easier-to-use model for creating robust multitiered applications and for delivering them on highly available systems. The need for application developers to create operating-system-specific and database-specific "cluster agents" has been eliminated in the new middle tier as this complexity has become the responsibility of the J2EE server provider. Indeed, the quality of a highly available deployment of a J2EE application offers a vendor a differentiator compared to other J2EE server providers.

A

REFERENCES

The information presented in this book was drawn from a variety of sources apart from my own experience. I was fortunate to have access to a range of Sun internal whitepapers and field notes, information posted on internal web pages, and a substantial quantity of research data that has never been formally documented. I also made extensive use of the web-based product manuals posted by all the database vendors and referred to a number of technical books. These reference materials are detailed below.

Web-Based Product Manuals

Database product manuals can be found at the locations listed below:

- **Oracle**. Database manuals can be found on the Oracle Technology Network at
  http://otn.oracle.com/docs/content.html

  A free registration is required.

- **Sybase**. Product manuals are found at
  http://www.sybase.com/support/manuals

- **DB2**. DB2 Universal Database manuals can be found at
  http://www-4.ibm.com/software/data/db2/library

- **Informix**. Informix XPS manuals are found under Servers on
  http://www.informix.com/documentation/

Technical Books

The technical books listed below cover the four database products, Sun products, and general computer architecture. I have indicated where I found a title to be particularly useful.

Oracle Texts

Oracle technical books are readily available, and some of them are very good. My list included the following books:

Oracle 24x7, Tips & Techniques, Venkat S. Devraj. Oracle Press, 2000. An excellent reference book.

Oracle Performance Tuning, Tips & Techniques, Richard J. Niemiec. Oracle Press, 1999. Also excellent.

Oracle8 Advanced Tuning & Administration, Eyal Aronoff, Kevin Loney, Noorali Sonawalla. Oracle Press, 1998.

Oracle8 Data Warehousing, Michael J. Corey, Michael Abbey, Ian Abramson, and Ben Taub. Oracle Press, 1998.

Oracle8 Tuning, High Performance Series, Don Burleson. Coriolis Group Books, 1998.

Oracle Performance Tuning, Peter Corrigan and Mark Gurry. O'Reilly & Associates, Inc, 1993. Of historical interest primarily. It highlights the changes that have taken place in the Oracle database in recent years.

Sybase Texts

Sybase technical books are a little harder to find. I used the following books:

Understanding Sybase SQL Server 11, A Hands-on Approach, Sridharan Kotta, Gopinath Chandra, and Tanya D.Knoop. Sybase Press, 1997.

Sybase SQL Server 11 Unleashed, Ray Rankins, Jeff Garbus, David Solomon, and Bennett McEwan. Sams Publishing, 1996.

DB2 Texts

The number of DB2 books is increasing rapidly. I own the book listed below, although it may not be the best choice for a general architectural overview.

A Complete Guide to DB2 Universal Database, Don Chamberlin. Morgan Kaufmann, 1998. Mostly focused on SQL.

Informix Texts

Informix technical books are not likely to be a growth industry. I referred to the titles listed below:

Informix Unleashed, John McNally, Glenn Miller, Jim Prajesh, Jose Fortuny, et al. Sams Publishing, 1997. Comprehensive, but not much on XPS.

Informix DBA Survival Guide, 2nd Edition, Joe Lumbley. Informix Press, 1999. Nothing on XPS.

Sun Texts

Sun Microsystems Press boasts many useful reference books. The titles that complement this book are listed below. If you don't own them already, go buy them!

Solaris Internals, Jim Mauro and Richard McDougall. Sun Microsystems Press, 2001. A must-have book for anyone with an interest in Solaris internals.

Configuration and Capacity Planning for Solaris Servers, Brian L. Wong. Sun Microsystems Press, 1997. Becoming old, but still a classic.

Sun Performance and Tuning, Java and the Internet, 2nd Edition, Adrian Cockcroft and Richard Pettit. Sun Microsystems Press, 1998. Another classic.

Resource Management, Richard McDougall, Adrian Cockcroft, Evert Hoogendoorn, Enrique Vargas, and Tom Bialaski. Sun Microsystems Press, 1999. Contains a useful section on Solaris Resource Manager and resource management generally.

Computer Architecture Texts

The following list represents a small selection from the wide range of titles covering computer architecture:

High Performance Computing, Kevin Dowd and Charles Severance. O'Reilly, 1998. Addresses RISC architectures, optimization, and benchmarks.

Computer Architecture A Quantitative Approach, 2nd Edition, John L. Hennessy and David A. Patterson. Morgan Kaufmann, 1996. Excellent, and very detailed.

Performance Analysis Texts

Both of the following books are useful if you have some statistical interest or background:

The Art of Computer Systems Performance Analysis, Raj Jain. John Wiley and Sons, 1991.

The Practical Performance Analyst, Neil J. Gunther. McGraw-Hill, 1998.

INDEX

483